Philosophers in Depth

Series Editor
Constantine Sandis
Department of Philosophy
University of Hertfordshire
Hatfield, UK

Philosophers in Depth is a series of themed edited collections focusing on particular aspects of the thought of major figures from the history of philosophy. The volumes showcase a combination of newly commissioned and previously published work with the aim of deepening our understanding of the topics covered. Each book stands alone, but taken together the series will amount to a vast collection of critical essays covering the history of philosophy, exploring issues that are central to the ideas of individual philosophers. This project was launched with the financial support of the Institute for Historical and Cultural Research at Oxford Brookes University, for which we are very grateful.

More information about this series at
http://www.palgrave.com/gp/series/14552

Garry L. Hagberg
Editor

Stanley Cavell on Aesthetic Understanding

palgrave
macmillan

Editor
Garry L. Hagberg
Bard College
Annandale-on-Hudson
NY, USA

Philosophers in Depth
ISBN 978-3-319-97465-1   ISBN 978-3-319-97466-8 (eBook)
https://doi.org/10.1007/978-3-319-97466-8

Library of Congress Control Number: 2018952592

© The Editor(s) (if applicable) and The Author(s) 2018
This work is subject to copyright. All rights are solely and exclusively licensed by the Publisher, whether the whole or part of the material is concerned, specifically the rights of translation, reprinting, reuse of illustrations, recitation, broadcasting, reproduction on microfilms or in any other physical way, and transmission or information storage and retrieval, electronic adaptation, computer software, or by similar or dissimilar methodology now known or hereafter developed.
The use of general descriptive names, registered names, trademarks, service marks, etc. in this publication does not imply, even in the absence of a specific statement, that such names are exempt from the relevant protective laws and regulations and therefore free for general use.
The publisher, the authors and the editors are safe to assume that the advice and information in this book are believed to be true and accurate at the date of publication. Neither the publisher nor the authors or the editors give a warranty, express or implied, with respect to the material contained herein or for any errors or omissions that may have been made. The publisher remains neutral with regard to jurisdictional claims in published maps and institutional affiliations.

Cover illustration: © loonger/ Getty Images

This Palgrave Macmillan imprint is published by the registered company Springer Nature Switzerland AG
The registered company address is: Gewerbestrasse 11, 6330 Cham, Switzerland

Contents

Part I Understanding Persons Through Film   1

1 I Want to Know More About You: On Knowing and
   Acknowledging in *Chinatown*   3
   Francey Russell

2 Other Minds and Unknown Women: The Case of *Gaslight*   37
   Jay R. Elliott

3 The Melodrama of the Unknown Man   57
   Peter Dula

Part II Shakespeare, Opera, and Philosophical Interpretation   73

4 Cordelia's Moral Incapacity in *King Lear*   75
   David A. Holiday

5 Disowning Certainty: Tragic and Comic Skepticism in
   Cavell, Montaigne, and Shakespeare   109
   V. Stanley Benfell

6	Must We Mean What We Sing?—*Così Fan Tutte* and the Lease of Voice Ian Ground	133

Part III	Aesthetic Understanding and Moral Life	165
7	What Matters: The Ethics and Aesthetics of Importance Sandra Laugier	167
8	Achilles' Tears: Cavell, the *Iliad*, and Possibilities for the Human David LaRocca	197
9	Wittgenstein "in the Midst of" Life, Death, Sanity, Madness—and Mathematics Richard McDonough	239

Part IV	Reading Fiction and Literary Understanding	263
10	Fraudulence, Knowledge, and Post-Imperial Geographies in John Le Carré's Fiction: A Cavellian Postcolonial Reading Alan Johnson	265
11	Must We Do What We Say? The Plight of Marriage and Conversation in George Meredith's *The Egoist* Erin Greer	293
12	Within the Words of Henry James: Cavell as Austinian Reader Garry L. Hagberg	321

Index	357

Notes on Contributors

V. Stanley Benfell is a Humanities Professor of Comparative Literature at Brigham Young University, where he is the Head of the Comparative Literature Program. He is the author of *The Biblical Dante* (2011) as well as articles and book chapters on medieval and early modern literature and its relationship to religious and philosophical texts and ideas. He is currently at work on a study of philosophical skepticism and early modern comedy.

Peter Dula is Professor of Religion and Culture and Chair of the Department of Bible and Religion at Eastern Mennonite University in Harrisonburg, Virginia. He is the author of *Cavell, Companionship, and Christian Theology* (2011).

Jay R. Elliott is an Assistant Professor of Philosophy at Bard College. He is the author of *Character* (2017) and co-editor of the *Norton Anthology of Western Philosophy: After Kant: The Analytic Tradition*.

Erin Greer is an Assistant Professor of Literature at the University of Texas at Dallas. Her current book project stages a dialogue between literary and philosophical texts in order to develop a theory of "conversation" as a medium central to intimate and political life. Her fields of research and teaching include late Victorian through contemporary British and Anglophone literature, new media, ordinary language philosophy, political philosophy, and gender and sexuality studies.

Ian Ground has, over the last 30 years, taught philosophy at a number of institutions including Newcastle, Durham, the Open University, Edinburgh, and Sunderland University. He has published in the philosophy of mind, especially our understanding of animal minds, in the philosophy of art, and on the thought and life of the philosopher Ludwig Wittgenstein and is a regular reviewer for *The Times Literary Supplement*. His books include *Art or Bunk?*, *Can We Understand Animal Minds?*, and *Portraits of Wittgenstein*, a comprehensive collection of memoirs. He is currently a Visiting Research Fellow in Philosophy at the University of Hertfordshire, a Visiting Lecturer at Newcastle University, and Vice-President of the British Wittgenstein Society.

Garry L. Hagberg is the James H. Ottaway Professor of Philosophy and Aesthetics at Bard College and has also been Professor of Philosophy at the University of East Anglia. Author of numerous papers at the intersection of aesthetics and the philosophy of language, his books include *Meaning and Interpretation: Wittgenstein, Henry James, and Literary Knowledge*; *Art as Language: Wittgenstein, Meaning, and Aesthetic Theory*; and *Describing Ourselves: Wittgenstein and Autobiographical Consciousness*. He is an editor of *Art and Ethical Criticism* and of *Fictional Characters, Real Problems: The Search for Ethical Content in Literature*, co-editor of *A Companion to the Philosophy of Literature*, and editor of the journal *Philosophy and Literature*. He is presently writing a new book on the contribution literary experience makes to the formation of self and sensibility, *Living in Words: Literature, Autobiographical Language, and the Composition of Selfhood*, as well as a series of articles on the exploration of self-constitution in film and a monograph on aesthetic issues in jazz improvisation.

David A. Holiday received his B.A. in Philosophy and Psychology from Balliol College, Oxford, an M.Sc. in Philosophy from Edinburgh University, and a Ph.D. from the University of Chicago. He is currently serving as a Postdoctoral Ethics Fellow in the Jackson Center for Ethics and Values at Coastal Carolina University, South Carolina. He teaches and conducts research in normative ethics and moral philosophy, concentrating on moral psychology, action theory, and the history of ethics, and the philosophy of human rights, where he focuses on the foundational normative concepts that help orient, shape, and direct contemporary discourse and practice in global justice.

Alan Johnson is a Professor of English at Idaho State University, where he specializes in postcolonial literature, with a focus on India, where he was raised. He did a Fulbright there in 2010, and again in 2016–17. He has published on a range of topics, and his 2011 book *Out of Bounds* focuses on the role that ideas of colonial Indian spaces played in the literature of British India. He is currently working on forest imagery in Indian literature. His chapter here grew out of an introductory class on spy fiction he taught as part of a series on the genre sponsored by ISU's College of Arts and Letters, and instigated by his colleagues Jennifer Attebery, Pamela Park, and Dan Hunt.

David LaRocca is the author of *On Emerson* and *Emerson's English Traits and the Natural History of Metaphor*, co-editor of *A Power to Translate the World*, and editor of *The Bloomsbury Anthology of Transcendental Thought: From Antiquity to the Anthropocene*, Stanley Cavell's *Emerson's Transcendental Etudes*, *Estimating Emerson: An Anthology of Criticism from Carlyle to Cavell*, *The Philosophy of Charlie Kaufman*, *The Philosophy of War Films*, and, most recently, *The Philosophy of Documentary Film: Image, Sound, Fiction, Truth*. He has served as Visiting Assistant Professor in the Cinema Department at Binghamton University, Visiting Assistant Professor in the Department of Philosophy at the State University of New York College at Cortland, Visiting Scholar in the Department of English at Cornell University, and Lecturer in Screen Studies in the Department of Cinema, Photography, and Media Arts at the Roy H. Park School of Communications at Ithaca College. Educated at Buffalo, Berkeley, Vanderbilt, and at Harvard, where he was also Sinclair Kennedy Traveling Fellow in the United Kingdom, his articles have appeared in *Afterimage*; *Epoché*; *Liminalities*; *Post Script*; *Religions*; *Transactions*; *Film and Philosophy*; *The Senses and Society*; *The Midwest Quarterly*; *Journalism, Media and Cultural Studies*; *The Journal of Religion and Business Ethics*; *The Journal of Aesthetic Education*; and *The Journal of Aesthetics and Art Criticism*. More details at www.davidlarocca.org.

Sandra Laugier is a French philosopher working on moral philosophy, philosophy of language, philosophy of action, and gender studies. She is currently a professor at the University of Paris I Pantheon-Sorbonne, member of Institut Universitaire de France, and Deputy Director of the Sorbonne Institute for Legal and Philosophical Sciences (ISJPS), after being a professor at the University of Picardie Jules Verne in Amiens, France (until 2010). She has worked extensively on J.L. Austin and

Ludwig Wittgenstein and has introduced several aspects of American philosophy to French readers (Emerson, Thoreau, and above all Stanley Cavell.) Having translated eight of Cavell's books into French, she is now working on moral philosophy, the ethics of care and gender studies, and aesthetics of popular culture (film and TV series).

Richard McDonough received his B.A., *summa cum laude*, major in philosophy and minors in chemistry and mathematics from the University of Pittsburgh in 1971, his M.A. from Cornell in 1974, and his Ph.D. from Cornell in 1975. He has taught at Bates College, the National University of Singapore, the University Putra Malaysia, the Overseas Family College (Singapore), the University of Maryland, and Arium Academy (Singapore). He has taught philosophy, psychology, physics, humanities, and writing courses in various university programs around the world. He has authored two books, 60 articles in refereed journals, about 11 book reviews and critical notices, and several encyclopedia and dictionary entries.

Francey Russell is a Postdoctoral Associate and Lecturer in the Philosophy Department and Humanities Program at Yale University. Her research is in ethics and moral psychology, broadly construed, as well as Kant, Continental philosophy, and the relationship between ethics and aesthetics. She also writes art and film criticism for the *Los Angeles Review of Books and the Boston Review*.

Introduction

Stanley Cavell, the Walter M. Cabot Professor Emeritus of Aesthetics and the General Theory of Value at Harvard University, past President of the American Philosophical Association, MacArthur Fellow, recipient of numerous honorary doctorates and many other honors, and widely regarded as among the most important and increasingly influential philosophers of recent decades, began his academic life not as a philosopher, but as a musician and composer. And throughout his life in philosophy, he has retained the ability that musicians take as essential to who and what they are, the ability to listen.

In his uniquely sustained engagement with the engrossing intellectual malady called skepticism, where a person comes to see him- or herself as hermetically sealed off from the world and thus from any genuine knowledge of it, Cavell has shown the great philosophically therapeutic value of listening, with the finest and most acute attention, to the multiform ways in which language positions us *within*, and not apart from, that world. Language, he has shown (inheriting and extending the tradition of Wittgenstein and J.L. Austin), is not merely a cold instrument for describing that world from afar; rather, it is what one might call (and Wittgenstein has called) a form of life that, in wondrously and irreducibly complex ways, can both make us who we are and make us who we are to each other, and in a multitude of ways (although, as he has shown, the articulation of this point requires great caution), it makes the world what and how it is.

The most extreme manifestation of skepticism is a state of being that philosophers call solipsism, where a person takes hermetic isolation from every other human mind as a brute fact of the human condition. Cavell, with a vision of and insight into this problem many believe to be unique in the history of philosophy, has seen this picture of solipsistic isolation as central to the making of tragedy (in literature and in life), and with a composer's ear, he has shown us that, in truth, the absorbing subtleties of the language we humans use to make ourselves known to each other make it so that we not only are not, but indeed could not, ever be so metaphysically alone.

Just as language, properly understood, is not separate from the reality it describes, so, Stanley Cavell has shown, the style in which philosophy as well as literature is written is not merely a matter of rhetorical decoration or the happenstance verbal presentation of content separate from that presentation, but is rather internal to, and thus inseparable from, its content. This is shown in his writings on Beckett, on Kierkegaard, on Wittgenstein and Austin, on opera, and his extensive writings on Shakespeare, in which that author is newly seen as confronting the skepticism that was for him the then-awakening precondition of early modern thought. Whether we see or do not see a dagger before us is, for Cavell and now for many of us, the modern question in microcosm that asks if we see and know the contents of an external world objectively independent of the contents of our present consciousness. But all of this, for Cavell, is intricately interwoven with aesthetic experience and the nature of aesthetic understanding.

Macbeth's relation to his dagger is in interesting ways like the audience's relation to the world portrayed in a film they are viewing—they in a sense have room to both believe and not believe it. (We whisper to children frightened by a scene in a film, "Remember it's only a movie!") In Cavell's groundbreaking book *The World Viewed*, he gave us what Wittgenstein would call a grammatical investigation into the nuanced language we use to identify, and in cases to create, the relations that exist between the viewer, the actor, the film image of the character, and the portrayed world within which that character acts in deed and word. In his later writings on film, he explored the help that psychoanalysis can offer in illuminating the structures within which a mind can know, not only another mind but also, indeed, itself. And this has led in turn—for one whose scholarly and personal life are in an exemplary way on such intimate terms—to autobiographical writing of an expansive kind that articulates for us the larger significance of a life spent plumbing the depths of film, literature, and music where they intersect not only with psychoanalysis but also with American transcendentalism, with images of moral perfectionism, with the depths of the philosophical legacies of Wittgenstein, Austin,

Kierkegaard, Heidegger, and numerous others, and, more broadly, with the depths and power of the language within which we become who we are. And bringing a human voice back into philosophy, he has also plumbed the depths of the moral language within which we not only become who we are but also who we aspire to be. Cavell's investigations into works of literature and film are at once aesthetic and ethical, just as his work interweaves issues in the philosophy of language and of mind into indissoluble unions with works of art.

The chapters presented here explore all of these issues, together offering a sense of the central position that aesthetic understanding—its character, its cultivation, its reach out into human life in so many ways—occupies in Cavell's extensive body of work.

In Part I, "Understanding Persons Through Film", in her opening chapter, Francey Russell asks: What is the difference between knowing someone and acknowledging them? Is it possible to want to be acknowledged and yet remain unknown? And if one's desire to know another person is too consuming, can this foreclose the possibility of acknowledgment? She shows how and why Cavell argues that we sometimes avoid the ethical problem of acknowledgment by misconceiving our relations with others in the narrow or restrictive terms of knowledge alone and how and why this epistemic misconception or reduction can actually amount to a form of ethical harm. Russell explores this through a close reading of Roman Polanski's *Chinatown*, which she shows helps us understand the ethically deep difference between knowing and acknowledging. And Russell shows in turn that Cavell's fundamental concepts, as tools for aesthetic understanding, help us to better appreciate the ethical significance of *Chinatown*.

Jay Elliott begins by observing that Stanley Cavell's approach to film is distinguished by his insistence on a deep connection between the recurring preoccupations of certain classical Hollywood genres, on the one hand, and the philosophical problem of other mind's skepticism, on the other. In Cavell's groundbreaking 1981 *Pursuits of Happiness*, he argued that a series of films he dubbed "comedies of remarriage" represents profound and original sources of thought about the conditions in which one can come to know the subjectivity of another. According to Cavell, these films demonstrate how this knowledge is achieved, not through an abstract intellectual argument, but through a certain mode of living together: a practice of marriage that Cavell calls, following John Milton, a "meet and happy conversation." Elliott here focuses on Cavell's attempt in his 1996 book *Contesting Tears*, to elaborate a "companion genre" to the remarriage comedies, one that he terms "the melodrama of the unknown woman." Elliott emphasizes that this later work is remarkably ambitious in its attempt to bring the themes of Cavell's earlier writings on film into a closer conversation with some of the characteristic concerns of feminism, where this is especially true in the structural injustice built into traditional forms of marriage. Elliott argues that through his renewed openness to doubt about whether marriage can constitute a scene of genuine acknowledgment between men and women, the Cavell of *Contesting Tears* presents a profound challenge to his own earlier work. But Elliott also shows that, for all of its ambitions, *Contesting Tears* has the air of an unfulfilled promise: it has neither found a comfortable place in Cavell's oeuvre nor been warmly received by the feminist thinkers he hoped to engage. Nevertheless, Elliott aims to celebrate the ambitions of *Contesting Tears*, to explain why the project in the senses he describes failed, and to draw a number of lessons for how we should inherit Cavell's approach to aesthetic understanding.

Peter Dula initiates his chapter by observing that the sustained attention that Cavell gives to artistic modernism in his early work seems to fade from his later work. But while the specific language of "modernism" becomes infrequent, nevertheless the same themes, Dula observes, remain present. Dula argues that the modernist artist becomes a type of moral perfectionist—especially in the account of perfectionism provided in the melodramas of the unknown woman. Read together, Dula claims that it becomes evident that modernism is melodramatic. He then explores whether the connections between modernism, perfectionism, and melodrama can help us be better readers of Cavell's memoir, *Little Did I Know*, a text which can sometimes seem to invite a subtitle resonating with the problem of self-understanding, "The Melodrama of the Unknown Man."

In Part II, Shakespeare, "Opera, and Philosophical Interpretation", David Holiday, noting that Cordelia's moral character is hotly contested in *King Lear* criticism, offers a new Cavellian reading of her words and deeds in the tragedy's opening scene, showing them to be expressive of a morally inflected inability to harm her father. Holiday contrasts this portrait of Cordelia with those in two major interpretative traditions: one, following Coleridge, viewing her as proud and willful; another, after Johnson, insisting on her otherworldly, sainted goodness. Holiday shows how both readings are instructively flawed, in a debate that also elucidates the ethical notion of "moral incapacity" and yields some Cavellian lessons about methodology in moral psychology.

V. Stanley Benfell, observing that Cavell has influentially argued that a particularly modern form of skepticism can be found in Shakespeare's great tragedies, suggests that attending to different, early modern notions of skepticism, especially as found in the writings of the essayist Michel de Montaigne, can lead us to a different notion of skepticism with different dramatic possibilities. These include a comic skepticism, where comedy offers a playwright the opportunity of working through the dramatic implications of skeptical thinking. Benfell, significantly extending Cavell's discussion, richly illustrates this possibility through an analysis of *Twelfth Night*.

Ian Ground begins his chapter by observing that Cavell writes about opera as a medium in which the skeptical threat to the meaning of what we say is rescued by music. But as Ground also observes, curiously—despite passing references to *Don Giovanni* and *Le nozze di Figaro*—*Cosi fan tutte* escaped Cavell's direct attention. Yet of all the three Mozart/Da Ponte collaborations, as Ground argues, it is *Cosi* which most intricately examines Cavellian themes of skepticism, sincerity, and alienation. And as he shows, this opera notoriously deploys incongruities between voice, action, and music to achieve its larger ethical purpose. Ground also shows that the opera features a philosopher in active pursuit of a project to "epistemologize" human relationships that in recent years has also attracted philosophical attention. So in this chapter, Ground argues that *Cosi fan tutte* is the most Cavellian of operas and a fitting arena in which to test Cavell's thought against rival accounts of his central themes.

In Part III, "Aesthetic Understanding and Moral Life", Sandra Laugier begins the section by exploring in her chapter the mutations in conceptions of popular culture brought about by attention to one's experience of its objects. According to Cavell, the value of a culture lies not in its "great art" but in its transformative capacity, the same capacity found in the "moral perfectionism" of Emerson and Thoreau. Cavell, Laugier observes, was the first to account for the necessity of theory and criticism brought about by serious reflection on Hollywood film. However, as she also observes, Cavell is less concerned with reversing artistic hierarchies or inverting the relation between theory and practice than with the self-transformation required by our encounters with new experiences, what he defines as the "education of grownups". This does not for her imply what she describes as a false revolutionary inversion of aesthetic values, but rather a new assessment of importance, one which Wittgenstein also called for when he asserted the importance of ordinary language philosophy and attention to ordinary practices and life.

Laugier argues that this displacement of values towards *the important* and *the personal* defines popular culture and its genres. And so she sees that the injunction to appropriate and re-collect one's experience and what counts within it defines the new demand of the *culture of the ordinary*—far from laments about the alienation caused by so-called mass culture. Creatively extending Cavell's observations, Laugier proposes that we may discover a form of perfectionism within the aesthetic demand to find and invent an audience, where this is viewed as a personal search for the words to describe and accept our experience. Thus taken as a whole, Laugier presents her chapter, as she explains, as a new requirement for ordinary criticism of a kind deriving from, and of a piece with, ordinary language philosophy.

David LaRocca, bringing Cavell's work into contact with the forms of human understanding woven throughout ancient epic, asks: Is Achilles a narcissist? Can he feel for his fellow man in a way that we humans know as our own? And more particularly, what does this half-god's behavior—the way he is moved to tears by the plea of another man—tell us about the nature of human empathy more generally, our knowledge of how others feel, and the possibility of the human as such? Sometimes, LaRocca observes, it is those who are not fully human—Gods, half-gods, animals—who demonstrate and reinforce (our presumed) human traits. Drawing primarily from the work of Stanley Cavell, yet in company with disparate scholars, including Simone Weil and her remarkable reflections on *The Iliad*, LaRocca shows how we can be pushed to ask whether it is possible to genuinely weep over others, or whether tears are necessarily only shed over one's own pain and losses. Why and how this scene of male weeping recommends this troubling thought lies at the heart of his investigation in this chapter. LaRocca concludes with some notes on criteria for human emotion and expression, linking all of his discussion to the question asking whether we may mediate ourselves out of our own narcissism.

Richard McDonough begins with one of Cavell's most striking themes, which Cavell associates with Wittgenstein *Remarks on the Foundations of Mathematics* (IV. 53): it is the claim that there is a close connection between philosophy and madness and that madness lurks just beneath the surface of ordinary life. However, McDonough notes that Cavell does not quote the final remark of that section which suggests that just as madness permeates sanity so also death permeates life (a claim he abbreviates as MDM). The extensive religious-literary history of MDM all leading to Cavell's claim, a tradition including Augustine, Luther, Milton, and Rilke (several of which were particularly admired by Wittgenstein), is explored by McDonough. McDonough then views MDM in the light of Wittgenstein's remark to Drury that he (Wittgenstein) cannot help looking at problems from a religious point of view, and he contrasts the view of death in Wittgenstein's later philosophy with his view in the *Tractatus Logico-Philosophicus*. McDonough investigates how Wittgenstein uses MDM to bring the deceptive sublimity of mathematics "down to earth" (where the people and the madness are). And finally in his chapter and weaving his themes together, McDonough shows how these insights suggest that mathematics is, within limits, akin to literature and, following Cavell, that some great literature can be seen as making what Wittgenstein calls "grammatical" points.

In Part IV, "Reading Fiction and Literary Understanding", Alan Johnson provides a reading of John le Carré's spy novel *Tinker Tailor Soldier Spy* in the light of themes from Cavell. The novel, Johnson argues, intricately describes a sham world in which little separates Western from Soviet practices. However, as many spy stories make the same point, what, Johnson asks, distinguishes le Carré's work? Johnson observes that, instead of simply describing Cold War espionage as an exercise in truth detection, this novel shows that version of espionage to be symptomatic of an inherently contingent post-imperial world. The novel thus reflects Cavell's point that by fundamentally acknowledging this contingency, we make meaning of the world—one whose historical fallout this novel's author's generation acutely sensed. The novel's global setting is therefore an integral part of its moral vision, a vision where ethical and aesthetic understanding inseparably intertwine.

Erin Greer begins with the observation that for Stanley Cavell, John Milton's seventeenth-century description of "a meet and happy conversation" as the goal of marriage hints at the intellectual reciprocity enacted in good conversation that Cavell terms "acknowledgment." Greer sees that George Meredith's 1879 novel *The Egoist* simultaneously evokes and disrupts this implicit association between conversation and intimate partnership, contextualizing romantic aspirations with a prescient dramatization of what twentieth-century philosophers would call "speech performativity." And as Greer shows, *The Egoist* reverses the familiar nineteenth-century marriage plot, exposing the intersection of social power, intimacy, and language use in the Victorian institution of marriage by depicting a woman's efforts to escape from the consequences of her promise to marry. Reading *The Egoist* in dialogue with J.L. Austin and against the backdrop of Cavell and Milton, this chapter articulates the historical and material conditions governing the "happiness" of both conversation and the "forms of life" it may index.

Garry L. Hagberg begins with the observation that throughout his work Stanley Cavell has maintained, with the kind of special vigilance that is connected to his understanding of the power and nature of absorbed aesthetic experience, an acute and tireless awareness of the expressive nuances of speech. And it is not only that such nuances are expressive; they are also, and perhaps still more deeply, self-constitutive. This explains why Cavell sees a fellow traveler in this enterprise in Henry James, and Cavell's observations concerning what it is to be "haunted" by past experience, to have such experience "carry with it an after-sense" in James's phrase, describe at one and the same time (a) our relations to our words and past words (as Cavell has written about at length), (b) the unsettling experience James had coming back to America after 25 years (as chronicled in his *The American Scene*), and, as Cavell explains, intimately connected with this, (c) the experience psychologically investigated in James's "The Jolly Corner", where the protagonist returns not only to New York, and not only to a former house, but indeed to the spectral image of the person he would, or might, have become had he never gone abroad years earlier. These themes are further pursued in James's "The Beast in the Jungle."

In making these connections, James refers to what he calls "the widening circle" of resonances, meaning-determining connections, and deepened meaning; this, Hagberg suggests here, is Cavell's approach to aesthetic experience, the process of continually grasping and articulating a "widening circle". And this experience, as Cavell shows in his philosophical-critical writings, and as James shows in the minds of his characters, is the content, the substance, of aesthetic understanding, of interpersonal understanding, and indeed of self-understanding. At one point Cavell catalogues James's self-descriptive phrases in *The American Scene* ("the indiscreet listener", "the hovering kindly critic", "the seeker of stories", "the visiting shade", "the restored absentee", among many others), and Hagberg suggests that we see here in microcosm the relation between the nuances of language and the nuances of self-identity as they weave themselves together. Cavell's work as reader, as interpreter, is the work of discovering and articulating "the widening circle", and the character of this work, when contained within the aesthetic realm, is both Austinian in its acuity and Wittgensteinian in its discernment of meaning-creating and meaning-shading nuance.

Taken as a whole, the dozen chapters brought together here offer a comprehensive view of one of the conceptually deepest and most culturally encompassing philosophers of recent decades, one specially alive to the contribution the arts and aesthetic experience can make to philosophical understanding.

Bard College Garry L. Hagberg
Annandale-on-Hudson, NY, USA

PART I

Understanding Persons Through Film

CHAPTER 1

I Want to Know More About You: On Knowing and Acknowledging in *Chinatown*

Francey Russell

Throughout his writings Stanley Cavell brings our attention to the difference between knowing and acknowledging, and has urges philosophers to recognize that the skeptical, epistemic problem of other minds might actually be part of an effort to avoid the ordinary, ethical difficulties of acknowledgment. What makes the latter so challenging to understand is Cavell's suggestion that acknowledgment cannot be elucidated via definition or conceptual analysis; instead, we can come to appreciate what acknowledgment means by learning to recognize instances of its success and cases of its failure, both in life and in art.

An exemplary case study of the problems of knowing and acknowledging would involve an exploration of both the temptation to treat another human being as an object to be known—figured out and laid bare—and an effort to grapple with the human need to acknowledge and be acknowledged. Such a case study would illustrate how the effort to know a person can obscure the ethical underpinnings, and how concrete opportunities for acknowledgment can be missed or seen too late, illustrating not only the

F. Russell (✉)
Yale University, New Haven, CT, USA

difficulty of recognizing the need for acknowledgment generally speaking, but the difficulty of realizing that *this gesture* or *this comment* or *this silence* constituted an expression of that need. It would have to show, as Cavell repeatedly emphasizes, the costs of knowing and acknowledging, a cost that Cavell sees philosophy as tending to forget. My proposal in this chapter is that we can find such an exemplary case study in Roman Polanski's *Chinatown*[1] and in the genre of film noir more generally. The genre and this instance afford us a kind of aesthetic understanding which, since acknowledgment is the issue, also constitutes a kind of self-understanding.

* * *

A descendent or perversion of the detective genre (see Durgnat 1998), film noir takes as part of its basic thematic motivation the problem or pursuit of knowledge (see "Towards a Definition of Film Noir" in Borde and

---

[1] What are the ethics of turning to a film by Roman Polanski as part of an exploration of the dynamics of acknowledgment? What are the ethics of turning to his films at all anymore, after everything we know? Speaking for myself, this difficulty is compounded in that not only do I think that *Chinatown* is one of the greatest films ever made, I also think Polanski has made a number of important films about women and their protest against the world: in addition to *Chinatown*, there is *Repulsion* (1965), *Rosemary's Baby* (1968), *Tess* (1979), even *The Tenant* (1976). But of course, thinking about these films, it is impossible not to think of the women in Polanski's life, most significantly Samantha Gailey, whom Polanski was charged with raping at Jack Nicholson's house while she was 13 years old, and in more recent years: Charlotte Lewis, a woman identified as Robin M., Renate Langer, and Marianne Barnard. How on earth do we reconcile what this man has done or been accused of doing to women, with an appreciation of his films, let alone the idea that some of his films make interesting, important claims about women's lives? Some might justifiably take Polanski's actions as more than enough reason to give up on his movies, certainly ground enough to give up any expectation that his films could display sensitivity to women's lives. I myself do not know how our thinking about his movies should be informed by our knowledge of the facts of Polanski's life, what he did or what he suffered (his mother, Bula, was murdered while pregnant in Birkenau; his wife, Sharon Tate, was murdered while pregnant by the Manson family). For me this remains an ever open, always troubling question. I do not think it is strictly *fallacious* to understand a work in light of the artist's life (the idea that it is is known as the "biographical fallacy"; see also "The Death of the Author"); I also do not feel prepared to reject works of art once I've learned that their creators were awful. These issues raise properly philosophical questions about the role that an artist's character should play in thinking about his or her art (a question that takes unique form when it comes to a collaborative medium like film). For now I believe it is possible to engage critically with movies made by Polanski while avoiding the cult-of-(male)-genius and without ignoring what he did. For further discussion of this problem, see Dederer (2017) and the Daily Nous roundtable discussion "Philosophers on the Art of Morally Troubling Artists" (2017).

Chaumeton 2002). The hero, or anti-hero, is usually in the business of knowing and discovering—for example, a private eye (the majority of noirs, including *The Big Sleep*, *Out of the Past*, and *Kiss Me Deadly*), a police officer (*Touch of Evil*), a journalist (*Ace in the Hole*), and so on—and the plot hinges on his being plunged into a disorientated state of not knowing. Unlike Sherlock Holmes whose neutrality and isolation[2] allow him to solve mysteries brought to him by and of concern to others, the noir hero is himself implicated in the mystery he is meant to solve; the pursuit of knowledge becomes a matter of not just professional but personal significance, the success or failure of which has consequences for who he takes himself to be and the world he takes himself to inhabit.

Noir presents a world in which our confidence in human knowledge and knowing is tested under the pressure of certain difficult "realities";[3] not only the reality of human corruptibility and the implications of war (noir is often understood as a uniquely "post-war" phenomenon), but even more intimately and philosophically, noir grapples with the reality of human separateness, the difficulty of knowing an other, and the possibility that in the realm of human relationships knowing, conceived as a matter of gathering information (the detective's or PI's *modus operandi*), will neither suffice nor satisfy. Following Cavell, we might say that the dissatisfactions of knowledge *would* be supplemented by acknowledgment, but that such human responsiveness to one another is rarely achieved in the world of noir—which is to say that noir evidences acknowledgment and the need for it primarily through its failure.

The archetypal characters of noir are representatives of human knowing, types recognizable for their particular epistemic postures. The decent detective, as one example, is a knowledge seeker whose moral uprightness is expressed in his commitment to discovering the truth (*The Big Heat*, *Laura*); in cases where the detective is corrupt, his corruption or moral failure lies not just in his violent crimes but in his efforts to distort or conceal some truth (*L.A. Confidential*). One's relationship with truth and knowledge, then, has implications for one's ethical orientation and

---

[2] In "The Hound of the Baskervilles," for example, Holmes tells Watson: "it is a singular thing, but I find that a concentrated atmosphere helps a concentration of thought. I have not pushed it to the length of getting into a box to think, but that is the logical outcome of my convictions." Holmes radically isolates himself in order to think, a posture and possibility which is unthinkable in noir.

[3] Cora Diamond discusses the idea of the "difficulty of reality" as a challenge to traditional moral philosophy in her essay "The Difficulty of Reality and the Difficulty of Philosophy," *Partial Answers: Journal of Literature and the History of Ideas* 1, no. 2 (2003).

capacities. The private eye is presented as especially morally ambiguous precisely because his business consists in selling the truth, making a profit off of knowledge, and in so doing disrespecting our faith that truth and knowledge rest rightly outside the realm of capital (*The Maltese Falcon*, *Chinatown*).[4]

With respect to the general plots of noirs, even after truth has been revealed or a case has been cracked, the morally unstable universe that we are left to live in is a world in which we no longer believe that truth is tethered to the good. In noir, the revelation of truth, when and if it comes, rarely provides redemption; we might say that in this world truth has lost its appeal or efficacy, or that we have been shaken from our fantasy of its power. Even in instances where a relatively good or upstanding character finally ascends to a position of power (*The Big Heat*, *L.A. Confidential*), or love wins out (*Gilda*), the question we are left with is whether moral principles or a love of truth are still meaningful or efficacious (rather than naïve, wilfully blind, risky, or impotent) in the world of film noir.

Finally, of the highly general claims we can make of the genre, the standard economy of imagery in noir involves a play of space and light that creates an atmosphere of inescapable duplicity and disorientation: dark back alleys, noisy clubs, claustrophobic interiors, blinding police lights, shadows dissecting faces, photographs and mirrors, repetitions and doublings. The city becomes a prison, safe and dangerous spaces become indistinguishable, and the human form—primarily the face—is darkened or obscured, compromising our familiarity and confidence as its disfigurement, whether by shadow or more literally, through violent action, intimates a fearsome unknowability.[5]

Of course, critics like Paul Schrader and Raymond Durgnat have suggested that film noir is best conceived not as a genre at all but as a *tone* that a film can take, a tone that dominated a certain period in the history of

---

[4] Of course, Sherlock Holmes also sells his knowledge. But the private eye sells private knowledge for private gain—often husbands and wives wanting information on one another, individuals seeking some sort of treasure—and he often has a tarnished history in a more legitimate form of sleuthing or policing; this presents him as morally suspect in a way that Sherlock Holmes is not. Additionally, while Holmes is everywhere showered with praise, noir private eyes are met with derision, skepticism, fear, even laughter.

[5] Consider in *The Big Heat* Gloria Grahame's face is horribly burnt right as Glenn Ford and we discover that we had misjudged her, wrongly taken her as a double-crosser. She is presented as who she really is, then, only by way of grotesque disfiguration.

American filmmaking and that finds its most apt expression in dark imagery and dark plots. As Schrader (2003) writes, "since film noir is defined by tone rather than genre, it is almost impossible to argue one critic's descriptive definition against another's. How many noir elements does it take to make a film noir noir?" (230). That is, since any list of marks or features common to noirs would be ultimately arbitrary, the task of grouping these films under a commonly defined genre becomes impossible.

In fact, Schrader's approach to noir is not out of step with Cavell's reworked conception of genre. Cavell suggests that we should imagine a genre not as a set of elements common to a class, but more like "a medium in the visual arts, or a 'form' in music" (1984, 28). He writes:

> the idea is that the members of a genre share the inheritance of certain conditions, procedures and subjects and goals of composition…each member of such a genre represents a study of these conditions, something I think of as bearing the responsibility of the inheritance (ibid.)

For both Schrader and Cavell, then, "film noir" should identify a sustained study of tone, cinematic procedure, goals of composition, and—perhaps against Schrader—the exercise of certain critical questions concerning the reach and limits of human knowledge and morality. Film noir offers, we might say, not the repetition of a fixed set of plots but a distinctive way of posing certain questions or, as Schrader puts it, a tone of inquiry.

Both Cavell's and Schrader's approaches attend closely to the fact of generic or tonal development, the fact that the tenor or pitch of noir changes over time, responding both to internal and external conditions, engaging in a kind of cinematic self-reflection that transforms the very thing it seeks to make reflectively explicit. This is not to suggest that what was once noir, imagined as something complete or determinate, eventually becomes something else. Rather, noir would always represent one tone in concert with others, never fully extricable from the full and diverse expression of which it is a part. Thus any transformation in noir is not peripheral or external to the genre but instead newly constitutes that very genre or tone.

One distinctive variation on noir, of which we can regard *Chinatown* (1975) as an instance, puts a specific emphasis on what can and cannot (or should not) be known, suggesting that the cinema's obsession with turning its gaze on every intimacy or perversity of human life results not in ever more knowledge, but in its undoing. In staging an almost Oedipal quest to know at any cost, these films unfold the implications of a perversity or secrecy at the heart of individuals or society; the perverse core of the family, for instance, or the corruption that animates authority. The suggestion, delivered in tone or style as much as plotting, is that the desire to know is too often a desire to know too much, a desire as excessive and perverse as the secret to be revealed. Thus this variant takes noir's abiding concern with the dark and hidden side of the human—and with the audience's desire to encounter it—and renders it horrifically explicit. This is a kind of *uncanny noir*, a noir concerned with the desire to bring to light, or to screen, what ought to remain hidden. Examples of uncanny noir include, for instance, Welles' *The Trial*, Aldrich's *Kiss Me Deadly*, Hitchcock's *Vertigo*, Lynch's *Blue Velvet* and *Mulholland Drive*, Fincher's *Se7en*, and Polanski's *Chinatown*.

In *Chinatown* the impulse to know that finds expression in so much of noir meets its resounding, terrifying, and ultimately tragic limits. The conceptual and ethical need for acknowledgment, as Cavell articulates it, is felt just at the place where the capacity for knowledge is outstripped in the face of another person, and the need for a form of relating *other* than knowing becomes pronounced. What would it mean for Jake to *know* Evelyn, and how is this different than knowing *what* she knows? What would be gained by learning her secret? The film suggests that, in fact, very little is gained by this new knowledge. Instead something is lost: the possibility for something like acknowledgment.

* * *

Chinatown, I want to suggest, really involves two films, two ways of seeing or two worlds. The preoccupation with or privileging of the first film drives the plot, head-on and violently, into the second; and in our attempt to attend to and keep pace with the first film, we everywhere miss the signs of the second. As I will try to show, the first film concerns questions of knowledge, the second the possibility of acknowledgment; and, in our fixation on the promise of knowledge, we, along with the protagonist, miss the opportunity for acknowledgment. Hence its tragic ending.

Chinatown's plot, based in part on the California Water Wars, is notoriously complicated and almost impossible to follow on a first viewing; "it is maybe the last of the great complicated story lines that movies dared" (Thompson 1994, 754). I have included a summary in the Appendix, but

I will offer this plot capsule here: in *Chinatown* a private detective is caught up in a scandal the reach of which he never fully comprehends; in his attempt to clear his own name, he encounters pervasive and profound corruption, at both public and private levels. This private investigator (PI), Jake Gittes (Jack Nicholson), believes that Evelyn Mulwray (Faye Dunaway) is holding information that could help him solve the mysteries of who set him up; of Water and Power's secret plot; of the role of her father, Noah Cross (John Huston); and of the murder of Evelyn's husband, the chief engineer of Water and Power, Hollis Mulwray. The film's plot consists largely in tracking Jake's efforts to understand these relations, the results of which fail to provide the kind of epistemic satisfaction he'd sought (which means here that the audience too is unsatisfied). That is, in classic noir fashion, the revelation of truth neither fully dissolves the mysteries nor provides anybody's salvation. Instead we find that Jake's pursuit of truth is undermined when brought to bear on the nature of the corruption he was convinced he could understand, even defeat.

In fact the viewer's experience of struggling to follow the plot, of feeling that unless one knows what is going on, one will miss what's important about the film, represents a conviction and commitment to a certain form of understanding that parallels the protagonist's own trajectory. When, in the film's famous last line, his partner tells Jake to "forget it…it's Chinatown," he seems to suggest that even the best collection of knowledge, even the most careful attention to detail, could neither prepare for nor prevent this particular turn of events: total loss is inevitable here, very little can be redeemed. Since some of these characters have worked this beat before and seen things turn similarly sour, the suggestion seems to be that there is nothing to gain from trying to imagine what could have been done differently, nothing to learn. The advice from one detective to another is that to live with Chinatown, it must be forgotten.

So what is "Chinatown"?

What is it about this series of events that accounts for Jake's apparent devastation? Is it just especially sad that a woman with a tragic history should meet a tragic death? Why, in response to a man evidencing such lifelessness, such a terrifying absence of response, would one advise him to just "forget it"? Does Jake know something that is best forgotten? Does Jake now, looking at Evelyn's corpse, *know* something he did not know before, has this tragedy *taught* him anything?

I will suggest that Jake's devastation is precisely not a response to new knowledge; rather, if Jake has learned anything (and this remains an open question), his devastation at Evelyn's killing is a registration of the thought that in his pursuit of knowledge, he failed to see or hear Evelyn at all, he failed to acknowledge her. "Chinatown" signifies not only, say, the fatedness of human life, the inevitability of corruption, the triumph of the criminal, or the ultimate inconsequence of certain human lives and deaths; rather "Chinatown" can be also understood to signify that a myopic preoccupation with certain kinds of knowledge can obscure solicitation for acknowledgment, and that when the latter goes unmet, there is a real human cost.

In *The Claim of Reason* (1999), Cavell discusses a presupposition of ordinary language philosophy, namely that our desire to know, and our skepticism about the reliability of our knowledge, must be justified by the concrete context in which this desire emerges; that is, there must be good reason why I would want to know something, and why I would question the reliability of my knowing (see "Austin and Examples," 1999). This represents, Cavell suggests, Austin's attempt to localize and contain skepticism, such that it cannot be loosed on knowledge *überhaupt*. The idea is that when generalized beyond the particular circumstance that inspired a skeptical attitude, that attitude loses its sense, hence its threatening force.[6]

With respect to *Chinatown*, this would mean that Jake's suspicious desire to know more about, say, Water and Power, and his conviction that his usual methods for acquiring such knowledge (relying on the testimony of employees, for example) are not trustworthy, must be reasonably justified by those circumstances. And indeed he does have good reason to be suspicious: not only was he set up, but the circumstances surrounding the setup are peculiar: the night time water dumping, Mulwray's mysterious trips to the riverbed, the implausible story about Water and Power benevolently irrigating the farmlands. The problem is that Jake assumes that the reasonableness of his suspicion in *this* case can extend to every circumstance in which he seeks knowledge; and, as I will claim, in the case of Evelyn, his desire for knowledge (to know what Evelyn knows), and his suspicion of the source of that knowledge (what

---

[6] Cavell of course believed that skepticism *can* be loosed on knowledge as such, but he follows Austin in suggesting that some actual and "local" experience, encounter, or feeling motivates skepticism about knowledge "generally." That is, whereas Austin believes that the skepticism about knowledge or the world as such is incoherent, Cavell wants to take seriously the thought that the philosopher may have "a special reason, anyway a good enough reason, for raising the question of reality [or knowledge]" (1982, 59).

Evelyn says), Jake's skeptical posture is inappropriate. Or rather, Jake's mistake is to take Evelyn to be a problem of knowledge, he believes that some piece of knowledge or information could allay his skepticism, and so he fails to recognize that, to use Cavell's words, our "relation to the world as such is not that of knowing, anyway not what we think of as knowing" (1999, 241).

Another way of putting this is that Jake wants to bring his professional detective's attitude, which is to say a skeptical attitude, to bear on all of his encounters. Three features of Jake's attitude are worth noting. First, his method is invasive yet detached; he follows individuals without their knowledge, he photographs them in private moments of which he is not a part, his métier as a PI is "matrimonial work," which is to say he specializes in observing the workings of marriages without being himself involved in an intimate relationship. Second, Jake is suspicious by habit and by trade, ready to regard any apparently ordinary situation as suspect. It is this general posture that allows him to perceive the mysteriousness of a drunk who drowned in a dry riverbed or to assume that the deputy chief of Water and Power is lying when he claims that his department is irrigating farmland out of pure goodwill. Finally, Jake takes himself to be an expert in matters of observation and acquiring evidence, much of which involves being skilled at reading other human beings. His work as a PI has taught him (he thinks) much about marriages, about relationships, about individuals and what they hide from one another, and about what it means to discover such hidden things. His confidence in his own expertise, then, allows him to imagine what someone might be hiding or lying about. Insofar as he thinks that his relation to the world is fundamentally a suspicious yet authoritative relation of knowing, we might say that, crucially and fatally, Jake thinks he knows what it is he doesn't know. If he accuses someone of hiding something, it is because he already has a sense of what that thing might be.

Jake's general attitude is well displayed in his first private meeting with Evelyn Mulwray. He arranges to meet with her after his nose has been cut following his snooping into the dealings of Water and Power, and after her husband has been found drowned. Jake, nose bandaged, meets Evelyn, veiled, in a dark bar; significantly, in this intimate meeting, both faces are obscured.

Jake tells Evelyn that what she's told him so far "isn't good enough...I think you short-changed me on the story. Something besides the death of your husband was bothering you." In so saying, Jake suggests first, that he can tell she is lying and has an idea of the kind of thing she is concealing; second, he suggests that he was able to make this adept conclusion based on what he takes to be an unconvincing expression of grief. "You were upset," he says, "but not that upset." Evelyn responds, "Mr. Gittes, don't tell me how I feel."

Pressing her—"I think you're hiding something"—Evelyn confesses that she hasn't been fully honest. She tells Jake that she knew about her husband's affair and that, far from being upset, she was "grateful." To this Jake responds, "look, I do matrimonial work, it's my métier. When a wife tells me that she was relieved her husband was cheating on her, it runs contrary to my experience," implying here, as he does in his accusation, that she did not display sufficient feeling, that he knows best what it means to grieve a husband and what it means to discover infidelity. When Evelyn tells him that she too was cheating—or rather, she does not disconfirm Jake's assumption—he asks still more questions, until she finally tells him, "I think you know all you need know about me...is that all?" Outside, Jake will aggressively accuse her again of "hiding something," but he abandons her, drives away in frustration too quickly to hear her calling after him. What has frustrated him? Even though he is in the arena of his expertise, there is something about Evelyn that does not conform to Jake's idea of what the situation should look like. He probes her private life, accuses her of withholding information, and suggests that he knows best how a woman in her circumstances should respond. Yet Jake's professional attitude does not here provide results, Evelyn cannot be adequately "read" in accordance with his pictures of marriage, women, grief, deceit, secrecy. In response to this failure of knowledge, his only recourse is to leave in anger, as though her unreadability were a personal affront, a form of aggressive withholding.

Cavell describes how a certain picture of our knowledge of others, of other minds, can suggest the skeptical conclusion that we might *never* know them. According to this picture, knowing another mind is impossible because that mind can keep to itself, withhold from me: "He's in; I'm out. Is something *keeping* me out, excluding me? *He* could be" (1999, 367). Such a picture fixes the other's mind, or the person, quite literally *inside* of a body, which itself functions as a wall—a veil, a bandage—making access to the other impossible; moreover, insofar as *he* keeps me out, he excludes me, an antagonistic refusal. Cavell notes two distinctive features of this picture of our relations with others, features that transform the real frustrations of our relationships—others really *can* be withdrawn, and they really *are* separate from us—into metaphysical constraints.

First, in this picture we conceive of knowing another person as knowing *what they know* (cf. 1999, 102) or experiencing what they experience; and given that we cannot inhabit another's position or live their life, it then seems that we can therefore never know them. If "he can keep his thoughts to himself" and "hide his feelings" (1999, 367), a suspicious picture will conflate knowing those "things" (thoughts and feelings) with knowing *him*; and again, upon realizing that other people can conceal those things, knowledge of others seems impossible.

As is already clear from this description of knowing another as knowing what they know, this picture describes the problem of knowing another as a problem of *access*; this is the second feature. We imagine the other's mind as, for example, "a garden which I can never enter" (1999, 368), and in so doing we literalize our genuine experiences of separation or powerlessness (2002, 261); we take our feeling of inability with respect to another person and conclude that there is some *thing* we cannot do (i.e., enter him). With this picture, the real practical difficulty of coming to know another is disavowed and replaced by a speculated metaphysical limitation. We generate an idea that "to know or be known by another is to penetrate or be penetrated by another, to occupy or be occupied. This idea would be prepared by the idea…of the self as private (hence, as said, as guilty)" (1999, 470).

That a PI's business is to find evidence for guilt, that his methods involve invading privacy in order to disclose what his target knows, that the only way to know another person is to produce evidence of her personal life, to occupy her personal space, and in so doing undermine any attempt at hiding or deceit, all this makes the PI a ready exemplar of the skeptical position as Cavell understands it. It is Cavell's contention that oftentimes a philosophically or metaphysically backed skepticism represents a defense against the ordinary disappointments that characterize human relationships, the everyday ways we fail to recognize, listen to, or acknowledge one another. Metaphysical limitations are preferable because ordinary limitations and difficulties are *our* responsibility. It is easier to hold that we *cannot* know each other than to accept that, in some cases, we simply do not or will not.

Jake assumes that something determinate, like a secret, is keeping Evelyn from being fully knowable to him, that they are separated for *some reason* (cf. 1999, 369); as a detective, he assumes that she is withholding what she knows, that she is resistant to his questions because she has some *thing* to hide. Since, in Jake's world, a human being is a source of evidence to be penetrated, and because resistance or withholding communicates a guilty disposition, Evelyn's evasiveness and her direct appeals that Jake stop questioning her can only be interpreted as an admission of guilt and so a solicitation for further invasiveness; there is no possibility, as far as he is able to see, that Evelyn might have a good, *not guilty* reason to keep things to herself. On a PI's model, human relationships only take the form of interrogation and confession, where privacy is secrecy, and secrecy guilt. For this reason, noirs are especially adept at working out the skeptical picture of knowing other minds.

Jake thinks he knows what it is he doesn't know. And he thinks he can obtain that knowledge as he obtains all his knowledge: invasively, suspiciously, accusingly, and calculatingly. When Evelyn asks him why he wants to know what her middle initial stands for—it is C for Cross, her father's name, something she bears—he says, "no reason, I'm just a snoop." That is, in being suspicious of everything by trade, no question stands in need of any specific justification. Jake's professional suspicion licenses him to ask any question he likes, no matter the cost for whomever he's interrogating.

If, following Cavell, skepticism masks a more fundamental disappointment or even horror in response to the exigencies of human relationships, then we might say that Jake is attempting to know Evelyn while evading the costs or consequences. He just wants to know (he's "just a snoop") the intimate details of her life, the nature and cause of her feelings toward her dead husband and toward her father, where she goes at night, the nature of her relationship with the young girl. He wants to know all of this, believing that he has the right, and that she, given the circumstances (murder and extortion), has a duty to tell. Despite the many signs she gives, both intentional and involuntary, that the aspects of her life that she wants to keep private have no bearing on his case, in generalizing his skeptical detective's attitude Jake assumes that he has right of access to Evelyn, to know what she knows, without any duty to take on the consequences of so knowing. He wants to know her *irresponsibly*. In fact, as viewers, so do we.

* * *

One of Cavell's central ideas in his *The World Viewed*, where he outlines his ontology of film, is that photography and film "maintain the presentness of the world by accepting our absence from it. The reality is a photograph is present to me while I am not present to it" (1979, 23): a world so viewed is a world without me. The cinema, Cavell suggests, provides pleasure, not by endowing the viewer with unlimited power—say, a voyeuristic power to view the world at will—but by providing us a time and space *without* the need for power, an experience where we do not have to bear the burden of power (ibid., 40). We can be witness to a world without responsibility.

While Cavell has reservations about cinematic modernity, and the idea that movies eventually come to reflect on their conditions, he also observes that "film has brought itself into question" (ibid., 123). That is, it seems that at a certain point in its history or development, film lost its conviction in its promise of a candid exhibition of the world itself (ibid., 119). In this post-lapsarian state, movies are now tasked with voicing this wavering conviction within the strictures of narrative cinema itself.[7]

Now it might seem that film's full realization or acknowledgment of its conditions and capacities must involve a form of conspicuous self-awareness or self-reference, by, for example, calling attention to the camera's interventions. The point, for Cavell, though, is not that the camera should acknowledge its presence in the world it records, by, for example, putting a camera in the scene itself (or putting the director in the film, as Polanski himself does); rather the point is that the camera is *absent* from the film's world. As Cavell puts it, the camera's calling attention to itself or otherwise winking to the audience "is not an acknowledgment but a denial of withdrawal. You cannot sidestep the claims of a position with a trick" (ibid., 130). This means that "the camera must now, in candour, acknowledge not its being present in the world but its being outside the world" (ibid.). By extension, we the audience must acknowledge not our secret involvement or implicit sanctioning of this world,[8] but our absence

---

[7] A full discussion of film's avoidance of the condition of modernity would take me too far afield, into topics of theatricality, automatism and mechanism, presentness, and so on. For my purposes, I think it is sufficient to make note of Cavell's concern about film's taking on the burden of modernism, while at the same time pointing out that he nonetheless sees that such a burden is being assumed.

[8] Michael Haneke, for instance, is an example of a filmmaker who takes it that his task is to bring to the viewer's awareness her secret and ongoing endorsement of what she sees. He is concerned to make the viewer feel the full extent of her power as a viewer, a power he thinks is suffered through the grueling violence in his films, and a power he thinks would be best exercised by walking out of his movies. Though I think he has matured beyond the interrogative and direct-address techniques of *Funny Games*, even in a film like *Caché*, he calls the camera's *presence* in that world, and so *our* presence, to explicit attention, suggesting that by revealing or unconcealing the camera and its powers to reveal and record, so too are we revealed to ourselves, we are asked to face up to our power as viewers. This is precisely neither the predicament nor the task of cinema for Cavell.

and powerlessness. But if recognizing presence seemed to call for a kind of self-conscious display, what would it mean to recognize absence? And *what of* that absence? Just what about absence needs acknowledging?

Cavell suggests that in making a world present to us in our absence from it, film relieves the viewer of the burden of power. I suggest that film thereby fulfills or plays out a certain fantasy of irresponsibility: it permits us to look and to know without consequence. What needs acknowledgment (which is not the same as calling for correction) is our passive presence with respect to a film, and the kind of relationship to knowing and acknowledging, or the fantasies of such a relationship, this passivity might invite.

Noir is perhaps especially apt for exploiting this fantasy of moviegoing insofar as one of its orienting thematic preoccupations is the fantasy, and impossibility, of separateness or neutrality as a condition for knowing. Indeed noir consistently suggests that it is the protagonist's fantasy of his own distance from the object of his interest that will be his ultimate undoing. *The Big Heat*, for instance, demonstrates this with devastating force: Det. Bannion assumes that he can investigate with immunity a sergeant's suicide and its connection with the mob, that he can face human criminality and cruelty within the confines of his profession while leaving his home life untarnished. In light of this fantasy, his wife's murder (intended for him) represents an assault not only on his effort to reveal the relations between the police force and the mob, but also on his conviction that he could maintain distance, that he could attain profoundly consequential knowledge without personally bearing any of those consequences. It is also an assault on his belief that the only person he puts at risk through his efforts is himself, as though in his investigation he could extricate himself cleanly from those with whom he is otherwise inextricably bound.

Noir's dark suggestion that no human knowledge is born without burden can be understood as, in part, a reflection on and challenge to one of the conditions of cinema, the viewer's belief or fantasy that she will not suffer what she sees, or that aesthetic suffering is somehow not real. In *Chinatown*, the painfulness of Evelyn's revelation and of the film's final scene is that in both we must recognize in ourselves the assumptions we'd made about her (like Jake, we thought we knew the kind of thing we didn't know) and about our own immunity from involvement or burden. Here, cinema's promise of passivity, its promise to relieve us of our need for power and grant us a kind of knowledge without responsibility, does not finally provide the satisfactions we perhaps felt entitled to.

* * *

Cavell writes that "being human is the power to grant being human" (ibid., 397). His point is that no fact or bit of knowledge will convince one of another person's humanity. Rather, seeing another person as human or in their humanity is something it is in our power to do and also in our power to refuse. But Cavell's point is also that if I withhold my power to grant being human, not only do I fail adequately to acknowledge others, my own humanity is also thereby compromised.

There is no better figure of a compromised humanity in *Chinatown* than Noah Cross. Of course, Evelyn is the one who is truly compromised, yet in attempting to maintain her privacy, in her effort to assert her separateness even in her intimacy with Jake, in her care for her daughter, in all this Evelyn demonstrates her humanity while it is everywhere denied by others. But the specific nature of Cross' cruelty proves his almost total incapacity for acknowledging others, thus the almost total loss of his own humanity.

Cavell suggests that what spurs skepticism is a disappointment with the criteria for knowing the world and knowing others. With respect to the latter relationship, the sense of disappointment in criteria is itself a response to human finitude or separateness: it is disappointing that no amount of knowing or intimacy can finally overcome our separateness. Being with others places "infinite demands on finite resources" (1999, 470); we are asked to live with unknowing as a constant feature of our knowing, to accept privacy as a condition for intimacy, separateness as a condition for attunement. Cavell's thought is that when these demands are felt to be intolerable, we imagine how we might be relieved of them, by fantasizing ways of overcoming our condition and conceiving our practical burdens as metaphysical limitations. Again, the fantasy Cavell returns to again and again is one in which the other is metaphysically walled off from me and the only way I can reach her is by penetrating that barrier.

"It is to be expected that the idea of knowledge as a violation of privacy (or punishment for it) will be eroticized, enacted in forms of sexual life" (1999, 470) writes Cavell. He notes sadism and masochism as evidence, and we should also recall Melanie Klein's concept of the "epistemophilic instinct" (Klein 1987, 69), an aggressive response to the (m)other's separateness that expresses itself as the desire to access her body and know its contents. It is possible to understand parent-child incest, or even less extreme dissolutions of generational, familial boundaries, as an inversion of this instinct, a destructive parental response to an awareness of the child's growing autonomy and separateness, a response that views separateness and privacy as a violation of the bond. With this anxious interpretation of otherness, access and symbiotic union present the only solution.

Noah Cross is in fact everywhere governed by a bloated sense of his entitlement to access, to literally *cross* all boundaries: social (both in his incest and in his desire to privatize and own crucial human resources), generational (in his relationships with Evelyn and Katherine), geographical (in his plans to "incorporate" the valley into the city of L.A.), and temporal (in his desire for immortality, for nothing less than "the future"). As the only character in *Chinatown* with knowledge of both stories (his corruption of the city and his corruption of Evelyn), Cross represents the literalizing or living-out of the fantasy of total access and the possession of complete knowledge. Indeed, while Cross is only in three scenes (his lunch with Jake; the confrontation at Evelyn's house; and the showdown in Chinatown), his presence saturates the film: once one knows what he's done, and so knows what Evelyn wants to keep private, it begins to seem like his terrifying omnipotence haunts every scene.[9]

Following a device common to many noirs, Jake finds his double not only (more obviously) in the thuggish hired gun Mulvihill, and in Lt. Escobar, an old colleague and newly appointed lieutenant; *Chinatown* also suggests a relation of doubling or kinship between Jake and Noah Cross.

In noir, doubles often offer glimpses of how life for the protagonist might have been, and thereby offer a distorted kind of mirror or opportunity for reflection; additionally, these doubles add to the uncanny, nightmarish quality of noirs, lending the world of noir a tenor of inescapability (David Lynch's films, for instance, take this element of noir and exploit it to hallucinatory effect). Attending to the relations of solidarity and mutual mirroring that are articulated between Cross and Jake allows us to see Cross as a fully realized, exaggerated version of the kind of posture adopted by Jake. That is, Cross represents the very omniscience Jake desires. Indeed, by consistently describing Evelyn as a "disturbed woman," Cross presents himself as a better authority on her state of mind and sense of self

---

[9] Another fictional character that similarly embodies this superhuman, almost metaphysical degree of power and control is The Judge, in Cormac McCarthy's *Blood Meridian*. Both men have perverse sexual appetites, both wield uncanny control over the events in which they participate, both desire, and take, the future; and both stories concern something like the founding or the maintenance of America, where being an American male licenses one to access all (the West, the people in it, the future).

than she is (as Jake had done when he judged her to be "upset but not that upset"). In so doing, Cross intimates that he knows what she knows, which is just what Jake seeks.

As we will see, consulting Cross constitutes Jake's greatest betrayal of Evelyn. In many noirs, the plots and more general thematic orientations pivot around a betrayal of intimacy; usually another character, often a woman, either betrays the protagonist or is seen to. With such a betrayal revealed, we are exposed to the thought that any human relationship is an opportunity for manipulation and capitalization. The femme fatale uses what she knows about the protagonist to exploit the relationship as a means to some end. And in films where the woman we expect to betray the hero does not (e.g., Gloria Graham's character in *The Big Heat*), the protagonist and audience must live with the guilt of having assumed her duplicity; that is, in assuming her deceitfulness, it is *we* who have reduced intimacy to manipulation, it is *our* faith in expressions of solidarity and offers of friendship that has weakened. In *Chinatown*, insofar as the audience also looks to Cross as a possible source of insight into Evelyn's secrets, by the film's end we also must live with the burden of having assumed her duplicity, of having conflated her privacy with some imagined guilt, of having believed that her father, of all people, could help us understand her. Doubting Evelyn's account, and turning to Cross for his, constitutes exactly the kind of "second injury" that victims experience when their claims are not heard or treated as authoritative (see Walker 2006). We see evidence of the impact of this second injury when, upon hearing that Jake went to see her father, Evelyn covers her naked body and recoils from Jake, her face crumbling in pained incomprehension.

If noirs frequently suggest that objective or complete knowledge is no longer possible, *Chinatown* recognizes that, when indulged, absolute knowledge takes a horrific shape. As Cross calmly informs Jake, with regard to the "loss" of his daughter: "I don't blame myself. You see Mr. Gitts [Cross never correctly pronounces Jake's last name], most people never have to face the fact that at the right time and the right place, they're capable of *anything*." With this it seems clear that the omniscience and omnipotence we thought we wanted is realized here in a frightening capacity to do "anything," which is to say a total *in*capacity to recognize anyone that would stand to suffer from that power, anyone who would constitute a legitimate limit to that capacity. With *Chinatown*, we discover that the absolute success of knowledge and power is not "humanly satisfying" (1999, 455), it denies the finitude, which is to say the humanity, in oneself by denying the authoritative presence and demand for acknowledgment, which is to say the humanity, of others.

* * *

At the beginning of my discussion of *Chinatown*, I suggested that there were really two films here, two stories or two worlds. I said that in our efforts to make sense of the first, we miss the signs of the second, which is to say that in our effort to secure knowledge, we neglect a claim to acknowledgment. Now it is standard in Hollywood filmmaking to run two parallel plots: the "action" plot and the "romance" plot.[10] But *Chinatown*'s second storyline isn't exactly Jake's and Evelyn's romance, as it is simply *Evelyn's story*, and though her brief intimacy with Jake is part of it, that intimacy is not its central current or point. Evelyn's story concerns the threat of her life unraveling (again) thanks to the investigation of a nosey PI; it concerns her recognition of him as someone similarly suffering from the past, and his consistent misrecognition of her; finally it concerns her compassionate struggle, against the efforts of her father, to maintain in her daughter a *lack* of knowledge, as part of her effort to ensure for her daughter and herself the future to which Cross feels cruelly entitled. In each of these efforts, what is owed to Evelyn is some form of acknowledgment.

As should be clear, my own discussion—in its concern to clarify Jake's project and the idea of knowledge that governs it, and in its effort to indicate how cinema itself plays out a certain fantasy of knowing without responsibility—has also sidelined Evelyn, not yet acknowledged her. It is as though consideration of *Chinatown* repeats the very dynamic of misrecognition staged by the film itself, as though a preoccupation with everything besides Evelyn was our fate as viewers, until it is too late. That our evasion of Evelyn constitutes such an instructive failure of acknowledgment helps clarify why Cavell thought that concept could be equally well elucidated by its failure as by its success: we learn something about what acknowledgment is when we can recognize its absence. What, then, would it be to pay attention to Evelyn? Can *Chinatown* also tell her story?

---

[10] Thanks to Daniel Morgan for calling my attention to this.

If we can see in *Chinatown* also the staging of her story and not just its consistent neglect (and I am still not sure if we can),[11] then *how* we tell her story will be quite different than how Jake's is told. The plot of which Jake is the hero, however anti-heroic and unsuccessful he may be, is told in his actions (even if failed) and through the circumstances in which he finds himself: we follow Jake's story by following what he does, what he looks at, or by learning what he knows (often *as* he comes to know it); we follow him into reservoirs and orange groves and public hearings, and we work alongside him to piece together a story. That is, in order to know him, we attend to the world toward which he is actively oriented. For all this outward-facing action, there are really only two moments when we are asked to consider Jake as a character with an inner life and a history: the first is in bed with Evelyn, the second is in the film's closing moments.

For the most part, Evelyn's story is told, not primarily by what she says and does as either a self-determining agent or an agent struggling to be so (like Jake), but rather in her face, in the ways in which it speaks for her and in spite of her. Viewing the film again, that is, after one knows *what* she is trying to both keep to herself and communicate, it is striking to see how much is there on the surface of her body. While we cannot know Evelyn by looking at the world around her, we do not for that matter have to look *into* her, to access her mind or know the contents of her thoughts; rather we can look at her face. There, we can quite literally see her struggle to inhabit two worlds, to play a part in two stories—hers and Jake's, or hers and the rest of the world's—right there in her faltered gaze, or in her stutters, or in her clenched jaw.

Or again, at Jake's mention of her father in the former's office, Evelyn blanks, and in attempting to recover herself, she lights a second cigarette, her first still burning in the ashtray. When Jake asks if his mentioning her father upsets her, she launches into a canned explanation having to do with a fight between her father and her husband, but stutters on the word "f-f-father," her face slackening, deadening, as she does so. It looks as if the film has frozen her in an awkward moment between determinate movements or expressions, as though the photograph was taken a moment too

---

[11] A worthy question for another paper on *Chinatown* would be whether we could regard it as representative, at least in part, of the melodrama of the unknown woman. See Cavell's *Contesting Tears: The Hollywood Melodrama of the Unknown Woman*. University of Chicago Press, 1997.

late or too soon. Yet while I think she *is* occupying something like an in-between zone, between being present with Jake and following out her associations with the word "father," she in fact holds this look for several seconds. That is, this look is part of her repertoire of looks; *as* a moment between determinate expressions, this is itself one of her forms of communication. Only with multiple viewings is one able to see how consistently Jake fails to really look at her face. And so while the film as a whole makes possible an aesthetic understanding of acknowledgment, this is in part by way of staging Jake's *lack* of aesthetic intelligence, his inability to look and see what is there on Evelyn's face.

Writing on Cavell's work on photography and film, Richard Moran argues that by simply placing a human being in its range, the camera will find there forms of expression unknown or unendorsed by that person. As he writes (Moran 2016), speaking of a character in Terrence Malick's *Badlands*: "the very fact of the camera's presence makes his very inarticulateness, the very grain of his silences and hesitations, into unavoidable vehicles of expression" (30). This inevitable expressivity, or to put the emphasis on the other side, this endless legibility, is both liberating and confining, "since within [the camera's] gaze, not even holding still and keeping silent, can count as withholding expression" (ibid, 31).

For Wittgenstein (2001), the body, photographed or not, stands as "the best picture of the human soul" (178); as Cavell puts it, "the soul is there to be seen" (1999, 368). Photographic media make explicit or thematize this fact of animate embodiment, namely that the body is not a veil but a voice for the soul. But if the soul really is there on the surface and in the movements of the body, Cavell continues, then "what hides the mind is not the body but the mind itself" (1999, 369), and that may be the other's mind or my own. That is, hiding myself or missing another are not our fates but our capacities, possibilities for our form of life; if this is so, then if we are unknown to one another, this isn't because we are confined within veil-bodies but because being unknown is a human possibility: we can wear veils or fail to look, but "we have a choice" (ibid., 107).

Evelyn then *is* concealing herself, is withholding from Jake, yet this work, the effort of which manifests in stutters and glances and fidgeting, functions against her best intentions by giving her away, or at least by making herself available to be read and acknowledged. In every instance, however, Jake is ready to account for Evelyn's apparent eccentricities with a story that fits what he already has in mind, which is to say that he exactly *fails* to read the expressivity of Evelyn's face. When, for example, Evelyn is beside herself and confesses that the girl in her house is her sister—she claws at her own hair, knocking her head portentously on the car's horn, a foreshadowing of her fate in the final scene—Jake responds to her intense remorse, first, by accusing her of being unnecessarily secretive ("take it easy—she's your sister, she's your sister. Why all the secrecy?"), then, after Evelyn cries quietly that she "can't," he takes the opportunity to answer his own question: "is it because of Hollis? Because she was seeing your husband? Is that it?," to which she eagerly nods her head, gratified for Jake's story, for the shift of attention away from her, back to, essentially, himself and his ideas. This is in fact their dynamic for much of the film: Evelyn, intentionally or not, gives something away, and Jake, rather than pay attention to her, uses this as material for his own speculative construction. In his professed effort to know more about her, he turns away from her, more interested in his own theories gleaned from his prized expertise; to this we want to say, with Wittgenstein (2001), "don't think but *look*!" (§66). We might call this Jake's urge to misunderstand (ibid., §109): he has brought a picture of how to understand Evelyn and cannot get outside it, he will not allow that Evelyn, and whatever she has to tell, might be capable of shaking his beliefs.

Chinatown provides us with one scene of intimacy, one moment of possible friendship. It is, of course, almost requisite for the protagonist of film noir to become emotionally or physically entangled with a woman involved in the case; such couplings, while they may relieve a kind of building tension between the characters and in the audience, nevertheless spell doom for the hero, dashing whatever hope he may have had for extracting himself or surviving the case unscathed. This is true of *Chinatown*, but this scene also offers a glimpse of something like another way in which Evelyn and Jake could be together. So while it does seal both of their fates, this moment is especially tragic because it also seems a fleeting respite from their fate, an opening, however brief, of a space for mutual acknowledgment. But this space cannot be maintained, and its imminent end is kept in view from the start: as the swell of music dies down, a stopwatch can be heard ticking throughout their quiet conversation in her bed.

What is important about this scene is not that Evelyn and Jake have sex, but that here Evelyn is finally doing the talking, and she is asking the questions. Outside on her patio, following their day of investigating the orange groves and being attacked at the retirement home, Jake toasts her for saving his "a-a-...., for saving my neck," correcting his vulgar language yet again, inspiring a sympathetic, even endeared smile from Evelyn. She asks him whether this often happens to him, clarifying that she means this kind of active afternoon, and he, gazing and smiling at her says, "actually this hasn't happened to me in a long time." This provokes a series of questions from Evelyn, where she turns Jake's own defense against him—"it's an innocent question"—and in this exchange we first hear about Chinatown, where Jake did "as little as possible." When Evelyn asks why he left, Jake touches his wounded nose and asks for peroxide.

Inside Evelyn tends to his cut; "it must be painful," she says, and in response Jake asks what's wrong with her eye—"there's something black in the green part of your eye"—again, deflecting attention from himself as an object of inquiry or concern. As he looks intently at her, she holds his gaze and smiles genuinely: "oh that. It's a f-f-flaw, in the iris," stuttering over "flaw," like "father." They embrace. In bed, the clock ticking, Evelyn turns to ask Jake, who faces forward, whether he wore a uniform, saying he must have looked cute in blue and she says, looking at him, "I want to know more about you." When he says "not now," she replies, "you don't like to talk about the past do you? ... why does it bother you to talk about it?" He says it bothers everyone that works in Chinatown, because "you can't always tell what's going on; like with you," making explicit that what bothers him about Evelyn is nothing about her as a person but that *he* can't tell what's going on, that he feels powerless and confused, a representative experience of the motivation for skepticism. As he says this, he turns to face her, and now Evelyn shifts to face forward, as though their proximity would be too much to bear if they were face to face. When Jake explains to Evelyn what happened—"I was trying to keep someone from getting hurt; I ended up making sure that she was hurt"—they do face each other. Jake's description can be interpreted as a memory, a comment on their present circumstances, and a prediction.

What does Evelyn want to know about Jake? In a sense, this scene represents her turning the tables, putting Jake on the receiving end of intimate questions. It might seem that, like his questions regarding Evelyn's feelings for her father, Jake experiences these questions about Chinatown as invasions of privacy or suspicious inquiries. But if this is a correct description of Jake's experience—and his response to her that he's "tired" indicates his real discomfort—it seems that his is a partial, or defensive, assessment of their exchange. For what Evelyn wants to know is *not* the kind of thing Jake wants to know, or her wanting to know is not animated by the same suspicious spirit. What Evelyn sees here is an opportunity for friendship, not for confession, whereas Jake's only understanding of conversation is as interrogation. That is, he can only understand an intimate relationship from within the perspective of his professional métier.

In the penultimate chapter of *The Claim of Reason*, Cavell explores skepticism of other minds, and proposes that it is properly conceived as consisting in two forms, active or passive skepticism: the former characterizes the more familiar form of skepticism regarding others and whether one can know them, the latter represents skepticism as to whether *I* can ever *be known* by others. Cavell then not only clarifies what it is we want, as opposed to what it is we think we want, when it comes to knowing another; he also meditates on what would count as being or feeling known. And as Moran rightly develops this thought, when it comes to human beings (as opposed to things) *we have a say* in whether we are truly known, one must be able to "*find oneself* in the knowledge that others claimed to have achieved" (Moran 2011, 252): to really be known, one must feel known. Trying to make sense of what it would mean to feel known, or find oneself in others' knowledge, helps dissolve the illusion that knowing others has anything to do with access, it makes "the fantasy of 'peering into the mind of another' seem not just fantastical and out of reach, but as missing the fact of how the knowledge of another is a matter of relatedness or responsiveness to that person" (ibid., 251). Taken from the other side, it makes the fantasy of, say, "opening up to the gaze of the other" (or being opened up by it) seem likewise misguided (and both versions now seem quite paranoid). Reconceived with Cavell, being known by someone not drive by this fantasy of access makes that person "not an ideal Confessor (because to a Confessor one must confess, make oneself known) but an ideal Acceptor…the Friend" (ibid., 460).

When Evelyn looks at Jake and asks about his past, it seems like she is trying to be a friend, not a confessor; she wants to know *him* and not "what he knows." It also seems that precisely in his reluctance to talk, a form of withholding that gives him away as someone with a past painful enough to suppress, Evelyn perceives in Jake someone with whom a kind of understanding might be possible. That is, she sees a kindred spirit, someone who likewise suffers from memory, who withholds from others (recall that she's told Jake that she "never stays with anyone very long"); she gazes at him with a longing not to possess but to understand or acknowledge, that is, to connect in the balance of separateness and intimacy.[12]

But the attraction of wounded people to wounded people is often animated by a fantasy of mutual recognition shaped by those very wounds; that is, with this fantasy we are in the grip of repetition, despite imagining that we are working through it. So if Jake is governed by a picture of knowing as accessing, and if, as we have seen, Noah Cross is likewise so governed, then Evelyn's attraction to Jake is in part a repetition of the dynamics with her father. After all, she is attracted to a man whom she has attempted to fight off or reject (she asked him to drop the case, she asked him to stop questioning her), who has not respected but in fact feels entitled to her privacy, who is crude (Jake uses foul language; Cross tells Jake he likes his "nasty reputation") and self-absorbed (both Jake and Cross are concerned primarily with their own success). So despite the perceived promise of acknowledgment, despite Evelyn's holding out for a friendship with Jake, in fact nothing suggests that this could be anything but painful, and familiar. And for Evelyn the familiar does not comfort, and if it can, then for the wrong reasons.

In any event, the clock is ticking, and their conversation about Jake's past is interrupted by a call from what we might understand as both her past and their future or fate. The rest of the film is an unfolding of that destiny, from her revelation of her sister/daughter, to Jake's confrontation of Cross which leads to the reunion of Cross and Evelyn, to Evelyn's death and Cross' absconding with Katherine. Though in some way a respite, Evelyn and Jake's union in fact solidifies their capture in repetition: she

---

[12] Obviously, in imagining what she wants, I am taking some interpretive liberties here with the character of Evelyn. Yet from what we know about her, and what we know about people, I think this interpretation is fair. On the topic of the relationship between how we understand what we and others do, and how we understand characters in movies, Robert Pippin (2012) writes: "there are certainly great gaps between [these cases]…but while screen images are not persons, and film narration is sui generis, there cannot be two completely distinct modalities of such sense-making: one for ordinary life and another governed by an incommensurable movie or dramatic or diegetic or aesthetic logic" (2). Being able to regard and understand movie characters in accordance with the same logic or framework with which we understand ourselves and others is, as Pippin puts, "the minimum conditions for the intelligibility of filmed action" (3). If we can understand Evelyn's lying in bed, speaking to Jake, as action, then I think it is fair to bring to bear both what we know about who she is and what she's done or been through, and what our best thinkers have to say about human motivations and experience, in order to imagine both what she is doing and what she takes herself to be doing.

repeating the dynamic of resistance and penetration enacted with her father, he repeating by endangering someone he cares about through his very efforts to care. To use words of Cavell's meant for another of Polanski's films, here we feel "the power of the past to join hands with the future behind the back of the present" (1979, 87).

When Jake finally confronts Evelyn in the house where Katherine is kept, he is again certain that he knows some secret that Evelyn has been keeping; moreover, he is again certain that in so keeping it, her biggest crime is putting *him* at risk, this time by putting his detective's license on the line. By this point in their relationship, his suspicions and selfishness seem especially cruel, even punishing. After being forced to confess the nature of her relationship with the girl, Jake thereby reinstating their dynamic as one of interrogation and confession, not friendship, and after he responds to her confession by beating her, Evelyn sits on the couch and draws it all out. "My father and I…"—and here she juts her face toward him, taunting him, indignant that he has demanded so much from her— "understand? Or is it too tough for you?"

When Jake states (he does not ask) that her father raped her, she looks at him both pleadingly and pityingly, as though it would be so easy if that's all it was, as if rape would be a much simpler thing—and then she shakes or twitches her head, and it isn't clear whether she is disconfirming his statement or rejecting his gaze, rejecting the place to which they've come. When Cavell insists that the soul is there to be seen, or that only the mind can hide the mind, he is, to reiterate, not suggesting that this makes knowing or acknowledging or showing a soul an easy task, but he does mean that the body is where the full complexity of the soul will show itself, if it does: "nothing is hidden" (Wittgenstein 2001, §435).

* * *

In "Knowing and Acknowledging" Cavell asserts that "from my acknowledging that [for example] I am late it follows that I know I'm late (which is what my words say); but from my knowing I am late, it does not follow that I acknowledge I'm late—otherwise human relationships would be altogether other than they are" (2002, 257). Acknowledgment, on Cavell's understanding, is logically dependent knowledge and goes beyond it, "not," he qualifies "in the order of knowledge, but in its requirement that I *do* something or reveal something on the basis of that knowledge" (ibid.). My acknowledgment that I am late, for example, takes responsibility for what I (we both) know, owns up to a failing, responds to your disappointment, develops what could be a merely epistemic awareness into a component of an ethical relationship.

In a sense, then, Jake does, or tries to, acknowledge Evelyn when he responds to her narrative with a flurry of activity. With his new "knowledge" ("he raped you"), Jake immediately tries to *do* something about it, to help Evelyn by arranging for her escape. Because he understands what's happened as the acquisition of important knowledge, Jake thinks there is something he can do about it. Additionally, Jake feels the need to do something for himself: he decides to confront Cross—to assuage his own guilt by insisting that Cross face his—a confrontation which will ultimately lead Cross to Evelyn, to Evelyn's death and Katherine's abduction. Thus Jake works to go beyond his mere knowledge by doing something practical, attempting to exorcize or exercise knowledge through the efficacy of action.

As I have been arguing, however, it appears that Jake does *not* successfully acknowledge Evelyn: he remains too committed to the orders of knowledge and action—qualifying her experience as (simply) rape, acting on this new knowledge by confronting her "rapist"—to properly acknowledge her, to attend to what *she* might want or need or how *she* might conceptualize her experience. Her derisive eye-roll in response to Jake's conclusion that her father raped her, and her conviction that the police can do nothing to help her because her father "owns the police," suggest that in her world knowledge and action are not domains that offer any opportunity. Indeed, the nature of Cross' abuse, their ongoing relationship, and the extent of her traumatization suggest that knowledge and action have been devoid of their potentiality, Cross having established himself as in firm control of both spheres of human life. Is Cavell correct, then, in claiming that acknowledgment "requires" that I *do* something *on the basis of knowledge*? Is he right that real acknowledgment rests on knowledge? Might not launching into action based on what he "knows" be precisely another way in which Jake avoids the profound difficulty of acknowledgment?

If the concept of acknowledgment is not given in advance but evidenced in its instances, if in appreciating acknowledgment we must not think but *look and see*, then from the case that *Chinatown* presents it would seem that we may need to amend or reject Cavell's provisional requirement that acknowledgment involve knowledge and action. Perhaps, instead, we can imagine gestures of acknowledgment that are not predicated on knowing and doing.[13] What would be acknowledged by such

---

[13] I am very grateful to José Medina for this suggestion.

gestures would be not what one knows and can do, but what one can stand *not* knowing and not doing, so it would acknowledge the space of separateness and the limits of action. Evelyn herself recognizes that acknowledging her daughter involves protecting her ignorance, at least for now. Might acknowledging Evelyn also involve Jake accepting *his* ignorance? Jake could then know that Evelyn was raped—whatever he thinks that means exactly—and still accept the limits of what that tells him, hence what he knows, hence what he can do about it. Acknowledgment without knowledge might then express a kind of trust: Jake's trust that Evelyn has reasons for her insistence on privacy, which might in turn inspire Evelyn's trust in Jake's ability to accept, to acknowledge her. This form of acknowledgment might be minimal, but when the world is such that knowledge and action can be so swiftly corrupted, a different requirement for acknowledgment might involve a capacity for silence and stillness. This would also indicate a domain of practical, ethical life that did not so immediately funnel us into actions and projects.

In one of the first scenes of interrogation between Jake and Evelyn, the former pressing for more information and confession from the latter, Evelyn fabricates the story of her affairs in order to divert Jake's penetrating attention. There is, though, an element of truth in her lie when she states, "I don't see anyone for very long, Mr. Gittes." With this, Evelyn reveals the cost of Cross' abuse, its disrupting the possibility of her being with others, since presence to others seems to require a revelation of her history for which she is not prepared; seeing anyone commits her to being seen, which she sees as too risky. As we have seen, Jake can only interpret Evelyn's privacy and reticence as secretive, guilty. Of this (mis) interpretation of what's involved in acknowledgment, Cavell writes:

> If the need to acknowledge presents itself as an urge to confess, it may *therefore* present itself as an urge not to, an urge to secrecy. Then one will have to have something to keep secret. Hence the crime, if only of imagination, will be for the sake of the guilt. For in a disordered world guilt will be proof of privacy, hence of one's possession of a self, hence of the nature of one's self. It will be the making known of oneself to oneself. So the desire for sanity can drive one mad. (1999, 460)

If the knowledge required for acknowledgment is expressed in the mode of interrogation and confession, acknowledgment may be avoided *for that reason*, with the need for acknowledgment recoiling and giving rise to a need for secrecy. Here the one who seeks to be acknowledged retreats under the threat of exposure, that very retreat functioning to organize the self around what is now kept as a secret, and so kept guiltily. It would seem that it is in an effort to avoid *this* dynamic of intimacy and avoidance, exposure and withdrawal, needfulness and guilt, that Evelyn wont "see anyone for very long," her apparently guilty withholding a testament to her real need of acknowledgment.

Jake and Evelyn are thus trapped in this self-satisfying circle: Jake's suspicion of guilt is confirmed by her evasiveness, Evelyn's fear of exposure and vulnerability is compounded by his interrogation. My suggestion is that so long as they are gripped by the economy of knowledge (and action), Jake and Evelyn will miss their opportunity for acknowledgment. Against some of Cavell's own claims, then, it would seem that acknowledgment can but *need not* (it is not a "requirement") be based in knowledge or find completion in action. In certain cases, acknowledgment may find expression in the ability to tolerate not knowing, or in a willingness to suspend the drive to do something.

* * *

Recall Cavell's words: "in a disordered world guilt will be proof of privacy, hence of one's possession of a self, hence of the nature of one's self. It will be the making known of oneself to oneself. So the desire for sanity can drive one mad."

Chinatown's world seems something like a "worst case" of the kind of "disordered world" that concerns Cavell. With Evelyn's revelation, we see that this particular world is disordered to the point of imminent collapse: if adequate boundaries are a condition for social life as such (even if those very boundaries can drive us to skepticism), then *Chinatown* offers a vision of a world where such boundaries are destructively weakened. Note that Evelyn never explicitly says what happened with her father, as though whatever possibility for world and future is left to her is predicated on her not invoking that trauma; certainly when Evelyn tells her father that Katherine will "never know" of the conditions of her conception, she is demonstrating her conviction that a world is possible, is fit for flourishing, only *without* that kind of knowledge. Sometimes ignorance holds space for possibility. This is why, when Jake tries to interpret Evelyn's confession as a story of rape, it seems trite, as though he were trying to turn Evelyn's experience into some readily knowable thing in his still stable universe. He tries to remain unchanged by her revelation, to hold his world together. He is able to sustain that hope just until Evelyn tells him the address of where they are going, and in the film's most ominous zoom, we watch as the realization that they are returning to Chinatown dawns over Jake's face.

We can regard the rest of the film as the gradual unraveling of whatever coherence was left of this world; or rather, it unfolds the consequences of a world of human relationships structured according to the dynamics of skepticism, invasiveness, guilt, confession, corruption, rampant capitalism, gendered violence, and, as I have been suggesting, an ongoing failure of acknowledgment. When Jake stares lifelessly at Evelyn's bloodied body hanging out of her car, when he murmurs to himself, "as little as possible," can we conclude that he's finally recognized the logic that he'd been following all along? Has he realized that in doing what he took to be as much as he could, he did (again) as little as possible, and so failed Evelyn? Is this the face of a man who comprehends that this is the second time he's been at this scene? Can he now acknowledge Evelyn, since, even if is too late for her, his capacity to finally grant her humanity will have consequences for his own? Or will he forget it, since it's Chinatown?

If the film does not answer these questions, I hope to have shown that insofar as *Chinatown* dramatizes the dynamics of knowing and acknowledging, we know at least that these are the questions that Jake, and we, are left with. As Jake, and perhaps the viewer, is counseled to "forget it," the music swells and the camera arches upwards, scanning the faces of a gathering and curious crowd; a policeman yells into a loudspeaker to "clear the area!", to leave Chinatown, just as a production assistant might instruct the crew to clear the set, or as an usher might ask the audience to exit the theater, to leave *Chinatown*. It's over. Now we must decide what to do with this experience, what if anything we will let this film teach us, what kind of responsibility—aesthetic? ethical?—is required in order acknowledge this world without us. Cavell writes that it is through fantasy "that our conviction of the worth of reality is established" (1979, 85). If this is so, and if movies offer something like the opportunity for shared fantasy, then we might understand the empty or gutted feeling *Chinatown* leaves us with as a kind of nausea in response to the prospect of trying to work out in what ways this film has transformed our conviction in the worth of the world.

Chinatown, I've argued, explores the possibility and cost of avoiding acknowledgment, and how a faith in knowledge can obscure just what one seeks to know. Additionally, we can see in *Chinatown* a consideration of and challenge to the fantasy of passivity we viewers enjoy with respect to the worlds and pleasures offered by the movies. In the cases of persons and movies we can ask: what do we want to know, what are we *willing* to know or *forego* knowing, when we want to know more about them? The organizing difficulty of this film is that if we evade the ethical and aesthetic demands of relationships, to others and to films, if we are unwilling to see what is revealed to us, then the poignancy and possibility of these relationships is missed. Cavell writes, "the only justification for the knowledge of others is the willingness for complete knowledge. That is the justice of knowledge" (1979, 127–28). We might amend this with the suggestion that this willingness must, paradoxically, include a willingness for *in*complete knowledge, a willingness to tolerate the limits of what will be known, or shared, and the limits of what we can do. The unwillingness to take on those burdens, Jake's and our unwillingness, is the injustice of *Chinatown*.

Appendix

In 1937 Los Angeles, a private eye, Jake Gittes (Jack Nicholson), is hired by a Mrs. Mulwray to investigate the indiscretions she suspects of her husband Hollis Mulwray, chief engineer of the Los Angeles Water and Power Company. After following Mr. Mulwray, Gittes obtains photos of him with a girl, pictures published in the papers without his consent. As it turns out, the woman who hired Gittes was not Mrs. Mulwray; the real wife of Mulwray, Evelyn (Faye Dunaway), visits Gittes at his office to introduce herself (by confirming that they have never met and that she certainly never hired him) and inform him of her intent to take legal action against him.

The mystery begins here: who was the woman pretending to be Mrs. Mulwray and what was her motive? While Gittes may have been able to maintain a level of distance and professionalism in his work as a PI, this new investigation concerns him personally; his curiosity about why anyone would want to slander Mulwray is second to his desire to know who set him up and to clear his name. In a meeting with Evelyn where he announces his intent to bring this information to light, she tells him that she will drop the lawsuit if he will stop his investigation. When he resists, she asks, "is this a business or an obsession for you?" Eventually, she complies and tells Gittes that he might find her husband at a certain water reservoir. When Gittes arrives, the police are already on the scene, as Hollis Mulwray was found drowned.

The mystery deepens. On the one hand, a murder needs solving, but on the other, there is another even less straightforward problem concerning Mulwray. L.A. is suffering from a drought, a drought severe enough to bring farmers into the city to protest and accuse Water and Power of stealing crucial resources. Yet in following Mulwray, Gittes discovers that fresh water is being secretly emptied into the ocean in the middle of the night. In his efforts to uncover more information, Gittes is apprehended by another PI apparently under the employment of Water and Power (Gittes' seedier double) and an unassuming heavy (played by Polanski himself) who cut his nose for being "nosey."

As it turns out, Evelyn's father, Noah Cross (played by occasional noir director John Huston), was once a co-owner of Water and Power (along with Hollis Mulwray) before it was turned over to the public. Over a lunch visit, Cross offers to double Gittes' pay to find the girl with whom Mulwray was apparently having an affair, warning that Jake does not know what he's dealing with (advice, Jake muses, that he was given while a cop in Chinatown). Jake discovers shortly after that the drought is in fact a fabrication of Cross', with an end to buying the dried-up land from farmers at a low price in order to later replenish the area (with the water that was never in low supply) and sell it for a profit.

There is, following this development, a respite from the investigation, as Jake and Evelyn make love in her house. The scene is intimate not simply because they sleep together, but because Evelyn tries to find out more about Jake as a person, about his time working as a police officer in Chinatown where he did, as he puts it, "as little as possible." "I want to know more about you," she says, to which he replies that he is tired. He does, however, disclose that Chinatown was a place where one could never quite tell what was going on ("like you," he says to Evelyn), and while he was there he suffered a great loss; in trying to keep a woman from getting hurt, he ended up making sure that she was.

The final, crucial developments happen quickly, and I'll simply lay them out. Evelyn receives a call, her mood changes drastically, and she tells Jake she needs to leave; she also asks that he "trust" her, and warns him that her father is "crazy." Jake follows Evelyn to a house where Mr. Mulwray's girl is in bed and forced to take pills at Evelyn's behest. Confronting her, Evelyn admits, reluctantly and tearfully, that the girl is her sister. In an exchange with a (newly appointed) lieutenant with whom Jake worked in Chinatown (Jake's apparently more respectable double), he is told that Mulwray drowned with salt water in his lungs, despite being found in a river reservoir. Back at Evelyn's house, Gittes discovers that a pond in their backyard is filled with saltwater, and in that pool he finds a pair of men's glasses—or, indeed, he re-finds, as, in his first visit to this house, the Chinese gardener told him that salt water is "bad for the grass," which, with his accent, sounds like "bad for the glass."

From here, Jake concludes that Evelyn killed her husband and confronts her at the house where the girl is staying. The most troubling and unexpected and disorienting scene in the film, Evelyn reveals a secret, but not the one Jake believed he would extract from her: the girl is indeed Evelyn's sister, but also her daughter. In response to this, Jake slaps her and screams that he "wants the truth." She answers: "my father and I… [looks him in the eye, I would say cynically]…understand? Or is it too tough for you?" To Jake's quiet response—"he raped you?"—she practically rolls her eyes. Later I will discuss this scene, and its centrality to what I will call the second film, Evelyn's film, at length. But note now that Jake came to Evelyn with a definite idea about how she was betraying him, about the kind of knowledge she's been keeping, about the kind of deceptive woman she is, and about the kind of clarity and satisfaction he will achieve when she tells the truth. Compare these expectations with her revelation. What satisfaction does this provide? What kind of world does this information clarify? What does it mean to know *this*, to know what Evelyn knows?

Evelyn is planning on running away with the girl, departing from her butler's home in, of all places, Chinatown, the disorienting and unlucky place of Jake's past, where attempts to help only guarantee harm. Of the glasses found in her backyard pond, Evelyn mentions that they did not belong to Hollis, "he didn't wear bifocals." Going quickly now, Jake contacts Noah Cross, making plans to meet him by offering information about the girl Cross had hired Jake to find. In their confrontation, Cross does not deny Jake's accusations regarding his crimes against Evelyn, the city, and Hollis Mulwray. Mulvihill, hired by Cross, puts a gun to Gittes' head, and, after warning that "it really isn't worth it," they force Gittes to lead them to Evelyn. In Chinatown, Evelyn does everything she can to protect the girl from Cross, who claims that the girl is "his too." When Jake calls to Evelyn that he's brought the police to help, Evelyn cries that Cross "owns the police," and gets in her car to drive away. The police shoot her in the head, which lies noisily on the car horn. In the confusion, Cross easily makes away with the girl, covering her eyes to protect her seeing her dead mother; indeed the film calls so little attention to his escape that it is only upon realizing that the girls screams have faded away, that we realize that Cross has re-possessed her. Jake is fully expressionless as he stares at Evelyn. Finally, under the lieutenant's orders ("just get him the hell out of here!"), Jake's partners lead him away, and as Jake glances back, one says, in the film's most famous line, "forget it Jake, it's Chinatown."[14]

References

Borde, Raymond, and Etienne Chaumeton. 2002. *A Panorama of American Film Noir: 1941–1953*. Translated by Paul Hammond. San Francisco, CA.
Cavell, Stanley. 1979. *The World Viewed: Enlarged Edition*. Cambridge, MA: Harvard University Press.
———. 1999. *The Claim of Reason: Wittgenstein, Skepticism, Morality and Tragedy*. Oxford: Oxford University Press.
———. 1984. *The Claim of Reason: Wittgenstein, Pursuits of Happiness: The Hollywood Comedy of Remarriage*. Cambridge, MA: Harvard University Press.
———. 2002. *Must We Mean What We Say*. Cambridge, UK: Cambridge University Press.
Dederer, Claire. 2017. What Do We Do with the Art of Monstrous Men. *The Paris Review*, November 20.
Durgnat, Raymond. 1998. Paint it Black: The Family Tree of Film Noir. In *The Big Book of Noir*, ed. Ed Gorman, Martin Greenberg, and Lee Server. New York: Carroll & Graf Pub.
Klein, Melanie. 1987. *The Selected Melanie Klein*. London: Free Press.
Moran, Richard. 2011/2. Cavell on Outsiders and Others. *Revue internationale de philosophie*, n° 256, 239–254.
———. 2016. Stanley Cavell on Recognition, Betrayal, and the Photographic Field of Expression. *The Harvard Review of Philosophy* XXIII: 29–40.
Pippin, Robert B. 2012. *Fatalism in American Film Noir*. Charlottesville, VA: University of Virginia Press.
Schrader, Paul. 2003. Notes on Film Noir. In *Film Genre Reader III*, ed. Barry Keith Grant. Austin, TX: University of Texas Press.
Thompson, David. 1994. *A Biographical Dictionary of Film*. 3rd ed. New York.
Walker, Margaret Urban. 2006. *Moral Repair: Reconstructing Moral Relations after Wrongdoing*. Cambridge, UK: Cambridge University Press.
Wittgenstein, Ludwig. 2001. *Philosophical Investigations*. Translated by GEM Anscombe. Hoboken, NJ.

---

[14] Thanks to participants at the 2012 Wittgenstein Workshop at the University of Chicago, and the participants at the "Experience, Intimacy, and Authority" at the Carlos III University in Madrid in 2012. I also thank Katie Kelley, Gregg Horowitz, Dan Morgan, Robert Pippin, and Joel Snyder for their insight and conversation.

CHAPTER 2

Other Minds and Unknown Women: The Case of *Gaslight*

Jay R. Elliott

1 Introduction

Among the most distinctive and fruitful aspects of Stanley Cavell's writings on film has been his insistence on a deep connection between the philosophical problem of other minds, on the one hand, and certain classical Hollywood genres, on the other. He first developed this connection in detail in his 1981 book *Pursuits of Happiness: The Hollywood Comedy of Remarriage*.[1] There he argued that a group of comedies from the 1930s and 1940s—films such as *It Happened One Night*, *The Philadelphia Story* and *The Awful Truth*—are centrally concerned with the question of how human beings (in particular men and women) can come to know one another. According to Cavell, these films propose a certain practice of marriage—what Cavell calls "remarriage"—as an answer to this question.

---

[1] *Pursuits of Happiness: The Hollywood Comedy of Remarriage* (Cambridge, MA: Harvard University Press, 1981). Hereafter abbreviated *PH*.

J. R. Elliott (✉)
Bard College, Annandale-on-Hudson, NY, USA
e-mail: jelliott@bard.edu

© The Author(s) 2018
G. L. Hagberg (ed.), *Stanley Cavell on Aesthetic Understanding*, Philosophers in Depth,
https://doi.org/10.1007/978-3-319-97466-8_2

On Cavell's reading, these films represent marriage as the paradigmatic example of a relationship that affords the intimacy and expressiveness required for genuine interpersonal knowledge. This argument forms the basis of Cavell's later treatment of a set of contemporaneous Hollywood melodramas, in his 1996 book *Contesting Tears: The Hollywood Melodrama of the Unknown Woman*.[2] In this later work, Cavell sought to show that films such as *Gaslight*, *Stella Dallas* and *Now, Voyager* are likewise centrally concerned with the conditions under which a human being can be known. But Cavell argues that the melodramas crucially differ from the comedies, insofar as they are concerned to depict the possibility of interpersonal knowledge—in particular, knowledge of a woman—outside of marriage.

Like many sympathetic readers of Cavell, I find *Contesting Tears* both admirable for the ways it promises to extend Cavell's thinking and at the same time frustrating in its failure to fulfill its promises.[3] As a result of this frustration, *Contesting Tears* has come to occupy a somewhat marginal place in Cavell's oeuvre. While I agree with many of Cavell's readers in finding it frustrating, I regard its relative neglect as a mistake, and I suspect that closer attention to what exactly went wrong in this late work can help us to think through how we might best carry forward Cavell's project of aesthetic understanding. I agree with Cavell that classical Hollywood movies, and the movies he discusses in particular, are characteristically concerned with the problem of other minds. He has also been quite perceptive in recognizing the deep connections between this problem and questions of marriage and gender.[4] Furthermore, he was right to revisit and complicate the treatment of these issues in *Pursuits of Happiness* through a consideration of the melodramas. But I disagree with Cavell's central claim about the melodramas: that they depict conditions of

---

[2] *Contesting Tears: The Hollywood Melodrama of the Unknown Woman* (Chicago: University of Chicago Press, 1996). Hereafter abbreviated *CT*.

[3] For the reception of Cavell's work on melodrama among students of his work generally, see Timothy Gould, "Review of *Contesting Tears*," *Philosophy in Review* 17 (1997): 241–43; Espen Hammer, *Stanley Cavell* (London: Polity, 2002), pp. 113–18; and Richard Eldridge, *Stanley Cavell* (Cambridge: Cambridge University Press, 2003), pp. 221–30.

[4] Cavell has explored these connections in a number of contexts: in addition to his film work, perhaps the other most notable example is his writings about Shakespeare's plays; see especially "Othello and the Stake of the Other" and "Recounting Gains, Showing Losses: Reading *The Winter's Tale*," both collected in *Disowning Knowledge in Seven Plays of Shakespeare* (Updated ed., Cambridge: Cambridge University Press, 2003).

successful interpersonal knowledge outside of marriage. Rather, on my reading, these films are concerned to show how the failure of marriage is deeply connected with failures of interpersonal knowledge.[5] While I admire Cavell's reading of these films on many points, I take his overall argument to fundamentally mischaracterize them and to obscure their real aesthetic and philosophical significance. Moreover, I will argue that this failure in Cavell's treatment of melodrama reveals deeper shortcomings in his treatment of the other minds problem more generally.

The chapter unfolds in three main parts. In the first part, I provide an overview of Cavell's argument in *Contesting Tears*, focusing on the way that argument draws on longstanding features of his approach to the problem of other minds. In the second part, I present my critique of Cavell's argument, beginning from a renewed examination of key scenes in *Gaslight* and building to the claim that Cavell's misreading of this film reveals fundamental limitations in his overall approach to the problem of other minds. In the third part, I draw out two further lessons from my critique of Cavell's work on melodrama: one about how best to bring Cavell's concerns into conversation with feminism, the other about what it means to take popular artworks such as Hollywood movies seriously.

2 OTHER MINDS AND UNKNOWN WOMEN

In order to understand Cavell's approach to other minds in *Contesting Tears*, we need first to appreciate how it builds on his earlier treatments of the problem of other minds, going back to the 1960s. Cavell introduced his fundamental ideas about other minds in his seminal essay "Knowing and Acknowledging."[6] In that essay, Cavell argued that the traditional philosophical framing of the problem of other minds fundamentally mischaracterizes the problem. According to the traditional framing, the problem is essentially epistemological. It concerns the question of on what epistemic grounds I can legitimately perform a certain inference, namely

---

[5] In this sense, my reading of the melodramas actually brings them much closer to the remarriage comedies than Cavell does: in my view, both genres uphold (successful) marriage as a privileged scene of acknowledgment, in particular acknowledgment between men and women. In the melodramas, the failure of this scene corresponds to a general failure of acknowledgment.

[6] "Knowing and Acknowledging," in *Must We Mean What We Say? A Book of Essays* (Cambridge: Cambridge University Press, 1969).

the inference from external, bodily behavior that I observe to the conclusion that behind the behavior lies another subjectivity like my own. Cavell's approach begins from the thought that the problem, cast in this form, cannot be solved. There simply is no epistemic principle by which I can be assured that I know another, and so attempts at interpersonal understanding inevitably carry an element of risk.

More fundamentally, Cavell argues that the traditional framing involves a misrepresentation of the true nature of the problem. In Cavell's view, the fundamental source of the problem is not an epistemic shortcoming but rather a metaphysical limitation: the fact of our separateness from one another. As Cavell puts it, the traditional framing mischaracterizes our "metaphysical finitude as an intellectual lack."[7] When we worry that we cannot know what another person thinks, wants or feels, according to Cavell, what we are really coming up against is the metaphysical distinctness of one human life from another. When we insist that there must be a solution to this problem, we are in effect rebelling against the finitude that is part of the human condition.

Cavell insists that there is no overcoming this separateness; to overcome it would in fact be the destruction of humanity. But Cavell does not despair of the possibility of interpersonal understanding. Rather, he seeks to show that the traditional framing of the problem misunderstands the grounds of that understanding. The lesson of the insolubility of the traditional problem, for Cavell, is simply that when one human being comes to know the mind of the other, he does so not on account of having good reasons to infer that there is a mind behind the other's behavior. In Cavell's view, the recognition of another's behavior as an expression of mindedness is not fundamentally a matter of making a certain discovery about what is going on inside her, but rather one of taking a certain attitude toward her. Rather than seeking to know the other, as if that could close the distance between ourselves and her, we can come to *acknowledge* the other, where that means coming into a relationship with her in which both intimacy and distance can be preserved. Thus for Cavell the epistemological framing of the traditional problem is to be replaced by an ethical problem, the problem of how to resist the tempting fantasy of overcoming human finitude and to instead cultivate forms of relationship based on mutual acknowledgment. Note that this ethical problem for Cavell is pitched at an

---

[7] "Knowing and Acknowledging," 263.

essentially anthropological register: it is a fact about the human that it is finite, and that it rebels against its finitude. The ethical task is thus understood as one of reconciling ourselves to our humanity, and the ethical struggle is a struggle against the denial of humanity as such.

Cavell's aim in *Pursuits of Happiness* was to present marriage, as depicted in the comedies, as a solution to this problem of acknowledgment. On Cavell's reading, the comedies solve this problem by reformulating the relationship of marriage essentially as a mode of conversation. As Cavell puts it, "in these films talking together is fully and plainly being together, a mode of association, a form of life."[8] In this form of life, conversation reveals each partner to the other intimately, while also preserving his or her separateness. As Cavell notes, these films are particularly beloved for the way the principal man and woman speak to each other, in a language that is playful but at the same time vulnerable and generous. Cavell particularly emphasizes the role that this mode of conversation plays in opening up certain possibilities for the woman: he says that the central concern of these comedies is the woman's demand for an education, where by this he means both her finding a language in which to express what she wants (especially but not only in marriage) and finding a partner in the man with whom she can express herself. The threat to interpersonal understanding in these films appears in the form of a lifeless, conventional marriage, of the sort of that, for example, Katharine Hepburn's Tracy Lord almost enters into in *The Philadelphia Story*. By contrast, these films represent the possibility of interpersonal understanding in terms of the creation of a new form of marriage in which the woman's desire can be expressed and recognized.

Between *Pursuits of Happiness* and *Contesting Tears*, Cavell became newly receptive to feminist doubts about marriage as a scene of liberatory possibility for women, recognizing that marriage has often been a source of "social and psychological violence"[9] in women's lives. Furthermore, Cavell came to appreciate that this violence is not an accidental or marginal phenomenon, but is built into how marriage in sexist societies works. In *Contesting Tears*, he thus makes the striking claim, in light of his previous argument in *Pursuits of Happiness*, that marriage in fact functions as a "structure of unhappiness."[10] From this point of view, the happy couples

---

[8] *PH* 88.
[9] *CT* 54.
[10] *CT* 117.

depicted in *Pursuits of Happiness* should be seen as lucky exceptions rather than as representatives of marriage generally.[11] In response to these doubts, Cavell formulated the "melodrama of the unknown woman" as a "companion"[12] genre to the remarriage comedy, a genre which centers on the failure of marriage in a woman's life, and thus explores the possibilities for female agency and expressiveness outside of marriage. In terms of the other minds problem, the question of the melodramas becomes the question of whether a woman can become known outside of the marital conversation that Cavell had previously upheld as the paradigmatic scene of acknowledgment.

Cavell's relationship to feminism in the project of *Contesting Tears* is complex. On the one hand, as I have noted above, he wants to recognize feminist doubts about marriage and to explore the possibility of female agency outside of it. With these concerns in mind, he identifies the read-

---

[11] In *CT*, Cavell introduces two more specific doubts about the marriages depicted in the remarriage comedies. First, he points to the persistent "privileging of the male" in the education of the woman: "In these comedies the creation of the woman ... takes the form of the woman's education by the man; hence a critical clause in the story these films tell and retell is the discerning of what it is about this man that fits him to be chosen by this woman to provide that authorization of her, of let us say her desire. This suggests a privileging of the male still within this atmosphere of equality. The genre scrutinizes this in the ways, even in this atmosphere, the male is declared, at his best, to retain a taint of villainy. This so to speak prepares the genre for its inner relation to melodrama" [*CT* 5]. Second, he notes the absence of the mother-child relationship in the remarriage comedies: "The woman is virtually never shown with her mother and is never shown to be a mother. Whether the absence of literal mothering is the permanent price or punishment for the woman's happiness, or whether a temporary and mysterious aberration of a disordered world, is not decided. What is decided is that the happiness achieved in remarriage is not uncontaminated, not uncompromised" [*CT* 116]. Both the "villainy" of the male and the mother-child relation are central themes of the melodramas.

[12] *CT* 4. Cavell largely defines the relation between companion genres as one of negation: thus characteristic features of the remarriage comedy are negated in the melodrama of the unknown woman. For example, the melodramas negate the role of marriage in the education of the woman. As Cavell puts it: "The chief negation of these comedies by these melodramas is the negation of marriage itself—marriage in them is not necessarily reconceived and therewith provisionally affirmed, as in remarriage comedy, but rather marriage as a route to creation, to a new or an original integrity, is transcended and perhaps reconceived" [*CT* 6]. The concept of companion genres seems to me in general a rich and promising one. But I suspect that thinking of the relation between companion genres as one of negation is overly narrow and itself a cause of Cavell's difficulties in *CT*. Here it leads Cavell to assume that both genres must contain "a route to creation," but in one case this route leads through marriage, in the other not.

ings that he offers in *Contesting Tears* as "feminist"[13] ones. At the same time, he is centrally concerned to resist what he takes to be a widespread tendency in feminist scholarship about these films: the tendency to approach them with an attitude that Cavell calls "condescension" and "contempt."[14] In Cavell's view, there is a tendency in feminist film studies to regard these films as both artistically superficial and politically reactionary. According to this style of reading, the aim of films such as *Gaslight* or *Now, Voyager* is essentially to reconcile women to the disappointing conditions of their lives under sexist injustice. In opposition to this style of feminist reading, Cavell aims to produce his own alternative feminist readings of the films, ones that reflect his sense of their artistic richness and liberatory potential.[15]

Cavell's central claim in *Contesting Tears* is that the principal women of the melodramas undergo a transformation analogous to that of the principal women in the remarriage comedies. In each case, Cavell argues, the women become known, that is, they become capable of giving expression to their thoughts and desires and claiming recognition of them. But in the case of the melodramas, this transformation occurs outside of marriage, not merely outside of the conventional marriage abjured by the women of the comedies, but outside of marriage altogether.[16] Speaking in the voice of the women in melodrama and imagining them addressing their comedic counterparts, Cavell writes:

---

[13] *CT* 127.

[14] *CT* 33. These characterizations of feminist film scholarship are disputed by E. Ann Kaplan, "Review of *Contesting Tears*," *Film Quarterly* 52 (1998): 77–81.

[15] Cavell identifies Tania Modleski's "Time and Desire in the Woman's Film" *Cinema Journal* 23 (1984): 19–30 and Laura Mulvey's "Visual Pleasure and Narrative Cinema," *Screen* 16 (1975): 6–18, as paradigmatic instances of the kind of feminist criticism he seeks to resist in *Contesting Tears*. Cavell's writing on melodrama has in turn been criticized by feminist scholars: see Modleski, "Editorial Notes: Reply to Cavell", *Critical Inquiry* 16 (1990): 237–44, and *Feminism without Women: Culture and Criticism in a 'Postfeminist' Age* (New York: Routledge, 1991); E. Ann Kaplan, "Review of *Contesting Tears*"; and Lauren Berlant, *The Female Complaint: The Unfinished Business of Sentimentality in American Culture* (Durham, NC: Duke University Press, 2008).

[16] Cavell sometimes presents the withdrawal of the melodrama women from marriage only as a necessary prologue to the reconfiguration of marriage in their worlds. Thus he writes that "the experience of being unknown" as it appears in the melodramas may be regarded as a starting point, after which "marriage is to be reconceived" [*CT* 22]. From this point of view, however, he should not say that the women of the melodramas themselves complete a transition to integrity, or that they have transcended marriage.

> You may count yourselves lucky to have found a man with whom you can overcome the humiliation of marriage by marriage itself. For us, with our talents and tastes, there is no further or happy education to be found there: our integrity and metamorphosis happens elsewhere, in the abandoning of that *shared* wit and intelligence and exclusive appreciation.[17]

The opening of this dense passage speaks to the feminist doubts newly at work in *Contesting Tears*. Cavell speaks of "the humiliation of marriage," as if this were the natural condition of women within marriage, and of those who escape this humiliation within marriage as "lucky." As an alternative to this structural unhappiness within marriage, the women of melodrama seek their "happy education" elsewhere, in fact precisely in the *refusal* of marriage as a possible site of their "integrity and metamorphosis." The essential lesson in the education of the comedy women was the discovery of what kind of marriage they wanted, or what was possible in marriage for them. By contrast, the essential lesson in the education of the melodrama women will be precisely that marriage is not for them, cannot offer them the integrity they seek. Cavell does not doubt that the melodrama women find a happy education. Elsewhere he speaks of them as "transcending marriage"[18] and as finding an "alternative route to integrity and possibility."[19] Both of these formulations suggest that for the women of the melodramas, the failure of marriage does not represent a genuine source of loss, disappointment or frustration in their lives. Indeed, by connecting these women's "metamorphosis" with the attainment of "integrity," Cavell suggests that they experience abandoning the possibility of marriage not as the splitting off of a set of lost possibilities for the self, but rather as the regaining of wholeness, in the face of a threatened fragmentation or dissolution represented by marriage. For women with certain "talents and tastes," Cavell proposes, the project of "shared wit and intelligence and exclusive appreciation" represented by marriage simply does not apply or rather represents a danger that needs to be warded off. For the women of the melodramas, abandoning that project is the key to expressing their desires and claiming acknowledgment of them.[20]

---

[17] *CT* 6.
[18] *CT* 47.
[19] *CT* 7.
[20] In a similar vein, Cavell speaks of the melodrama women as making a "certain choice of solitude... as the recognition that the terms of one's intelligibility are not welcome to others" [*CT* 12]. Like the language of "talents and tastes," this language of choice seems at once to

3   The Case of *Gaslight*

Cavell's account of the melodrama genre is appealing, in the sense that it places that genre in a clear and striking contrast to the remarriage genre: in the remarriage genre, marriage is affirmed as the scene of a woman's happy education; in the melodrama, by contrast, her education centers on the abandoning of marriage. This reading of the films is also naturally appealing from a feminist perspective, since it seems to celebrate the women of the melodramas and to affirm that women can find integrity and possibility outside of marriage. Cavell's reading also has the advantage of taking these popular works of art as serious sources of thought about the conditions of women's agency, rather than seeing them as merely sentimental or regressive. In all of these ways, it would be natural for an admirer of these films to be attracted to Cavell's account of them.

The difficulty, however, is that his account does not succeed in doing justice to the complexity of the films themselves. It therefore falls short both in characterizing the films and in taking the full measure of the intellectual provocation they can afford. In this section I first describe what Cavell's overall argument about the melodrama genre misses in the films, drawing on a close reading of certain scenes in *Gaslight*, and then diagnose why his argument has gone wrong in this way, tracing the difficulty to a limitation in his framing of the problem of other minds.

Cavell's treatment of the melodrama genre centers on the idea that the central women in these films undergo a transformation analogous to that undergone by the central women of the comedies. I agree with Cavell that the women of the melodramas undergo a transformation, and that this transformation can helpfully be characterized as an abandoning of marriage. But I disagree with him insofar as I see this transformation as fundamentally disanalogous to the one depicted in the comedies. The women of the comedies succeed in finding a language in which they can express their desires and make them understood; their transformation can thus rightly be characterized as one in the direction of greater integrity and possibility. By contrast, the transformation of the melodrama women consists essentially in their loss of hope for such a language; these women come to reconcile themselves to the fact of being inexpressive and being misunderstood

---

underestimate the degree to which the melodrama women are limited from the outset to a set of bad options, and to overstate the degree to which they succeed in finding "terms of intelligibility," even for themselves.

by those around them, especially men. As a result, they come to cultivate oblique modes of expression, in particular irony.[21] Rather than representing a route to integrity and possibility, I take the abandoning of marriage to represent a loss of integrity and possibility for these women, in particular loss of the prospect of a relationship of trust and vulnerability in which their desires could be expressed and understood. Likewise, I reject Cavell's suggestion that the difference in the experience of the comedy and melodrama women is to be accounted for in terms of a difference in "talents and tastes"; as I see these films, the central women in them have as much talent and taste for marriage as their comedy counterparts. The difference in their experience is rather one of luck: while the comedy women are fortunate to find a partner with whom they can escape the structural unhappiness built into marriage, the experience of the melodrama women brings this structural unhappiness to light.

The strains in Cavell's reading of *Gaslight*[22] illustrate the difficulties in his account especially clearly. The film centers on Paula Alquist (Ingrid Bergman), an orphan who is raised in a London townhouse by her aunt Alice, a celebrated opera singer. One night Alice is strangled to death in a botched jewel theft. The case is never solved. Paula flees London and seeks refuge in Milan with Signor Guardi, her aunt's former voice teacher. Ten years pass, during which she tries and fails to follow in her aunt's footsteps as a singer. But in Milan she meets a young pianist and composer named Gregory Anton (Charles Boyer). They fall in love, marry, and return to live in the townhouse in London, which has sat vacant since Alice's death. During a visit to the Tower of London with her new husband, Paula draws the attention of Brian Cameron (Joseph Cotten), a young detective from Scotland Yard. He had met and admired Alice in his youth, and is struck by Paula's resemblance to her; he becomes fascinated by her and decides to reopen the investigation into Alice's murder. Meanwhile, Gregory becomes increasingly cruel toward Paula: he forbids her to go out or to receive company; accuses her of forgetting, losing and hiding things; and ultimately plans to have her committed to an insane asylum.

---

[21] Cavell notes that irony is the distinctive mark of the unknown woman's language. He writes that "Something in the language of the unknown woman melodrama must bear ... the weight borne by the weight of conversation in the case of remarriage comedy... I identify this opposing feature of language as that of irony" [*CT* 47]. He goes on to note that it "serves to isolate the woman of this melodrama from everyone around her" [*CT* 117]. It seems to me he fails, however, to take full account of the implications of this observation.

[22] *Gaslight*, George Cukor, dir., 114 minutes, MGM Studios, 1944/2006, DVD.

Trapped in the house with only the deaf cook Elizabeth (Barbara Everest) and the scheming maid Nancy (Angela Lansbury), Paula becomes increasingly weak and despondent, and begins to accept her husband's description of her as mad. With help from a gossiping spinster (Dame May Whitty), Brian begins to understand the misery of Paula's marriage. After Brian forces his way into the house, he and Paula find evidence proving that Gregory is in fact Sergius Bauer, the jewel thief who murdered Alice. Paula realizes that Gregory plotted their marriage from the beginning only in order to return to the house, where he hoped to find the jewels and complete his unfinished crime. In the film's climactic scene, Paula, alone with Gregory/Sergius in the attic of the house, confronts her husband with this newfound knowledge. When he asks her to help him escape, she refuses, appropriating for herself his idea that she is mad, this time as an explanation for her lack of pity toward him. In the film's final moments, Gregory/Sergius is led away by the police, while Brian attempts to comfort Paula.

Cavell's reading of the film centers on the climactic scene between Paula and her husband. He refers to this scene as "Paula's aria," as a way of proposing that in this scene Paula finds her voice in a way that had previously eluded her both in her lessons with Signor Guardi and in her life with Gregory. For Cavell, this is the key scene that makes this film support his overall account of the melodramas, the scene that reveals Paula's transformation over the course of the film from humiliation by marriage to integrity outside of it. Here is how Cavell describes it:

> The woman confronts her husband alone… and delivers to him her *cogito ergo sum*, her proof of her existence… I call this late moment Paula's aria, and its declaration causes, or is caused by (that is, it is the same as) her metamorphosis, or creation, which is what we should expect of the assertion of the *cogito* that, as in Descartes, puts a close to skeptical doubt.[23]

In Cavell's view, the transformation that Paula reveals here is one in which, like Descartes in the *cogito*, she affirms her own existence. By defying and mocking her husband in this scene, Paula is, on Cavell's reading, declaring her existence as separate from his, and thus making herself known.

I agree that this scene represents a kind of transformation in Paula. But that transformation is a peculiar one, in ways not captured by Cavell's

---

[23] *CT* 48.

reading. The comparison with Descartes suggested by Cavell is illuminating, but as much for the points of contrast as for those of similarity. In Descartes, the performance of the *cogito* is meant to put a close not merely to skeptical doubt, but also to the threat of madness with which that doubt is associated. He knows that madmen's mad imaginings often seem perfectly real to them, just as dreams do to those asleep. He therefore seeks in the *cogito* a thought that cannot be mere appearance, cannot possibly be mad, whatever else may be. By contrast, Paula's declaration of herself in this scene takes precisely the form of an avowal of madness, as if for her the only way to overcome the terrible unreality of her life is to descend further into it. I agree with Cavell that this scene represents Paula's separation from her marriage, and indeed from marriage as such. But what strikes me, and what Cavell seems to miss, is that for Paula this separation appears not as a positive, Cartesian affirmation of self, but rather as an acknowledgment of loss, in particular loss of her capacity for love, pity and trust.

Let's look in detail at Paula's words in this scene. Gregory has ordered, and then begged, her to help him escape. The key portion of her speech runs as follows:

> If I were not mad, I could have helped you. Whatever you had done, I could have pitied and protected you. But because I am mad, I hate you. Because I am mad, I have betrayed you, and because I am mad I am rejoicing in my heart, without a shred of pity, without a shred of regret, watching you go with glory in my heart!

Paula is being ironic here: part of the thrill of the scene lies in the way that she skillfully turns her husband's treatment of her against him. But we should not be too quick to assume that we know just what this irony means. Irony is not sarcasm; it is not a matter simply of meaning the negation of what one says. Here, as often, ironic speech involves appropriating the words of another, so as to reveal a different meaning those words can have in a different voice. Here, as often, that different voice finds a different kind of truth in those words, one that the original speaker may not have recognized or may not have been in a position to assert. Does Paula really believe in this moment that she is mad? I find that this is the wrong question to ask. Rather, what I find striking is that this language of madness is the language that she finds to express her separation from her husband and her marriage. She marks the moment as one in which she discovers how deeply he has disfigured and damaged her, to the point that she is filled with hate, can feel no loyalty, and has lost all sense of pity. This is not the statement of a woman who has overcome the humiliation of marriage. It is rather the statement of a woman who recognizes that her marriage has been a fraud, while at the same time finding herself deeply scarred by that discovery. For her, the failure of the marriage represents the shearing off of a whole dimension of her affective self, the part that was capable of love and trust. The loss of this part of herself is what she calls her madness. If there has been a transformation here, it is a bitter one: out of a humiliating marriage, but not out of the humiliation or its effects.

Cavell expresses his own reservations about his reading of the film, noting that the scenes following the "aria" lead us to wonder how fundamentally Paula's escape from her marriage can shift the terms of her existence. But absent the kind of reconsideration of the "aria" itself that I have been offering here, these reservations fail to reckon with what is most unsettling about the ending of the film. Cavell writes, concerning Paula in the film's final moments:

> She is back where she started, or stopped, at best—the place from which she was to be rescued from her fears and her ignorance of the world by marriage to a mysterious stranger. Her identification, through the aria, with her dead aunt has rescued her from that rescue, but the world of women here seems to hold no further hope; it cannot conceive of it. Women's options in this universe…are the flirtatiousness of the maid, the deafness of the cook, or the shocked spectatordom of the spinster; a set of options perfect for maintaining the perfect liberty and privilege of the male.[24]

In this passage, Cavell raises two doubts about Paula's future possibilities, based on the two scenes that follow the "aria": on the one hand, the scene of Gregory/Sergius being led away by police, in which he walks slowly downstairs and through the house, pausing to acknowledge the cook and the maid, as if to approve the hopeless "world of women" they represent; and on the other hand, the final conversation between Paula and the "mysterious stranger" Brian, which takes place elsewhere, on the housetop, yet is overheard by the spinster.

In drawing our attention to these final scenes, Cavell points out the key role played in the film by the other female characters: the cook, the

[24] *CT* 60–61.

maid and the spinster. They represent this film's world of women and the options it affords. As Cavell notes, these options offer no hope of relief from the "perfect liberty and privilege of the male." But why does Paula's aria not offer that hope? The true hopelessness of Paula's situation only properly comes into view once we see that her affirmation of her existence in the aria does not represent a positive affirmation of a newfound integrity, but is rather an expression of her sense of abandonment and mutilation following the loss of marriage as a scene of interpersonal acknowledgment.

Regarding the second scene, between Paula and Brian, Cavell recognizes that any hope offered by this scene is highly equivocal, given its unnerving aura of repetition. Once again, she has been rescued by a mysterious stranger, indeed yet another stranger who is haunted by a past connection with her aunt. On a first viewing of the film, we may welcome this rescue; on a second viewing, we may dread it, as suggesting a cycle of dependence—on men, on her aunt's memory—that Paula seems unable to escape. Cavell's reservations seem to end here, but as a result I think they fall short of capturing the real darkness that shadows this final scene between Paula and Brian. For the real focus of this scene is not the danger of a cycle of repetition, but rather how this film envisions that this cycle can be broken: only by the deadening of the heart itself. On a third viewing, I think we come to see the two reactions described above as deliberately elicited, and at the same time undercut, by the film: our preoccupation with Brian, and our tendency to take up his point of view, is in fact an artful misdirection, yet another reminder of the "perfect liberty and privilege of the male." Cameron is of course in love with Paula, or thinks he is. He offers to console her in the film's final lines: "Let me come here and see you and talk to you." To this she responds with only a polite "You're very kind." The spinster closes the film with a scandalized "Well!"

All of this invites us to see Paula, for better or worse, as destined to marry Brian. But I take it we are also invited to recognize and suspect that invitation. First, because of what we know about the spinster: that she is a vain and idle speculator who for all of her "interest" in Paula's case has no real sympathy or understanding of her. And second, because of what we know about Brian: that his own relation to Paula is largely a projection of his imagination. The first time he sees her, Brian refers to Paula as a "ghost," and that is essentially how he regards her throughout: as a haunting from his past and as a mystery to be solved. Most importantly, the film pointedly shows Paula excluding him from the revelation of the "aria."

Paula asks to speak with her husband alone; Brian forbids her; she insists and then bolts the attic door against him. Paula even assures us that "he is not listening" at the door. Thus he does not know what she is, or has become, how the failure of her marriage has maddened her heart. He imagines that he sees, knows and loves her; but this is only a misrecognition, and that is the real darkness of the film's final scene.

I have focused here on the case of *Gaslight*, because it is the film in which Cavell most emphatically identifies a transformation in the woman, in the moment of Paula's "aria"; I have argued that this transformation is not quite what Cavell takes it to be. But this case is representative; similar things could be said about his reading of each of the melodramas. Why does Cavell's account go wrong in these ways? I suspect that the source of the difficulty lies not merely in his readings of these films, but at a deeper level in his work, in his way of framing the problem of other minds. In this light, Cavell's difficulties with the melodramas are not limited to these films alone, but are revealing and symptomatic of a larger limitation in his philosophical project. As a result, Cavell's difficulties with these films have broader implications for thinking about how we should inherit that project.

Cavell assumes that the women of the melodramas can establish satisfactory terms of acknowledgment for themselves. I take this assumption to rest on a further, more fundamental assumption he makes: that the problem of other minds arises exclusively in an anthropological register, as a problem that derives from the universally human urge to deny the human as such. When the problem is framed in this way, it looks as if a solution to it is equally available to every human being: namely to affirm one's humanity along with that of others. But this way of thinking fails to recognize that structures of injustice can systematically impede the possibility of interpersonal knowledge. Within these structures, the denial of human subjectivity arises not merely from a generic horror at human finitude as such, but from specific forms of horror connected with specific ways the human gets marked for injustice, for example, by gender. These structures have not merely imaginary or ideological but real-world effects; they create conditions in which human subjectivity cannot be properly acknowledged. Furthermore, these conditions are systematic and pervasive; they give those who live under them only bad options. For women under sexist injustice, for example, they restrict their possibilities both within and outside of marriage.

I take the melodramas to demonstrate precisely this lack of possibility for their central women, as a way of dramatizing the deeply dehumanizing effects of gender-based injustice. This argument does not cast doubt on Cavell's general thought that these films are deeply concerned with conditions of interpersonal knowledge. Rather, it takes that thought as a starting point for a fresh reading of the films, one in which we see that the denial of human subjectivity arises not merely from metaphysical horror at the anthropological fact of human finitude, but also from more specific structures of injustice. In order to overcome this latter form of denial, we require the transformation, not merely of individuals, but of the terms and relations in which recognition is expressed. Only in this way, I propose, can the "unknown woman" become known.

4 Cavell, Feminism and Popular Art

In this brief final section, I want to draw out lessons for two further topics that I take my argument to illuminate: the question of how to bring Cavell's project fruitfully into conversation with feminism; and the question of what it means to take popular art seriously. As I mentioned at the outset, I see Cavell as having rightly and productively insisted on the deep connection between the philosophical problem of other minds and feminist concerns regarding marriage and gender. The starting point for making this connection is recognizing that traditional forms of marriage essentially involve the denial of women's subjectivity. The difficult questions in this area concern the next step, imagining what it might look like to overcome this "humiliation of marriage." I take Cavell's approach to melodrama to represent one way of doing that: to affirm women as independent human beings and to insist that they can find routes to "integrity and possibility" outside of marriage.

I don't wish to deny that this is possible, and I am certainly far from suggesting that the women of the melodramas should enter into, or persist in, the sorts of disastrous marriages their worlds afford. But it is significant to me that, as I have been arguing above, this sort of positive affirmation of independence is not in fact what the melodramas are concerned to depict. I take this fact about the films to suggest a different mode of feminist response to the humiliation of marriage. To insist, as Cavell does, on the availability of integrity outside of marriage is to neglect the pervasive structural violence of sexism, which gives women only bad options, whether inside or outside of marriage. To overcome those bad options, we need to think about the way specific social structures distort the terms of interpersonal knowledge, and to picture the work of acknowledging the human as not merely ethical work, but as constructive social and political work as well.[25]

The other question I want to touch on briefly here concerns what it means to take popular art seriously. Cavell has rightly championed products of popular culture, such as Hollywood movies, as works of art that invite and reward sustained attention and interpretation. He has been especially helpful in showing how to fruitfully place these popular artworks in dialogue with philosophical texts.[26] Throughout his career, Cavell has admirably resisted the urge to dismiss popular art as "low" and unserious, whether this urge is based on a preference for "high art" and "avant-garde" modes, or on the sort of political suspicion of popular culture that can be found in some forms of literary and cultural studies. Cavell's way of making the case for popular artworks, however, has its own characteristic limitations. He tends to frame his defense of the artwork as a defense of the central character or characters: hence his habit of referring to the women of both the comedies and melodramas as "heroines." His readings are largely organized around tracing the arc of the principal character or characters through a transformation he sees them undergo in their values and attitudes. I take Cavell's interest in affirming the integrity of the central women in the melodramas as an instance of this tendency.

---

[25] For other approaches to deepening the dialogue between Cavell's work and feminism, see Nancy Bauer, *How to Do Things with Pornography* (Cambridge, MA: Harvard University Press, 2015); Teresa De Lauretis, *The Practice of Love: Lesbian Sexuality and Perverse Desire* (Bloomington: Indiana University Press, 1994); Sandra Laugier, "The Ethics of Care as a Politics of the Ordinary," *New Literary History* 46 (2015): 217–40; and Toril Moi, "'I am a Woman': The Personal and the Philosophical," in *What is a Woman? And Other Essays* (Oxford: Oxford University Press, 1999) and "Literature and Philosophy, Cavell and Beauvoir," in Richard Eldridge, ed., *Stanley Cavell and Literary Studies: Consequences of Skepticism* (New York: Continuum, 2011).

[26] One of the great merits of Cavell's approach in this area is that it resists the tendency, prevalent in much other work on philosophy and film, to read already fully formed philosophical questions into films and to ask how a given film "answers" those questions. Cavell instead takes the films as, among other things, an invitation to shift our sense of what a certain familiar philosophical question is really about; see, for example, his remarks on his juxtaposition of Capra and Kant in *PH* 9–10. I say more about this difference in ways of connecting philosophy and film in "The Meaning of Life and the Pottersville Test," *Film and Philosophy* 17 (2013): 38–46.

But a serious interpretation of a popular artwork need not be oriented around character in this way. Popular artworks—and especially Hollywood films—can in some cases be profitably viewed as depictions of a world, where a world in the relevant sense consists in a certain set of social structures, roles and relationships. The characters and events depicted in the film can then be seen as representative of what happens in this world, what is possible (and not possible) within it. I take the melodramas to depict worlds in this sense, in particular worlds that define a constricted set of possibilities for women, or perhaps more generally a constricted set of possibilities structured around notions of gender, sexuality and family. Taking a popular art work seriously in this way is not so much a matter of admiring the central characters, nor of admiring the world depicted, but rather of taking the film to provide a compelling aesthetic vision of the way a world can hang together, the way it can define possibilities not only of behavior but also of thought, feeling and imagination.

Even where popular artworks are concerned to represent their characters as admirable, the way they do so can elude the expectations of character-centered readings. A film may represent a character as admirable, for example, in the way she explores or tests the limits of what is possible within the film's world.[27] This is certainly true about the central women of the melodramas. That effort of testing necessarily involves extremes, and it is often costly, as the melodramas show. The result is that these characters are not quite the models of virtue we tend to expect in character-centered readings: what may be exemplary about them, for example, is not their integrity in the face of betrayal, but rather their exposure to that betrayal, even to the point of madness. I take the melodramas to present their central women as at once admirable *and* profoundly damaged. Taking popular works of art seriously, in my view, means recognizing that they can contain that degree of complexity.[28]

---

[27] For an exemplary treatment of a character archetype in this spirit, see Robert Warshow, "The Gangster as Tragic Hero," in *The Immediate Experience: Movies, Comics, Theatre and Other Aspects of Popular Culture* (Enlarged ed., Cambridge, MA: Harvard University Press, 2001).

[28] In "Virtue Ethics and Literary Imagination," *Philosophy and Literature* 42 (2018): 244–56, I raise a set of related worries about philosophers' tendency to focus on character in their readings of literary texts.

5 Conclusion

Much of this chapter has been critical, but its real aim is constructive. I have been critical of Cavell's account of the melodramas in *Contesting Tears*, focusing as a representative example on his reading of *Gaslight*. Drawing on fresh consideration of key moments in the film, I have argued against Cavell's claim that the melodramas represent their central women as effecting a transition from humiliation by marriage to integrity outside of it. Rather, I have argued that the melodramas should instead be seen as representations of women who suffer by the failure of marriage in their lives, a failure that stands in for a failure of interpersonal understanding more generally. I have proposed that this shortcoming in Cavell's approach to the melodramas reflects a deeper underlying limitation in his treatment of the other minds problem. Cavell treats the problem of other minds as arising from human nature as such; as a result, he tends to assume that a solution to it is equally available to every human being, simply by acknowledging the fact of human finitude. I propose that we should instead see the problem of other minds as taking on a particularly vicious and intractable form within structures of injustice. In such circumstances, successful terms of interpersonal acknowledgment simply may not be available. Only change in those circumstances can make genuine acknowledgment possible.

This criticism is meant not so much to undermine Cavell's project as to show us a way forward from it. I take Cavell to have rightly drawn our attention to the promise of the melodramas as a source for thinking through a range of issues: the depth of classic Hollywood genres, the seriousness of popular art, the possibilities of feminist criticism and the conditions of interpersonal knowledge. I intend my argument here to suggest that these films can fulfill that promise, in ways that can even take us beyond the confines of Cavell's project. By advancing beyond Cavell's readings of these films, we can begin to fulfill the promise that he saw in them.[29]

---

[29] This chapter started life as my contribution to a colloquium on Cavell held at The New School for Social Research in the fall of 2016. I am grateful to Zed Adams for organizing that event and to my audience for thoughtful discussion. I have also benefitted from subsequent exchanges about Cavell, melodrama and feminism with Norton Batkin and Sandra Laugier. The chapter was improved enormously by perceptive comments from Erica Holberg and Dan Wack. Finally, I am indebted to Garry L. Hagberg for suggesting that it might find a home in this volume.

CHAPTER 3

The Melodrama of the Unknown Man

Peter Dula

Early in his memoir, *Little Did I Know*, Cavell wonders about the right to tell his story. Anxious about an impending catheterization of his heart, he asks, "Am I using the mortal threat of the procedure, and of what it may reveal, to justify my right to tell my story?"[1] A page later he writes of wanting "authorization" to tell his story. He is still raising the question 500 pages later: "So it comes to the question, what gives us the right to single ourselves out and open our mouths in all seriousness?" (540). Attentive readers of Cavell may recognize the phrasing. It recalls the opening of his book on melodrama.

> I claim that the four films principally considered in the following chapters define a genre of film, taking the claim to mean, most generally, that they recount interacting versions of a story, a story or myth, that seems to present itself as a woman's search for her story, or of the right to tell her story.[2]

---

[1] *Little Did I Know: Excerpts from Memory* (Stanford: Stanford University Press, 2010), p. 2. Subsequent page numbers will be noted parenthetically in the text.
[2] *Contesting Tears: The Hollywood Melodrama of the Unknown Woman* (Chicago: University of Chicago Press, 1996), p. 3.

P. Dula (✉)
Eastern Mennonite University, Harrisonburg, VA, USA

In Cavell's long engagement with skepticism, he turned again and again to works of literature and film that interpreted and reinterpreted the same problems that philosophy since Descartes had been interpreting as skepticism. Given the centrality of such texts and films to Cavell's work, one promising approach to reading *Little Did I Know* (*LDIK*) is to ask if it might plausibly be situated within, or placed in relation to, one of the genres with which he was so preoccupied: Shakespearean tragedy, the comedies of remarriage and the melodramas of the unknown woman. *LDIK* is not a tragedy, but it does have elements of comedy and, I argue, clear and striking elements of melodrama.

That said, my title is admittedly an overstatement. I don't quite mean to assert a new genre called the melodrama of the unknown man, still less to shoe-horn Cavell's massive and complex autobiography into a pre-cut category. But I do think it relatively uncontroversial to imagine that Cavell's writing about his own life would be inevitably, often unconsciously, saturated with tropes, images and themes from the genres that he spent so much time thinking about, much like Augustine's *Confessions* is saturated with scriptural allusion. Pursuing those links is useful because it helps place the memoir within Cavell's entire body of work and helps us know what it might mean to read a memoir philosophically, even to begin thinking about how in *LDIK* philosophy knows itself even as it is becoming literature.

It is instructive to briefly compare *Little Did I Know* with Cavell's account of the melodramas of the unknown woman. There are some pertinent parallels to be drawn with the list of characteristics Cavell outlines early in *Contesting Tears*. The first characteristic of the melodramas that he mentions is that in the melodramas, unlike the comedies, the father is present "not on the side of [the heroine's] desire, but on the side of law."[3] Early in *LDIK*, shortly after we find Cavell wondering if his first and pivotal story about one of his father's rages was told too "melodramatically," he tells another story about his father, one that places him squarely on the side the law. Early in Cavell's time at Berkeley, he returned home to Sacramento to visit his parents. When his mother agrees to let him use the family car to visit friends, his father reminds her that she had promised to lend the car to neighbors the next morning. She responds, "But then I hadn't known Stanley would be here." His father's response is witheringly sarcastic, "Oh I see. Stanley is here. Therefore all obligations, all friend-

---

[3] *Contesting Tears*, p. 5.

ships, all right and wrong are to be suspended for the duration… But if I am alive tomorrow morning, that promise will be kept" (20).

Perhaps more importantly, along with the differences between the roles of fathers and mothers in melodramas and comedies, the second characteristic Cavell mentions is "a difference in the role of the past and of memory: in the comedies the past is open, shared, a recurring topic of fun, not doubt somewhat ambiguous; but in the melodramas the past is frozen, mysterious, with topics forbidding and isolating."[4] Cavell's childhood is a painful one. He describes one of his father's inexplicable rages as "the moment at which I realized that my father hated me" (14). Recalling the move from the extended family home he describes as "paradise," he writes, "the catastrophe of the move broke over me in waves that I have periodically felt have never entirely stopped breaking" (17). He continually refers to his childhood as isolated and excluding. Cavell is all but explicit about this when he says that his experience of psychoanalysis prompted him "to consider my early life in relation to ideas of childhood abuse and abandonment and neglect, in other words, in relation to isolation and despair" (110).

The third characteristic with which Cavell announced the genre of melodrama has to do with the way they end. "In the remarriage comedy the action of the narration moves … from a setting in a big city to conclude in a place outside the city, a place of perspective, in melodramas of unknownness the action returns to and concludes in the place from which it began or in which it has climaxed, a place of abandonment or transcendence."[5] *LDIK* ends where it began, with Cavell back in the city of his birth, Atlanta, in a difficult conversation with his father at his hospital bedside, immediately following an extended meditation on transcendence. Moreover, the final line of *LDIK*—"I walked out to find my mother"—gestures toward a "fundamental feature" of the melodramas which Cavell calls "the search for the mother" (14).

1   Perfectionism and Comedy

But these are at most clues. A checklist of features is not an argument, especially since the most important features—what these films do with marriage and with conversation between men and women—have not yet been approached.

---

[4] *Contesting Tears*, p. 6.
[5] Ibid.

Before attempting to investigate those features, it is useful to step back to a much less controversial claim. Whether or not *LDIK* is a comedy or melodrama or neither, it is clearly a *perfectionist* text. The fact that it is so obviously a perfectionist text is part of what raises the question of comedy or melodrama because they are the perfectionist genres to which Cavell committed so much energy. In fact, it seems that these films are not just examples of perfectionism, they are the resources from which Cavell came to develop his account of perfectionism. "When I thought about [deontology and utilitarianism] in connection with the lives depicted in the grand movies I had been immersed in, the theories and the depicted lives passed one another by, appeared irrelevant to each other."[6]

Perfectionism is the moral commitment to life as a continual journey, not toward a fixed state called perfection, but from what he calls the "attained self" to the "attainable self." Making that transition requires that we become ashamed of our current, attained self and dedicate ourselves to our next, further, attainable self even if in the moment that can only seem to us like a betrayal of the self. Cavell considers this an elaboration of what Emerson meant by "self-reliance," but since that term has become so easily mistaken for the most baleful kind of individualism, it is worth noting two aspects of self-reliance. First, this transformation is occasioned by another, helping make sense of what Cavell will mean when he writes, "How do we become self-reliant? The worst thing we could do is rely on ourselves."[7] Second, the perfectionist self is doubled, split as it were, horizontally. Self-reliance in this case is reliance on one's next self, not on one's attained self. Because this process is never ending, or ends only with death, it does not rely on an account of a "true self" toward which one is working, but a self perpetually doubled.

Reading *LDIK* as a perfectionist text means reading it as a story of movements from attained selves to attainable selves, as journey of a self repeatedly finding itself lost but also finding its way to further states of that self in the company of exemplary friends. Cavell invites us to understand several pivotal transitions in this life in precisely this way.

> For the third explicit time in my life I found myself creatively stopped, not understandably challenged and inspired, but at a dead end: the first time in

---

[6] *Cities of Words: Pedagogical Letters on a Register of the Moral Life* (Cambridge, MA: Harvard University Press, 2004), p. 9.

[7] *Conditions Handsome and Unhandsome: The Constitution of Emersonian Perfectionism* (Chicago: University of Chicago Press, 1990), p. 47.

New York after music at Berkeley; the second time at Harvard with the appearance of Austin and his work; the third time with hundreds of pages of acceptable pages recognizably my own that I could not lead to a conclusion in the present (451).

In the first, when he drops out of Juilliard, Cavell betrays his attained musical self, the self which everyone, especially his family, thought destined for a successful career in the music industry, a career denied his mother and his beloved uncles Mendel and Meyer. In the second, when J. L. Austin comes to Harvard and he gets "knocked off his horse,"[8] Cavell betrays the philosopher he had been (mostly) educated to be in favor of Austin, whose reputation, at least in the US, was and is ambiguous, not least for two of Cavell's closest philosophical interlocutors (Bernard Williams and Thompson Clarke). In the third, though his dissertation had long ago been accepted for publication, he finds himself unable to consider it finished or find a way to finish it.

Now we can sharpen the question. Instead of "is *LDIK* a comedy or a melodrama?" the question becomes "does Cavell's perfectionist journey proceed comically or melodramatically?" The argument for comedy begins with the role of conversation in making this journey. "Mode of conversation" is the first feature in Cavell's list of the elements of perfectionism[9] and it is the crucial link between the perfectionism of the remarriage comedies and the perfectionism of *LDIK*. Over and over, Cavell makes a case for the importance of conversation in the remarriage comedies. "Pervading each moment of the texture and mood of remarriage comedy is the mode of *conversation* that binds or sweeps together the principle pair. I suppose that this is the feature that comes in for the greatest conceptual development in *Pursuits of Happiness*."[10]

LDIK is comedic just insofar as it partakes of this chief feature of the remarriage comedies. Pervading *LDIK* are numerous accounts of lengthy transformative conversations with Thomas Kuhn, Bernard Williams, Kurt Fischer, Seymour Shifrin, Michael Fried, Thompson Clarke and others. The friends and colleagues that left indelible imprints on Cavell are invari-

---

[8] The reference is to Acts 9 and Paul's confrontation with the risen Jesus on his journey to Damascus after which Paul goes through his own period of lostness somewhere in Arabia (Galatians 1.17) before returning to Damascus.

[9] *Conditions Handsome and Unhandsome*, p. 6.

[10] *Contesting Tears*, p. 5.

ably presented as masters of the art of conversation. He writes of Kurt Fischer's "capacity for eliciting conversation" and of Clarke, "we talked about everything of interest to us," and of "enter[ing] unknown territory together" (367). Without the daily conversation with Clarke, Cavell would never have come to a dissertation, still less *The Claim of Reason*. The first time Cavell met Bernard Williams, "we arranged to have dinner together that night, and we talked until dawn" (149). When Mary Randall returned to Berkeley, Cavell writes, "Our conversations began again…" (398). On meeting Michael Fried for the first time he writes, "From perhaps 8 o'clock as the party was still forming until… after midnight…Fried and I stood in our relatively private corner…talking about anything and everything.… We found ourselves pushed to not merely to new subjects but were led steadily to speak at the limits, and sometimes as it were just the others side of what we knew and could judge" (406–07). Rogers Albritton "craved conversation … keeping concerted conversation going for hours, once that I know of for seven hours, even when he was in pain and in order to get a modicum of relief had to lie flat on his back on the floor" (490). Among the students gathered in Emerson Hall in his early years on the Harvard faculty, "Standards of philosophical conversation, of intellectual conversation more generally, were established whose powers of inspiration remain, I trust, alive for me" (422).

In the Foreword to *The Claim of Reason*, he describes some of these conversations with Kuhn, Fischer and Clarke:

> I do not think I can exaggerate the continuity of the discussions over those years; I know I cannot exaggerate the importance of that intellectual companionship. We seemed at times almost in possession of something you might call an intellectual community, and sometimes one or other of us said as much. It is an essential part of my indebtedness to the work of Austin and Wittgenstein that it, for a time at least, helped make possible such a visible community, or the concrete hope of one."[11]

At this point, I suspect, readers may be growing exasperated with a discussion of comedy and melodrama that hasn't even mentioned the most important, defining feature: marriage. Who cares if *LDIK* is, like the comedies, a triumph of transformative conversation if those conversations

---

[11] *The Claim of Reason: Wittgenstein, Skepticism, Morality and Tragedy* (New York: Oxford University Press, 1979), pp. xxii–xxiv.

are not with a wife? Take as a counter-example, another 2011 memoir by an academic, Duke University theologian Stanley Hauerwas's *Hannah's Child*.[12] Hauerwas clearly allows his second marriage to Paula Gilbert to be the climax of his memoir, making *Hannah's Child* a comedy. Not classical comedy because it is a second marriage, and not a comedy of remarriage either, but a comedy all the same. In *LDIK*, Cavell's second wife, Cathleen Cohen, doesn't play the same role as Paula in Hauerwas's memoir. This is not to diminish her role nor to slight the finely crafted and moving scenes which introduce her: leaning against the archway smoking a cigarette, charming the elite and intimidating company of Rawls and Dworkin at the bar of the Algonquin Hotel. But unlike a comedy, the trajectory of *LDIK* is not toward marriage but toward a different place of rest and/or happiness. Its climax is not marriage to Cathleen but the completion of the fourth part of *The Claim of Reason*.

This raises the possibility, already suggested by the kinds of conversations I highlighted, that the woman in question in *LDIK* is Lady Philosophy. Where the women of the comedies and the melodramas have a decision to make about whether a particular man is worth spending a life with, Cavell has a decision to make about philosophy. In his writing before Part Four of *The Claim of Reason*, he states: "I had the unmistakable sense of having said hello a number of times without anyone saying hello back... It had become a matter of taking things far enough. Far enough for what? To arrive where others are. To achieve, that is, to participate in a public" (521). He also says that completing *The Claim of Reason* had given him a way out of his sense, expressed in *Must We Mean What We Say?* that "philosophy is in one of its periodic crises of method" (459). So we have something like a remarriage to philosophy. A first marriage in the heady days at UCLA where he had "found something like a home, call it a neighborhood, anyway a place to remove my shoes and lay aside my staff" (242, also 284). A crisis occasioned by his encounter with Austin and no clear way out. And a remarriage represented by the publication of Part Four.

2   The Melodrama of the Unknown Man

But if *LDIK* is a comedy, or, better, can be helpfully read as participating in the genre of remarriage comedy, what are we to do with melodramatic characteristics, especially of isolation and transcendence, with which I

---

[12] *Hannah's Child: A Theologian's Memoir* (Grand Rapids, MI: Eerdmans, 2010).

began? The fact of isolation itself may be no argument against *LDIK*'s status as a comedy. The remarriage comedies also end with isolation, what Cavell calls "an isolating happiness."[13] An important difference between the remarriage comedies and Shakespearean comedy is that in the latter the reconciliation of the couple comes hand in hand with the reconciliation of the entire community, often even in multiple marriages (*Much Ado About Nothing*, *Twelfth Night*, *Midsummer Night's Dream*, *As You Like It*). In the remarriage comedies, the couple may be reconciled, but not to a wider community (hence they so rarely end with a wedding scene). The conversation they achieve is set in contrast to the impossibility of such conversation, call it democratic conversation, among the society's citizens.

So the isolation at the end of *LDIK* may be just this kind of isolation. Immediately prior to Cavell's remarks about completing *The Claim of Reason* at the beginning of Part XIV of *LDIK*, he recounts presiding over the wedding of a former student, Alice Crary. The wedding is on September 15, 2001, four days after the destruction of the World Trade Centers. In the hotel that morning Cavell encounters an unsettling example of war fervor that leaves him worried that "the possibility of community, of anything like constitutional democracy, is negated, gutted" (521–22). Immediately after the remarks about *The Claim of Reason*, he turns to Blanchot. So Part XIV opens with the image of a wedding that, like in *Pursuits of Happiness*, takes place in contrast to a society in which community is not possible. And it may be that the remarks about *The Claim of Reason* exist there analogously to the wedding, suggesting that it is not Cavell alone who is isolated but philosophy that is isolated from a culture unwilling or unable to put itself in question. Transcendence, then, exists as an element of melodrama, but not a decisive one because "In each of these comedies some element of melodrama variously makes an appearance without getting to the point of shattering the comedic universe."[14]

I am almost, but not quite, satisfied with that. I am not sure that the theme of transcendence can be so easily placed as one element. It plays too large a role in *LDIK*'s conclusion and it seems to me that Cavell is as much isolated from philosophy as with it.

---

[13] *Pursuits of Happiness: The Hollywood Comedy of Remarriage* (Cambridge, MA: Harvard University Press, 1981), p. 151.

[14] *Cities of Words*, p. 10.

Earlier I emphasized the role of conversation in Cavell's philosophical journey as it parallels the role of conversation in the remarriage comedies. But that account may have been too simple. After another passage in which he "marvel[s] at the depth and sweep of sheer talent and sociability" of his graduate students and their sense of common purpose, he pauses to recall

> a recurrent topic of exchange between Tom Clarke and me in our first years at Berkeley concerning our sense of the lack of community in our experience of studying philosophy, a sense of paradox in this circumstance since philosophy was obviously and irreducibly bound to the possibility of continuous, perhaps interminable, exchange. At this distance the topic seems plainly to express his and my individual senses of isolation. (477)

He goes on to describe an exchange with Hilary Putnam as "a fair instance causing my own recurrent feelings of isolation among the members of my own generation of teachers" (478).

Recall that Cavell wrote, "It is an essential part of my indebtedness to the work of Austin and Wittgenstein that it, for a time at least, helped make possible such a visible community, or the concrete hope of one."[15] This account of philosophical community can exist alongside his and Clarke's sense of isolation because such community was made possible by two philosophers, Austin and Wittgenstein, were isolated from the larger community of professional philosophy.

It is important here that in two of the three crises Cavell describes, he sought out psychoanalytic help. The conversations I have been highlighting seem to mostly play a transformative role in Cavell's movement to further attainable selves in the first two crises Cavell describes. The third, the completion of *The Claim of Reason*, was not made possible by philosophical conversation but by psychoanalysis. In the winter of 1976, despairing of ever finishing *Claim*, he begins to meet once a week with Eugene Smith and "the mere months of more or less aimless talk—what else was it?—… produced a breakthrough" (434). By fall of 1977, 16 years after the original dissertation had been submitted, the manuscript is at the press.

The entrance of the analyst here is another important link to the melodramas, especially to *Now, Voyager*. Both the comedies and melodramas

---

[15] *The Claim of Reason*, p. xxiv.

regularly feature therapists. But without exception, in comedies like *Bringing Up Baby* or *His Girl Friday*, the therapist is a butt of jokes, himself apparently in need of therapy as much as his clients. In melodramas like *Gaslight* and *Now, Voyager*, the therapist plays a central and even leading role. Cavell accounts for this difference, the only difference for which he claims there is no exception, this way: "In a comic world, where desire is present, joyous, but disruptive, to mistake it for madness is itself comic; it will find its own way out. In a melodramatic world where desire is denied, or fixated, perhaps a source of horror, liberation must come from the outside."[16]

3 Transcendence and the Disaster

In conclusion, I want to pursue one final, unavoidable, link between the melodramas of unknownness and *LDIK*: transcendence. Each of the melodramas end with a moment when "the woman's isolation is associated ... with some register of her relation to the transcendent—grounded in a cosmic symbology of light and darkness, of enclosure and the imagination of freedom,"[17] most famously at the end of *Now, Voyager* when Bette Davis says, "Let's not ask for the moon; we have the stars."

Cavell cites this line as he begins the discussion of Blanchot which serves as a springboard for Part XIV, the closing section of the memoir. Blanchot seems like a curious choice here. Cavell's forays into twentieth-century French philosophy (Derrida, Foucault, Lacan) have been occasional and usually seem done out of a sense of obligation, because someone has demanded that he do so, not because of his own volition. Why Blanchot and why here, "seeking a way to take my leave" (538)?

Little Did I Know is a writing of at least four disasters. Cavell is explicit that he is writing in anticipation of his own death. Much of the end of the text is preoccupied with the disaster of 9/11 and the US response to it. His turn to Emerson's "Fate," makes it also about the disaster of slavery. The closing pages about his father take us back to the devastations of Cavell's childhood.[18] Blanchot's disaster marks "our being dissociated or

---

[16] *Cities of Words*, p. 240.
[17] *Contesting Tears*, p. 37.
[18] For Blanchot it is above all the Holocaust, a fact which alerts us, if we hadn't noticed already, that his book by a Jew born in 1926 has said nothing about the Holocaust. This

disconnected or disengaged from the pertinence of the stars... For Blanchot disaster is revealed metaphysically to be, or to have become, the normal state of existence, marked by a release from our ties to the stars, say from our considered steps beyond, a release that partakes of an oblivion of the transcendental draw of words" (522). From here Part XIV begins a kind of contrapuntal polyphony—Christopher Johnson calls it a fugue[19]—in which the voices of Blanchot, Derrida and Schlegel are met with the voices of Wittgenstein, Thoreau and Emerson, all repeating and developing in different keys a number of themes that run throughout Cavell's work and themes that appear multiple times here at the end of *LDIK*: consideration, understanding and awkwardness. In what follows, I trace some of this fugal structure in order to understand just what Cavell means by "transcendence."

When Cavell writes that Blanchot thinks we are released "from our considered steps beyond," he is recalling another Blanchot text, *Le Pas au-delà*. Part of what interests Cavell is the way that this title can be variously translated as *The Step Not Beyond* or *The Step Beyond* or *The Non-Step Beyond*. It interests Cavell because it is the way he describes acknowledgement. When Austin says that "I know" is similar to performative utterances like "I promise" or "I bet," he means "that just as saying you promise takes a step, makes a commitment, beyond saying that you fully intend to, so saying that you know takes a step beyond saying that you are, for your part, absolutely sure" (320). It will be ten years after his initial encounter with Austin that Cavell comes to formulate this as "acknowledgment."[20] "Acknowledgement goes beyond knowledge. (Goes beyond not, so to speak, in the order of knowledge, but in its requirement that I *do* something or reveal something on the basis of that knowledge.)"[21]

---

omission is too stunning to be unintentional. I read the turn to Blanchot, in part, as Cavell's way of signaling the one disaster for which words fail him, for which he is grateful for the words of another.

[19] Johnson writes, "he creates indeed a kind of fugue on the theme of *consideration*," *MLN*, 125, no. 5 (Dec. 2010): 1150. I am grateful for this image, but I find it harder to single out one fugal theme. It also seems to me a fugue on the themes of disaster, awkwardness and understanding, though Johnson might persuasively argue that these are all part of the development of the theme of consideration.

[20] See *Must We Mean What We Say?* (Cambridge: Cambridge University Press, 1967), p. 257.

[21] Ibid.

The multiple possible translations of *Le Pas au-delà* nicely capture the way acknowledgement is a step beyond knowledge in the way it demands that I do something with my knowledge. Gloucester knows Edgar is his son but must acknowledge it. To know your pain is to respond to it. But acknowledgement doesn't go beyond knowledge in the sense that it isn't what the skeptic wants. It isn't certainty. In that sense, it is a non-step or a step not beyond.

But these are not just any steps beyond, they are *considered* steps beyond. If we are dissociated from the stars, Cavell writes, then that means consideration is no longer a usable mode of thought. The seemingly odd claim makes sense when we see that Cavell is invoking the etymological root of consideration: the sidereal. "Consideration (and reconsideration) speaks of a careful attention to the framework of stars... [But] there is now no sidereal orientation" (529). But just as Cavell stepped beyond or stepped not-beyond Blanchot's dissociation from the stars toward Wittgenstein's contrapuntal dissociation from our words, Cavell again changes keys, describing consideration as "placing a constellation of ideas within whatever other constellations you divine" (530). Now consideration is just what he is doing, no more transcendent than reading intertextually. Yet the language of "divine" suggests something more complicated. So does the fact that his constellation of ideas (Wittgenstein, Thoreau, Emerson, *Now, Voyager*) is being placed within a relatively new constellation (Blanchot, Proust, Ruskin, Hemingway, St. Paul, *Only Angels Have Wings*) in this farewell chapter.

Consideration takes another turn a few pages later. In a manner that manages to encapsulate the lessons of the melodramas, he is explaining Emerson's claim that "To be great is to be misunderstood," as part of Emerson's recognition that being misunderstood may be a way of avoiding "the violent desire of others to grasp oneself" through false understanding. It may be that one may only maintain a grasp on oneself by avoiding the grasps of the understanding of others. "Emerson in effect questions whether we know what it is to understand each other, perhaps to consider, say take account of, be considerate of, one another" (532).

This may seem to be another way of withdrawing consideration from the sidereal, but again, Cavell complicates things by turning immediately back to the sidereal. Cavell has discovered that Proust, in his translation of Ruskin's *Bible of Amiens*, cites Emerson's essay "Civilization," "whose subject is evidently our needing to be reminded or our relation to what in reading Wittgenstein's *Investigations* I have called the farther shore of human existence and its language...; I have sometimes called it the transcendental shore" (533). Specifically, Proust cites Emerson's line, "Hitch your wagon to a star." Proust does not reduce Emerson's claim to a platitude about thinking big and aiming high but writes:

> [In such a cathedral as that at Amiens] men of the thirteenth century came to seek ... a teaching which, with a useless and bizarre luxury it continues to offer in a kind of open book, written in a solemn language where each letter is a work of art, a language no longer understood. Giving it meaning less literally religious than during the Middle ages or even an aesthetic meaning only, you have been able, nevertheless, to relate it to one of those feelings that appear to us as the true reality beyond our lives, to one of 'those stars to which its well that we hitch our wagon.' (533)

Where Blanchot thinks we are released from the stars, Cavell, with Proust and Emerson, still urges us to hitch our wagon to a star. But that is not exactly a contradiction, for just insofar as the hitch is not already in place, Cavell concedes the fact of being released.

Proust's remarks on Amiens prompt a Proustian recollection of Cavell's own. At Logan Airport, "a distinctive, unmistakable aroma" of kerosene reminds him of the aroma of a horse-drawn wagon's lamp in his childhood Atlanta.

This much should make clear what Johnson meant by calling this a fugue. But what work is it doing? There is more here than just a lovely way to end a book. To understand what Cavell is doing, I turn to one of Cavell's last essays, written around the same time as *LDIK* and cited twice in Part XIV, "The *Investigations*' Everyday Aesthetics of Itself."[22] The essay is trying to figure out what Wittgenstein meant by "perspicuousness" since, in the *Investigations*, it can no longer mean formal logic. Philosophy as Cavell has come to understand it begins with lostness: Emerson's "Where do we find ourselves?", Dante's dark wood. "It is, accordingly, as the philosophical answer to this disorientation that Wittgenstein proposes the idea of perspicuousness."[23]

> How shall we place the farther shore of perspicuousness, the literary? Let us say it is, alluding to Kant, a standpoint from which to see the methods of the

---

[22] In John Gibson and Wolfgang Huemer, eds, *The Literary Wittgenstein* (New York: Routledge, 2004), pp. 21–33.
[23] Ibid., p. 23.

Investigations, their leading words home, undoing the charms of metaphysics, a perspective apart from which there is no pressing issue of spiritual fervor, whether felt as religious, moral, or aesthetic. Standpoint implies an alternative, a competing standpoint, a near shore. For professional philosophers this shore is that of philosophical 'problems,'

I wish I could make the two shores equally palpable, and sufficiently so to make questions as to which shore is the more important seem as foolish to us as it must seem to the river of philosophy that runs between.[24]

All of this language—farther shore, the literary, Kant's standpoints, leading words home, metaphysics, spiritual, religious, the river of philosophy—reappears in Part XIV of the memoir almost as if a display of the everyday aesthetics of itself. The back and forth between Blanchot and Wittgenstein, stars and words, airplanes and horse-drawn wagons, is the back and forth between the near and far shores, the metaphysical and the ordinary. It is Cavell's way of making the two shores "equally palpable" in his life. In terms of the melodramas, it is his way of identifying himself "with some register of her relation to the transcendent—grounded in a cosmic symbology of light *and* darkness, of enclosure *and* the imagination of freedom."[25]

Furthermore, if it is a fugue, that may help understand how this chapter has a claim to being perspicuous. On a first reading it seems convoluted and disorganized, anything but clear. Cavell is aware of this. Immediately after the smell of kerosene, he turns to Schlegel's "Über die Unverständlichkeit" and notes that Schlegel is aware of the irony of writing an essay on understanding that will be called incomprehensible. It is in fact his topic: "Of all things that have to do with communicating ideas, what could be more fascinating than the question of whether such communication is actually possible?" (535).[26]

The word "understanding" appears again and again in this final section. Blanchot has a "horror of knowledge" which Cavell formulates as a "horror of understanding." Where skepticism as Cavell most often understood it was a fate to be avoided, in Blanchot's hands, becomes a refuge from the unbearable knowledge of the disaster. To put it differently, and so get at

---

[24] Ibid., p. 26.

[25] *Contesting Tears*, p. 37 (italics mine).

[26] Compare to *Contesting Tears*, "The concluding position of the women of the unknown woman melodramas...now associate with an incommunicability of the transcendent, might perhaps usefully be studied in conjunction with [Nietzsche's death of God parable]" (43).

the full range of Cavell's development of "understanding," some knowledge must be stood, the way we say we "stand (or can't stand) the pain" ("like what? like a trial or like ground before an enemy?").[27] Schlegel understands that he may have to stand up under the pain of being misunderstood. So does Cavell. "My 'standing' has, from the first writing I published that was meant to establish it, been in in question professionally" (182).

But this worry does not exhaust Cavell's anxiety. "Standing" is also a key term in Cavell's moral philosophy, one that comes up for significant development in one of his essays on *Now, Voyager*. The importance of Charlotte and Jerry's closing conversation is its contribution to moral perfectionism, "most particularly the question of what constitutes one's standing in confronting another person with moral questioning."[28] Cavell's concern now is with his own standing in confronting us with an autobiography, the very act of which declares himself to "stand here for humanity" as Emerson put it. "What gives us the right to single ourselves out and open our mouths in all seriousness?" (540), the same question that opened *Contesting Tears*.

Like many fugues, Part XIV has a clear coda. In it, at his father's hospital bed, the philosophical, literary, scriptural and cinematic voices have dropped out. It is just Cavell and his parents, back in Atlanta.[29] "Whereas in remarriage comedy the action of the narration moves as said, from a setting in a big city to conclude in a place outside the city, a place of perspective, in melodramas of unknownness the action returns to and concludes in the place from which it began or in which it has climaxed, a place of abandonment and transcendence."[30]

This longest stretch of dialogue in the book begins:

> Do you *understand* me?
> You mean can I hear you? Yes.
> No, I mean am I making sense to you right now?

---

[27] *The Claim of Reason*, p. 80.
[28] *Cities of Words*, p. 235.
[29] I have written at length about the closing conversation with his father in "Six Scenes of Instruction in Stanley Cavell's *Little Did I Know, Philosophy and Literature*" 2016. What follows borrows from that essay.
[30] *Contesting Tears*, p. 6.

His father goes on to ask Cavell to speak for him, to represent him to the doctors, to stand for him, a task Cavell awkwardly refuses but then goes on to reconsider before he walks out "to find my mother." The ironies that Cavell has been circling around pile up here and the burden on the reader is hard to bear because we are in the same position vis-à-vis him as he is vis-à-vis his father. And we know from Schlegel that a lack of understanding is due "to the lack of an ear for ironies of various kinds" (535). Cavell establishes his standing by confessing a failure to stand. He shows understanding by displaying his misunderstanding. In exposing his awkwardness, he demonstrates tact. Standing is awkward. "The subject of the melodrama of the unknown woman [is] the irony of human identity.... [T]he narrative drive of the genre is a woman's search for the mother."[31]

---

[31] Ibid., p. 210.

PART II

Shakespeare, Opera, and Philosophical Interpretation

CHAPTER 4

Cordelia's Moral Incapacity in *King Lear*

David A. Holiday

1 Cavell, King Lear and Moral Incapacity

Stanley Cavell's great essay "The Avoidance of Love" is an important contribution to the rich corpus of critical thought on *King Lear*.[1] The paper concentrates on a reinterpretation of *Lear's* central metaphor, the dual image of sight and blindness, but in doing so it casts new light over much of the play. Cavell develops this reading along multiple axes: resolving interpretative puzzles; connecting Lear to the deep cultural undercurrents of modern scepticism; and reflecting on the possibilities of expressing, depicting and effecting human presence in the theatre.

For my purposes, Cavell's reading is important because it informs a novel understanding of the ill-fated interaction between Cordelia and Lear in the play's opening scene. This moment is the breaching point from which the terrible flood of calamity, chaos and destruction which makes up the rest of the play gushes forth. Importantly, Cavell's interpretation

---

[1] Stanley Cavell, *Disowning Knowledge: In Seven Plays of Shakespeare*, 2nd ed. (Cambridge: Cambridge University Press, 2003).

reveals that the words which precipitate the catastrophe—Cordelia's simple "Nothing, my lord."—are the expression of a *moral incapacity*, an inability to perform a perceived wrong, in which Cordelia's moral nature, character and distinctive fineness show themselves. The notion of moral incapacity is developed in Bernard Williams' eponymous paper, Harry Frankfurt's "Rationality and the Unthinkable" and other recent work in moral psychology on "volitional necessities."[2] A moral incapacity is a volitional limit, pertaining to intentional action (to that which can be done knowingly by a person), which holds as a matter of a person's moral character and which partly gives their character its colour, shape and style. Put plainly, our moral incapacities are those limits on our free agency which help make us the kinds of people, morally speaking, that we are. As the notion is hard to make clear in the abstract, and as a central aim of this chapter is to elucidate it by means of a rich case study, it will be best to turn our attention to the example of Cordelia.

Surveying the critical literature on *King Lear*, one is struck by how deeply divided commentators are on this critical moment in the tragedy. In particular, there are deep rifts in how to understand Cordelia's words in the opening scene, and her moral character as it is expressed through them. As Anna Jameson puts it:

> Speak of Cordelia to a critic... all agree in the beauty of the portrait...; but when we come to details, I have heard more... opposite opinions relative to her than any other of Shakespeare's characters—a proof... that, from the simplicity with which the character is dramatically treated, and the small space it occupies, few are aware of its internal power or its wonderful depth of purpose.[3]

---

[2] Bernard Williams, *Making Sense of Humanity: And Other Philosophical Papers 1982–1993* (Cambridge University Press, 1995); Harry G. Frankfurt, *The Importance of What We Care About: Philosophical Essays* (Cambridge University Press, 1988). See also Craig Taylor, "Moral Incapacity," *Philosophy* 70, no. 272 (1995): 273–85, and Craig Taylor, "Moral Incapacity and Huckleberry Finn," *Ratio* 14, no. 1 (2001): 56–67; Robert J. Gay, "Bernard Williams on Practical Necessity," *Mind* 98, no. 392 (1989): 551–69; Dwight Furrow, "Schindler's Compulsion: An Essay on Practical Necessity," *American Philosophical Quarterly* 35, no. 3 (1998): 209–29; and "Volitional Necessities" in Gary Watson, *Agency and Answerability: Selected Essays* (Oxford, New York: Clarendon Press, 2004).

[3] Extracted from Jameson's "Shakespeare's Heroines" (1832), in Susan Bruce, ed. *Columbia Critical Guides: William Shakespeare King Lear* Columbia (1998), p. 91.

Having first outlined my Cavellian reading of Cordelia, I will then contrast it with two alternative, conflicting traditions in *King Lear* interpretation—traditions to which Cavell also responds in "The Avoidance of Love." Each tradition has distinguished origins in the works of Coleridge and Johnson, but I will argue that both are mistaken. I disagree with Coleridgians over the matter of whether Cordelia truly *cannot* or rather *will not* flatter her father. On the other hand, while I share their moral admiration for Cordelia, I will argue that Johnsonian readers also misinterpret her inability to do as Lear demands in my view and are thereby led to a distorted picture of her character which does her a serious disservice.

Each of these critical contrasts reveals significant aspects of moral incapacity in itself, and in relation to our broader conception of human nature and the moral life. The distortions of the Coleridgian reading, which mistakes her incapacity for a *refusal*, demonstrate the depth of difference between these two practical concepts, and the degree to which this difference impacts judgements of character. The error in Johnsonian readings, in contrast, is that of confusing Cordelia's moral limitation—a matter of her character and context, as a situated moral agent—for an abstract form of conceptual impossibility. The breakdown of this reading, then, illustrates the importance of keeping to a personal or humanized conception of moral agency as we think about character.

2 Cavell's Hermeneutic Proposal—The Central Metaphor of *King Lear*

Before turning to Cordelia's "Nothing," it will be necessary first to do a little stage setting regarding Cavell's reading of Lear's agenda as the play opens. Cavell's re-reading of the play concentrates on its central metaphor of sight and blindness. These concepts not only permeate the language of the play but are also enacted in one of its most visceral moments, the appallingly protracted and interrupted blinding of Gloucester. Cavell's revolutionary interpretation of *King Lear* centres on the innovation of turning Shakespeare's metaphor on its head, reading these notions not as primarily concerned with the *act* of seeing and its failure, but as being about vision in its passive aspect of *being seen* and *being hidden from view*. This inversion has particular resonances for Lear, who Cavell reveals to be a man governed by an overwhelming desire to avoid (hide or flee from) the penetrating gaze of love.

Cavell's reading illuminates Lear's behaviour in the opening scene, which is strange on any account and presents various puzzles for critical readings of the play. Lear demands that his three daughters profess their love for him before the royal court, performing an act of courtier's flattery, in order to "win" their inheritance (a third of his kingdom). This is motivated, Cavell argues, by a deep-seated dread of being seen by another with the eyes of love. The connection between being seen and being loved is that to be seen by someone who genuinely loves you is to be seen for *what you really are*, in your entirety, with all of your successes and strengths, and all of your faults, failures and weaknesses. Appearing to another's loving gaze is a form of appearing naked before them. This exposes Lear's fear of being seen as, at bottom, a fear of an encounter with *himself*—of being forced to confront what he now is, what he has become. His attempt to hide from love is the expression of a powerful drive to self-deception.[4]

For Lear, being seen lovingly means appearing stripped of the armour of political power and a fearsome reputation (earned through battle and harsh rule), and being exposed as the increasingly feeble and dependent old man he is becoming. Cavell's reading sheds an entirely new light on the significance of, and intention behind, Lear's demand:

> He feels unworthy of love when the reality of lost power comes over him. That is what his plan was to have avoided by exchanging his fortune for his love at one swap. He cannot bear love when he has no reason to be loved, perhaps because of the helplessness, the passiveness which that implies, which some take for impotence. And he wards it off for the reason for which people do ward off being loved, because it presents itself to them as a demand.[5]

---

[4] This turns the metaphor of sight into *being seen for what one really is*, in something like the sense of "She saw right through me." And its companion idea of *blindness* becomes about *hidden-ness*, being protected from the gaze of others, perhaps in the way that young children cover their eyes with their hands so as to become "invisible." This is a pertinent image to apply to Lear, because what is so terrifying about him is the tension between his fierce and violent power, and the childish fear and weakness at his core. As evidence that Cavell is on the right track, we can note that the fool also harps on Lear's having assumed the role of a child with respect to his daughters.

[5] Cavell (2003), p. 61. Cavell's suggestions as to *why* Lear cannot bear to be loved are rather rough, but they do hang together in a coherent and useful picture. His first suggestion—fear of impotence with age—seems to turn Lear's avoidance of love (of another's gaze) into a fear of confronting his own powerlessness (seeing himself reflected in the lover's gaze).

Behind Lear's demand, then, is his intention "to avoid recognition, the shame of exposure, the threat of self-revelation."[6] Driven by this wish, he tries to engineer a situation in which it will be impossible for his daughters to confront him with real love. Hence, in his official role as King, and exploiting the publicity of the court setting, he demands of his daughters that they trade empty professions of love, love's mere semblances, for their dowry, security and fortune.

Seeing Lear as motivated in this way, three key aspects of the opening scene become clearer. Firstly, it explains Lear's choice of venue. To hide from love, the venue of the court and the very public business of dividing up his kingdom provide near perfect shelter. The situation places a powerful incentive on his daughters to go along with his plan, as in this context his requests effectively have the force of a command. Any failure to comply will be conspicuous, and will appear as a refusal of his demand and a repudiation of his authority. In this way, Lear has secured, in advance, reason to be angry in the event that anyone does not play along with his scheme. The setting provides perfect psychic cover for someone wishing to avoid genuine interaction or communication.

Cavell's thesis also explains why Lear turns the private matter of family love into a business transaction. Although real love might be expressed in a courtier's speech, expressions of love cannot be rightly used as a form of coinage. Love is not the kind of thing to be bought, traded or measured in tracts of land.[7] But that is the point: Lear is trying to buy a false

---

That it is fear of self-recognition that lies at the root of his character is plausible because "rock bottom" for Lear, the lowest point in his slide into madness, comes precisely at the point when he is totally isolated and vulnerable (almost trapped in his own mind). However, a person may be powerless, feeble and so on and be able both to love and accept another's love, so this suggestion seems incomplete and in need of supplementation with a further account of how love, self-worth and power hang together for Lear. Love's being seen by Lear as (imposing) a *demand* seems to me to be closer to the mark. Although Cavell seems to mean by this "Lear sees love as something which is demanded of him," I would argue that Lear is more frightened by the impending threat of *his* need for the love of *others* (again because of fear of his own weakness and because he feels he does/cannot deserve such love when he is of no use) than by the possibility of their needing him. What Lear fears—his weakness, powerlessness and dependency—are all essentially *passive* states of being which grate with his sense of himself as sovereign, legislator, judge and self-made man of action.

[6] Cavell (2003), p. 58.

[7] I am not claiming that Cavell's reading gives us the whole story of Lear and the opening scene. There is a good case to be made that Lear's trying to engineer a situation in which he

semblance of love from his daughters, and he wants to destroy the possibility of encountering genuine love by forcing it into a barter.

Finally, Cavell's reading removes a key interpretative puzzle about Lear's behaviour in the opening scene: Why is Lear so easily gulled into accepting Goneril and Regan's grossly obsequious hyperbole as professions of their love?[8] It is true that Lear acts foolishly in the opening scene, but he is clearly no idiot. As Cavell puts it, he is possessed of a "powerful, ranging mind" which shines through even his later madness. The avoidance-of-love thesis explains Lear's acceptance of the professions of love offered by Goneril and Regan in a way which excuses him of credulously accepting them as heartfelt expressions of affection. Cavell's Lear sees right through his elder daughters' disingenuous words, just as Cordelia, Kent and we do, and accepts them warmly nonetheless because they give him precisely what he wanted. As Cavell puts it:

> Lear knows it is a bribe he offers, and—part of him anyway—wants exactly what a bribe can buy: (1) false love and (2) a public expression of love. That is, he wants something he does not have to return *in kind*, something which a division of his property fully pays for. And he wants to *look* like a loved man—for the sake of the subjects, as it were. He is perfectly happy with his little plan, until Cordelia speaks. Happy not because he is blind, but because he is getting what he wants, his plan is working.[9]

3 My Cavellian Reading of Cordelia

This provides the backdrop for my reading of Cordelia as experiencing, and expressing, a moral incapacity in the opening scene. Cordelia sees Lear's demand for exactly the disastrous play at self-deception and self-

---

can give Cordelia—clearly the most worthy successor to his throne, but the furthest from it by the conventional order of succession—the best part of his kingdom, so as to then retire with Cordelia (his favourite) and taking his troops along to help protect her from her sisters. Here, see P. Cantor's "Nature and Justice in King Lear," in Jeffrey Kahan, *King Lear: New Critical Essays* (Routledge, 2008), p. 236. There is no conflict between the two readings, although Cavell's better illuminates the core themes of the tragedy than Cantor's in my view.

[8] This thought leads to denials of Lear's intelligence, and proposals that this tone-deafness is the first sign of his failing mind, or a reflection of the tyrannical egoism which overpowers his reason. The last of these is closest to the mark, but it remains committed to the view that Lear really thinks Goneril and Regan really love him, which is very hard to square with his perceptiveness and sharpness.

[9] Cavell (2003), pp. 61–62.

avoidance that it is. She sees things as Cavell does. To make my case, I develop a full reading of the scene below, but as strong *prima facie* evidence for its plausibility we might note the following. First, Cordelia is Lear's favourite daughter. They have spent great deal of time together, and she has good claim to know him "best of all." Secondly, we do not need to grant her any special powers of psychological insight to explain her realization that Lear is up to something nasty, ill-advised and dangerous: *all* of the characters in the opening scene can see that Lear is caught in folly, and all of them are disgusted, appalled or horrified by it.[10]

To pin down Cordelia's perception of Lear's disastrous injudiciousness precisely, it will be helpful to dwell a little longer on the metaphor of sight and blindness. Lear's demand is, in effect, an attempt to blind himself to the truth of his condition. Blinding, specifically the putting out of a person's eyes, is an apt image for the harm he does himself through his ploy because of its *permanence*. In turning his daughters' love into an item for barter, Lear means to undermine or destroy it once and for all. This trick will license him to regard any subsequent care and affection he receives from his daughters as merely his due (what he has paid for, what is owed him under a contract of purchase), thereby providing a psychic protection against ever having to experience the shameful revelation of a loving gaze again. Lear's demand is an attempt to create an illusion behind which he can hide from love, and so from himself, *always*.

All sales are final, as they say. But as the subsequent actions of Goneril and Regan reveal, there is a terrible flip-side to this for Lear too: once a purchase has been completed, the seller has no right subsequently to renegotiate the terms of sale. So, when Lear later comes to them seeking a comfortable retirement, they are entirely within their rights (if also utterly heartless) to refuse to share what they have bought from him. Instead of receiving their care and protection, Lear is humiliated, stripped of the entourage which is the last vestige of his former military glory, and cast into the wilderness where he descends into madness. Lear has sold comfort to avoid love, and he comes to realize the irrevocable harm he has thereby done himself only, tragically, after it is already too late.

The two elder sisters are enthusiastic accomplices in Lear's folly, offering a pandering show of "obedience" which really expresses their disdain.

---

[10] On the Cavellian reading, "everyone" includes Lear himself, although he sees confusedly and badly misjudges the plan.

Cordelia, in contrast, is pained by the scene from the outset. Her first words "What shall Cordelia speak? Love, and be silent." express an awful double recognition: that her father is on the road to ruin, dead set on doing himself a terrible harm, and, worse, that there is nothing she can do to help him. To meet Lear's demand with flattery would, after all, make her as complicit as her sisters in the grotesque spectacle of his self-destruction. However, Lear has ingeniously contrived the situation in such a way that any failure to do as he asks (effectively, demands) will appear as an insulting act of public defiance. And that, in turn, will only enrage the domineering King, driving him further into his deluded and disastrous ploy. Lear is damned if Cordelia does and damned if she doesn't, and she is consigned to watch powerlessly as he self-destructs.

Lear is embroiled in a plan so cleverly designed to make him immune from love that Cordelia's voice cannot reach him. He is, at this moment, beyond help. This places Cordelia in the awful situation of being witness to her father's self-harm and utterly powerless to do anything to save him. Shakespeare gives Cordelia the language of "nothing" and "silence," notions which become *leitmotifs* of the whole play, to express this devastating recognition.[11]

Cordelia's second aside "Then poor Cordelia! //And yet not so; since, I am sure, my love's//More ponderous than my tongue" expresses much the same predicament. Kenneth Muir's observation that "ponderous" has a dual sense of heaviness and greater worth is important here. Evidence for the predominance of the latter sense is that the *Quarto* has the line as "… more *richer* than my tongue." As Muir puts it, Cordelia here means to say that she "cannot produce golden words, cannot 'coin her heart in words', but her heart has love of a better and weightier metal."[12] She is "poor" in the sense that she cannot follow Regan and Goneril in parading "love" in gorgeous rhetoric so as to profit from complicity in Lear's folly; "yet not so…" because she alone possesses something of real intrinsic worth, her

---

[11] This points to the need for a thorough examination of the relationship between the metaphorical themes of silence, nothingness and sight/blindness.

[12] See Kenneth Muir, *King Lear* (Arden Shakespeare, 1964), p. 8. The connection between the two senses, of course, is the higher worth traditionally ascribed to heavier metals (iron over bronze, gold over silver, etc.). Another advantage of this reading is that it ironically echoes Regan's claim (immediately beforehand) to be "made of that *self metal* as my sister" (68). Cavell also acknowledges the *Quarto*'s use of "richer," but prefers the *Folio*'s "heaviness."

filial love. Cordelia's love is more valuable than her tongue because no words can help her father. In this situation love must keep silent, because speaking will only further harm the beloved.[13]

This brings us to the heart of the scene, a passage which bears quoting at length:

> LEAR:... Now, our joy,
>   Although the last, not least; to whose young love
>   The vines of France and milk of Burgundy
>   Strive to be interess'd; what can you say to draw
>   A third more opulent than your sisters? Speak.
> CORD: Nothing, my lord.
> LEAR: Nothing!
> CORD: Nothing.
> LEAR: Nothing will come of nothing: speak again.
> CORD: Unhappy that I am, I cannot heave
>   My heart into my mouth: I love your majesty
>   According to my bond; nor more nor less.
> LEAR: How, how, Cordelia! Mend your speech a little
>   Lest it may mar your fortunes.
> CORD: Good my lord,
>   You have begot me, bred me, loved me; I
>   Return those duties back as are right fit.
>   Obey you, love you, and most honour you.
>   Why have my sisters husbands, if they say
>   They love you all? Haply, when I shall wed
>   That Lord whose hand must take my plight shall carry
>   Half of my love with him, half my care and duty:
>   Sure I shall never marry like my sisters,
>   To love my father all.
> LEAR: But goes thy heart with this?
> CORD: Ay, good my lord.
> LEAR: So young and so untender?
> CORD: So young, my lord, and true.

---

[13] Here, she contrasts most starkly with Goneril, who loudly *proclaims* herself unable to voice her devotion to Lear because its greatness outstrips language (55), and promptly goes on to describe the greatness of her love. Even Goneril's opening denial phrase is a mere rhetorical figure, the hackneyed *disclamatio* "I love you more than words can say." Her words are empty of love, a pure semblance. She has mastered "...that glib and oily art,// To speak and purpose not" (244–55) and uses the outer forms of love to express contempt.

Lear asks Cordelia for a profession of love, and in return she gives him *nothing*. The interaction is jarring, stilted and awkward. It brings the theatrical histrionics which preceded it to a crashing halt. When Cordelia is forced by Lear to speak, she speaks as a loving daughter: truly, directly and simply. Her tone seems flat and lifeless by contrast with her sisters' splendid rhetoric and vulture-like enthusiasm: she speaks sadly and sorrowfully, seeing that her words are bound to fail. But then Cordelia's words *should* grate and feel unfitting in this context, because there *is* no place for a devoted, loving daughter here. The proceedings orchestrated by Lear are devised so as to leave no room for such a one. His demand is designed to abolish love, or to stifle it by removing the air on which it depends for its life: genuine, heartfelt expression, real communication, and the direct and intimate personal connections that these involve.[14]

My central claim is that Cordelia *cannot* flatter Lear. Seeing the terrible wrong in fulfilling his demand, she "shrinks from it as an impossibility" to borrow Mill's phrase.[15] Textual detail provides strong evidence for taking Cordelia's "Nothing" as the expression of a moral incapacity.[16] Lear initially demands of all three daughters, "Which of you shall we say doth love us the most?" and after Goneril's speech he asks Regan, "What says our second daughter…" Both of these questions are capacity-neutral in their wording. Lear asks only what the daughters *will* do. However, when it comes to Cordelia, he asks her "…what *can* you say to draw//A third more opulent than your sisters?" The juxtaposition in phrasing between Lear's third question and the first two seems to be both deliberate and significant, as this shift in wording is retained exactly in the *Quarto* and *Folio* editions of the play, with the additions to Lear's speech in the *Folio* all being inserted before the questions, leaving their sense unaffected. Lear means this "can" as a challenge to Cordelia's powers of rhetoric. He is trying to egg her on to outdo her sisters. But as a direct reply to the specific question that Lear has asked her, Cordelia's "Nothing, my Lord" means that she can say nothing, that there is nothing she can say, to win

---

[14] I am here drawing on the development and extension of these Cavellian themes in Sarah Beckwith's *Shakespeare and the Grammar of Forgiveness* (Cornell: Cornell University Press, 2012).

[15] J.S. Mill, *Utilitarianism and the 1868 Speech on Capital Punishment*, ed. Sher, 2nd ed. (Hackett, 2002), p. 28.

[16] The author has not encountered a reading in which this point of textual detail is noted explicitly.

her inheritance. Cordelia actually *tells* Lear that she is incapable of the flattery he demands. And this is a moral matter, to do with love, rather than a mere function of her lack of skill or opportunity. She knows what he wants her to say, and she has the words of flattery to hand. She simply cannot bring herself to *say* these words, in light of the harm that this would bring.

How should we judge Cordelia, if this is what she means to say? What kind of a person would such an incapacity show her to be? Here, it is crucial to note how prevalently "love" features in her words in the opening scene, from her very first aside to her claim that "Nothing" is itself the expression of love. The sentence, "I love your majesty//According to my bond," can be misleading in this connection. Many commentators hear this as an unfeeling reference to mere filial obligation, a grim-faced "going through the motions" of daughterly love. However, this belies the clear evidence from Acts IV and V of Cordelia's devotion to Lear. There, she gathers an army to rescue Lear and ultimately lays down her life for him. These actions outstrip the requirements of filial duty, and anyway all come subsequent to Lear's severing of the ties of familial obligation by banishing and disowning her. Long after he has ceased to behave like a father to her, Cordelia cherishes and protects him as a daughter. I would suggest that Cordelia's phrasing "According to my bond" is deliberately ambiguous, leaving open how it is that a daughter should love. Thus, I prefer Danby's proposal that we read the line as expressive of her filial love: "For Cordelia 'bond' means 'natural tie', a duty willingly accepted and gladly carried out because it answers to right instinct."[17]

Cordelia's devotion to Lear, something which various characters in the play attest to, sits in stark contrast to the mercenary wickedness of her sisters. Regan and Goneril profess love with relish, but express only their greed and contempt for their father. Cordelia, in contrast, loves her father as a daughter should: without incentive, selflessly, bravely and truly. Her love shows itself nowhere more plainly than in her inability to join in the spectacle of his self-harming, and her pain in acknowledging that she is helpless to stop it. We should therefore read her "Unhappy that I am" with the sense of "hapless," prey to wretched ill-fortune. Cordelia's situation has the character of an affliction before which she is bowed, helpless

---

[17] John F. Danby, *Shakespeare's Doctrine of Nature: A Study of King Lear* (Faber & Faber, 1965), p. 129.

and miserable.[18] Cavell captures all of this wonderfully in the comment that "All her words are words of love; to love is all she knows how to do. That is her problem, and at the cause of the tragedy of *King Lear*."[19]

4   A WILFUL CHILD: THE COLERIDGIAN VISION OF CORDELIA

The picture of Cordelia which I have drawn out of Cavell's reading of *King Lear* is far from standard in the critical literature on the play. A very different view of Cordelia is to be found in the tradition of readings originating with Coleridge. It will be best to start with a famous quotation from his comments on *King Lear*:

> There is something of disgust at the ruthless hypocrisy of her sisters, and some little faulty admixture of pride and sullenness in Cordelia's 'Nothing;' and her tone is well contrived, indeed, to lessen the glaring absurdity of Lear's conduct, but answers the yet more important purpose of forcing away the attention from the nursery-tale, the moment it has served its end, that of supplying the canvass for the picture.[20]

I think it is natural to see Cordelia as suffering a tragic fate *in spite of* her goodness and tenderness, and thus as a pitiful figure destroyed by the dark and terrible world of broken, limited and wicked people around her. Coleridge's view of her, in contrast, is severe and unforgiving. In his view, whilst Cordelia may be less corrupted than her thoroughly wicked sisters, she is nonetheless equally culpable for setting in motion the disastrous course of events that will eventually swallow them all up. Coleridge holds Cordelia to *blame* for throwing her family and her kingdom into madness, murder, war and chaos. He does not see her as the innocent cause of a

---

[18] Cavell comes very close to this reading when he claims that Cordelia is "shuddering with confusion, with wanting to do the impossible" in the opening scene. Although I agree that Lear demands the impossible of Cordelia, I find that Cavell's explanation of the impossibility leaves it too close to a form of *inconceivability*, rather than a primarily a matter of love (the will and heart). His reading here veers too close to the Johnsonian interpretation I criticize below.

[19] Cavell (2003), p. 292.

[20] S.T. Coleridge, *Shakespeare and Milton* (1811–12) in Kermode, Frank. *Shakespeare: King Lear : A Casebook* (Macmillan, 1992), p. 37.

calamity, the author of a well-meaning mistake that is in itself faultless, but which has disastrous unintended and unforeseeable consequences. Rather, he takes the tragedy to originate in substantial part with Cordelia's moral shortcomings; her vices of pride, and childish and resentful wilfulness.

It is a virtue of Coleridge's interpretation that he retains a very lively sense of Cordelia's humanity. He does not reduce her to an allegory. She is not for him primarily a symbol of anything, but just another morally flawed and limited player caught in a dirty game of family relations and political power. Coleridge is very much alive to Cordelia's intelligence and perceptiveness. He sees that she is fully conscious of the absurdity and inappropriateness of Lear's demand, and how nauseatingly disingenuous her sisters' words are. Moreover, I think he correctly identifies Cordelia's tone when she speaks at length to Lear in I.i. She *is* unabashedly critical of her sisters and, thus, by implication, of what her father has allowed and encouraged them to do. Coleridge, however, finds her tone *too* blunt, and takes this to reflect a harsh and intolerant nature. He sees no way for this anger to be an expression of love.

This perspective is shared by Ulrici. In some respects, he is even more critical of Cordelia, ignoring Coleridge's suggestion that Cordelia speaks as she does partly to *distract* the court from the shameful behaviour of her father:

> Cordelia pays the penalty of the fault she has committed, when, instead of affectionately humouring the weakness of her aged father, she met him with unfilial forwardness, and answered his, no doubt, foolish questions with unbecoming harshness, and asperity; a father's curse lights upon her head, and its direful consequences cannot afterwards be avoided. The slighter her failing may appear, the deeper is the tragic effect of its heavy penalty.[21]

Ulrici shares both Coleridge's ear for Cordelia's tone in the opening scene, and his sense that she is seriously at fault there. Thus Ulrici is also led to a vision of Cordelia in I.i. as a wilful, petulant child.

This perspective is retained in Legatt's more recent interpretation. He also finds no warmth or affection in Cordelia's words, writing of her "initial, unsettling coldness…" and her "cold, limited statement of love in the first scene." In his view, Cordelia in the opening scene is a "plain-spoken

---

[21] Danby (1965), p. 115.

but cold and prickly girl."[22] Coleridgian readers, in general, share this sense of the unforgiving harshness of Cordelia's tone to Lear in the opening scene. They hear her words as cutting, biting and icy, and see this as revelatory of a character flaw like obstinacy or sullen pride. In this way, she comes to appear to such readers as thoroughly unfilial.

The most fundamental point of connection between these readings, however, is their interpretation of the meaning of and intention behind Cordelia's "Nothing, my lord." Indeed, their understanding of Cordelia's reply to Lear is the main grounds for their claims about her character and tone. Every critic in this tradition hears Cordelia's words as a *refusal* to play any part in her father's foolishness. Take, for instance, Stanley Stewart's characterization of Cordelia's reply as a "refusal to engage the ceremonial occasion with speech...."[23] Most Coleridgian readers also see this refusal as an act of self-assertion, a juvenile act of rebellion against a parent's authority; or a declaration that she is above both the craven obsequiousness of her sisters and Lear's disgraceful demand. Such a view is explicitly articulated by P.A. Cantor in the following passage:

> Cordelia objects to the hypocrisy of her sisters, the way they simply say what is conventionally demanded by the situation in order to gain as much of the kingdom as they can. *She refuses to be put in the same class with them, and thereby confused with them in public...* Cordelia *rejects* precisely the way Lear's scheme runs together nature and convention, working to confuse her genuine love for her father with her sister's artificial expressions of a purely customary affection. Unfortunately, Cordelia's *refusal* to tell her father what he wants to hear triggers the worst possible response in him... [my italics][24]

This brings into focus the two distinctive features of Coleridgian readings. First, such readers see Cordelia as *refusing* Lear's demand, viewing her failure to flatter as a deliberate and stubborn omission, an act of will. Second, they trace this behaviour back into her character, finding it to be expressive of, and explained by, some degree of vice or combination of character flaws. In Coleridge and Cantor's view, it is a prideful desire to maintain her superiority over her sisters, for others, it is just lack of filial

---

[22] *Harvester New Critical Introductions to Shakespeare* (Harvester, 1988), pp. 15, 65 and 66 (respectively).
[23] Kahan (2008), p. 289.
[24] From his essay *Nature and Justice in King Lear*, in Kahan (2008), p. 237.

warmth or juvenile defiance against convention or authority. These two features of the reading are complementary and it is helpful to see how they hang together.

Characterizing Cordelia's words in I.i. as a *refusal* commits Coleridgian readers to the claim that she *could* have done otherwise, but *chooses* to act as she does. After all, one can only refuse to do that of which one is capable. It makes no sense for me to *refuse* to jump over the Tower of London, for instance. (I take this to be a grammatical point and not in the least controversial.) Seen as a deliberate, intentional act of refusal, Cordelia's "Nothing" is remarkable for its tremendous *imprudence*. By it she not only risks alienating her father, whose love and favour she has always enjoyed, but also gambles with her inheritance, the cost of losing which should not be underestimated. Cordelia's inheritance is her dowry, her best chance at marriage, and thus her only secure guarantee of a safe and stable life.[25] (And this is not even to mention that the fate of a whole kingdom, for which she, as a princess and heir, is partly responsible, hangs in the balance!) Given just how much is staked on Cordelia's meeting Lear's demand, the view that Cordelia refuses to do so raises a pressing question of why on earth she would choose to do so.

What is it about Lear's demand that could prompt such imprudence, and the cold, harsh tone that Coleridge and his followers hear in Cordelia's words? In the first place, it is true that Lear's actions are inappropriate and ill-advised. Everyone in the scene *but* Lear sees this: Regan and Goneril mock Lear disdainfully for his ridiculous behaviour once he leaves the scene, noting that "… he hath ever but slenderly known himself" and that "The best and soundest of his time hath been but rash" once they are alone. And Kent bravely confronts Lear for the madness of bowing his power to flattery (147), an act which he says shows that Lear's majesty has fallen to folly (148). That Lear acts foolishly is, then, uncontentious. This does not yet provide adequate motivation for Cordelia's purported "refusal" to play along, but Coleridgians need only press on a little further to come at a convincing psychological explanation.

There is, after all, something truly shameful or disgraceful about the proceedings in the court that Lear engineers. It befits neither Lear nor his

---

[25] As it turns out, Cordelia is married in spite of her father's disowning her, but this is a stroke of luck which she cannot have expected in the opening scene—she risks a lot there and knows that she does so.

princesses to conflate serious political matters with the intimate and private matters of familial love as they do. Lear's demand trivializes and degrades the two eminently serious matters. First, it transforms the division of his kingdom, which should be a solemn matter of giving his heirs their divinely ordained birthright, into a carnival of fawning sycophancy. Second, the demand perverts and destroys familial love by turning it into a commercial transaction. The inappropriate, even base, character of Lear's demand is reflected in Regan and Goneril's rapacious eagerness to seize their chance for personal profit. All three of them act shamefully, in a manner insulting to their elevated station, and under the auspices (and in the full view) of the royal court.

Coleridge's Cordelia has a sharp sense of the indignity and shamefulness of her family's behaviour. But while this helps explain her sharp and cold critical *tone* in the opening scene, it does not yet satisfactorily explain her behaviour there, because it seems insufficient grounds for the wilful, reckless gambling with her fate that Coleridgian readers will ultimately convict her of. As a result, they project onto her a character flaw pernicious enough to entirely undermine her discretion, tact and prudence. Consequently, Coleridgians see Cordelia as lashing out at Lear and her sisters in disgust, resentment or spite, a response which reveals in her some vice related to an inflated sense of self; pride, vanity, rebellious hubris or wilful contrariness, say. In short, Coleridgian readers see Cordelia (in I.i.) not as acting and speaking from love, but rather as childishly lashing out from a wounded ego. Theirs is the doppelgänger of the Cordelia revealed by Cavell's reading, and I will next endeavour to show that something is seriously awry with the Coleridgian interpretation.

5   Objections to the Coleridgian Reading

The Coleridgian depiction of Cordelia is extremely hard to square with the details of the text. One strident discordance is between Cordelia's use of the notion of love, in both of her asides (63 and 76) and her elaboration on what she meant by "Nothing, my lord" (95, 112), and the total absence of love in the Coleridgian reading of her words, actions and character. In seeing Cordelia as refusing to debase and disgrace herself at Lear's command, the closest Coleridgians can come to finding love in Cordelia is to see her as animated by a self-congratulatory sense of being above her family's antics. But this is only preciousness or vanity, a perversion of self-love.[26]

We see this clearly when we apply the Coleridgian interpretation to Cordelia's asides. It renders the first aside sarcastic, self-involved and resentful, as if she were there saying: "This low, awful business might be fine for my sisters, who have no sense of decency, but what about *me*? How can I be expected to lower myself in this way?" In order to make Cordelia's resolute silence accord with their sense of her wilfulness and pride, Coleridgians will hear in these words a bitter sense of superiority over her sisters. Similarly, these readers hear Cordelia's second aside as expressing her sense of the difficulty of choosing between sinking to the shameful level of her family and risking her inheritance. And once we judge Cordelia's character to be governed by wilfulness and pride, she can only think of herself as "Poor Cordelia!" in self-aggrandising and self-pitying contrast to her sisters, who jump at the chance to dance for their dinner. In this way, Cordelia's words *all* come to seem like expressions of an inflated ego for Coleridgians—their reading forces all of her claims of love into the distorting mould of self-absorbed moral preciousness.

We should also note how Cordelia's "Nothing, my lord" and subsequent explanation of these words (90–96) seem, once they are interpreted as a refusal. Coleridgian readers find these wilfully proud: her brevity and plainness, especially when taken in contrast with her sisters' eloquence, seems to them deliberately contrary, even spiteful. Heard thus, her words seem to reflect her intention to insult Lear with an obstinate denial and thereby to provoke him. In this way, her ambiguous "I love your majesty//According to my bond; nor more nor less" takes on the cutting sense of "You'll get from me only what I owe you, not a shred more!" Again here, Cordelia's words and her character seem cold, harsh and barren of filial tenderness.

The strain here over how to hear "love" in Cordelia's mouth is, I think, particularly significant, given how prominently notion features in her lines and how little she says in the play. However, it is not yet sufficient to demonstrate that the Coleridgian reading is internally inconsistent or impossible to square with textual details. To do so, I offer three arguments for

---

[26] It is certainly a perversion of the conception of self-love we find in Weil and Murdoch's writings: that under which the self disappears as a substantive presence in moral perception, enabling a clear (unimpeded) view of one's beloved or object of devotion.

the claim that Cordelia *cannot* rather than *will not* flatter her father; that is, that her failure to fulfil his demand is not a willed omission or refusal, but rather a moral incapacity, a limit to what she can will herself, or bear, to do.

The first argument, which I mentioned above, is that there is direct textual evidence in favour of my view: Cordelia tells Lear that she cannot give him the flattery that he demands. Given that Cordelia's claim to incapacity is written into the text of the play itself, it is surprising that so many critics wish to insist that Cordelia *refuses* to rise to Lear's demand. Of course, a committed Coleridgian, determined to insist that Cordelia is acting from wilful pride can claim that she is being insincere or sarcastic here, just as she is in her asides. But now the reading leaves almost nothing that she says in the opening scene as available to be taken as a literal or direct expression of her outlook, which is hermeneutically problematic. (For a start, Shakespeare's characters have no need to dissemble in asides.) Moreover, there are two further significant problems with the Coleridgian vision.

First, Coleridgians accept a picture of Cordelia which is almost indistinguishable from Lear's view of her. He too fails to perceive any love behind Cordelia's words, and feels them as harsh and cutting ("untender"). He also sees Cordelia as deliberately trying to hurt him, and takes her words as a pointed and entirely uncalled for affront. Lear sees Cordelia's "Nothing" as an intentional refusal to cooperate, a "will not" instead of a "cannot." And later in the scene it is made clear that he regards this refusal as the expression of her *pride*. For after initially replying to her with "…thy truth, then, be thy dower," shortly afterwards he comments to Kent, "Let pride, which she calls plainness [honesty], marry her…." Lear sees no way for Cordelia to be speaking truly, from the heart. He hears only pride, vanity and the intent to hurt him in her words. As a result, he charges her with precisely the same vices as Coleridge and Cantor do.

Surely, though, it is Lear who cannot see beyond *his* pride in the opening scene: it is *his* fragile ego, and the situation which *he* designs to protect it, that make him incapable of seeing past the embarrassment Cordelia causes him to the genuinely loving concern that it expresses. The distorting influence of Lear's pride is plainly visible in his interaction with Kent in the opening scene. Kent bravely defends Cordelia by explaining to Lear that her words were *not* a hurtful attack meant to belittle him but the only truly honourable, respectful and devoted response to his deeply unwise scheme: "To plainness honour's bound, //When majesty stoops to folly…."

Where Kent is alive to the noble filial concern behind Cordelia's words, however, Lear just accuses Kent, in turn, of trying "with strain'd pride// To come between our sentence and our power...."

Cavell's reading shows that Lear's perception of pride in all those who do not cooperate with his plan is a projection of the unhealthy self-relation in which he is trapped. His strange demand is designed to protect a fragile and threatened self-image, and Cordelia's failure to play along threatens to expose it, not merely to the court, but more frighteningly to Lear himself. Lear, of course, responds to Cordelia's "Nothing" and Kent's council, by lashing out at both in a childish tantrum.[27] It should be a strong warning against Coleridgian readings that their view of Cordelia ends up virtually indistinguishable from Lear's radically distorted perspective.

The final stumbling block for Coleridgians is the massive dislocation between Cordelia's character as they construe it in the first scene of the play, and how she appears when she returns in the fourth act.[28] There, Cordelia is unmistakably the loving daughter in everything she does and says. She returns to fight for her father in a war against her sisters, having raised an army on his behalf. She shows no trace of resentment for the harm Lear has done her, and never rebukes him for his mistreatment of her, but is gentle and kind to him. Remarkably, when he asks her forgiveness, she simply dismisses his self-accusation:

> **Lear:** Be your tears wet? Yes, faith. I pray, weep not:
> If you have poison for me, I will drink it.
> I know you do not love me; for your sisters
> Have, as I do remember, done me wrong:
> You have some cause, they have not.
> **Cordelia:** No cause, no cause.
>
> (IV. viii. 76)

The purity and strength of Cordelia's dedication to Lear is revealed here in the fact that she sees no need to forgive her father. Her words absolve him of his transgressions against her, or show him to have *been* absolved; they erase his wrongdoing by denying that it ever even hap-

---

[27] Cavell has it that it is Cordelia's confronting him with the honest gaze of love that sends Lear into his rage. Here I only mean to be fleshing out this suggestion at greater length.

[28] She re-enters at IV.iv (or, at IV.iii in the *Quarto* edition—a scene deleted in the *Folio* edition).

pened.[29] Cordelia's love for Lear is movingly expressed in the last two acts of the play. There, she fits perfectly the descriptions of her offered by other characters, who consistently portray her as quiet, calm and gentle, Lear's one truly devoted daughter.

This creates a severe tension for Coleridgian readings, a pressure to accuse Shakespeare of dramatic incoherence. The Cordelia of Acts IV and V is unrecognizably different to the wilful, proud and vain girl that Coleridge finds in the opening scene. Consequently, Coleridgian readers must infer a radical transformation of her character; from a wilful, foolish and proud child, into a dedicated, kind and mature woman. But this is not supported by textual evidence, and anyhow seems psychologically implausible because it comes only *after* Lear has disowned and banished Cordelia, ruining her (original) prospects for marriage and a stable life, and turned over his kingdom to her wicked sisters. Why would Cordelia be willing to risk her life to help Lear here, when she was earlier prepared to throw away her fortune and future rather than lower herself by doing as he asked?

The text itself offers nothing that might account for such a radical shift in character. We do not see Cordelia in the intervening scenes, and we hear little of her. There is certainly no mention anywhere in the text of her having undergone any conversion experience or serious reformation of character. Furthermore, Cordelia does not return in a spirit of atonement for her earlier wrongdoing, as she should if she had come to recognize, and repent, her refusal to comply with Lear's plan. She comes back, rather, to rescue her father from the pitiful (literal and spiritual) hinterland into which her sisters have thrown him, and to win back a part of his kingdom in which he can take up his rightful home.

Recognizing this tension, some Coleridgian readers have gone so far as to accuse Shakespeare of inconsistency or incompleteness in imagining Cordelia.[30] We should, I think, be loathe to accept a reading which denies

---

[29] This is a remarkable moment, which encapsulates Cordelia's whole loving attitude towards Lear. Her response to him is reminiscent of the Socratic convictions that all wrongdoing is grounded in ignorance or error, and that the wrongdoer should be pitied.

[30] This is how she appears on Salvini's reading of the play, for instance. He sees her in the first scene as Coleridgians do—as discourteously and irreverently (i.e. unfilially) rebuffing Lear's offer—and only later in the play is she revealed to be a loving, caring daughter. See Porter's critique of Salvini in her "The Drama 'Ay, every inch a King.'" "*Shakespeariana*" Vol. 1, no. 2 (Nov. 1883).

the unity of *King Lear* as a dramatic work. The most plausible response for a Coleridgian at this point would be to claim that Cordelia has simply undergone a change of heart in a response to news of the terrible treatment Lear has suffered, and the wickedness of her sisters. That would still leave Shakespeare to blame for not making that change dramatically (or psychologically) convincing, but it at least avoids the untenable charge of dramatic incoherence. In contrast, the Cavellian reading can comfortably capture Cordelia's motives in returning, the spirit in which she returns and how she treats Lear when she does so. For on this interpretation Cordelia returns just as she left, guided by her love for her father and her concern for his well-being. The smoothness and coherence of this imagining of Cordelia surely counts in its favour.

6 A Vision of Otherworldly Goodness: Johnsonian Readings of Cordelia

In radical contrast to the harsh critical attitude taken by Coleridge, Dr. Johnson found Cordelia's death at the end of *King Lear* simply too awful to bear.[31] Cordelia was, for him, too pure and perfect to suffer the violent, profitless death to which Shakespeare subjects her. Consequently, Johnson read the play only once and never reopened it until, many years later, he was asked to edit it for a new publication.[32] His opposition to Shakespeare's original ending is also reflected in his warm endorsement of Nahum Tate's "Hollywood" re-writing of the play, in which Cordelia escapes death and returns to the stage, a triumphant symbol of the triumph of virtue over vice.[33]

Johnson's horror at the original ending ties in with his allegorical reading of *Lear*, under which its characters are seen to be representations of aspects of "Nature," the divine moral order of things. This Enlightenment

---

[31] Samuel Johnson, ed. *King Lear* in *The Works of William Shakespeare* (1765).

[32] "And if my sensations could add anything to the general suffrage, I might relate that I was many years ago so shocked by Cordelia's death that I know not whether I ever endured to read again the last scenes of the play till I undertook to revise them as an editor" (*Samuel Johnson on Shakespeare* (Penguin Books, 1989), pp. 222–23).

[33] N. Tate. *The History of King Lear* (1681). In Tate's version, Cordelia also has a romance with Edgar that ends in their marriage. Dickens, a man with a considerable sweet tooth for the sentimental, calls Tate's version of the play "disgusting," and Charles Lamb designates it (with amusing precision) as "ribald trash" (see Bruce (1998), p. 84 and p. 49, respectively).

tradition of allegorical interpretation is common to most of the readers I will class as "Johnsonian." Johnson views Cordelia as a representative or paradigm of transcendental perfection and purity; she is, for him, virtue itself. Her failure to save Lear and brutal unredemptive death struck him as an appalling denial of the power of the divine, the good and the noble to defeat the powers of evil. Shakespeare, Johnson wrote, "has suffered the virtue of *Cordelia* to perish in a just cause, contrary to the natural ideas of justice, the hope of the reader, and, what is yet more strange, to the faith of the chronicles."[34] We might sum up Johnson's stance thus: if Cordelia is the embodiment of divine moral perfection, then her unjust death is an abomination. His vision of Cordelia as a symbol of moral perfection or saintliness is a shared feature of the readings in this tradition. Despite his outright denunciation of Tate's *History*, for instance, Schlegel also describes Cordelia as an otherworldly spiritual ideal: "Of Cordelia's heavenly beauty of soul, painted in so few words, I will not venture to speak; she can only be named in the same breath with Antigone."[35]

A hundred years later, Bradley also saw Cordelia as a devoted disciple to virtue, truth and the good:

> ..Cordelia's is a higher nature than that of most even of Shakespeare's heroines... Her assertion of truth and right, her allegiance to them, even the touch of severity that accompanies it, instead of compelling mere respect or admiration, become adorable in a nature so loving as Cordelia's. She is a thing enskyed and sainted....[36]

Bradley's reading of Cordelia is both more sensitively responsive to details of the play and less thoroughly allegorical than those of Johnson and Schlegel. Consider, for instance, his claim that it is Cordelia's *allegiance* to

---

[34] From *Johnson on Shakespeare*, ed. Walter Raleigh (Oxford University Press, 1925), pp. 161–62. Johnson's attitude is also clearly visible in this quote: "A play in which the wicked prosper, and the virtuous miscarry, may doubtless be good, because it is a just representation of the common events of human life: but since all reasonable beings naturally love justice, I cannot be easily persuaded, that the observation of justice makes a play worse; or, that if other excellences are equal, the audience will not always rise better pleased from the final triumph of persecuted virtue." (Ibid. p. 161).

[35] Frank Kermode, *Shakespeare: King Lear : A Casebook*, rev. ed. (Macmillan, 1992), p. 32.

[36] A.C. Bradley, *Shakespearean Tragedy: Lectures on Hamlet, Othello, King Lear, Macbeth*, 2nd ed. (London: Macmillan, 1905), pp. 316–17 (my italics). See also p. 320 where he calls Cordelia "heavenly true."

truth and right that makes her "adorable." Bradley's Cordelia is a woman whose soul is governed by her commitment to moral ideals, rather than being a dramatic representation of the ideals themselves. He even sees some degree of fault and failure in Cordelia, calling her speech in I.i. "unhappy," for instance, which suggests either imprudence or limited capacity to express herself in public speech. He also accuses her of misrepresenting the truth when she claims that she would have to "divide" her love between Lear and her husband when she gets married.[37] And he even detects a touch of *pride* in her words. However, all of these faults are ultimately minor and entirely forgivable, not really clouding her virtue but serving rather to magnify it and to place her beyond moral condemnation:

> And the cause of her failure—a failure a thousandfold redeemed—is a compound in which imperfection appears so intimately mingled with the noblest qualities that—if we are true to Shakespeare—we do not think either of justifying her or of blaming her: we feel simply the tragic emotions of fear and pity.[38]

Despite his resistance to a purely allegorical reading, then, strong echoes of Johnson ring throughout Bradley's commentary.[39] His characterizing her as "nobl*est*" marks her virtue of the highest order, and his references to Cordelia's "higher" or "enskyed" nature and to redemption suggest that Bradley also saw saintliness or divinity in her.

This Johnsonian tradition continued well into the twentieth century, becoming increasingly unrestrained in its allegorical, symbolic and explic-

---

[37] In fact, I think he misreads Cordelia here. She is referring to how one has to divide the *duties* of love between one's loved ones, and her comment is not really about the amount of love that each receives. (That would imply that love can be scaled, which conflicts with her sense of the deep disjoint between love and the commercial interaction Lear invites her to make with him.) Nevertheless, I here mean only to show that Bradley is not afraid to see some flaws in Cordelia.

[38] Bradley (1905), p. 318.

[39] Bradley comes very close to an allegorical reading, writing, for instance, that in Shakespeare's work: "...the characters are there to express the natures, and not the natures the characters. It is how they stand with regard to nature that gives each character what importance it carries in the play" (Kermode (1992), pp. 120–21). However, that he does not quite subscribe to a purely allegorical reading has interesting and revealing consequences, as we will see shortly.

itly Christian interpretations. For instance, Bickersteth sums up the opening scene thus: "Divine love, symbolized by Cordelia, enters a kingdom already divided against itself, which is the Christian definition of hell..."[40] And G. Wilson Knight, writing in the 1930s, reads Cordelia as a purified representation of the principle of love, hence "...the death which Dostoevsky's Stavrogin singled out as of all the least heroic and picturesque, or rather, shall we say, the most hideous and degrading: this is the fate that grips the white innocence and resplendent love-strength of Cordelia."[41]

Knight's explanation of Cordelia's behaviour in I.i. helps to reveal the core common features of Johnsonian readings. He writes: "Sincerity forbids play-acting, and Cordelia cannot subdue her instinct to any judgement advising tact rather than truth."[42] The link he draws between the notion of instinct and this claim about Cordelia's incapacity is significant. For Knight, Cordelia's inability to fulfil Lear's demand is explained by a kind of non-reflective, almost automatic, impulse to speak the truth. Tact or prudence may be what her rational judgement advises, but she has an irresistible psychic drive to sincerity and fidelity. Notably, Cordelia's incapacity to flatter Lear is not explained in terms of what she cares about, her attitudes, relationships and sense of the harm she would do in meeting Lear's demand. Rather, the impossibility boils down to a conflict between the virtue of fidelity, which Cordelia represents, and the nature of the flattery—*qua* act of dissembling and thus falsification—demanded by Lear.

Similarly, Jameson's comment "It appears to me that the whole character [of Cordelia] rests upon the two sublimest principles of human actions—the love of truth and the sense of duty..."[43] is presented as if it were an exhaustive explanation of why Cordelia is incapable of flattering Lear. Here again, Cordelia's inability to act is explained without any reference to her particular relationship with Lear. The Cavellian vision of Cordelia as a daughter and young woman fully alive to what is at stake in the opening scene (in particular to the shamefulness of Lear's demand) goes missing altogether on this reading. Cordelia's character is subsumed by the moral principles to which she is devoted, and her incapacity to act

---

[40] Kermode (1992), p. 165.
[41] Kermode (1992), p. 98.
[42] Kermode (1992), p. 84.
[43] Bruce (1998), p. 92.

is fully explained by their incompatibility with Lear's demand. Revealingly, Jameson goes on to argue that because these two virtues of fidelity and dutifulness can seem "severe and cold" when presented in isolation, Shakespeare has "wreathed them round with the dearest attributes of our feminine nature, the power of feeling and inspiring affection."[44] In other words, Shakespeare's depiction of Cordelia as a young woman is really no more than attractive packaging for the "sublime" moral principles for which she stands—her femininity becomes a mere sugar-coating used by Shakespeare to make these lofty ideals more palatable to his audience. The fact that Cordelia is Lear's *daughter* thus becomes inessential to her character, situation and the explanation of her incapacity to flatter him.

On the Johnsonian reading, and most clearly in its strongly allegorical forms, the opening scene of *King Lear* does not show a clash of wills, intentions or desires between a king and his youngest daughter. Instead, the play opens with a confrontation within an abstract realm of moral values: a conflict between Truth and Falsehood, quiet virtue and dreadful force, the noble and the base. So while Johnsonian readers acknowledge that Cordelia is incapable of doing as her father bids, they understand this limitation as a manifestation of the conceptual incompatibility between the wrongdoing which Lear commands, and the pure morality for which Cordelia stands or allegorically *is*.

The core of this view is retained even in J.F. Danby's highly sensitive and illuminating reading of *Lear*. Danby takes the play as a depiction of the Elizabethan conception of Nature (in a double socio-political and moral sense), and interprets its characters as manifestations of the key elements of this conception.[45] Of Cordelia he writes:

> Cordelia, for Shakespeare, is virtue. Like Wordsworth's Lucy she stands for wholeness... Cordelia is Shakespeare's version of singleness and integration... She constitutes the apex of the pyramid... She is the norm itself. And she is not only Nature—the Nature violated in society. She is also Art—the

---

[44] Bruce (1998), p. 92.

[45] Danby is explicit on this point, writing that "...the characters are there to express the natures, and not the natures the characters. It is how they stand with regard to nature that gives each character what importance it carries in the play" (Danby (1949), p. 198). He differs from others in the tradition in taking Shakespeare's vision of Nature to have a *dual* aspect: the moral, private and personal; and the social or public.

Art pledged to present and express the wholeness society violates. Cordelia is the apex of Shakespeare's mind.[46]

It is, perhaps, unsurprising then that Cordelia appears to Danby as "not a complex character." As a representation of virtuous unity of soul and social order, she *must* be in harmony with herself, as undivided and simple as those ideals. Thus, he comments elsewhere that "Cordelia expresses the Utopian intention of Shakespeare's art" and that she seems close to Chaucer's Griselda insofar as each character "stands in the framework of [medieval/Elizabethan] allegory and acquires meanings that transcend psychology."[47]

Ultimately, though, even Danby makes Cordelia out to be an essentially otherworldly figure and loses sight of her as a human individual—a concrete, particular, situated young woman, princess and daughter, with a heart, life and moral perspective all of her own. That Cordelia's humanity loses its centrality and significance in Danby's reading is apparent when he summarizes Cordelia as "literally a woman; allegorically the root of individual and social sanity; tropologically Charity 'that suffereth long and is king'; analogically the redemptive principle itself."[48] The opening phrase, "literally a woman," seems just a thinly disguised way of saying that only on a superficial reading of the play is Cordelia's femininity (her identity as a daughter) relevant to her character and role in the tragedy.[49] Just as in Jameson's reading, then, Danby's Cordelia ends up as a female shell filled with all the highest and most exalted abstract concepts in the putative Shakespearean moral scheme.

As a class, Johnsonian readings either underplay, or outright deny, the relevance of Cordelia's humanity to her character. Cordelia ends up con-

---

[46] Danby (1949), p. 128.
[47] Danby (1949), p. 117.
[48] Danby (1949), p. 125.
[49] Despite commenting that "the Nature [Cordelia] stands for is essentially human and requires incarnation" (Danby (1949), p. 125) and that "...she is intended for a fully human integration" (Ibid., p. 137), Danby ultimately concludes that Cordelia "stands for no historically realizable arrangement. Her perfection of truth, justice, charity requires a New Jerusalem. She is in a transcendent relation to the political and the private. *She is the norm itself. As such she belongs to the utopian dream of the artist and of the good man*" (Ibid., p. 138, my italics).

sumed by transcendent virtue or values, in a manner most clearly visible in the commentary of François Guizot:

> Of the five personages subject to the action of misfortune, Cordelia, a heavenly figure, hovers almost invisible and half-veiled over the composition, which she fills with her presence, although she is almost always absent from it; she suffers, but never complains, never defends herself: she acts, but her action is manifested only by its results; serene regarding her own fate, reserved and restrained even in her most legitimate feelings, she passes and disappears like a denizen of a better world, who has traversed this world of ours without experiencing any more earthly emotion.[50]

In this way everything about Cordelia other than her virtue—her age, gender, family history, fairness, gentleness and softness of speech—seems to idle in the play: at best they are inessential dramatic devices for securing a morally unsophisticated audience's empathy. The Johnsonian Cordelia does not belong in the world, and never fully inhabits it. She stands for the divine, and her heart and mind are directed upwards at the heavens and not focused on the messy, dirty world of real people and problems, "the fury and the mire of human veins" as Yeats puts it, that will ultimately engulf and destroy her.[51]

7 Objections to the Johnsonian Reading

The core error of the Johnsonian tradition of reading Cordelia is its failure to fully acknowledge her perception of the specific moral quandary she confronts in the opening scene of the play. The reading fails, in other words, to bring into view exactly what it is that Cordelia professes herself incapable of doing with her "Nothing, my lord." This is compounded by the reading's explanation of Cordelia's incapacity purely in terms of abstract moral ideals and models of virtue, and failure to acknowledge her more down to earth, human identity as a young woman and daughter. The connecting thread between these two shortcomings is that the Johnsonian reading fails to recognize the importance of Cordelia's love for her father in explaining her words and deeds.

---

[50] Bruce (1998), p. 79.
[51] William Butler Yeats, *Byzantium* (originally 1928), from *The Poems of W. B. Yeats: A New Edition*, ed. R. J. Finneran (Macmillan, 1989).

In the first place, Johnsonians fail to capture Cordelia's sense of the harm she would do in fulfilling Lear's demand. It is uncontroversial that there is *something* unfitting or shameful about his request and the obsequious show Goneril and Regan perform in response to it. As we saw above, Coleridgian readers take this to be the motivation for Cordelia's proud refusal to play along. Despite their antagonism to this reading, Johnsonian readers in fact take a very similar view to Coleridgians on the matter of the moral significance of Lear's demand. They also focus solely on the *insincerity* and *falseness* of the show of flattery which he demands, and ignore the fact that here a father is asking his daughters' complicity in doing him a great harm.

On the allegorical reading, of course, this incapacity is a direct expression of the metaphysical structure of the value scheme which the play depicts and explores. But to consider, for a moment, the less abstracted Johnsonian readings in which Cordelia is a devotee of truth rather than Truth itself, we can see that she now appears as a high-minded young woman of principle taking a stand for the right and good against her craven family. She becomes, more or less, a perfected version of Isabella in "Measure for Measure": cleansed of the hypocritical prudishness to which Isabella falls prey there, but nonetheless consumed by an overwhelming concern for moral rectitude.[52]

This view of Cordelia distorts the significance of her appeals to filial duty and her daughterly bond with Lear. It also fits poorly with how Cordelia appears on stage and is described by the other characters in the play who know her well. Cordelia is described throughout the play as a gentle, soft-spoken and devoted daughter. Not once, even by her sisters who have neither fondness nor respect for her, is she characterized as a prude or a self-righteous moralizer. Cordelia's reserve, her unassuming and quiet nature, is a central aspect of her character and part of her dramatic power. Moreover, in the opening scene, although she is directly critical of her sisters and Burgundy, she does not engage in self-righteous posturing or preaching. She is certainly frank in accusing her sisters of hypocrisy and clearly angered and pained by the harm they thereby do to Lear, but she only speaks when forced to do so, and never proclaims herself to be an example of moral virtue in contrast to them. Rather, she

---

[52] Isabella's key line in this connection is said to herself, almost as a consolement: "Then, Isabel, live chaste, and brother die; // More than our brother is our chastity" (II.4).

focuses on ordinary aspects of her person and situation (e.g. how her moral duties will be split as a daughter and a wife), and laments her powerlessness to help her father.

When we follow out this Johnsonian line of thought, Cordelia's reply to Lear's demand begins to look like she is taking a stand for truth and right. This, however, conflicts with the claim that she genuinely *cannot* do as Lear demands, as it makes no sense to refuse to do something which you (know that you) couldn't do even if you tried. Here, in other words, the less allegorical Johnsonian readings run into tension with the claim, central to the tradition, that Cordelia cannot flatter Lear. For instance, Bradley's comment that Cordelia is making an "*assertion* of truth and right," that is, putting her foot down, leaves him very close to the Coleridgian claim she *refuses* to meet Lear's demand; the difference being that for Bradley this manifests her virtue of fidelity, rather than a vice of pride. This shows that it is very hard for a Johnsonian reader both to maintain the claim that Cordelia is unable to flatter Lear, and to view her as a real human being (with cares, commitments and an outlook of her own) as opposed to a symbolic representative of moral concepts.

Furthermore, where Johnsonian readers tell us that it is Cordelia's virtue or moral fineness that makes her incapable of flattering Lear, Cordelia herself says, repeatedly, that it is *love* which prevents her from acting as her sisters do. It is surprising that Johnsonian readers offer little or no explicit account of the link between these explicit claims and their allegorical account, especially given the clear connections between Love, Truth and the Good in the Christian Elizabethan moral scheme. In fact, the deepest shortcomings of Johnsonian readings are in their omissions. For although they hold Cordelia in the highest esteem, such interpretations often fail to engage with what she actually says in much depth or detail. Consideration of Cordelia's especially close relationship with her father is conspicuously absent from these readings, as is any attempt to flesh out her understanding of what moves Lear to his strange demand or her concern for how it will harm him. Perhaps their assumption is that no such common-or-garden psychological explanation of Cordelia's actions is necessary, because the play concerns (and thus can be explained entirely by reference to) the moral-conceptual scheme of Nature which it represents. This seems to explain why Cordelia's incapacity tends to be characterized by Johnsonian readers as in the first place an inability to dissemble or speak falsely *as such*, rather than a specific inability to say a certain falsehood to a particular person in a determinate context. We should note that the text offers no evidence for the broad claim that Cordelia simply cannot lie. Moreover, this makes the fact that it is *Lear's* demand which Cordelia cannot meet seem to be of little real significance. Her situation would be just the same if she were asked, or ordered, to lie by anyone, anywhere: her devotion to (or identification with) Truth would render her equally incapable of doing so.

The danger here is that Lear appears on the Johnsonian reading as the *mere occasion* for Cordelia's incapacity. The reading divorces her incapacity from her love by explaining the former in terms of the abstract wrongness of dissembling, leaving no work to be done by Cordelia's sense of the harm that her father would suffer if she answered his demand. Johnson's Cordelia is ultimately so consumed by devotion to Truth and the Good, that she becomes essentially detached from her father: she seems blind to his desperate folly and need, and unconcerned with protecting him or coming to his aid. In my view, this is as ill-fitting a picture of Cordelia's actions in the opening scene as that of the Coleridgians. One reading sees human fault and vice where the other finds saintly purity, but neither succeeds in bringing Cordelia herself into view.

Despite their attempts to sanctify Cordelia, Johnsonian readers actually miss the remarkable selflessness of her incapacity. By "selfless" I mean more than simply to mark Cordelia's courage in risking her fortune, although she is certainly admirable in that. Her incapacity, as it is revealed by the Cavellian reading, is morally inspiring because it focuses solely on Lear: it is, in the first place, an inability to harm *him*. The purity and depth of Cordelia's filial love—and *her* purity and depth as such a daughter and such a lover—consists in her being so alive, so sensitive, to the harm that Lear does himself in the court, that she simply cannot bear to participate in it. (In contrast, the Johnsonian reading tends to view Cordelia as in the first place incapable of violating her own nature.)

I would like to expand a little on this point about the different explanatory directions in which we can develop an understanding of Cordelia's moral incapacity. In taking her incapacity to dissemble as an entry point *into* her character and moral psychology, Johnsonian readers are led to a picture of Cordelia as exhausted by the moral ideals she represents or is committed to. This is often the way that moral-psychological explanations tend to go: we follow a person's deeds inwards to their psychological underpinnings in the agent's character (such as dispositions, emotions or beliefs). An alternative approach has been suggested by Raimond Gaita. He argues that the real significance of "saintly" deeds, those which inspire wonder by their undeniable moral purity, lies not in what they show about their agents but in what they reveal about their *objects*.[53] He proposes, in other words, that instead of tracing such actions inwards to the minds and hearts of those who perform then, we often learn more by following them *outwards* to the people (creatures, projects, ideals etc.) to which they are addressed. Saintly deeds, to paraphrase for a minute, illuminate the common humanity of their objects.

Gaita's suggestion allows us to see that there is more to say about the remarkable fineness of Cordelia's filial love than that it shows her purity of heart. Cordelia's incapacity to harm Lear does reveal her to be brave, unselfish, tender, kind and caring. She is a remarkable young woman, princess and daughter. However, the purity of her love, and her perfection as such a lover (both of which Johnsonian readers sense, we should note), actually lie in their power to reveal Lear's humanity. Cordelia's incapacity is revelatory of her fineness but *also of Lear's preciousness*. Her inability to harm him shows him to be someone whose suffering matters, one whose pain can be shared and calls out to be assuaged. Cordelia also reminds us that this preciousness is not something earned or deserved: she loves Lear simply for being her father, and regardless of the folly and cruelty that he displays.

Cordelia is fully responsive to her father's need for care from the very beginning of the play: she sees through his shameful scheme to the weakness, frailty and vulnerability that drives it. Importantly, she is sensitive to all of this when it is hardest for us to see. She is alive to the pitiful, frightened old man that Lear has become long before he undergoes the erosive process of humiliation and abuse that drives him to insanity—the process by which Shakespeare helps *us* (as audience) to see Lear in this way. We need to see Lear isolated, humiliated and reduced before the depth of his folly at the play's opening becomes clear. He must first appear to us as broken before we can respond to him as pitifully weak and in need of sanctuary and comfort. But Cordelia's love makes her alive to this from the

---

[53] I take this to be a central upshot of his discussion of the powerful example of Charles and Ladmaker from Primo Levi's *If This Is a Man* (see the "Preface to the second edition" in Gaita's *Good and Evil, An Absolute Conception*, 2nd ed. (Routledge, 2004) p. xv ff). The ideas here come up elsewhere in his work and are closely connected to Simone Weil's conception of justice and compassion for the afflicted (degraded and ruined) as *miraculous* and Gatia's work on the ideas of intrinsic worth and inalienable dignity at the core of contemporary conceptions of human rights (Kantian and otherwise).

outset. Even when Lear is at his most manipulative and tyrannical, he is, to her, a father in need of her love and help.

We can acknowledge all of this without making Cordelia into something transcendent or otherworldly. What makes her a powerful dramatic depiction of love is not that she manifests the elated perfection of the angels, but that she displays the naturalness, purity and beauty of a daughter's love for her father. Cordelia's loving vision combines an unflinchingly honest sense of Lear's folly, a penetrating empathetic sense of the human shortcomings that underlie it, and an unconditional affirmation of his worth.

On my reading of *King Lear*, which owes its spirit and much of its detail to Cavell's revelatory reading of the play, Cordelia is above all else a daughter who cannot bring herself to do a serious harm to the father she loves. There is something remarkably fine about this, but nothing superhuman. That human beings are capable of loving one another in such a way that their love can impose strict moral-volitional limits on what they can do to one another is certainly mysterious, in the sense that it should strike us as wondrous, and demands our acknowledgement and attention. However, it needn't be explained by appeal to divine ideals or transcendent schemes of value, and we should be wary of reaching too quickly for such devices in responding to her. From another vantage point, after all, there's nothing unfamiliar or superhuman in the idea of a person's sacrificing everything for their beloved, or bring unable to wreak dreadful suffering on them even under the threat of great harms or losses. These are not daily happenings, but they are also not restricted to the lives of the saints.

In forcing Cordelia up into the heavens, Johnsonian readers miss what is at once most human and most wondrous about her. Cavell's great contribution to the aesthetic and moral understanding of *King Lear* is that it allows us to see that Cordelia's goodness consists in her exemplifying an eminently human form of love. He is thus correct to claim, against Johnson and his successors, that Cordelia's "grace is shown by the absence of any unearthly experiences; she is the only good character whose attention is wholly on earth, on the person nearest her."[54]

---

[54] Cavell (2003), p. 74.

8 Conclusion

Cavell's reading reveals *King Lear* as a more compelling and more human tragedy than it appears on either of the other two interpretations. Coleridgian readers see human failings, all around, to be the cause of the tragedy. Theirs is the grim cynicism of La Rochefoucauld, a thoroughgoing denial of the human potential for real goodness, which sees it as always undermined by our proneness to self-deception, vanity and the powerful illusions behind which our vice hides itself from view. Johnsonian readers, in contrast, take the play as a dark comment on the impossibility of maintaining or protecting heavenly purity in an ugly world of morally weak and corrupted players.[55] For them, Lear presents an image of the losing battle between transcendent virtue and baseness.

Seen under a Cavellian light, *King Lear* revolves around an agonizing double acknowledgement: of the purity and fineness of the unconditional love of a daughter, on the one hand; and of the utter impotence of such love to withstand the destructive forces of delusion, fear and wickedness, on the other. To paraphrase Simone Weil, Shakespeare captures the "unlimitedness of woe" in *Lear* by at once testifying to love's supreme beauty and truth, and its helpless subjugation to the pull of gravity, the merciless necessity of force.[56] Cavell's reading places Cordelia right at the heart of the tragedy. She is no longer just another limited player swept up in a tumult of vice that is largely of their own making. Rather, she is the very site of the tragedy itself: blameless victim of her family's folly and foulness; and powerless bystander to her father's degradation, humiliation and dissolution. As such, Cordelia is a painful reminder that even the best kind of love and the finest ethical character may be insufficient to protect those we treasure from catastrophe. She reminds us that sometimes to love someone can only be to share in their suffering. Schlegel captures this point when he writes: "According to Shakespeare's plan the guilty, it is

---

[55] Some Johnsonian readers, however, have tried to see King Lear as a play about *redemption* through sacrifice (with Cordelia being at the heart of this story). For instance, Speaight responds to Johnson "by asserting that the conclusion of the play as Shakespeare originally wrote it is sufficiently happy insofar as it suggests that the death of Cordelia is an image of saving grace, not a revelation of meaninglessness" (R.V. Young, *Hope and Despair in King Lear* in Kahan, p. 255).

[56] See Simone Weil, *The Notebooks of Simone Weil*, 1st ed. (London and New York: Routledge, 2004), p. 210 ("a tragedy of gravity") and p. 620.

true, are all punished, for wickedness destroys itself; but the virtues that would bring help and succour are everywhere too late, or overmatched by the cunning activity of malice."[57] To my mind, Cavell's vision of *Lear* is filled with both a brighter light, and more impenetrable darkness, than those of Coleridge or Johnson. It is, as it were, shot in starker tones, on higher contrast film stock.[58]

---

[57] Bruce (1998), p. 72.

[58] I owe a debt of thanks to my father (an English teacher) for many of the fine details in this reading of *King Lear* and for help with charting and navigating the vast critical literature surrounding the play. I would also like to thank Raimond Gaita for his help in developing some of the moral-philosophical implications of the reading; Candace Vogler, Dan Brudney and Ben Laurence for their supportive supervision of the doctoral research project at the University of Chicago from which this essay is taken; and James Conant and David Wellbery, whose graduate seminar at the University of Chicago on Cavell's aesthetic, epistemological and moral philosophy greatly deepened my appreciation of the importance and richness of his thought.

CHAPTER 5

Disowning Certainty: Tragic and Comic Skepticism in Cavell, Montaigne, and Shakespeare

V. Stanley Benfell

Numerous scholars have explored the relationship between early modern skepticism and Shakespearean drama, and their studies often depend for their force on a historical narrative dominated by the idea of crisis. The outlines of the narrative can be stated briefly: with the advent of the Protestant Reformation and the rise of Renaissance humanism, old certainties break down, and dissension and violence result. And while the arc of this narrative reinforces the traditional view of the early modern period as the origin of modernity, the story itself is not a happy one. It is perhaps for this reason that these studies invariably link skepticism to tragedy.[1]

---

[1] See, for example, Millicent Bell, *Shakespeare's Tragic Skepticism* (New Haven: Yale University Press, 2002): "tragedy results from skeptic disillusion" (p. 4). Other important studies of Shakespearean tragedy and skepticism include Benjamin Bertram, *The Time is Out of Joint: Skepticism in Shakespeare's England* (Newark: University of Delaware Press, 2004); and William H. Hamlin, *Tragedy and Scepticism in Shakespeare's England* (New York:

V. S. Benfell (✉)
Brigham Young University, Provo, UT, USA
e-mail: benfell@byu.edu

© The Author(s) 2018
G. L. Hagberg (ed.), *Stanley Cavell on Aesthetic Understanding*, Philosophers in Depth,
https://doi.org/10.1007/978-3-319-97466-8_5

Stanley Cavell thus locates the origin of his work on Shakespeare in the "thought that this mode of tragedy is a response to the crisis of knowledge inspired by the crisis of the unfolding of the New Science in the late 16th and early 17th centuries." And while he here implies that in *King Lear* and the other tragedies Shakespeare was responding to a contemporary historical crisis, he goes on to express his particular interest in a skepticism that post-dates Shakespeare: "especially as [this skepticism was] articulated so decisively for philosophy in the next generation following those tragedies by Descartes's articulation of modern skepticism."[2] In this study I propose, however, to come at skepticism from the other side of history, looking toward Shakespeare from the ancient skepticism as expressed in the Academic and Pyrrhonist traditions and in early modern thinkers, especially the essayist Michel de Montaigne, influenced by those ancient traditions.[3] Here one finds different dramatic possibilities for skepticism, or at least possibilities that are hardly exhausted by tragedy—a "comic" skepticism, in other words, where comedy offers the opportunity of working out the dramatic implications of skeptical thinking.

1 Skepticisms: Ancient, Modern, and Early Modern

As we will see, Cavell's philosophy, with its rejection of Cartesian skepticism and its assertion of the necessity of reciprocity and acknowledgement, insists on the contextual and finite nature of human knowledge.

Palgrave Macmillan, 2005). Alternate conceptions of skepticism in Shakespearean drama include Graham Bradshaw, *Shakespeare's Scepticism* (Brighton: Harvester Press, 1987), who finds skepticism to be characteristic of Shakespeare's "poetic-dramatic thinking" as a whole and not limited to one genre; Richard Strier, in "Shakespeare and the Skeptics," *Religion and Literature* 32, no. 2 (2000): 171–96, explores skepticism in *The Comedy of Errors* and *A Midsummer Night's Dream*, as well as in *King Lear*, noting, for example, that *The Comedy of Errors* has "an extraordinarily dark view of human intellectual capacity." See also Ellen Spolsky, who argues "against the inevitability of a tragic interpretation of the conditions of human knowing," and considers tragicomedy (but not comedy) in her analysis in *Satisfying Skepticism: Embodied Knowledge in the Early Modern World* (Aldershot: Ashgate, 2001); and James Kuzner, *Shakespeare as a Way of Life: Skeptical Practice and the Politics of Weakness* (New York: Fordham University Press, 2016).

[2] From the "Preface" to *Disowning Knowledge In Seven Plays of Shakespeare*, Updated ed. (Cambridge: Cambridge University Press, 2003), xiii. Future references to *Disowning Knowledge* will occur in the text.

[3] For an extended essay on what the shift from Montaigne to Descartes means in the history of culture, see Stephen Toulmin, *Cosmopolis: The Hidden Agenda of Modernity* (Chicago: University of Chicago Press, 1990).

We can only know something here and now, at this time and in the context of the relationships with which we are engaged. It is no wonder, therefore, that Cavell sees drama (and film) as ideally suited for philosophical exploration. In his view a text such as a Shakespearean tragedy, while usually viewed as "literary" and therefore as "aesthetic," nevertheless opens up the possibility of philosophical exploration. For Cavell, as other scholars such as David Rudrum have noted, "the [Shakespearean] play itself, rather than 'exemplifying,' 'illustrating,' or 'instantiating' a philosophical idea, becomes an invitation to or occasion for philosophy in its own right."[4] In Cavell's work on Shakespeare, it is difficult to determine where "aesthetic" reflection ends and more strictly "philosophical" exploration begins. Aesthetic understanding works hand in hand with philosophical exploration. In this paper, I follow Cavell's lead in this endeavor, although I will argue below that Shakespearean comedy is also available in a similar way for philosophical exploration, a possibility Cavell acknowledges in his work on film comedy.[5] Before moving to comedy, however, we must first understand why Cavell finds skepticism to be inescapably tragic.

For Cavell, skepticism is not just historically important for a playwright working in the wake of the Reformation and on the cusp of the scientific revolution, it is characteristic of virtually the entire modern philosophical tradition.[6] Cavell sees skepticism as fundamentally human, at least in the modern world, "whether," as he writes in "Hamlet's Burden of Proof," "in Descartes's or Hume's or Kant's pictures of that inescapably, essen-

---

[4] David Rudrum, *Stanley Cavell and the Claim of Literature* (Baltimore: Johns Hopkins University Press, 2013), pp. 55–56.

[5] See Cavell's *Pursuits of Happiness: The Hollywood Comedy of Remarriage* (Cambridge, MA: Harvard University Press, 1984).

[6] Cavell has been concerned with skepticism for virtually his entire philosophical career. In his own writings, see especially "Knowing and Acknowledging," in *Must We Mean What We Say?* (New York: Charles Scribner's Sons, 1969), pp. 238–66; and *The Claim of Reason: Wittgenstein, Skepticism, Morality, and Tragedy*, new ed. (New York: Oxford University Press, 1999). For accounts of his skepticism, see Michael Fischer, *Stanley Cavell and Literary Skepticism* (Chicago: University of Chicago Press, 1989); Gerald Bruns, "Stanley Cavell's Shakespeare," *Critical Inquiry* 16 (1990): 612–32; and James Conant's response to Bruns's article, "On Bruns, On Cavell," *Critical Inquiry* 17 (1991): 616–34; Espen Hammer, *Stanley Cavell: Skepticism, Subjectivity, and the Ordinary* (Cambridge: Polity Press, 2002), esp. chaps. 2 and 3; and David Rudrum, *Stanley Cavell and the Claim of Literature*, esp. chap. 7.

tially human possibility" (179). When he surmises, therefore, "that not only was tragedy obedient to a skeptical structure but contrariwise, that skepticism already bore its own marks of a tragic structure" (5), it was perhaps natural for him to turn to Shakespeare, whose "writing is engaging the depth of the philosophical preoccupations of his culture" (2). Indeed, early in the Introduction to *Disowning Knowledge*, Cavell claims an intuition that "the advent of skepticism as manifested in Descartes's *Meditations* is already in full existence in Shakespeare" (3). Cavell's skepticism is particularly concerned with the skepticism of other minds. As he states the idea in the "Foreword" to *The Claim of Reason*, "skepticism concerning other minds is not skepticism but is tragedy."[7]

Descartes proves to be a key thinker in Cavell's understanding of skepticism, which on the face of it may seem surprising, since, as William Hamlin phrases it, for most readers "Descartes is ultimately less remarkable for his doubt than for the certainty that his doubt enables him to obtain."[8] Descartes is nevertheless key for Cavell precisely because it is in Descartes's writings that skepticism becomes a problem, that is, a lack. Whereas Montaigne repeatedly insists on "the emptiness, the vanity, the nothingness of Man,"[9] he does so not to despair but ultimately, as I suggest below, to learn to live without certainties; for Descartes, however, skepticism is a corrosive that inhibits one from attaining any knowledge that deserves the name, and which in turn produces a paralysis of thought and action. He engages in a project of radical doubt, shaking every assumption in order to find something that cannot be shaken, and on that solid ground he proposes to build his philosophy. Nevertheless, even at that point, building upon his certainty regarding his *cogito*, his ultimate defeat of skepticism depends upon proving the existence of a benevolent, omnipotent being who can guarantee the validity of both the Cartesian subject's sense impressions and his clear and distinct ideas. His certainty depends, that is, on the existence of a God who will not deceive him. As Descartes writes in his Third Meditation, "for without a knowledge of these two

---

[7] *The Claim of Reason*, p. xix.

[8] "What Did Montaigne's Skepticism Mean to Shakespeare and His Contemporaries?" *Montaigne Studies* 17 (2005): 195–210.

[9] This citation is from "An apology for Raymond Sebond," from *The Complete Essays*, trans. M. A. Screech (Harmondsworth: Penguin, 1991), p. 500. All citations of the *Essays* in English refer to this edition. The original French text is cited according to *Les Essais*, ed. Pierre Villey (Paris: Presses Universitaires de France, 1924).

truths [God's existence and his truthful nature] I do not see that I can ever be certain of anything."[10]

For Cavell, a skeptic is a Cartesian unable to move past the phase of radical doubt, to ground his or her knowledge in the existence of a transcendent God. Confronted, then, with his or her own intellectual limitations, the skeptic refuses to accept finitude. In his essay on *Othello*, Cavell draws on a definition of skepticism that he first proposed in *Must We Mean What We Say?*: "the conversion of metaphysical finitude into intellectual lack."[11] Cavell finds a skeptic in this tragic sense in Othello. Forced to confront Desdemona as a separate, autonomous individual who exists outside of his control even though committed to him through a marriage vow, he comes face to face with his own finitude. As he laments, "O curse of marriage, / That we can call these delicate creatures ours / And not their appetites!" (3.3.266–68).[12] When Othello implies his wish to control or, rather, actually own Desdemona and her appetites ("call these…creatures ours"), he is, for Cavell, skeptically rejecting her. That is, his inability to know whether Desdemona is faithful to him with absolute certainty is interpreted by him (with some help by Iago) to be a failure—an unacceptable lack. Othello's finitude could result in his acknowledging Desdemona fully as a separate individual with her own appetites, but whom he trusts to be faithful to him without demanding an absolute, and hence inhuman, knowledge of her. Instead, Othello refuses to acknowledge her and in fact rejects or disowns the knowledge that is readily available to him, a rejection that constitutes an inescapably tragic refusal: "Tragedy is the place we are not allowed to escape the consequences, or price, of this cover: that the failure to acknowledge a best case of the other is a denial of that other" (138). As James Conant describes the importance of acknowledgment for Cavell, "This failure of acknowledgment is then interpreted by the philosopher in us (call him Othello) as a failure of knowledge. *It is converted into an intellectual difficulty*, so that its solution now appears to require a further application of the intellect: a search for more and better knowledge."[13]

---

[10] René Descartes, *Discourse on Method and Meditations on First Philosophy*, ed. David Weissman (New Haven: Yale University Press, 1996), p. 72.

[11] *Disowning Knowledge*, p. 138. The phrase originally appears in his chapter, "Knowing and Acknowledging," in *Must We Mean What We Say?*, p. 263.

[12] Citations of Shakespeare's plays refer to *The Norton Shakespeare*, ed. Stephen Greenblatt et al., 3rd ed. (New York: Norton 2016).

[13] Conant, "On Bruns, On Cavell," 631, emphasis mine.

By refusing to acknowledge Desdemona, Othello becomes all too susceptible to Iago's "proofs" of her infidelity, since only then can he be out of the unendurable situation of depending on another human being. As Cavell states the idea, "He cannot forgive Desdemona for existing, for being separate from him, outside, beyond command, commanding, her captain's captain" (136). Othello disowns or rejects the kind of knowledge available to him, knowledge fit for a finite being, and demands instead an absolute knowledge, the "ocular proof," as he states it (3.3.357). Othello the skeptic is unavoidably tragic because while he cannot achieve certainty, he longs for it to such a degree that he will kill the person that confronts him with his own limitations: "skepticism's 'doubt' is motivated not by (not even where it is expressed as) a (misguided) intellectual scrupulousness but by a (misplaced) denial, by a self-consuming disappointment that seeks world-consuming revenge" (6).

In his reading of *Othello*, Cavell finds a thoroughly modern skepticism at work, a skepticism tragic at its core. As suggested above, however, Cavell's modern(ist) skepticism is not the only way of viewing skepticism, and certainly not the only skepticism available to Shakespeare, assuming that Cavell is right that this (post-) Cartesian skepticism was already apparent in Shakespeare's great tragedies. From the other side of history, we find a skepticism formulated in the French essayist Michel de Montaigne that differs in significant ways from Cavell's understanding of skepticism as a fundamentally modern and tragic temptation. Montaigne becomes crucial in considering Shakespeare's grasp of skepticism because he was the most influential and persuasive early modern writer who attempted to work through the implications of skeptical thought, and we find as we attend to him that his conclusions, and the ways that he works through skeptical ideas to reach them, differ markedly from what more recent thinkers often understand the implications of skepticism to be.

Montaigne's skepticism derives ultimately from ancient, Pyrrhonist skepticism, which arose not as an attempt to work out or frustrate epistemological inquiries, but as a *practical* teaching, similar to the other Hellenistic philosophies that arose at the same time. Martha Nussbaum notes that the "Hellenistic philosophical schools in Greece and Rome—Epicureans, Skeptics, and Stoics—all conceived of philosophy as a way of addressing the most painful problems of human life. They saw the philosopher as a compassionate physician whose arts could heal many pervasive types of human suffering."[14] The form of skepticism most influential for Montaigne was attributed to the third-century BCE thinker Pyrrho of Elis, although our best account of Pyrrhonist skeptical thought is found in the writings of Sextus Empiricus, whose dates are unknown but is perhaps best placed in the late second century CE. For Pyrrhonist thinkers,[15] skepticism was an ability or mental skill that enabled a thinker to assemble evidence on both sides of any question involving belief or knowledge. Because of the conflicting evidence, skeptics felt compelled to suspend judgment on the question being considered only to discover that they had obtained *ataraxia*, the tranquility that was the goal common to most Hellenistic philosophy.[16] Skepticism, as Richard Popkin phrases it, "was a

---

[14] Martha Nussbaum, *The Therapy of Desire: Theory and Practice in Hellenistic Ethics* (Princeton: Princeton University Press, 1994), p. 3. In addition to Nussbaum's volume, in gaining an understanding of ancient skepticism I have benefitted from R. J. Hankinson, *The Sceptics* (London Routledge, 1995); Alan Bailey, *Sextus Empiricus and Pyrrhonean Scepticism* (Oxford: Clarendon Press, 2002); Julia Annas and Jonathan Barnes, *The Modes of Scepticism*; Charles Brittain's translation of and commentary on Cicero, *On Academic Scepticism*, (Indianapolis and Cambridge: Hackett, 2006); and Richard Bett, ed. *The Cambridge Companion to Ancient Scepticism* (Cambridge: Cambridge University Press, 2010).

[15] Ancient skepticism is traditionally divided into two main "schools": Academic skepticism, which flourished intermittently in the Platonic Academy after the time of Plato, and Pyrrhonist skepticism, which was held to derive originally from Pyrrho. In broad terms, the difference most commonly cited between these two schools is that while the Academic Skeptics argued (one might even say dogmatically) that knowledge was not possible, the Pyrrhonists observed that one could not even make the claim that knowledge was not possible, and so they favored suspending judgment on all questions of knowledge and belief. Many scholars of Academic skepticism point out that the distinctions between the two schools are actually much more complex. For a recent discussion of the differences between them, see Gisela Striker, "Academics and Pyrrhonists, reconsidered," in *The Cambridge Companion to Ancient Scepticism*, 195–207. Montaigne, for his part, in "An apology for Raymond Sebond," remarks that the Academics, while accepting that it was impossible to know the truth of things, did argue that certain things were more likely, "and concede to judgment the power to incline towards one probability rather than another." The Pyrrhonists, on the other hand, held that "it is pointless for our judgement to be influenced by [our faculties], no matter what 'probabilities' it seems to present us with." Montaigne declares the Pyrrhonist position "more true-seeming" (*"plus vray-semblable"*) (633).

[16] Here I paraphrase Sextus's own definition of skepticism from his best-known work, *Outlines of Scepticism* (usually abbreviated as *PH*, after its Greek title, *Pyrrhōneioi hypotypōseis*): "Scepticism is an ability to set out oppositions among things which appear and are thought of in any way at all, an ability by which, because of the equipollence in the opposed objects and accounts, we come first to suspension of judgement and afterwards to tranquility" (I, iv,

cure for the disease called dogmatism, or rashness."[17] Montaigne, too, seems to think dogmatism a kind of affliction, writing that "there is a plague on Man: his opinion that he knows something."[18]

Pyrrhonist skepticism did not have a significant following in the Middle Ages or in the first decades of the early modern period, although Academic skepticism, primarily through the writings of Cicero, found adherents, most famously in Erasmus.[19] Henri Etienne's Latin translation of the works of Sextus Empiricus, published in 1562, changed the landscape of European thought; many thinkers were drawn to Sextus's account of Pyrrhonist philosophy as a response to the intellectual upheavals caused by the Reformation and its aftermath. That is, as with ancient skepticism, many early modern thinkers turned to skepticism as a "cure for the disease called dogmatism." For Montaigne, the alarming troubles of the sixteenth century were not caused by a lack of "knowledge" or "certainty," but by an excess of them; the French religious wars came about because of the certainty of radical Huguenots and extremist Catholics, who felt, without doubt and without compunction, that their understanding of Christianity was God's own truth, that their opponents were perverting it, and, finally, that violence to protect such a sacred truth was fully justified. Montaigne welcomed skepticism, at least as an initial step, because it undercut the deadly certainties to which so many of his countrymen were devoted.[20] Through Montaigne, many others found the appeal of skepticism.[21]

---

8). I cite the translation by Julia Annas and Jonathan Barnes in Sextus Empiricus, *Outlines of Scepticism* (Cambridge: Cambridge University Press, 2000), p. 4.

[17] From his classic account, Richard H. Popkin, *The History of Scepticism: From Savonarola to Bayle*, rev. ed. (Oxford: Oxford University Press, 2003), p. xix.

[18] From "An apology for Raymond Sebond," p. 543.

[19] For example, in the introduction to his *De libero arbitrio* (written to combat Luther's teachings against free will), Erasmus calls himself a skeptic: "And I take so little pleasure in assertions that I will gladly seek refuge in Scepticism whenever this is allowed by the inviolable authority of Holy Scripture and the church's decrees." I cite the translation by Peter Macardle, found in volume 76 of the *Collected Works of Erasmus* (Toronto: University of Toronto Press, 1999), p. 7.

[20] For example, see the brief essay, "Qu'il faut sobrement se mesler de juger des ordonnances divines," translated by Screech as "Judgements on God's ordinances must be embarked upon with prudence" (1.32).

[21] See chapters two and three, "The Revival of Greek Scepticism in the Sixteenth Century," and "Michel de Montaigne and the *Nouveaux Pyrrhoniens*," in Popkin, *History of Scepticism*, pp. 17–63. Popkin argues that "through Montaigne, Renaissance scepticism became crucial in the formation of modern philosophy" (p. 43). Further treatments of the spread of skepti-

Montaigne studied the newly translated Sextus Empiricus carefully and was strongly influenced by his Pyrrhonist ideas. His most overt expression of skepticism is found in "An apology for Raymond Sebond," by far the longest of his essays. Montaigne defends the Spanish theologian of the essay's title by launching a skeptical attack on Sebond's critics, who demonstrate a faulty confidence in human reason. Montaigne tells us that he will "trample down human pride and arrogance, crushing them under our feet; I make men feel the emptiness, the vanity, the nothingness of Man, wrenching from their grasp the sickly arms of human reason" (500–01). Later in the essay he summarizes his discussion: "I have succeeded in showing, I think, how far reason is from understanding even itself. And what can anyone understand who cannot understand himself?" (628). Passages such as these have made Montaigne's Pyrrhonist skepticism a critical commonplace. Popkin, who concentrates his attention on the "Apology," finds Montaigne's thought to be "complete Pyrrhonism" (55), since Montaigne consistently undermines abstract philosophizing and links the human desire for absolute knowledge and certainty to "human pride and arrogance." Montaigne, noting how difficult it is for the "Pyrrhonist philosophers" to state their doubts in any positive form, suggests that "scepticism can best be conceived through the form of a question": "*Que sçay-je?*," in Montaigne's French, or in Screech's translation, "What do I know?" (590–91).

The standard account of Montaigne's Pyrrhonism seems to me, as it has to many others in the last few decades, to be an inadequate description of his thought as a whole and depends upon an over-reliance on the "Apology."[22] While Montaigne was profoundly influenced by his encoun-

---

cism in the sixteenth century include Myles Burnyeat, ed., *The Skeptical Tradition* (Berkeley: University of California Press, 1983); and Brian C. Copenhaver and Charles B. Schmitt, "Stoics, Sceptics, Epicureans, and Other Innovators," chapter 4 of *Renaissance Philosophy* (Oxford: Oxford University Press, 1992), pp. 196–284. For a specific consideration of how Sextus's writings spread, see Luciano Floridi, *Sextus Empiricus: The Transmission and Recovery of Pyrrhonism* (Oxford: Oxford University Press, 2002). Zachary Schiffman argues—against Popkin—that the rise of skepticism, especially in Montaigne's writings, was due to the breakdown of humanist assumptions about education. See "Montaigne and the Rise of Skepticism in Early Modern Europe: A Reappraisal," *Journal of the History of Ideas* 45 (1984): 499–516. For a biographical consideration of why Montaigne turned to skepticism, see Sarah Bakewell, *How to Live, Or, A Life of Montaigne in One Question and Twenty Attempts at an Answer* (New York: Other Press, 2010), especially pp. 123–53.

[22] There are too many studies to enumerate in full here. Some important studies in English include: Donald Frame, *Montaigne's Discovery of Man: The Humanization of a Humanist*

ter with Sextus's writings, he was not a thoroughgoing Pyrrhonist. Indeed, one can find, especially in his later essays, the possibility of knowledge—a different kind of knowledge, to be sure, than the dogmatic knowledge that he rejects in the "Apology"—but knowledge nevertheless: a knowledge that embraces metaphysical finitude while rejecting certainty. "On Experience," the final essay of his three-book collection, perhaps advocates this finite knowledge most clearly.

Montaigne opens his final essay in a way that echoes the beginning of the "Apology," by making a claim for the value of knowledge with an allusion to the opening of Aristotle's *Metaphysics*: "No desire is more natural than the desire for knowledge." But he uses this Aristotelian opening to move in an un-Aristotelian direction, arguing that diversity and variety are much more common than likeness and unity. He will, in fact, undermine common humanist teachings concerning ethics, striking at traditional notions of exemplarity, for example, which assume that we can learn from studying the lives of great men, since their lives are similar to those of other men. Nevertheless, while philosophical reason does not fare much better in this essay than it does in the "Apology," Montaigne does argue for the validity of experience. "When reason fails us, we make use of experience," he writes, even though it is "a weaker and less dignified means" (1207). And while this statement may seem to denigrate experience, throughout the course of the essay he consistently claims for experience the ability to achieve a limited knowledge: "Were I a good pupil there is enough, I find, in my own experience to make me wise" (1218). He questions traditional exemplarity in this essay, but he finds that our own lives provide the material we need to attain wisdom, preferring for this purpose his own life to that of Caesar.[23] In an earlier essay of the third book, "On

---

(New York: Columbia University Press, 1955); David Quint, *Montaigne and the Quality of Mercy: Ethical and Political Themes in the "Essais"* (Princeton: Princeton University Press, 1998); M. A. Screech, *Montaigne & Melancholy: The Wisdom of the "Essays,"* new ed. (Lanham, MD: Rowman & Littlefield, 2000); and, especially, Ann Hartle, *Michel de Montaigne: Accidental Philosopher* (Cambridge: Cambridge University Press, 2003). A briefer statement of Hartle's argument can be found in her chapter, "Montaigne and skepticism," in *The Cambridge Companion to Montaigne*, ed. Ullrich Langer (Cambridge: Cambridge University Press, 2005), pp. 183–206.

[23] For a consideration of how Montaigne undermines and transforms humanist notions of exemplarity, see Timothy Hampton, *Writing from History: The Rhetoric of Exemplarity in Renaissance Literature* (Ithaca: Cornell University Press, 1990), pp. 134–97, although Hampton finds Montaigne's notion of the self much closer to Descartes's than I do.

Repenting," Montaigne compared the two great exemplary lives—Alexander and Socrates—and found Socrates's achievement to be greater, because it contains more universal lessons on how to live. "Ask Alexander what he can do and he will reply: 'Subdue the whole world.' Ask Socrates, and he will answer, 'Live the life of man in conformity with his natural condition': knowledge which is more generous, onerous, and right" (913).

To return to "On Experience," Montaigne devotes a good deal of attention at the end of the essay to the question of his own health and the medical treatment needed to sustain it. His discussion is telling: medicine for Montaigne is a resolutely practical science, and his discussion contrasts this practical focus with that of "the learned [*les sçavans*]," who "arrange their ideas into species and name them in detail. I, who can see no further than practice [*l'usage*] informs me, have no such rule, presenting my ideas in no categories and feeling my way" (1222). The lessons he has learned come through paying close attention to his own body and following the lessons that it teaches him. We frequently read statements such as the following: "Experience has taught me that we are ruined by impatience" (1235).

While crucially informed by Pyrrhonist skepticism, then, Montaigne stops short of advocating the complete suspension of judgment for which Sextus argues. Given Montaigne's use of skepticism, but his refusal to follow Pyrrhonist conclusions to their end, we must qualify what we mean by his skepticism. Instead of suspension of judgment in all things, he seeks a limited, finite wisdom that will teach him how we should live, a goal that moves beyond the desire for tranquility sought by Pyrrhonists. In a discussion of the ethical implications of skepticism, Richard Bett has argued that suspension of judgment seems a good way to achieve the goal of tranquility. "But someone with that attitude does not seem to be, in the usual sense, an ethically involved agent."[24] Montaigne, however, is ethically involved; his words near the end of "On Experience" seem foreign to the

---

[24] Richard Bett, "Scepticism and ethics," in *The Cambridge Companion to Ancient Scepticism*, p. 193. For a consideration of whether Pyrrhonist skepticism is in fact "livable," see M. F. Burnyeat, "Can the Sceptic Live His Scepticism?" from *Doubt and Dogmatism: Studies in Hellenistic Epistemology*, ed. Malcolm Schofield et al. (Oxford: Clarendon Press, 1980), pp. 20–53. He argues ultimately that it is not possible to live a skeptical life as Sextus describes it; Sextus, according to Burnyeat, fudges the question of belief, since it proves to be impossible to live a life without beliefs, as Sextus claims to be able to do.

detachment praised by Sextus: "Nothing is so beautiful, so right, as acting as a man should: nor is any learning so arduous as knowing how to live this life naturally and well" (1261). The knowledge he seeks, in other words, is not absolute or theoretical, but practical and finite, well suited to his own condition. Ann Hartle calls this limited, non-dogmatic wisdom "accidental philosophy," which Montaigne opposes to the dogmatic philosophizing of abstract thinkers. For the purposes of this chapter, I prefer "comic skepticism," which refers both to the skeptical step that is crucial to his inquiry and to the optimistic turn toward finite wisdom that ultimately characterizes his thought. For Montaigne, apt guides for living are patience and allowing nature to have its way. "Let us allow Nature to do something! She understands her business better than we do" (1236). The danger is trying to impose our wills on nature and on our lives, to insist on more, or on more absolute, knowledge than is possible to find. To use Cavell's phrase, "metaphysical finitude" is not avoided or despised by Montaigne, but embraced. Montaigne's thought proves to be skeptical in that he distrusts abstract knowledge in all fields, but it is comic in that he finds in his close attention to the realities of human existence a wisdom that allows him to live and even flourish. Cavell, interestingly, allows in his reading of *Othello* for the kind of skepticism that I am outlining here. He suggests that the "moral" of the play may be found in Montaigne, that "all these topics...are not tragic unless one makes them so; that we are tragic in what we take to be tragic; that one must take one's imperfections with a 'gay and sociable wisdom'" (139), referring to Montaigne's essays "On Some Lines of Virgil" and "On Experience" in this brief account of the tragedy's "moral."[25]

Before finally turning to Shakespeare, I would like first to return for a final reflection on Cavell's reading of skepticism and Shakespeare's plays. I have made the case that Cavell's skepticism diverges from the skepticism that has its roots in the ancient world and that flourished in early modern Europe. And yet there is an important aspect of Cavell's approach to skepticism that matches that of Montaigne and other early modern thinkers; for Cavell, the primary interest in skepticism is ethical. Or, rather, for

---

[25] In the Introduction to *Disowning Knowledge*, Cavell makes it clear, however, that the skepticism that interests him is not of the Montaignian variety: "However strong the presence of Montaigne and Montaigne's skepticism in various of Shakespeare's plays, the skeptical problematic I have in mind is given its philosophical refinement in Descartes's way of raising the questions of God's existence and of the immortality of the soul" (p. 3).

Cavell, the skeptic's problem is that he becomes obsessed with knowing to such an extent that when that obsession cannot be placated (as inevitably it cannot), the skeptic is brought up against his limitations in a fashion that he finds unendurable and so remakes his world by destroying those things (or persons) that elude his grasp. An epistemological dilemma results in ethical atrocity. What Cavell (and, Cavell argues, Shakespeare) wants us to do is to get past "knowing" in this absolute sense and accept the finite knowledge available to us. As Gerald Bruns describes Cavell's position, the claims of the world, or of love, force us "out of the mode of knowing into that of answering." And this is why, for all of its philosophical sophistication, Cavell's literary criticism seems old fashioned in its attention to Shakespeare's characters and what ethical lessons we can learn from them.[26] Cavell focuses on tragedy, where Othello, Lear, and others reject their human limitations with disastrous results. When we turn to comedy, however, we find characters similarly confronted with their own limitations, but their "answering" has a different end.

2 Skepticism, Comedy, and Shakespeare

William Hamlin, in his study of the place of philosophical skepticism in Elizabethan England, argues that skepticism takes diverse forms during the period; while we may not see much "pure" Pyrrhonism, we do find that skepticism exerts a broad influence across a wide range of writings. Hamlin thus acknowledges Paul Kocher's conclusion in his classic study, *Science and Religion in Elizabethan England*, that "only in a relatively small but illustrious group of lay intellectuals did classical skepticism have real force,"[27] but he nevertheless concludes that "skepticism in a less narrowly defined sense had far-reaching consequences during the period."[28]

---

[26] See Bruns, "Stanley Cavell's Shakespeare," pp. 617–19. Cavell most clearly lays out his case for attending to or confronting the characters of Shakespearean tragedy in the second half of his essay on *King Lear*. "The Avoidance of Love: A Reading of *King Lear*," in *Disowning Knowledge*, pp. 81–123.

[27] Paul Kocher, *Science and Religion in Elizabethan England* (San Marino, CA: Huntington Library, 1953), pp. 50–54.

[28] *Tragedy and Skepticism*, p. 70. Hamlin provides a careful and illuminating discussion of the evidence for skepticism in England during Shakespeare's day in Part One of this same study, "The Reception of Ancient Skepticism in Elizabethan and Jacobean England," pp. 15–115.

Similarly, we can assume a broad acquaintance with Montaigne's writings in Elizabethan England, even though the best early modern translation of the *Essays* into English—John Florio's—was not published until 1603, the year of Elizabeth's death. There were other English translations of the *Essays*, and evidence also suggests that Florio's translation circulated in manuscript form prior to its publication. It is likely that Shakespeare would have had access to this translation in manuscript, especially since both Florio and Shakespeare were part of the circle surrounding the Earl of Southampton.[29] Many, including perhaps Shakespeare, would have read Montaigne's *Essays* in French.[30] Whatever Shakespeare's precise knowledge of Montaigne's writings, it is fair to assume that skeptical thoughts and problems were "in the air," and that they drew Shakespeare's interest, not only later when he explores them through his tragedies, but also in his earlier plays, especially the comedies.

One problem in considering skepticism's influence on comedy is that we all too often think of comedy as too far removed from "reality" to be deserving of serious philosophical investigation. In his classic study of Shakespearean comedy and romance, Northrop Frye argued for the possibility of dividing all literary scholars into *Iliad* critics—interested in "tragedy, realism, and irony"—and *Odyssey* critics, who gravitate toward comedy and romance. And it is in comedy, he writes, that "the story seeks its own end instead of holding the mirror up to nature. Consequently comedy and romance are so obviously conventionalized that a serious

---

[29] See *Tragedy and Scepticism*, p. 60, as well as Hamlin's "What Did Montaigne's Skepticism Mean to Shakespeare and His Contemporaries?" and, most recently, his *Montaigne's English Journey: Reading "The Essays" in Shakespeare's Day* (Oxford: Oxford University Press, 2013). James Shapiro also argues that Shakespeare would have known Montaigne in some form as early as the composition of *Hamlet*, which Shapiro dates to the end of 1599. See *A Year in the Life of William Shakespeare: 1599* (New York: HarperCollins, 2005), pp. 292–302. For a brief history of studies of Montaigne and Shakespeare, see Warren Boutcher, "The Cultural Transmission of Montaigne's *Essais* in Shakespeare's England," in *Shakespeare et Montaigne: vers un nouvel humanisme*, ed. Pierre Kapitaniak and Jean-Marie Maguin (Paris: Société Française Shakespeare, 2003), pp. 13–27, especially pp. 13–17.

[30] Travis D. Williams makes the case for Shakespeare drawing on the French text of the *Essays* while composing the famous "to be or not to be" soliloquy in *Hamlet*, as it proves to be the only way to account for Shakespeare's use of the word "bourn" at 3.1.78–79. See "The *Bourn* Identity: *Hamlet* and the French of Montaigne's *Essais*," *Notes and Queries* 58, no. 2 (2011): 254–58.

interest in them soon leads to an interest in convention itself."[31] Tragedy, in other words, has a philosophical seriousness, so that in holding up a mirror to nature it engages us in questions about the world; comedy simply shows us the way to escape the world into an aestheticized realm of convention. In the words of one critic, "comedy suspends the moral law in order to substitute another, a purely aesthetic one."[32] Similarly, Hamlin argues that tragedy is the proper dramatic genre to explore when looking for skeptical influence, because "in tragedy…scepticism finds a particularly congenial environment, since questions of perception, knowledge, rashness and judgement already figure importantly in the genre."[33] Yet it does not take much deliberation to realize that these very questions are also central to *Twelfth Night*, as well as to many other Shakespearean comedies and romances. Nevertheless, critics typically resist this parallel between comedy and tragedy, because, in Graham Bradshaw's words, in comedy we find "no corresponding sense that momentous metaphysical issues are being engaged."[34] In this essay, I assume the reverse, that comedy often does engage questions of philosophical weight. There is not sufficient space here to justify this assumption through argument; the reader will therefore need to decide if the results bear out that assumption.

Many recent productions of *Twelfth Night* manifest this bias toward comedy as escapist entertainment, emphasizing the play's humor while glancing over the ways in which Shakespeare uses comic episodes of mistaken identity and faulty perception to explore issues that are at the heart of skepticism.[35] For example, in the fourth act, when Feste mistakes Sebastian for Cesario, Shakespeare has Feste explicitly raise questions of knowledge and perception by exclaiming to Sebastian, "Nothing that is so, is so" (4.1.7). The ubiquity of perceptual error within the play creates an ideal situation for the exploration, in a comic vein, of the abilities of the characters to come to a knowledge of the truth through their own facul-

---

[31] Frye lays out this dichotomy in the first chapter of *A Natural Perspective: The Development of Shakespearean Comedy and Romance* (New York: Columbia University Press, 1965), especially pp. 1–8.

[32] Catherine Bates, "Love and Courtship," in *The Cambridge Companion to Shakespearean Comedy*, ed. Alexander Leggatt (Cambridge: Cambridge University Press, 2002), p. 109.

[33] *Tragedy and Scepticism in Renaissance England*, p. 2.

[34] *Shakespeare's Scepticism*, p. 21.

[35] To take one prominent example, in his 1996 film of the play, Trevor Nunn frequently edits out passages that most intriguingly engage questions of meaning and language.

ties. Indeed, the question of mistaken identity as applied to *twins* proves to be particularly interesting within the skeptical tradition. Both Academic and Pyrrhonist skeptics criticized the confidence of Stoic thinkers in the reliability of sense perception, observing that even a distinct sense impression may be mistaken; a careful observer may mistake one object for another that is so similar to it as to be virtually indistinguishable. Twins provided skeptics with a readily available example of this phenomenon and hence as a proof of the unreliability of perception.[36] Similarly, the characters within the play are repeatedly placed in a situation where they mistake one thing (a person or, in Malvolio's case, a particular person's distinctive handwriting) for another, underlining the difficulty that the characters have in perceiving things accurately. As an audience or a group of readers, we are placed in a different situation, given additional information that allows us to know that the character in front of us is Sebastian rather than Viola dressed as Cesario, say, or that the letter Malvolio reads was actually penned by Maria rather than Olivia. This privileged epistemological position enables us to witness the fallibility of each character.

These epistemological issues of discernment are foregrounded within the play, but these epistemological dilemmas invariably lead to questions demanding ethical reflection: how, that is, should we live in a world devoid of certainty? This question, as I have suggested, proves to be central to the ancient and early modern traditions of philosophical skepticism. As we have seen, in both ancient and early modern skepticism, epistemology and ethics are intertwined. In considering how and what we know, we invariably confront the question of how to act. This brief analysis of *Twelfth Night* will therefore focus on particular characters, looking for the ways in which their (in)ability to understand the truth leads them to act; how, in other words, they turn "from the mode of knowing to that of answering."

Comedy, of course, is the genre of happy ends, but a distinctive feature of Shakespearean comedy is that some characters are invariably left out of the concluding reconciliation or "atonement" (and in later comedies, such as *All's Well That Ends Well* and *Measure for Measure*, even that final rec-

---

[36] For the Academic tradition, see Cicero, *On Academic Scepticism*, 2.83–88, as well as Brittain's discussion of the issue in his Introduction on pp. xix–xxiii. For the Pyrrhonist tradition, see Sextus Empiricus, *Against the Logicians*, trans. R. G. Bury (Cambridge, MA: Harvard University Press, 1935), pp. 218–21 (1.409–11).

onciliation is brought into question). This is true of *Twelfth Night*; at the play's conclusion, Olivia is betrothed to Sebastian, Viola is paired with Orsino, and even Toby and Maria end up married. Malvolio, however, is left out of the play's happy resolution of previous mistakes and divisions, and he exits the stage vowing revenge. And yet, as Malvolio's anti-festive personality works against the comic spirit, this denouement is to be expected. A. D. Nuttall argues that he "has no business to be wandering about in a happy comedy."[37] Malvolio's anti-festive personality seems nearly to demand a comic retribution. When he criticizes Feste's fooling and rebukes Sir Toby's "uncivil rule," we fully expect him to be shown up and humiliated. Nevertheless, Malvolio's anti-festive nature manifests itself not only through anti-comic scolding, but also in a false confidence in his own worth, especially in his own intellectual abilities. Shakespeare uses the comic situations that arise as a result to provoke reflection on the issues raised by skepticism. Malvolio's methods and personality, that is, should cause us to reflect on the difficulty—and the perils—of (mis)perceiving the truth, and so he is actually key not only to the working out of the comic plot but also to the exploration of the philosophical issues that Shakespeare implicitly raises in the course of the play.

Maria famously describes Malvolio as "a kind of puritan" (2.3.129), and many scholars have argued that his character corresponds to stereotypes of Puritanism.[38] When Olivia diagnoses him as "sick of self love," and who therefore "taste[s] with a distempered appetite" (1.5.82–83), she attributes to Malvolio a vice that he shares with Puritans and other schismatics, at least as defined by their critics. Another trait that Malvolio shares with the Puritans (again, as portrayed in anti-Puritan literature) is his penchant for engaging in tortured exegesis in order to make writings correspond to

---

[37] A. D. Nuttall, *Shakespeare the Thinker* (New Haven: Yale University Press, 2007), p. 241.

[38] C. L. Barber, for example, argues that Malvolio "is not hostile to holiday because he is Puritan; he is like a Puritan because he is hostile to holiday." See *Shakespeare's Festive Comedy: A Study of Dramatic Form and Its Relation to Social Custom* (1959; repr., Princeton: Princeton University Press, 2012), p. 291. The most extensive case for Malvolio as a portrait of the stereotypical Puritan is in J. L. Simmons, "A Source for Shakespeare's Malvolio: The Elizabethan Controversy with the Puritans," *Huntington Library Quarterly* 36 (1972–73): 181–201. For a more balanced attempt at defining Puritanism, see Diarmaid MacCulloch, *The Later Reformation in England*, 2nd ed. (Basingstoke: Palgrave, 2001), pp. 69–78. See also Maurice Hunt, "Malvolio, Viola, and the Question of Instrumentality: Defining Providence in *Twelfth Night*," *Studies in Philology* 90 (1993): 277–97.

his beliefs, as well as his corresponding certainty that his interpretive gymnastics uncover hidden truth. Puritans, that is, were criticized not only for thinking themselves purer or more righteous than their conformist peers, but also for believing that they had privileged access to the truth; they were, to put it briefly, thought to be dogmatists. Malvolio similarly reveals himself as a dogmatist when he claims certainty in his interpretation of the "hidden" meaning of the letter that Maria has forged to trick him. When he first notes the addressee, "M.O.A.I.," he exclaims, "If I could make that resemble something in me" (2.5.107–08). The ordering of the letters, however, does not quite match his name as he thinks it should, "and yet," he declares, "to crush this a little, it would bow to me, for every one of these letters are in my name" (2.5.123–24).[39] His language ("make" and "crush") reveals that in his mind, his own interpretive acumen uncovers the truth. As he works through the letter, his certainty increases; the letter is "open," and he claims, "I do not now fool myself to let imagination jade me, for every reason excites to this—that my lady loves me" (2.5.140–44). When he comes to Olivia cross-gartered and in yellow stockings, he similarly concludes from Olivia's confused behavior that "everything adheres together, that no dram of a scruple, no scruple of a scruple, no obstacle, no incredulous or unsafe circumstance—what can be said? Nothing that can be can come between me and the full prospect of my hopes" (3.4.72–76).

It is true enough that the letter is "open," since Maria has specifically composed it to trick him. And yet, Malvolio is far too confident of his ability to discover the truth without impediment, quickly concluding that the letter must be from Olivia: "By my life, this is my lady's hand" (2.5.77–78). But as the audience knows, he has in fact mistaken one object for another very much like it (Maria claims to be able to "write very like my lady" [2.3.147]). Similarly, he mistakes Olivia's distracted actions as confirmation of the letter, whereas we in the audience perceive them to be the result of his strange and seemingly unmotivated actions, which are out of character. As suggested above, Malvolio's mistaking Maria's hand for Olivia's could in fact be taken as a skeptical proof of the unreliability of

---

[39] Many theories have been proposed regarding the meaning of the puzzle "M.O.A.I" that Malvolio wrestles with. For a review of these theories, see Peter J. Smith, "M.O.A.I 'What should that alphabetical position portend?' An Answer to the Metamorphic Malvolio," *Renaissance Quarterly* 51 (1998): 1199–224.

human judgments—when two seemingly identical objects are brought before someone and they cannot be distinguished, we must conclude that sense impressions are unreliable.

Maria's ruse and Malvolio's inability to see through it (largely because of his false confidence in his own interpretive abilities) predictably turn to his humiliation, thwarting his own comic desires to fulfill those of Maria, Toby, and their fellow conspirators. In the play's final scene, Malvolio, having been humiliated and imprisoned in a dark room, is at last brought before Olivia, and he again asserts his certainty concerning the meaning of Maria's letter, now blaming Olivia for tricking him for some unknown purpose. He accuses Olivia, doubting her character rather than his own understanding of the evidence before him: "You must not now deny it is your hand. / Write from it if you can, in hand or phrase, / Or say 'tis not your seal, not your invention. / You can say none of this" (5.1.319–22). Olivia responds by showing that Malvolio in fact has mistaken one thing for another: "Alas, Malvolio, this is not my writing, / Though I confess much like the character. / But out of question, 'tis Maria's hand" (5.1.333–35). When the truth of the prank comes to light, Olivia expresses pity for him, emphasizing how mistaken he has been: "Alas, poor fool, how have they baffled thee!" (5.1.357). Earlier in the play, Malvolio had criticized Feste for his fooling, and when Feste reminds him of his taunting words, Malvolio exits, vowing revenge. And at this moment, we may be reminded of Cavell's skeptic—Malvolio, in his own way like Othello or Lear, seeks to revenge himself on those that force him to a realization of his own finite, limited self. But while Cavell sees Othello's actions as the fruit of skepticism, I would argue that Malvolio comes to an unhappy end because he *refuses* the lessons of comic skepticism we find in Montaigne.

The twins Viola and Sebastian provide more positive examples of how the lessons of skepticism can lead to successfully navigating the obstacles of an uncertain world. In contrast with Malvolio, Viola consistently avoids trying to control the events in which she is caught up, instead suspending judgment and exercising the kind of patience that Montaigne recommends. An apt illustration is found in Viola's soliloquy in the second act, where she rehearses the "tangled knot" that her "disguise" has wrought, since she has just been able to deduce that an unsuspecting Olivia has fallen in love with her in her disguise as "Cesario." Recognizing her own, equally confused state, since she loves Orsino, she concludes by disclaiming her ability to sort things out: "O time, thou must untangle this, not I. / It is too hard a knot for me t'untie" (2.2.39–40). Later, at the end of the third act, when Antonio, mistaking Viola for her twin brother, comes to her rescue, she wonders if Antonio has in fact seen her brother in her disguise, which could easily arise, since she dresses herself according to her brother's fashion ("for him I imitate"). The resemblance between the twins is so great that she claims to see Sebastian when she encounters her own reflection: "I my brother know / Yet living in my glass" (3.4.346–47). Viola recognizes that Antonio's mistake makes her brother's survival probable, and yet she does not express certainty, only expressing a wish: "Prove true, imagination, O, prove true" (3.4.342). And even when Sebastian and Viola are brought face to face, Viola refuses to jump from probability to certainty and encourages Sebastian to do the same, instructing him, "Do not embrace me till each circumstance / Of place, time, fortune do cohere and jump / That I am Viola" (5.1.241–43).

Viola's twin, Sebastian, acts in a similar fashion. Even more than Viola, he encounters situations that defy logic and expectation. But while Viola can suspend judgment for a time, Sebastian is frequently constrained to act, to answer the world that he encounters without fully understanding it. When Sir Andrew Aguecheek attacks him, he must defend himself. When he finds himself the object of the beautiful and wealthy Olivia's attentions, he initially attempts to forestall a decision, comparing his position to a dream state. "What relish is in this? How runs the stream? / Or I am mad, or else this is a dream. / Let fancy still my sense in Lethe steep. / If it be thus to dream, still let me sleep" (4.1.55–58). The question of whether one was awake or dreaming was a standard question for skeptical thinkers; Cicero, Sextus Empiricus, and Montaigne all explore the differences between a dreaming or sleeping state and a waking state, arguing that it is often more difficult to determine which state is real than we might initially expect. Even Descartes famously considers this question at length in his First Meditation.[40]

This skeptical frame becomes important again when, a few scenes later, in one of the longest soliloquies in the play, Sebastian muses on the unprecedented situation in which he finds himself, and again wonders if

---

[40] Sextus Empiricus discusses this issue in the fourth mode of ten modes of suspension of judgment at *PH* I, xiv, 104–13; Cicero considers it in *On Academic Scepticism*, 2.88–90; Montaigne considers the question in the "Apology" (see p. 674 in the Screech translation). Richard Strier notes that something very similar happens in *Comedy of Errors* (2.2.183–84), when Antipholus of Syracuse wonders if he married Adriana in his sleep. See "Shakespeare and the Skeptics," p. 172.

what he perceives to be real can possibly be so. Sebastian's reflection on what he may or may not know, what seems real but also unreal, is worth quoting at some length. He begins by rehearsing to himself things that seem beyond dispute:

> This is the air, that is the glorious sun.
> This pearl she gave me, I do feel't and see't,
> And though 'tis wonder that enwraps me thus,
> Yet 'tis not madness. Where's Antonio then?
> His counsel now might do me golden service
> For, though my soul disputes well with my sense
> That this may be some error but no madness,
> Yet doth this accident and flood of fortune
> So far exceed all instance, all discourse,
> That I am ready to distrust mine eyes
> And wrangle with my reason that persuades me
> To any other trust but that I am mad –
> Or else the lady's mad. Yet if 'twere so,
> She could not sway her house, command her followers,
> Take and give back affairs and their dispatch
> With such a smooth, discreet, and stable bearing
> As I perceive she does. There's something in't
> That is deceivable. (4.3.1–21)

Sebastian tries to account for his experience in different ways, reviewing to himself his own, distinct sense impressions, the unaccountable behavior of Olivia toward himself, and yet her rational government of her household. He is unable to come to a definite conclusion, saying only that something "is deceivable" (or deceptive). For skeptics, of course, Sebastian's concluding statement is true of all sense experience, indeed, of all experience. We cannot know if what we perceive is true or real. So here, it seems, is an ideal case for the suspension of judgment that classic Pyrrhonism recommends—if Sebastian were a thoroughgoing Pyrrhonist, he would refuse to commit himself since all he can do is suspend judgment.

Sebastian, however, does not have this luxury; when Olivia returns and asks him to come to her chapel and betroth himself to her, he must decide how to act, deciding to trust his nascent feelings and accept her offer: "I'll follow this good man and go with you / And, having sworn truth, ever will be true" (4.3.32–33). In considering this quick decision, one might agree with the Princess of France from *Love's Labour's Lost* that this is "A time…too short / To make a world-without-end bargain in" (5.2.774–75). There is a precedent, however, in the Academic skeptical tradition, where a skeptic "may accept a plausible or persuasive impression as a basis for decision or action, for example, as an informed guess, without actually being convinced of its truth," as Gisela Striker phrases it.[41] Sebastian makes a decision and agrees with Olivia when she confronts him with a claim of love, but he remains uncertain of the truth of the situation and acknowledges the possibility that he may be deceived. We may also find a precedent for Sebastian's willingness to accept his unprecedented situation in Montaigne, who frequently argues that we must not believe only that which is familiar to us and so automatically discredit things that are unfamiliar. Our certainty that we already know the truth actually inhibits our ability to find it. He thus criticizes in "On Experience" the "distressing and combative arrogance which has complete faith and trust in itself: it is a mortal enemy of finding out the truth" (1220). Sebastian's willingness to trust the appearance of things that are happening to him, even though there is something "deceivable" in them, helps lead him to his happily comic end. His patient acceptance of what he perceives seems to echo Montaigne's counsel in "On Experience" to trust patience and nature to work things out. When at the end of the play, Olivia realizes that she has betrothed herself to the twin brother of the (wo)man she fell in love with, Sebastian consoles her with the thought that it was the work of nature: "But nature to her bias drew in that" (5.1.250).[42]

Twelfth Night gives us in many ways a typical comic plot, with mistaken assumptions, discoveries of hidden identities, and the restoration of long-lost siblings to one another. But the way that Shakespeare goes about working out the plot's complications forces us to consider how the characters, and hence we, should respond to the uncertainties and ambiguities of earthly existence. The question becomes not how we can obtain knowledge, but, as it was for Montaigne, how we should live, given that we cannot attain certainty. I began this essay with a consideration of Stanley Cavell's notion of skepticism, which, for him, is tragic at its very core

---

[41] "Academics versus Pyrrhonists, reconsidered," pp. 200–01. She bases her account on a book by the Academic Clitomachus, which Cicero cites at *On Academic Scepticism*, 2.104.

[42] Of course, there are complex implications here about gender identity and sexuality that I do not have space to explore.

because it contains a yearning for an infinite or absolute knowledge that is unobtainable. For Cavell, modern skepticism is about a displaced understanding of what it means to be human, deriving from Descartes's defining humanity in one's ability to *know*, and to know with certainty. For him (and his Shakespeare), the "moral" is to get past skepticism. For Montaigne, however, being human is to *live*, and to live in accordance with the finite human condition. Montaigne (and, perhaps, Montaigne's Shakespeare) would probably argue that the answer is not to reject skepticism but to learn its lessons—that we are embodied, finite creatures, and so we can abandon our demand for certainty and learn to trust in patience, time, nature, and our own experience.

CHAPTER 6

Must We Mean What We Sing?—*Così Fan Tutte* and the Lease of Voice

Ci vuol filosofia—Don Alfonso

Ian Ground

Stanley Cavell writes about opera as a medium in which the sceptical threat to the meaning of what we say is pacified, though fitfully, by music. Curiously, despite passing references to *Don Giovanni* and *Le nozze di Figaro*, the third of the Mozart/Da Ponte collaborations—*Così fan tutte: La scuola degli amanti*—escapes his direct attention. Yet, as I wish to suggest here, there are reasons for thinking that in this operatic triptych, and just perhaps amongst all operas, it is *Così* which offers the most sustained exploration of Cavellian themes of scepticism and sincerity, alienation and acknowledgment. First, in its deployment of congruities and incongruities in voice, action and music in pursuit of its ethical and philosophical purpose, it is a work that is at once free from comfortable certainties and yet in thrall to an ideal of such certainties, echoing that very condition of human beings under modernity which Cavell's writing explores. Second, the opera explicitly features a philosopher in such active pursuit of a project to epistemologize human relationships so as to seem the very model of

I. Ground (✉)
University of Hertfordshire, Hatfield, UK

© The Author(s) 2018
G. L. Hagberg (ed.), *Stanley Cavell on Aesthetic Understanding*, Philosophers in Depth,
https://doi.org/10.1007/978-3-319-97466-8_6

the target of Cavellian critique. Finally, the work has attracted direct philosophical exploration and critique not just by musicologists and cultural historians but directly by philosophers[1] which gives resonance to a Cavellian re-reading of the opera. For these reasons and others, I argue that *Così fan tutte* is the most Cavellian of operas and a fitting arena in which to explore Cavell's central themes[2] and his related reflections on music, meaning and voice.[3]

If any claim is uncontroversially central to Cavell writings, and uniting of earlier and later work, it is that the philosophical problems of scepticism are not technical puzzles in epistemology. In particular, the problems of sceptical doubt about our knowledge of each other cannot be solved with classical resources such as the argument from analogy or indeed more recent theoretical innovations such as Theory of Mind.[4] Such "solutions" are merely further twists in the expression of the problems. Nor can the sceptical problems be dissolved, in line with some readings of Wittgenstein, as if the problem of other minds were a mere conceptual *faux pas*. Rather, for Cavell, philosophical scepticism about our knowledge of others is a shadow thrown by the shape and structures, fissures and fractures of our actual relations with one another and their attendant anxieties and agonies, responsibilities and commitments. Seen in this light, the Wittgensteinian concept of a psychological criterion, say for someone's being in pain (but also and relevantly here for being in love), is not, or at least not merely, a defeasible "standard by which to judge".[5] In Cavell, the Wittgensteinian concept of a psychological criterion acquires ethical force.

---

[1] Inter alia Cohen, *Die Dramatische Idee in Mozarts Operntexten*. Kivy, *Osmin's Rage*. Žižek and Dolar, *Opera's Second Death*. Williams, *On Opera*, chap. 5. The closest to Cavellian themes and an inspiration for this essay, though with no reference to Cavell, is Burnham, 'Mozart's felix Culpa'.

[2] Largely, Cavell, *The Claim of Reason: Wittgenstein, Skepticism, Morality, and Tragedy*. and Cavell, *Must We Mean What We Say?*

[3] Largely, Cavell, *A Pitch of Philosophy*. Cavell, 'Opera in (and as) Film" (2005)'.

[4] Leudar and Costall, *Against Theory of Mind*.

[5] "A standard by which to judge something; a feature of a thing by which it can be judged to be thus and so. In the writings of the later Wittgenstein it is used as a quasi-technical term. Typically, something counts as a criterion for another thing if it is necessarily good evidence for it. Unlike inductive evidence, criterial support is determined by convention and is partly constitutive of the meaning of the expression for whose application it is a criterion. Unlike entailment, criterial support is characteristically defeasible. Wittgenstein argued that behavioural expressions of the 'inner', e.g. groaning or crying out in pain, are neither inductive evidence for the mental (Cartesianism), nor do they entail the instantiation of the relevant

Our use of psychological criteria in our ordinary encounters with one another should be understood not as psycho-existential judgments but, via their role in the identification of the psychological, as expressions of our willingness, reluctance or failure to recognise the reality of the other through their claims upon us. The paradigmatic Cavellian claim is then that our relations with one another are both founded and flounder not on knowledge but on acknowledgment. Our going on being intelligible one to one another is guaranteed by neither evidential facts nor consoling theory but is a continuing ethical struggle and responsibility. Because scepticism about our knowledge of others is a shadow thrown by our condition, it is possible to reveal more about by what, in the human condition, casts that shadow by tracing its changing outline as it falls and moves over different surfaces and solids. This is one way to understand the rationale for Cavell's explorations in drama, literature, film and, our topic here, opera.

Cavell sees the development of opera as the attempt to rescue us from the threat of scepticism—about our relation to each other, language and the world—that marks, for him, the beginning of modernity. It needs to be said here that, at moments of juncture in his reflections, Cavell's treatments of opera are in the service of a larger quasi-historical thesis, articulating a competitive relation with a his more central passion, that of film. This larger thesis is that "what happened to opera as an institution is that it transformed itself into film, that film is, or was, our opera"[6] a thesis which sets the scene, though it does not assemble the cast, for Cavell's treatment of film, especially, of course, the comedies of remarriage.

But what concerns us here are the claims about opera itself. For what precedes this connection with film is the claim that music, in opera, embodies "the flame that preserves the human need [...] for conviction in its expressions of passion".[7] The thought here appears to be that opera, in its unique capacity to unite voice and drama in music, is the attempt to defeat or overcome the vicissitudes to which agency and speech are subject—or felt to be so—under the condition of modernity. This theme, with typically Cavellian inflections, is explored through discussions of or observations upon *Carmen, Der Rosenkavalier, Orfeo, Le nozze di Figaro,*

---

mental term (behaviourism), but are defeasible criteria for its application." P.M.S. Hacker in Honderich, *The Oxford Companion to Philosophy.*

[6] Cavell, *A Pitch of Philosophy*, p. 136.
[7] Ibid., p. 307.

Die Zauberflöte, Fidelio, Il Trovatore, La Traviata, Aida, Der Ring des Nibelungen and *Péleas and Mélisande* with, as we will see, particular emphasis on the struggles to hear or refuse to hear the voices of women.

As elsewhere in his writing, Cavell's claims about opera as such are more in the nature of moral claims on the reader and, even then, scattered and discursive, rather than determinate philosophical theses. Still, drawing from his treatment of individual operas, it seems possible to identify the following Cavellian contentions about opera as a medium. The first and perhaps most uncontroversial is that the very fact of seeing real or imagined human beings and their lives on the stage, as we might say, under the aspect of music, is transfiguring.

> I am counting here on an intuition of opera which… I imagine as widely shared…the intervention or supervening of music into the world as revelatory of a realm of significance that either transcends our ordinary realm of experience or reveals ours under transfiguration.[8]

It would indeed be hard to imagine a follower of opera lacking in this intuition. One may be far short of signing up to the Wagnerian ideal of *Gesamtkunstwerk*, and yet agree and, more importantly, *feel* at every performance, that opera is not and cannot be a matter of merely setting human drama to music. But as Cavell unpacks it, this intuition is twofold. The first thought, that the way in which music intervenes in the world is "revelatory of a realm of significance that…transcends our ordinary realm of experience" is, paradoxically perhaps, the more prosaic of the two. For it may be thought a commonplace that music gives a universal significance, or the sense of such, to the particular thoughts or feelings or acts occurring in the drama. One wants to say of that thought: well, yes, but almost *any* kind of artistic treatment of a particular human action will do *that*. For it belongs to the nature of regarding something as art, that otherwise ordinary acts or thoughts or speech are given a weight which, as actually occurring particulars, they would lack. Thus Wittgenstein:

> But only the artist can represent the individual thing so that it appears to us as a work of art. …The work of art compels us—one might say—to see it in the right perspective, whereas without art the object is a piece of nature like any other.[9]

---

[8] Ibid., p. 141.

[9] Wittgenstein, *Wiener Ausgabe Studien Texte: Band 1: Philosophische Bemerkungen*, pp. 17–18. Translation by Richard T. Eldridge (kindly offered in correspondence).

So, even if we concede that opera is peculiarly powerful in its capacity to give this significance to the particular, it still does so in virtue of being art, not in virtue of being opera. Moreover, it is possible to think of that transcending and enlarging as a weakness of opera or, at least, of opera in a certain stage of its history. That it tends always towards grandeur and thus risks grandiosity. The opposing intuition to that rightly identified by Cavell is that, unlike the novel or poetry, "the intervention or supervening of music" finds it hard to do what we most need to be done by art: to particularise or reveal the particular. Of course, this question of whether we aestheticise in order to generalise or particularise is a matter of philosophical contention. (It is also, and perhaps more importantly, a matter of taste.)

The question mark over the particularising power of opera is the target of the second half of Cavell's claim and surely the more interesting: that we feel, in our experience of opera, that music *reveals* the ordinary "under transfiguration". For this is the thought, or suggests the thought, that it is a condition of the possibility of opera that we be able to see human character and agency *through* and not merely *alongside* the music. That, to take the simplest possible cases, we experience a change in rhythm, perhaps placing a word on an offbeat, or else a change of key, perhaps to one from a connecting context, to be not an appropriate accompaniment, nor a mere drawing of attention—not, as it were, musically ostensive—but to be that very thought or feeling *revealed*. Of course, we can recognise that in many operas and more often in certain of its periods, music is also used as a commentary on the action, sometimes condoning, but more often ironically undercutting, disapproving or distancing (the most obvious and here pertinent examples are Mozart's use of hunting horns to signal a cuckolding unknown to the agents[10] or his use of woodwind to offer the indulgent and wry chuckles gently urging the moral indulgence of a character by the audience). But if opera consisted of nothing but a musical commentary upon drama, it would surely have never lasted as an independent art form, remaining merely a species of musical theatre. (Cavell claims that the role of opera was usurped by that of film but not, surely, in respect of the replacement of the operatic score by the film score.) It is tempting to say here, perhaps out of a commitment to a general claim about aesthetic form

---

[10] Including the horns in the recapitulation in Fiordiligi's second-act aria, *Per pietà* (No. 25 Rondo) which, even as we, the audience, are moved by the beauty of this piece, seem gently to mock us as much as they do Fiordiligi.

and content, that, in opera, the dramatic content is cast in musical form. But in the case of opera, that would leave the music competing for our attention with the actual words or action. And that is precisely what is not wanted. It seems more apt to say that the transfigurative function of operatic music to the drama, when it is essentially operatic, and sounds out of and not merely alongside the nature of the medium, is akin to the transfigurative function of a metaphor. A metaphor is not logically separable from its object and succeeds not by introducing a second object but by jolting or seducing us into seeing the same object under a new aspect and thus newly particularised. And it is perhaps this—opera's capacity to let us experience human action and feeling under the aspect of music—that best glosses the Cavellian notion of revelation under transfiguration and which, for such is the larger implication, rescues or attempts to rescue human meaning from scepticism. In opera, human action under the aspect of music succeeds where, in actuality, action under the aspect of language fails.

But how, exactly, is music meant to achieve what, under the condition of scepticism, seems to be a miracle? It cannot do so by being another kind of language. For then it would be subject to just the same sceptical threat that haunts natural language. We make no progress by simply replacing words with notes. One must perhaps suppose something like this thought which is not unfamiliar from the history of philosophical thought about music and which might here be given a Cavellian inflection: in contradistinction to the arbitrary character of linguistic signs, music as organised sound offers non-arbitrary significance. It is non-arbitrary because it functions in a way akin to the functioning of the direct expression of psychological states and to which our natural responses are direct and unmediated. Wittgenstein famously asks (or protests) "For how can I go so far as to try to use language to get between pain and its expression?".[11] What must be resisted here is the parallel thought that in opera, music too plays a mediating role. Rather, music, paradigmatically so in opera, presents us with the first-person in all its unmediated directness. The psychological is *made manifest* in music.

Such a thought can survive the charge that since music, and especially art-music, is a historical and cultural phenomenon, it is replete with conventions just as elaborate as the grammar of a natural language. For how

---

[11] Wittgenstein, *Philosophical Investigations: The German Text, with a Revised English Translation 50th Anniversary Commemorative Edition*, sec. 245.

music came to work as it does is not in question here. Only how it works on us now. However it came about, we experience music as offering significant structure. Significant of what? That, notoriously, we cannot say. But not because there is a semantic content lying below or behind the music. Wittgenstein asks us to consider the ways in which understanding a sentence is akin to understanding a musical phrase.[12] But the point of that remark is not to steer us towards thinking of music as more akin than we think to our (mistaken) paradigm of language: as quasi- or proto-semantic and so, we falsely think, essentially representational. It is instead to make us change our paradigm of the role of language to be more like that of music. We start in a better philosophical place if we think of the music of language rather than the "language of music". For then, we can come to see that language too does manifest and does not merely describe the psychological (and that it can do so is a condition of the possibility of linguistic description of psychological states). But we can take this lesson from Wittgenstein's remark about understanding music and understanding language only if we first accept the thought that music makes manifest. That it does so in a way that invites or compels us to take up the "attitude towards a soul".[13] And this is the connection with Cavell. In making the psychological manifest for direct apprehension, the possibility of sceptical doubt is, at least temporarily, suspended. Though it does so by introducing another doubt: that even if the human body is the best picture of the human soul,[14] it is not the only one.

A second Cavellian claim about opera is one that ties his treatment of the medium to his more general perspective and, at the same time, more precisely locates the medium's distinctive capacity in a way that helps us to see what it might be that *Otello* can do that *Othello* cannot:

> Opera's issues can be seen to be a response to, hence a continual illumination of, the divisions of self, the suffocation of speech, and the withdrawal of the world that have preoccupied philosophy since the advent of skepticism in Descartes, which is to say, explicitly since the generation after the invention of opera and the construction of the works of Shakespeare.[15]

---

[12] Ibid., sec. 527.
[13] Ibid., p. 178.
[14] Ibid., pts. II, iv.
[15] Cavell, *A Pitch of Philosophy*, p. viii.

This, of course, is very familiar Cavellian territory. But it is at this point that Cavell brings to bear what must be essential to any account of opera—for even the idea of music as a metaphorical transfiguration of human agency might fail to distinguish opera from ballet—but most especially to a Cavellian account. What matters, of course, is that opera *is sung*. For Cavell, singing in opera comes about "as though some problem has arisen about speaking as such".[16] That is, the function of opera is to put *speech itself* under the aspect of music. This matters because philosophical scepticism, under Cavell, has traction on our lives first and foremost as it has traction on speech, on what we say and what we mean. Epistemological scepticism of the traditional kind affects only our (imagined) knowledge of others. It is, classically, supposed to leave *ourselves* untouched. We—conceived as a plural "I"—are still speaking (only never heard), still meaning (only never understood). The Cavellian inflection is to show how scepticism is really the corrosive worry that we cannot *mean* or can no longer have confidence in the idea that *we* mean. One way to reconstruct that anxiety is the thought: if I have no grounds for others, then I have no grounds for thinking of my language as anything other than a private language. But there cannot be a private language. But then I have no grounds for thinking that I mean when I say (or even for thinking *that* thought). My words turn to mud in my mouth. I am left with only the "inarticulate sound" of *Philosophical Investigations* S 261.

The implied promise of opera then is that through singing, speech is rendered under an aspect that will guarantee its meaningfulness. That the sung words will intrinsically contain the revelation of others which makes possible and sustains the meaning of just those words. In the grip of music, words succeed in making their first-person significance directly available where, at least while we are in thrall to the philosophical pictures[17] of mind and meaning underpinning scepticism, speech alone fails. Cavell's point here seems to be that singing is the realisation of a "signature"—a unique way of showing oneself in the world—as the sign of "abandonment" to one's words. The sung words *lease*—grant possession of—meaning. And they do so by giving words the aspect of, expressive behaviour that, in actuality, make ourselves manifest and function in our criterial psychological ascriptions. The promise of the medium is that, manifesting

---

[16] Ibid., p. 136.
[17] For a sensitive account, see Hagberg, *Wittgenstein and Autobiographical Consciousness*, pp. 95–97.

meaning under the aspect of music, opera saves speech from scepticism. The issue then is whether opera honours that promise to us because it does so to its own protagonists whether we can experience "singing as the thinking which confirms existence".[18]

Cavell's method then may be regarded as testing the proposed distinctive power of the medium to rescue from sceptical threat the particular protagonists in their particular dramas. It matters then that we do so when operas are most "attuned to…moments of separation" between protagonists and between the protagonists and their worlds:

> We should think of the voice in opera as a judgement on the world on the basis of, called forth from, pain beyond a concept.[19]

That is, we are to examine those moments in which the medium is testing *itself* against its own promise (which is, perhaps, a standing obligation perhaps for any artistic medium).

An important waypoint in Cavell's reflections here is the question of how opera asks us to conceive of the relation between the singer and the role. In theatre, Cavell claims, we typically regard the character as being played by one actor amongst other possible actors. The character is instantiated by the actor. By contrast, in film, he claims, we come to the actor first and see the current character as one amongst others that she could play. (We may note that in literature, such a split between the character and its instantiation would be nonsensical). What then of the singer in opera? The crucial move here is Cavell's claim that the relationship is "undecidable": that in the case of opera, no clear precedence can be given between performer and protagonist. Why? Because that question is, within the audience response, rendered "unimportant" besides the fact of the way in which the voice is "located in—one might say disembodied within—this figure, this double, this person, this singer, whose voice is essentially unaffected by the role" such that it appears to introduce, as a condition of the possibility of opera:

> A Cartesian intuition of the absolute metaphysical difference between mind and body together with the twin Cartesian intuition of an undefined intimacy between just this body and only this spirit…[20]

---

[18] Cavell, *A Pitch of Philosophy*, p. 153.
[19] Ibid., p. 149.
[20] Ibid., p. 138.

This has an implication to which we return. For now, we should note that Cavell's perception of this condition of the possibility of opera as a medium is put to moral use by him in explaining—without excusing but, to a degree, expiating—a feature so common in opera as seeming also to belong to the very character of the medium: its much-remarked misogyny. Opera as the dying of women to music[21] by "suicide, murder, asphyxiation, drowning, execution, consumption, leaping off a balcony or dying in an avalanche".[22] Cavell brings together operatic misogyny and the distinctive function of operatic singing in the defeat of scepticism in the following:

> …singing exposes [the female protagonist] as thinking, so exposes her to the power of those who do not want her to think, do not, that is to say, want autonomous proof of her existence.[23]

The task now is to test these thoughts about opera in the one operatic work, which for all its overt and hidden Cavellian themes, Cavell does not discuss: that "deep and unsettling masterpiece…[playing] disquietingly across the formalities of its structure",[24] *Così fan tutte*.

The plot of *Così fan tutte* is easily outlined.[25] Two young men—Ferrando and Guglielmo—enter into a wager with a philosopher, Don Alfonso, that their fiancés will stay faithful to them if put to a test. In a deception orchestrated by Don Alfonso, the sisters Fiordiligi and Dorabella are told that their lovers are off to war. Ferrando and Guglielmo return in disguise as Albanians and, in absurdly histrionic terms, confess their passion for the sisters. Don Alfonso enlists the sister's maidservant Despina to win the sisters over. Both sisters protest their fidelity but allow that innocent flirtation will do no harm. As, they claim, a mere diversion, Dorabella, Ferrando's betrothed, chooses Guglielmo while Fiordiligi, Guglielmo's betrothed, chooses Ferrando. Thus, the original relationships are transposed. But to the horror of Ferrando, Dorabella is won over by Guglielmo.

---

[21] Clement, *Opera, Or, The Undoing of Women*.
[22] Kettle, 'Why Do Women Die in Opera?'
[23] Cavell, *A Pitch of Philosophy*, p. 146.
[24] Williams, *On Opera*, p. 45.
[25] The reader unfamiliar with the opera is recommended the video recording of the 2006 production for Glyndebourne featuring Topi Lehtipuu, Anke Vondung, Miah Persson and Luca Pisaroni conducted by Iván Fischer: Hytner, *Mozart*.

Fiordiligi resists but eventually yields to Ferrando, and a marriage ceremony is planned with Despina disguised as a notary. As a drumroll is heard in the distance, announcing the supposed homecoming of Ferrando and Guglielmo, the "Albanians" hide only to return in their true guise. They reveal the deceit, and, ostensibly, the drama ends if not in forgiveness then in understanding and a moral drawn.

Such a plot has, of course, attracted charges of absurdity (not least from Beethoven and Wagner).[26] We must believe that the sisters do not recognise their lovers in flimsy disguise (or their maidservant in two different garbs). But, for the most part, a modern temperament regards it as itself foolish to so criticise the opera. We should no more protest the silliness of the disguise mechanics in *Così* than protest how implausible it is that Figaro is the lost son of Marcellina and Bartolo in *Le nozze*. Audiences, both then and now, have been quite able to grasp the necessity of the disguise conceit to do the ethical work the opera has in mind and would and do recognise it as a well-known trope. Such mechanics are perfectly familiar in *opera buffa* (and also *dramma giocoso* which arguably is a more accurate description of *Così*). Themes of identity and role, disguise and pretence are common to all the central Mozartian canon[27] and marked in the very titles of even very early pieces (*La finta semplice* and *La finta giardiniera*). It is true that in *Le nozze di Figaro* and *Don Giovanni* (though not *Die Zauberflöte*'s Papagena), disguise is often aided by night but that darkness is as much ethical as efficacious.

Žižek suggests that the concept of disguise is an integral part of the Enlightenment groping after materialism:

> A person can be reduced to the function denoted by his or her clothes, and their relations can be reduced to conditional reflexes provoked by those external marks. The disguise is the beginning of behaviorist psychology.[28]

But if so, these operas carry within them an implied critique of Enlightenment philosophy running in parallel to their critique of Enlightenment class politics. In the *Le nozze* garden scene, the plot, the

---

[26] In an implied critique of Da Ponte's libretto, Wagner laments "if only [Mozart] has met the Poet whom he only would have had to help" Wagner, *Opera and Drama*, p. 37.

[27] Barry, *The Philosopher's Stone*, p. 92.

[28] Žižek and Dolar, *Opera's Second Death*, n. 68.

comedy and its ethical wheels turn on the point that the lust-blinded Count cannot recognise his own wife, disguised as Susanna, whilst, also in the dark, Figaro recognises his beloved Susanna, disguised as the countess, via not her appearance but her voice ("io conobbi la voce che adoro"—"I knew the voice that I adore").[29] This climactic case of disguise is surrounded by counterpointing cases. The Countess's and Susanna's disguise of Cherubino as a young girl is steeped in the erotic potential of fluid gender identity. A narrative crux hangs on the identity of the person who jumped out the window and the desperate claim that people look bigger when they jump. And of course, Figaro himself is really Rafaello, disguised but without pretence. It seems absurd to maintain that a librettist and composer who had dealt with themes of disguise with such sophistication in 1786 should have become entirely naïf about the matter in 1790. It may be supposed that some modern audiences still smile indulgently at the artifice of *Così*, forgiving the supposed absurdity because of the beauty of the music. But the truth is that, in the context of the opera as a whole, the disguise mechanics in *Così* are not silly at all but the self-conscious use of a trope, known and known to be known, creating a framework able to simultaneously support both the comedic and the ethical ambitions of the opera.

The use of disguise as an ethical probe is traceable to the opera's origins. As historians of the opera have noted,[30] the plot of *Così* is a conflation of two stories: first, the myth of Cephalus and Procris[31] in which a suspicious husband seeks, disguised, to seduce his own wife, and second, the Wager motif from the ninth novella of the second day of Decameron. Da Ponte melded these plot structures to bring his libretto in line with symmetries familiar from the theatre of Marivaux and added in the idea of pairs of contrasting and then transposed personalities lifted, fairly shamelessly, from Casti and Salieri's *La Grotta di Trofonio*. Thus, in *Così*, two sisters face two brother officers. In each pair, one is, ostensibly, presented as more superficial (Dorabella and Guglielmo) and one more serious (Fiordiligi and Ferrando). Moreover, Don Alfonso and Despina present two kinds of cynicism about human motives, the former supposedly in pursuit of truth but arguably in pursuit of power and the other ostensibly in pursuit of pleasure

---

[29] No. 28: Finale.
[30] Steptoe, 'The Sources of "Così Fan Tutte"'.
[31] Gombrich, 'Così Fan Tutte (Procris Included)'.

but arguably in support of a genuine humanity. In other hands, these symmetries would threaten to overwhelm our sense of the protagonists as anything other than moral types, as much manipulated by the librettist as each other. But in *Così*, that response is itself subverted so that, in cruxes of the opera (*Terzettino Soave sia il vento* No. 10, *Aria Come scoglio* No. 14, *Duetto fra gli amplessi* No. 29), an appropriate audience response is to feel our own shame at having, prior to these points, regarded the sisters as puppets ourselves and failed, ourselves, to acknowledge their appalling treatment by the men and with that, their subjective reality.

As this suggests, absurdity is perhaps the least of the reproaches against the opera. The moral critique is more damning. Thus, the nineteenth century found *Così* "distasteful, unfunny, morally ugly and unworthy of Mozart"[32] noting a gulf between the purity and beauty of the music and the vulgar cruelties of the action. The nineteenth century's rejection of the opera as morally ugly is echoed in Kerman's account of the opera's finale as "in the last analysis...improbable and immoral"[33] and in more recent feminist critiques of the opera. Thus Zalman[34] expands on Ford[35] in charging that "the opera is indeed an unfortunately misogynistic portrait of Enlightenment-era society". But Zalman goes further than nineteenth-century critics by asking us to maintain our resistance to Da Ponte's "offensive libretto" with a refusal to allow ourselves to be manipulated by the beauty of Mozart's score. Citing Ford's detailed demonstration of how subtleties in rhythm and key modulation underpin the opera's portrayal of gender, Zalman claims that:

> ...despite its magnificence, Mozart's music makes problematic statements about gender ideologies just as frequently as Da Ponte's libretto—the two complement each other in this way more than is usually recognized or acknowledged.[36]

Thus, for Zalman, the beauty of the music is not in (problematic) contrast with the offensive action but is implicit in that cruelty. The audience in *Così* are in the same trap as the benighted Donna Anna, Donna Elvira and Zerlina are to the meretricious charm of Don Giovanni. Zalman considers the

---

[32] Hensher, 'School for Lovers'.
[33] Kerman, *Opera as Drama, New and Revised Edition*, p. 98.
[34] Zalman, 'Critical Perspectives'.
[35] Ford, *Così?*
[36] Zalman, 'Critical Perspectives'.

defence that *Così* is "a parody, but none of these claims seem convincing enough to excuse the misogynistic attitudes the opera promotes". Thus, Zalman and, to an extent, Ford take the opera to be a reflection of the patriarchy of its times and with a value, which is, one supposes, at best, documentary. Fortunately, certainly for opera houses, Zalman eschews any recommendation that Così be denied performance since it "presents us with an opportunity to confront these issues and bring them into discussion".

To an extent, this feminist critique is of a piece with Cavell's analysis of operas other than *Così*. Thus, at the centre of Cavell's treatment (citing Clement[37] as a "welcome debt") of particular operas are his reflections on the "countless ways in which men want and want not to hear the woman's voice; to know and not to know what she knows about men's desires"[38] But reading the opera in a Cavellian light also enables us to reject the choice that Zalman insists upon: that we should treat the opera either at its (offensive) face value or (implausibly) as parody. As if that binary choice exhausted our response. As if laying out that choice to the audience were not central to the opera's ethical intent. One, obviously contentious, difference between some feminist critiques and a Cavellian reading is this: Cavell offers a diagnosis of what has gone wrong with men as human beings such that they are structured to engage in practices of oppression, denial and avoidance. One form that inner distortion of men takes is "that philosophical self-torment whose shape is scepticism, in which the philosopher wants and wants not to exempt himself from the closet of privacy: wants and wants not to become intelligible, expressive, exposed". It is this *shared* philosophical problem of male and female under modernity that *male* psychological structures egregiously project outwards in a denial of the possibility of "autonomous proof of [women's] existence".[39] Is there a danger of aggrandising patriarchy here, of aestheticizing it? A thought that the male refusal to acknowledge the female voice cannot be a straightforward epistemic injustice but must be the result of tragic entrapment in philosophical depths? Perhaps. Certainly, whether Cavell himself, as a man, has lease of a voice to address such issues would be a matter that, had he treated of *Così*, he surely would have been obliged to remark. But one way to throw light on such rightly contentious matters is to examine in

---

[37] Clement, *Opera, Or, The Undoing of Women*.
[38] Cavell, *A Pitch of Philosophy*, p. 132.
[39] Ibid., p. 146.

detail, as Cavell does, the artworks in which such issues are explored and the ways in which they implicate the audience, critics and commentators in their ethical interrogations.

Così fan tutte is one of the most frequently performed operas in the canon. Since just 2017, there have been 147 performances of 32 productions in 32 cities, and it is the 15th most produced opera in the world.[40] Like *The Taming of the Shrew*, or *Measure for Measure*, any production of *Così* must deal with pivotal points, and the treatment of these will be hooks upon which the ethical value of the opera and its vulnerability to contemporary critique will depend. Obvious points of interpretative decision include:

- The extent to which Don Alfonso traps the men into the experiment.
- Whether the men are presented as exploited by Don Alfonso as much as the women are by them.
- The extent to which and the manner in which Don Alfonso is himself caught up in the emotional realities of *Soave sia il vento*.
- The question of whether the maid Despina can be thought to know of the mechanics of the male plot and the nature of her relationship with Don Alfonso (a key element in the Peter Sellars 1984 production).[41]
- The contradistinction of the sisters. The wider the gap of character between the sisters, the more seriously we take Fiordiligi's *Come scoglio* and *Per Pieta* (*Rondo* No. 29) and the more difficult it is to read her "yielding" as a mere device. (Alternatively, the substitution of Dorabella's *E amore un ladroncello* (No. 28) by the concert aria

---

[40] 'Operabase'.

[41] Žižek observes: "The notorious production of *Così* by Peter Sellars took the bond between the maid and the philosopher as the guiding line, the assumption being that the real drama takes place there, buttressed by erotic and traumatic undertones. The crucial moment for their relationship is the subtle quartet 2.22 ('La mano a me datem') where Don Alfonso acts as a spokesman for the two men, while Despina speaks for the two women. They both act as interpreters of the desire of the Other and thus enter an ambiguous play of mediation. After the establishment of contact between the two couples, they quickly vanish, but what about their own desires? Is there such a thing as neutral mediation? What do vanishing mediators do after they vanish?" Žižek and Dolar, *Opera's Second Death*, n. 62. Sellars's production notes are discussed in Said, 'Peter Sellars's Mozart'.

Vado, ma dove (K. 583) can seem to put the two sisters back in balance at just the right time.)
- The perceived violence of the epistemic assaults by the men, the violence of their reaction to the news of "betrayal" and the extent to which they demonstrate casual disregard for women outside the main plot. (Christopher Honoré's 2016 colonial setting was thought sufficiently disturbing to warrant a warning being sent out to ticket buyers.)[42]
- The presentation of the new pairings against the old. After all, in the initial setup, a mezzo (Dorabella) is matched with a tenor (Ferrando) and a soprano (Fiordiligi) with a bass (Guglielmo).[43] Arguably that situation is already presented as an incongruity and the rearrangement is a move to a more "natural" pairing. Certainly, Fiordiligi and Ferrando seem more evenly matched in temperament. Moreover, presented that way, the initial lovelorn portrait gazing of the sisters can be seen as a case of protesting too much. There is indeed not overmuch hesitancy when Fiordiligi and Dorabella choose "il biondino" and "brunettino", respectively. It might, one supposes, even be possible to show, during the overture, the sisters scheming with the philosopher with the express aim of finding a way to transpose their relationships, perhaps to put right some terrible misunderstanding that had earlier occurred. (The nineteenth century did even more extreme things to the opera's story and worse things are done to other operas.)
- An apparent point of decision is the ending with multiple readings ostensibly consistent with the libretto. It would be an incompetent production which ended the opera without ambiguity and discomfort that failed to leave protagonists and audience in a very hard place. But it would be a poor production too that delivered that discomfort *ex nihilo*, with, say, a stolen glance between Fiordiligi and Fernando. The ending of *Così* needs to be earned, through the management of a multitude of small dramaturgic decisions regarding looks, expressions and positions of the singers, any and all of which may make profound differences to the opera's final ethical impact.[44]

---

[42] Molleson, 'Così Fan Tutte Review—Mozart's Frothy Opera Turns Nasty'.

[43] Jochnowitz, 'Reconsidering Così Fan Tutte'.

[44] In Don Giovanni and *Così fan tutte*, the end has often been seen as the problem. However, if there is a problem, in each case, that cannot be the full extent of it—it must reach back into understanding the work as a whole. Williams, *On Opera*, p. 21.

The possibility of such dramaturgic decisions, all consistent with the libretto, if not always the libretto and score together, underlines the extent to which the opera engages with natural objects of Cavellian reflection: themes of pretence and sincerity, identity and authenticity, acknowledgment and denial, the defeasibility of our psychological criteria for the sincere expression of feeling. Dramaturgic choices will interrogate our willingness to sustain those criteria even as we find them doubted, abused and compromised under the pressure of the philosopher's method.

That method, applied here to the subjective lives of others—their love and loyalties, friendships and fragilities—is, as Ford claims,[45] an expression of the Enlightenment project to disenchant nature and one which projects the contradictions of that project onto those very lives, especially those of women:

> …although the women are represented as mere specimens of Alfonso's experimental ethics, it is always their subjective perspective on situations that provides the musical interest. In treating women as inert matter, the experiment brings femininity into the scope of the Enlightenment's systematic disenchantment of nature. From this perspective, feminine responses should have no such immanent qualities, but be only the empty space in which male desires become incarnate as objective facts of nature. Whilst Enlightened women are torn apart by the contradiction between their lived experience, and the discourse that denies it, Enlightened men are fascinated and threatened by a conception of femininity that contradicts its experienced reality.[46]

Seen in this light, Don Alfonso is then a paradigm of the Cavellian "philosopher". Don Alfonso is manipulative and in denial of the conflicts which are produced by a picture of human life in which certainty and proof offer the only sure foundation: a picture both arising from and reinforcing a damaging dichotomy between "inner" and "outer" which is then projected onto others:

> I think this is something Nietzsche meant when he ridiculed philosophers for regarding life "as a riddle, as a problem of knowledge" (Genealogy of Morals, p. 682), implying that we question what we cannot fail to know in

---

[45] Ford, *Così?*, p. 29.
[46] Ibid., p. 176.

order not to seek what it would be painful to find out. This, of course, does not suggest that skepticism is trivial; on the contrary it shows how profound a position of the mind it is. Nothing is more human than the wish to deny one's humanity, or to assert it at the expense of others.[47]

Don Alfonso, in word, deed and note, is then everything that Cavell has struggled in thought against. The philosopher of *Così fan tutte*:

> ... insinuates that there are possibilities to which the claim of certainty shuts its eyes; or: whose eyes the claim of certainty shuts. It is the voice, or an imitation of the voice, of intellectual conscience. Wittgenstein replies: "They are shut." It is the voice of human conscience.[48]

The question is then whether and how the opera itself replies to Don Alfonso, and challenges us to reply back to him, in that "voice of human conscience".

As we have noted, one of the decision point for productions is the degree to which Don Alfonso is presented as manipulating the lovers from the start or as only driven to do so out of frustration by their reactions. In the coffeehouse *in media res* opening, the libretto invites us to believe that Don Alfonso has offered the possibility of infidelity in the context of some general philosophical discussion—say about the fragility of love or the crooked timber of human nature—and that Ferrando and Guglielmo have offered their beloved fiancées by way of a philosophical counter-example. Don Alfonso counters by denying the need for proof:

> *Tai prove lasciamo...*
> Let's not trouble with proof[49]

But it requires only the barest dramaturgic flicker from Don Alfonso at this point to persuade us that this is a very disengenous denial. The implication is that in the pre-opera. Don Alfonso set up the lovers, knowing just how they will react. What then does Don Alfonso want? Only for others

---

[47] Cavell, *The Claim of Reason: Wittgenstein, Skepticism, Morality, and Tragedy*, p. 90.
[48] Ibid., p. 431.
[49] All translations from the libretto are taken from 'Così Fan Tutte—Wolfgang Amadeus Mozart—Libretto in Italian with Translation in English—OperaFolio.Com'.

to live in the light of the truth he claims. But at the end of the opera, he sings:

> *V'ingannai, ma fu l'inganno*
> *Disinganno ai vostri amanti,*
> *Che più saggi omai saranno,*
> *Che faran quel ch'io vorrò*

> I deceived you, but my deception
> Undeceived your lovers,
> Who henceforth will be wiser
> And will do as I wish.

His ultimate ambition is revealed as control, and his strategy is to destabilise and delegitimise the young men and women's inner lives, from the inside, by epistemologizing the lover's relationships. It is a gaslighting of youth. Don Alfonso claims to be an empiricist for whom experience is foundational:

> *Ho i crini gia grigi,*
> *Ex cathedra parlo;*
> *Ma tali litigi*
> *Finiscano qua*

> My hair is already grey,
> I speak with authority;
> But let's have done
> With argument

To be sure, this leaves the nature of his authority—objective philosophical detachment or bitter personal experience—in question. But his voice remains that of Enlightenment rational doubt, lying darkly between the numbered sections of Wittgenstein's *Philosophical Investigations* and whose whispers are heard, all too keenly, by Cavell. But how can I *know* that she loves me, suffers, is happy?

Don Alfonso purports to offer up a vision of the human, accepting us in our natural finitude. But it is a false conception of finitude that defines it only as a kind of limit, surveyable, by calm reason, from both sides, from a privileged position. His advice at the end of the opera has a moment of what looks like acceptance—"Abbracciatevi e tacete" ("Embrace each other and say no more"). But, as an audience, we may well think that these words are—perhaps instead, perhaps also,—a desperate attempt to cover his horror at the outcome of his experiment. He wanted to show that reason is but *ought not to be* the slave of the passions. The result of his sideways view onto human felt experience is not to put the passions in harness to reason but to substitute one pair of passions for another. Ironically, his finale words express the very thought he might have offered at the opera's opening when the men defended their lover's fidelity. What they offered then were avowals, and in both senses: an affirmation of the truth of what they believe and also an acknowledgment or claim—an *Ausdruck* that is rung from them like a passionate cry.[50] Words that were then deeds have been distorted by Don Alfonso into a hypothesis.

But these are responses we have when we know the opera and we reflect upon it. As we *experience* the opera, our responses are unsettlingly unstable.

Perhaps our first-order response is to treat the opera as a critique of false sentiment. Inside that response, Don Alfonso initially has our sympathy as he seeks to puncture the callow idealisations of his friends. The sisters are first seen gazing at images of their lovers which we make take to underline the artifice of their affections. More than one production opens Scene 2 with Dorabella—standardly presented as the shallower of the sisters—reading a novel. Like the heroines of Jane Austen who came later, their current emotions are already conditioned by their culture and, for that reason, we think, false and inauthentic. Within this response, we find ourselves thinking that what is real is lust and bodily passion, for these at least are authentic. This will lend a significance to a much-remarked feature of the opera: just as Don Giovanni lacks a single self-reflective aria, so *Così* lacks love duets.[51] While there are solo arias, duets, trios, sextets and a chorus, at no point do any of the four pairings sing a straightforward love duet. The closest we come to this is *Quartetto La mano a me date* (No. 22) where the philosopher Don Alfonso and the *soubrette* Despina speak for the (disguised) young men and sisters, respectively. Within this

---

[50] Wittgenstein, *Philosophical Investigations: The German Text, with a Revised English Translation 50th Anniversary Commemorative Edition*, sec. 546.

[51] Jochnowitz, 'Reconsidering Così Fan Tutte.' in Jochnowitz, *The Blessed Human Race*.

first-order response, this will appear to confirm the mediated, theatrical character of the lovers' inner lives.

Of course, this first-order response comes with a moral kick. We may think it is hard to acknowledge our animal nature but acknowledge we must if we are to master it. This conventional Judaeo-Christian frame of course fits well with readings of other Mozart works. It is the theme, it will be said, of *Die Zauberflöte* (even more obviously so in its lesser-known sequel by Schikaneder and von Winter: *Das Labyrinth*). We are upright animals, but our very capacity to acknowledge that fact is what gives us hope that we are something more, or other, than "merely" animal.

But we may begin to suspect that such a reading has all the *faux* humility of Kantian moral philosophy producing a second-order response that to rest content with it is surely is to be as much gaslighted by Don Alfonso as the other protagonists. This response, which may develop as the opera goes on, or which may strike us in a different production, is that the emotions induced by Don Alfonso's artifice are shown to be no less real than those they disrupt. The philosophical and moral point of the opera is to undercut precisely that distinction between authentic "natural" feeling and the *merely* socially induced which is a central hypothesis of Don Alfonso's materialism. After Dorabella "yields" to her Albanian, Ford jibes that Fiordiligi "takes only another twenty minutes…to 'fall'",[52] as if this were a mere delay designed to nail home the misogynistic claim that "all women do thus"—even the apparently most resolute—and confirming the libretto's attack on female autonomy. But those "twenty minutes" contain a crux of the opera—*Come scoglio*—whose intensity of feeling and direct presentation of Fiordiligi's inner integrity and authority stays with us throughout and beyond the opera. Žižek is surely right here:

> This pseudo-dialectics of sincere and feigned emotions, although it is not entirely out of place, none the less fails to take into account the gap that separates the bodily machine from the surface of its effects-events. Alfonso's point of view is that of mechanical materialism: man or woman

---

[52] Ford, *Music, Sexuality and the Enlightenment in Mozart's Figaro, Don Giovanni and Così Fan Tutte*, chap. 4.

is a machine, a puppet; his or her emotions—love, in this case—do not express some spontaneous authentic freedom but can be brought about automatically, by way of submitting him or her to proper causes. Mozart's answer to this philosopher's cynicism is the autonomy of the 'effect' qua pure event emotions are effects of the bodily machine, but they are also effects in the sense of an effect-of-emotion (as when we speak about an 'effect-of-beauty'), and this surface of the effect qua event possesses its own authenticity and autonomy. Or, to put it in contemporary terms: even if biochemistry succeeds in isolating the hormones that regulate the rise, intensity and duration of sexual love, the actual experience of love qua event will maintain its autonomy, its radical heterogeneity with regard to its bodily cause.[53]

Žižek's reflections echo a central theme of Wittgensteinian reflection: "Not empiricism and yet realism in philosophy: that is the hardest thing".[54] What is at issue here is our capacity to acknowledge the reality of the subjective when our models of the real are designed on an objectivising, empiricist model which perforce renders those realities only as effects. The mistake is not to think that we are biological machines if that means only that we are indeed animals. The mistake is to misconceive the explanatory relation of that realistically grasped fact to lived experience. And to then to give that explanation lease to excuse us from our responsibilities to one another. How does this opera reply? In *Così*, in the midst of all this human mess and distress, stands a woman singing *Come scoglio immoto resta*—like a rock standing impervious.

It is at this point, beyond the easier and more obvious thoughts that this opera addresses the issues of sincerity and pretence, of the defeasible criteria of interpersonal ascription, of the moral moment of scepticism, that perhaps a third-order response and a more completely Cavellian reading becomes possible.

In his reflections on particular operas, Cavell singles out a "transfigurative moment" in *La Traviata*—the scene between Violetta and Germont in which Violetta's entrance on F-flat changes an expected cadence in

---

[53] Žižek, *The Metastases of Enjoyment*, p. 125.
[54] Wittgenstein, *Remarks on the Foundations of Mathematics, Revised Edition*, p. 325.

D-flat major into a D-flat minor leaving "the texture between the voices …momentarily unreadable".[55] For Cavell, this moment of Violetta's resignation exemplifies the ethical centre of this opera but also of opera as a medium: the presentation of the horror and terror of the "theft of expressiveness"[56] under modernity, in the suffering and resistance of an individual woman.

But there is equally such a moment in *Così* which speaks, and more profoundly so, to Cavell's earlier critique of the epistemological stance and the moral challenge of acknowledgment. In the famous *Terzettino Soave sia il vento* (No. 10), the grieving sisters, joined by the duplicitous Don Alfonso, wish their departing lovers calm seas and gentle winds.

> *Tranquilla sia l'onda,*
> *Ed ogni elemento*
> *Benigno risponda*
> *Ai nostri/vostri desir.*

> Gentle be the breeze,
> Calm be the waves,
> And every element
> Smile in favour
> On their wish.

As a standalone aria, the *terzittino* is widely regarded as quintessentially Mozartian, despite being, in E major, "at the exotic twilight realm at the far edge of the tonal world of Mozartian opera".[57] But in the context of the opera, the *terzettino* is its first psychological and ethical crux point, the key looking forward, significantly, to another such point: *Come scoglio* (No. 14).

Of course, *Soave sia il vento* is encased in irony and at multiple levels. At the most basic level, we feel the poignant intensity of the farewell, thinking perhaps of farewells we too have suffered. Yet at the same time we know that what we are being shown is built on illusion and deceit.

---

[55] Cavell, *A Pitch of Philosophy*, p. 155.
[56] Cavell, p. 154.
[57] Burnham, 'Mozart's felix Culpa', n. 35.

We may wonder what then lay beneath our own farewells. But again, if we the audience know the opera, we know that they are saying farewell to more than their lovers. It is a farewell at the very least to comfortable certainties if also, perhaps, to illusions. Not gentle breezes and calm waves but storms and high seas lie before the sisters. And "every element" will be set against *their* wishes. And of course, singing with them is Don Alfonso. Žižek remarks that Don Alfonso "becomes dupe of his own manipulation from time to time and is carried away by his feigned emotions, which unexpectedly prove sincere (in the trio 'Soave sia il vento', for example)". But Žižek underestimates the lasting profundity of this moment. It is true that before this scene, we the audience are perhaps complicit in Don Alfonso mocking laughter "Io crepo, se non rido!" ("I'll burst if I don't laugh!") and that immediately after this scene, Don Alfonso will remark: "Non son cattivo comico!" ("I am not a bad actor after all"). We are, nominally, returned to his world as he compares supposed female fickleness to wind and the seas if to usurp the terzettino's metaphor and rend it from our memories. But it is then too late: our sense of Don Alfonso as a superior infallible authority is, thankfully, gone, and we hear his invocation of natural forces as a cheap and fragile simile. As Burnham notes,[58] throughout this scene the dominance of Don Alfonso's cynical irony is reduced from absolute sway in No. 6 through to an internal aside in No. 9, and finally, in this *terzettino*, it is gone completely. We have been shown, as Montesano argues,[59] the possibility of "a feminine space over which Don Alfonso does not have full control". So, while the aria uses irony, it does so to move us beyond it, to show the possibility of a space other than "the empty space in which male desires become incarnate as objective facts of nature".[60]

Underpinned by a strangely forward moving bass pulse that speaks of movement and departure, undulating strings embody the calm waves that the sisters wish for their lovers. The three voices interweave in exquisite rising and falling counterpoint. And then comes the extraordinary dissonance at "desir". The diminished seventh here is hardly in itself unexpected. It has

---

[58] Ibid., p. 84.
[59] Brown-Montesano, *Understanding the Women of Mozart's Operas*, p. 222.
[60] Ford, *Così?*, p. 176.

perhaps been hinted at by the A#-B[61] at "ond" and even by the E#-F# of "benigna". Perhaps too, the double *appoggiatura* of "desir" at its first occurrence is a kind of preparation, though one we recognise only when we have already experienced what, at that moment, is still to come. But it is only with that dissonant "desir" that the intense chromaticism latent in the aria is revealed.

---

[61] My thanks to Dr. Naomi Barker for assistance with this account.

And the effect here is surely unique and shattering. Without this moment, the aria would undoubtedly be beautiful. But with it, the piece achieves an effect, widely recognised by musical analysts and audiences, as something of a different and quite profound order. The effect is of a suspended manifestation, not merely of emotional but of subjective reality. It seems to be a moment in which, within the web of deceit and contempt, of vanity and pretence, in the striving for proof in the name of reason, we, the audience, are brought into the presence of these women. It is a moment not of knowledge but, with a caveat that we explore shortly, of acknowledgment. That this dissonance should fall so determinatively on the word "desir", hinting at the sexual resonance but surely speaking out of a greater yearning in the sisters, and not excluding the striving after power of Don Alfonso, is perhaps the most striking testament, in this opera, to the fortunate genius of the Mozart/Da Ponte collaboration: that "Da Ponte produced one sort of thing and got from the hands of Mozart another, a very peculiar, kind of thing".[62]

This aria at the first fulcrum of the opera and that dissonance on "desir" at the fulcrum of this aria lies exactly on the line, as Burnham notes, "between truth and illusion and between emotional proximity and ironic distance"[63] so that in this moment:

> Mozart's music goes beyond the painting of individual characteristics and begins to assume the point of view of these puppets, with the result that the illusion that defines them as puppets becomes a truth that defines them as human.[64]

And this line is too, exactly, that "between acknowledgment and avoidance". Suspended in this dissonant moment on this line, we can still look to either side. To one side, we recognise the sisters as plot puppets, doubly so, with two sets of controlling strings: those of Don Alfonso *and* those of Mozart and Da Ponte. And yet, to the other, we are appraised of their real presence. On its own, the aria is a beautiful glory. But in the context of the opera to which it belongs, it is a profound one.

And one way to say this is that it precisely marks the difference or better, the transition, between Cavell's reflections on Shakespeare and those on opera and the lease of voice. Regarding the presences we encounter in theatre, Cavell writes:

---

[62] Williams, *On Opera*, p. 45.
[63] Burnham, 'Mozart's felix Culpa', p. 85.
[64] Ibid., p. 92.

> They are in our presence. This means, again, not simply that we are seeing and hearing them, but that we are acknowledging them (or specifically failing to)…But doesn't the fact that we do not or cannot go up to them just mean that we do not or cannot acknowledge them? One may feel like saying here: The acknowledgment cannot be completed. But this does not mean that acknowledgment is impossible in a theater. Rather it shows what acknowledgment, in a theater, is. And acknowledging in a theater shows what acknowledgment in actuality is. For what is the difference between tragedy in a theater and tragedy in actuality? In both, people in pain are in our presence. But in actuality acknowledgment is incomplete, in actuality there is no acknowledgment, unless we put ourselves in their presence, reveal ourselves to them. We may find that the point of tragedy in a theater is exactly relief from this necessity.[65]

Thus, whilst we *can* acknowledge the other in theatre, and indeed, for Cavell, Shakespearean drama trades in all the necessities and vicissitudes of that possibility, part of the point of theatre as a medium, for Cavell, is to show us what we cannot do there, but must in actuality, if we are to constitute our responses as acknowledgment *in actuality*.[66] This is a question which we must put to Cavell's reflections on opera. For it is clear now that if opera were to achieve the rescue from scepticism that is the promise he identifies in the medium, then it would have not just to make the other present to us but to reveal ourselves to them. Can it do that? Can *Otello* do what *Othello* cannot?

The confident philosophical answer is that surely it cannot. Protagonists in opera and drama are both and equally fictional. As we have seen, for Cavell, insofar as opera is speech under the aspect of music, insofar as sung opera gives words the shape of behaviour that compels unmediated response—our *Einstellung zur Seele*—then opera has an advantage over drama. Opera rescues us from scepticism in a way that drama cannot insofar as drama is, and opera is not, subject to the same problem about speech as actuality. But insofar as operatic characters are fictional, then drama and opera are on equal footing. The critical question then is whether "the intervention or supervening of music into the world as revelatory"[67] is, in any sense, revelatory of *our* presence. But now we can say this. The fiction-

---

[65] Cavell, *Must We Mean What We Say?*, pp. 332–33.
[66] For a discussion, see Mulhall, *Stanley Cavell*, pp. 198–200.
[67] Cavell, *A Pitch of Philosophy*, p. 141.

ality of operatic characters does not show that our revelation is impossible in an opera. Rather it shows what our revelation, in an opera, is. And it is precisely at this point that Cavell's perception that voice is "located in— one might say disembodied within—this figure, this double, this person, this singer, whose voice is essentially unaffected by the role", such that the relation between singer and character is "indeterminate", comes to the fore. If Cavell's insight is sound, then the fictional status of the character played is "unimportant", compared to the sung role, in a way that the spoken character cannot be in drama. Our relation, as audience, to the sung character in opera is not identical to our relation, as audience, to the enacted character in drama. Rather, our response as audience to what actually happens, not merely what is portrayed, on the operatic as opposed to the dramatic stage, is different in kind. (Is it perhaps, for this reason, that while it would be entirely alien to the medium to applaud an outstanding Shakespearean soliloquy, through-composed opera notwithstanding, such applause to an outstanding performance of an aria would be expected? We might reply: that is only for historical reasons. But it belongs to the essence of an artistic medium that it is historical.) If the relation between singer and character in opera is, as Cavell claims, *indeterminate* in a way that the relation between dramatic actor and character cannot be, then *so too* the question of our correlative presence as an audience is indeterminate. We might say: in a drama, no audience is implied by the action. For that reason, *Verfremdungseffekt* can only be parasitic on a theatrical medium in which it is not standardly deployed. For that reason, the final speech of *The Tempest*, given not by Prospero but the actor playing Prospero, making the audience present by revealing his own presence and inviting an ethical relationship between the two through the acknowledgment of applause, is an *exceptional* moment in drama. But in opera, the presentation of speech under the aspect of music always and immediately implies the audience who hear that music. For who else, we might ask, is the music for? The characters in opera do not hear the chuckling woodwind or the recurring *leitmotif*. We might object that no more do characters in film hear the musical score but that only reinforces Cavell's larger thesis that film has been able to usurp opera. It is in this sense—our responsiveness as an audience to the operatic voice—that *our* presence in the opera is vouchsafed.

What now of *Così* and the extraordinary *terzettino*? We are, in this aria, and profoundly so in that dissonant "desir", vouchsafed the perception of the reality of these women, in high and shocking relief to their ostensible role in the plot, in one sense as puppets of operatic convention, in another, as victims of voice-denying patriarchy. Our response is, or ought to be, direct and unmediated in contrast to the narrative ambiguities of sincerity and pretence that shape our response to the rest of the narrative. (To this extent, Zalman's insight is sound: we *are* as aesthetically controlled by the opera as the sisters are cognitively controlled by Don Alfonso). Seen in a Cavellian light, what allows *our* response, uninfected by the scepticism that structures the male characters' actions under the "guidance" of philosophy, is the transfigured manifestation of the sisters's subjective voice, under the aspect of music. But, for all its power and genius, the music in isolation cannot deliver what is needed for our genuine acknowledgment of the sisters. And for that, there must be a sense in which we too are present. Does *Così fan tutte* achieve *that*?

Here is a striking parity between Cavell's quasi-historical thesis regarding modernity—and the responding need for opera and, much later, for film—and Burnham reflections on this opera:

> Music will no longer be assimilated into the Enlightenment's primarily verbal world, and the demonstration of this incommensurability in *Così fan tutte* comes at precisely the time when music started to be heard to assert itself as a nonverbal counterlanguage, a locus for both human emotion and transcendent intimation.[68]

Though we might hesitate here at Burnham's choice of the term "counterlanguage"—for what is starting to be heard is not the assertion of another kind of language, however oppositional to our actual languages—the point of this remark is its noting of the transitionary status of the opera. This resonates with Cavell's remarks about the emergence of opera as a medium which is born out of modernity. Perhaps the answer here is that in this opera we stand a little down a road already taken but not so much that we cannot still look back in regret to the crossroads where this avenue was chosen. Perhaps, in delivering not just the presence of the protagonists to the audience but the possibility of acknowledgment dependent upon *our presence to the singers*, *Così* offers only the template of a promise: one that can only be fulfilled by the genius—the attendant spirit—of production and performance. One that, by putting speech itself

---

[68] Burnham, 'Mozart's felix Culpa', p. 93.

under the aspect of music, does not unfailingly produce our presence but gives us the lease to respond in the "voice of human conscience".

Così fan tutte is an opera which, certainly in the Mozart/Da Ponte triptych but perhaps—as its openness to productions, reflecting anew the anxieties of our times, continues to demonstrate—amongst all operas, marks not so much the rise of modernity as our fall into it. The singers/protagonists, indeterminately so, in superposition of actuality and fiction, bid farewell, in *Soave sia il vento*, to a time, perhaps idealised just as much as the lovers idealise each other but certainly, as the opera opens, already lost, when acknowledgment of others alone was enough and was not yet flanked and threatened by the desire *to know*. In which the reality of others was a precondition of knowledge, and not amongst its putative objects. For Burnham, the abiding value of the opera as a whole is its documentation of "a passage from faith to doubt, a fall from ideal grace to the struggle for reality...from natural grace to human consciousness".[69] In this most Cavellian of operas, so invisible and yet so present in his reflections, it is to us, under modernity and its descendants, to whom Dorabella, Fiordiligi and even Don Alfonso, the philosopher—Cavell's nemesis—in this moment reenchanted with and in the world, wish calm seas and gentle winds. To whom, now present, that dissonance on "desir" is sung, in love and regret and warning.[70]

References

Barry, Barbara R. 2000. *The Philosopher's Stone: Essays in the Transformation of Musical Structure*. Pendragon Press.

Brown-Montesano, Kristi. 2007. *Understanding the Women of Mozart's Operas*. Berkeley: University of California Press.

Burnham, Scott. 1994. Mozart's "Felix Culpa: Così Fan Tutte" and the Irony of Beauty. *The Musical Quarterly* 78 (1): 77–98.

Cavell, Stanley. 1996. *A Pitch of Philosophy*. Harvard University Press.

———. 1999. *The Claim of Reason: Wittgenstein, Skepticism, Morality, and Tragedy*. Oxford University Press.

---

[69] Ibid., pp. 91–92.

[70] My thanks to members of the *Heaton Opera* group for convivial conversation on this and many other operas.

———. 2002. *Must We Mean What We Say?: A Book of Essays*. Cambridge University Press.

———. 2005. "Opera in (and as) Film" (2005). In *Cavell on Film*, ed. William Rothman. SUNY Series, Horizons of Cinema.

Clement, Catherine. 1999. *Opera, Or, The Undoing of Women*. University of Minnesota Press.

Cohen, Hermann. 1915. *Die Dramatische Idee in Mozarts Operntexten*. http://onlinebooks.library.upenn.edu/webbin/book/lookupid?key=ha006675114.

Così Fan Tutte—Wolfgang Amadeus Mozart—Libretto in Italian with Translation in English—OperaFolio.Com. Accessed 4 March 2018. http://www.operafolio.com/libretto.asp?n=Cosi_fan_tutte&print=y&translation=UK.

Ford, Charles. 1991. *Così?: Sexual Politics in Mozart's Operas*. Manchester University Press.

———. 2016. *Music, Sexuality and the Enlightenment in Mozart's Figaro, Don Giovanni and Così Fan Tutte*. Routledge.

Gombrich, E.H. 1954. Così Fan Tutte (Procris Included). *Journal of the Warburg and Courtauld Institutes* 17 (3/4): 372–374.

Hagberg, Garry L. 2006. *Describing Ourselves: Wittgenstein and Autobiographical Consciousness*. Oxford University Press.

Hensher, Philip. 2009. School for Lovers. *The Guardian*, May 23, sec. Music. https://www.theguardian.com/music/2009/may/23/mozart-da-ponte-cosi-fan-tutte.

Honderich, Ted. 2005. *The Oxford Companion to Philosophy*. Oxford: Oxford University Press.

Hytner, Nicholas. 2007. *Mozart: Cosi Fan Tutte*. Opus Arte.

Jochnowitz, George. 2018. Reconsidering Così Fan Tutte. Accessed 17 February 2018. https://www.jochnowitz.net/Essays/ReconsideringCosiFanTutte.html.

———. 2007. *The Blessed Human Race: Essays on Reconsideration*. Hamilton Books.

Kerman, Joseph. 1988. *Opera as Drama, New and Revised Edition*. University of California Press.

Kettle, Martin. 2018. Why Do Women Die in Opera?, Music Feature—BBC Radio 3. *BBC*. Accessed 17 February 2018. http://www.bbc.co.uk/programmes/b00sw2p7.

Kivy, Peter. 1988. *Osmin's Rage: Philosophical Reflections on Opera, Drama, and Text*. Princeton University Press.

Leudar, I., and A. Costall, eds. 2009. *Against Theory of Mind*. New York: Palgrave Macmillan.

Molleson, Kate. 2016. Così Fan Tutte Review—Mozart's Frothy Opera Turns Nasty. *The Guardian*, August 26. http://www.theguardian.com/stage/2016/aug/26/cosi-fan-tutte-review-edinburgh-festival-theatre-mozart-cape-town-opera.

Mulhall, Stephen. 1994. *Stanley Cavell: Philosophy's Recounting of the Ordinary*. Clarendon Press.
Operabase. Accessed 17 February 2018. http://operabase.com/oplist.cgi?id=none&lang=en&is=cosi+fan+tutte&by=&loc=&stype=abs&sd=17&sm=2&sy=2018&etype=abs&ed=&em=&ey=.
Said, Edward. 2008. Peter Sellars's Mozart. In *Music at the Limits*, 87–90. Columbia University Press.
Steptoe, Andrew. 1981. The Sources of "Così Fan Tutte": A Reappraisal. *Music & Letters* 62 (3/4): 281–294.
Wagner, Richard. 1900. *Opera and Drama*. University of Nebraska Press.
Williams, Bernard. 2006. *On Opera*. Yale University Press.
Wittgenstein, Ludwig. 1983. *Remarks on the Foundations of Mathematics*. Rev. ed. The MIT Press.
———. 1991. *Philosophical Investigations: The German Text*, with a revised English Translation 50th Anniversary Commemorative Edition. Wiley-Blackwell.
———. 1999. *Wiener Ausgabe Studien Texte: Band 1: Philosophische Bemerkungen*. Vienna: Springer-Verlag.
Zalman, Paige. 2016. Critical Perspectives: Women's and Gender Studies. *Così Fan Tutte in Context* (blog), April 20. https://cosiincontext.wordpress.com/critical-perspectives-womens-and-gender-studies/.
Žižek, Slavoj. 2005. *The Metastases of Enjoyment: Six Essays on Women and Causality*. Verso.
Žižek, Slavoj, and Mladen Dolar. 2002. *Opera's Second Death*. Psychology Press.

PART III

Aesthetic Understanding and Moral Life

CHAPTER 7

What Matters: The Ethics and Aesthetics of Importance

Sandra Laugier

Stanley Cavell's work is a redefinition of ethics through aesthetic understanding: it transforms our view of the way ethics and knowledge bear on our ordinary lives. In this chapter, I am trying to show how Cavell's teaching on film—in the way he draws our attention to gestures, particulars, details of our ordinary lives—is the basis of such a transformation of ethics and of a different approach to morals. Cavell proposes an ethics of perception and sensitivity, of attention to what our moral life "looks like": what I want to call an ethics and aesthetics of importance.

I will first define this approach by the idea, expressed in the title of chapter 3 of *Pursuits of Happiness*, of "The importance of Importance". The expression comes from Austin:

> What, finally, is the importance of all this about pretending? I will answer this shortly, although I am not sure importance is important: truth is. [Austin, "Pretending", *PP* 271]

Austin is, as we all know, Cavell's first master, and also a very strong and lasting influence as appears in recent texts like "Performative and Passionate Utterances". My point here is that Austin's presence (importance) in Cavell's work is connected to this transformation of ethics and that such a transformation of ethics is a new understanding, or reinstatement, of the idea of importance, of the idea of importance, or of what matters, one's own relevance. The revelation of one's own relevance, of the possibility and the necessity of making use of who one is, is something that all of Cavell's readers and students owe him. As he said early in his work about Socrates:

> This discovery about himself is the same as the discovery of philosophy, when it is the effort to find answers, and to permit questions, which nobody knows the way to nor the answer to any better than yourself. (*MWM*, xxviii)

1 THE IMPORTANCE OF IMPORTANCE

The question that strikes me as most persistent in Cavell's work is "what is it to mean anything?", not, for example, as would be given in a semantical or psychological theory of meaning, but in terms of meaningfulness, of significance. To mean what we say is to know, or to tell, what matters. And the question of what matters becomes the question of what it is to *tell* anything. Much has been written, since *Must We Mean What We Say?*, about relevance. Cavell offers an actual theory of relevance, or pertinence, that takes into account the total speech situation, everything that is involved in speaking (especially the question: to whom?), in what Austin calls:

> A) The total speech act in the total speech situation is the *only actual* phenomenon which, in the last resort, we are engaged in elucidating (*HTW* 148)

This descriptive project clarifies the idea, expressed in the title of chapter 3 of Cavell's *Pursuits of Happiness*, of "The Importance of Importance". The phrase comes, again, from Austin:

> What, finally, is the importance of all this about pretending? I will answer this shortly, although I am not sure importance is important: truth is. (Austin, "Pretending", *Philosophical Papers*, 271)

Recounting what is important, taking up the details of where importance lies, is the task Cavell assigns to philosophy. The difficulty of the task, expressed systematically in *Little Did I Know*, is that the unimportant (the trivial, the accessory, the detail) is sometimes, and maybe often, what is most important. And that is what we call the ordinary. So how is importance important?

To matter is also to make a difference, and Cavell insists on Austin's insistence on the elucidating power of differences, or distinctions, reminding us that "in this crosslight the capacities and salience of an individual are brought to attention and focus". Austin says: "we are using a sharpened awareness of words to sharpen our perception of the phenomena". This awareness is the perception of what matters. Importance and truth are both important and internal to each other. Putting importance first means transforming our idea of what is important. Cavell follows Wittgenstein here:

> Where does our investigation get its importance from, since it seems to destroy everything great and interesting? (Wittgenstein, *PI* §118)

We have a "distorted sense of what is important (call it our values) that is distorting our lives" (*Cities of Words*, 40). We need a shift in our ideas of what is important, of what we are asked to let interest us (*CR*, XXI). In this way, *relocating importance* is then the new task for philosophy, and a task *Little Did I Know* takes up by *telling*. Telling, as Cavell often reminds us throughout his writings, is counting (and knowing what counts). The identification of telling and counting, importance and truth, is claimed by the presence of pawnbroking in the depiction of Cavell's early life, his task in his father's pawnshop—"Counting up the monthly interest owed, upon redemption".

Here we encounter certain opening suggestions of the philosophy of the concepts of pawnbroking. The concept of what we count, especially count as of interest or importance to us, is a matter fundamental to how I think of a motive to philosophy. (*LDIK* 115–16)

Cavell, in *Little Did I Know*, states clearly, and I think for the first time, a connection between these "ideas of redemption and grace and interest and importance (or mattering or counting)". The motif of counting as redemptive is important in Cavell's work—the idea of a literary redemption of language by telling, in *Walden*, or his comments on the perfectionist moment in *It Happened One Night* when Clark Gable makes a very precise account of the sum his road trip with Claudette Colbert has cost him, which Cavell correlates to the way Thoreau gives an accurate account of the cost of his cabin. The motif of counting is thus important in Cavell's work, and especially in his moral work on film (think, e.g., of the perfectionist moment in *It Happened One Night* where Clark Gable makes an account of the sum Claudette Colbert has cost him, which Cavell correlates to the way Thoreau gives an account of the cost involved in building his cabin).

Cavell writes:

Knowing what counts defines importance and truth by accuracy, *exactness*. To tell things right, in context, to find the right, relevant word (the pitch of philosophy) is a task that articulates the search for importance, and of truth, making awareness of importance part of the task of knowing the world. But it also transforms our ideas of importance. Wittgenstein's point is also that the importance of the grammatical investigation is precisely in this, in "destroying everything great and interesting", displacing our interests, our hierarchies.

What is strange is that I haven't been able to find in Cavell's chapter an explicit reference, or treatment, of Austin's idea of the importance of importance. The chapter as a whole is about importance, and reads as a crucial moment of the movie the declaration of the infamous Sidney Kidd about the event of the wedding as being of "national importance". The whole movie, and its narrative, may be seen as an acknowledgment of what the actual importance of this wedding is: what is happening at the end (what you see on Kidd's picture, the re-marriage) is what is "of national importance".

> It could mean for example that they understand their marriage as exemplifying or symbolizing their society at large, quite as if they were its royalty, and their society as itself embarked on some adventure. George is confusedly thinking something more or less like this when he declares towards the end that his and Tracy's marriage will be "of national importance". And Tracy has toward the beginning defended George to Dexter by claiming that he is already of national importance, in response to which dexter winces and says she sounds like Spy magazine. Yet George and Tracy may be wrong not in the concept of importance but in their application of the concept. (*PH* 147)

It takes a whole movie, and sometimes many years, to get clear idea of what is important, and to find the right application of the concept: and finding the right application of the concept of importance would, then, help in understanding what is important to you—what are the important turns, or moments, or movies, in your life, or what you care about. Finding the right application of the concept of importance would be understanding and perceiving the importance of importance.

> "Importance" is an important word for Dexter and throughout the film (*PH*, p.148).

It is an important word for Cavell, as is shown by the strategic reappearance of the motif of importance in *Cities of Words*. First about *The Philadelphia Story*:

> "Importance" is an important word for Tracy's former (and future) husband C.K. Dexter Haven, who applies it, to Tracy's chagrin, to the night she got drunk and danced naked on the roof of the house—it is her saying impatiently to him that he attached too much importance to that silly escapade that prompts him to say to her, "it was immensely important" (*CW* 40).

But we shouldn't understand the chapter, and Cavell's treatment of what importance is, as a rebuttal of Austin's seemingly ironic sentence "I am not sure importance is important". The question is not: is importance or truth important? The question is to understand—and, I may say, it is one of Cavell's greatest accomplishments to show—that truth and importance are one and the same, or that importance is just as important as truth, and just as demanding and precise a concept.

Just as Austin says parenthetically in a passage of the essay "Truth" which is later quoted parenthetically by Cavell:

> To ask 'Is the fact that S the true statement that S or that which it is true of?' may beget absurd answers. To take an analogy: although we may sensibly ask 'do we *ride* the word « elephant » or the animal?' and equally sensibly 'Do we *write* the word and the animal?' it is nonsense to ask 'Do we *define* the word or the animal?' For defining an elephant (supposing we ever do this) is a compendious description of an operation involving both word and animal

(do we focus the image or the battleship?) and so speaking about 'the fact that' is a compendious way of speaking about a situation involving both words and world (Austin, *PP* 124).

Cavell comments, or at least uses, this Austinian point in *Pursuits of Happiness* about the mutual expression of words and world:

> (J.L. Austin was thinking about the internality of words and world to one another when he asked, parenthetically in his essay "Truth", "do we focus the image or the battleship?") (*PH* 204)

The matter of importance is a matter of focusing, and film is a means to teach us how to focus, how to see what matters. Importance and truth are not separate things but are both *important*: the two words define the way my own experience matters (to myself and to the world), or counts. The motif of counting is thus important in Cavell's work, and especially in his moral work on film (the perfectionist moment in *It Happened One Night* which Cavell correlates to the way Thoreau gives an account of the cost of his cabin).

Recounting of importance, taking up the details where it lies, is the task of philosophy, and what connects it most closely to film. But it means transforming our idea of what is important.

> Where does our investigation get its importance from, since it seems to destroy everything great and interesting? (Wittgenstein, *PI* § 118)

Wittgenstein's point, explored thoroughly by Cavell in his work, is that, just as importance is about truth and vice versa, the importance of the grammatical investigation is precisely in this, that "it seems to destroy everything great and interesting", displaces our interests, focus, care. Here Cavell connects his teaching on film to his reading of Wittgenstein's *Investigations*:

> His answer in effect is that it is precisely philosophy's business to question our interests as they stand: it is our distorted sense of what is important (call it our values) that is distorting our lives (*CW* 40)

The idea is a shift in the task of philosophy, and (as in Emerson's "The American Scholar") in ideas of what is important, what we are asked to let interest us.

His consolation is to reply: "What we are destroying is nothing but structures of air. But after such consolation, what consolation?—What feels like destruction, what expresses itself here in the idea of destruction, is really a shift in what we are asked to let interest us, in the tumbling of our ideas of the great and the important" (Cavell *CR* XXI).

Relocating importance is the new, guiding task of philosophy.

This relocation of importance and interest is what in *The Claim of Reason*, following my reading of Wittgenstein's *Investigations*, I call the recounting of importance, and assign as a guiding task of philosophy (*CW* 262).

Ordinary ethics calls for a relocation and new hierarchy of importance. Ordinary has been variously denied, undervalued, or neglected (not seen, not taken into account) in theoretical thought. Such negligence has to do with widespread contempt for ordinary life inasmuch as it is domestic and female. The disdain stems from the gendered hierarchy of objects deemed worthy of intellectual research, deemed as *important*. And this is also the starting point of the ethics of care.

2 Ordinary Ethics

I want now to connect Stanley Cavell's approach of aesthetic understanding to a redefinition of ethics, and of moral life that has been proposed by Cora Diamond and Iris Murdoch, as refocused on our ordinary lives. Understanding what importance is, and that philosophy is about the recounting of importance, helps you understand what Wittgensteinian ethics is about. It means that depicting our ordinary lives does not mean simply describing our practices, what we do. Ethics cannot be described simply by reference to our customs, and our practices cannot form a foundation for ethics, because they themselves are unknown to us. Cora Diamond follows Cavell in her central idea that our practices are *exploratory* and not merely given, as if we had a complete view before us of what we think, say, and mean. The point is not so much to argue but as to explore, to "change the way we see things". This leads us to change our notion of justification. There is, for Diamond, no subject matter specific to ethics. This might seem to make ethics more general. But it does just the opposite: Diamond's aim, drawing on Wittgenstein, is to define an ethics and aesthetics of (attention to) the particular.

> I begin by contrasting two approaches to ethics. The first is characteristic of philosophers in the English-speaking tradition. We think that one way of dividing philosophy into branches is to take there to be, for every kind of thing people talk and think about, philosophy of that subject matter. Thus we may, for example, take psychology to be an area of thought and talk, a branch of inquiry, and so to have, corresponding to it, philosophy of psychology, containing philosophical consideration of that area of discourse. We may then think that there is thought and talk that has as its subject matter what the good life is for human beings, or what principles of actions we should accept; and then philosophical ethics will be philosophy of that area of thought and talk. But you do not have to think that; and Wittgenstein rejects that conception of ethics. Just as logic is not, for Wittgenstein, a particular subject, with its own body of truths, but penetrates all thought, so ethics has no particular subject matter; rather, an ethical spirit, an attitude to the world and life, can penetrate any thought and talk. So the contrast I want is that between ethics conceived as a sphere of discourse among others in contrast with ethics tied to everything there is or can be, the world as a whole, life. (C. Diamond, "Ethics, Imagination and the *Tractatus*", p. 153)

The aesthetics of the particular goes against the "craving for generality" and is based on careful attention to the ordinary and various, *different* uses of language. This is also an ethics of perception, of what our moral life *looks like*, the face or aspect of ethics. But that does not mean simply describing our practices, "what we do" as simplistic readings of Wittgenstein might suggest. Diamond criticizes them:

> Talk about moral things may include the telling of stories; as much as anything is, the telling of stories is communication or what we hope will be communication. (Communication about moral things, like that about many other things, includes exploration of what will enable the participants to reach each other: that is not 'given' by the existence of a 'practice'. Our practices are exploratory, and it is indeed only through such exploration that we come to see fully what it was that we ourselves thought or wanted to say.)
> That is not just what I take to be the true view; it is also clearly Wittgenstein's. (*RS*, p. 27)

Ethics cannot be described simply by reference to our customs. Our practice is itself shaped by what we expect from ethics, and ethics itself is shaped both by what we do, and by what we want or imagine. Our practices cannot form a foundation for ethics, because, as Cavell has beautifully put it, they themselves are unknown to us. This is connected with Diamond's saying that our practices are *exploratory* and not merely given, as if we had a complete view before us of what we think, say, and mean. The point is not so much to argue but as to explore, to "change the way we see things". This leads us to change our notion of justification, and of practice. Diamond here refers to Cavell:

> The force of what we are able to say depends on its relation to the life of the words we use, the place of those words in our lives; and we may make the words tell by argument, by image, by poetry, by Socratic redescription, by aphorism, by Humean irony, by proverbs, by all sort of old and new things. And the judgment whether we produce illumination or obfuscation by doing so, the judgment whether there is truth in our words or self-deception, is not in general something on which there will be agreement. Ethics *is not* like mathematics; the role of agreement, the kind of agreement that there is in ethical thought, is not to be laid down in advance on some general Wittgensteinian principles. We need to see—in ethics as in mathematics—what agreement *belongs to* the intelligibility of the language we use. (Compare the use of *gehören zu* in PI, §242.) (*RS*, p.)

Cavell is then the main source, for Diamond, Nussbaum, and others, of the ethical interest of literature, of examples, of riddles, and of stories: not because ethics should somehow become "descriptive" or determined by practice. One could generalize to ethics the point Cavell made about rules in "The Argument of the Ordinary" in Conditions Handsome and Unhandsome. The use of literature is not simply as illustration, but as with all *examples* (see the *Blue Book*), it helps us see something more clearly. It helps us to see what we expect from ethics, *say what we mean* by ethics.

Like Diamond, Hilary Putnam has recently placed himself in the tradition that aims to vindicate this kind of approach to ethics, his reference being here not only Cavell but mainly Iris Murdoch. It consists in paying attention to what we say, to the ways in which our common expressions guide us, or lead us astray. It is certainly not the same as falling back on our "practices" or conventions. What is interesting is the way Murdoch insists, as Cavell does, on the disagreement, misunderstandings, and distances, instead of community and agreement. I quote from an unpublished Putnam conversation with Jacques Bouveresse:

So it's interesting that the second generation of Wittgensteinian, people that were very close to W and their immediate followers, were strongly concerned with ethics. And one thing that is in common between Deweyan ethics and Wittgensteinian ethics is a dissatisfaction with the way ethics has become identified with a very cut and dry debate in philosophy departments. (…) Our ethical lives cannot be captured with a half a dozen words like « ought » « right » « duty » « responsibility » « fairness » « justice » and the like, and the ethical problems that concern us cannot be identified with the debates between these very abstract metaphysical propositions of the natural laws, utilitarian, common sense etc. schools, we have to break out of the ethics in these overly restrictive, not only overly restrictive but also overly metaphysical ways. [H. Putnam, interview with J. Bouveresse]

Diamond critiques a fascination in ethics comparable to that of Frege and Russell in logic, a fascination with an ideal of rationality that can "ground all moral arguments". But not everything in ethics happens by way of arguments. We imagine, like Frege, that "it would be impossible for geometry to formulate precise laws if it used strings as lines and knots in the strings as points". In the same way, we believe that ethics cannot be done without the idea of a norm and of an ethical must that are quite separate from ordinary reality with its strings and knots, the weave of our life that Wittgenstein evokes in various places (e.g., RPP II §862). This is the realistic spirit: seeing that what matters, what needs attending to, is the knots and strings, the weave of our ordinary lives. We find here an image shared by Henry James and by Wittgenstein, that of a tapestry, which evokes the weaving together of the conceptual and the empirical (something John McDowell is also trying to describe).

This is exactly what Cavell describes, in maybe his most quoted passage, as the "turmoil" of our ordinary lives:

We learn and teach words in certain contexts, and then we are expected and expect others to project them into further contexts. Nothing insures that this projection will take place (in particular, not the grasping of universals nor the grasping of books of rules)… It is a vision as simple as it is difficult, and as difficult as it is (and because it is) terrifying. (*MWM* 52)

Turmoil and details define what has to come to our attention. Wittgenstein uses his idea of family resemblance to dispute the idea of ethical concepts and of moral philosophy. He aims at an ethical "exploration"—cf. Diamond: "Our practices are exploratory, and it is indeed only through such exploration that we come to see fully what it was that we ourselves thought or wanted to say"—rather than at discovering an ethical reality. Above all this is an exploration of the way our ethical preoccupations are embedded in our language and our life, in an ensemble of words that extends beyond our ethical vocabulary itself, and their complex connections with a variety of institutions and practices. In order to describe ethical understanding we would have to describe all of this, all these particular uses of words, of which a general definition cannot be given. Cavell says every word, in the ordinary world, would need a transcendental deduction.

> It is what human beings say that is true or false, and they agree in the language that they use. That is not agreement in opinions but in form of life. If language is to be a means of communication, there must be agreement not only in definitions but also (queer as this may sound) in judgments. This may seem to abolish logic, but does not do so. (Wittgenstein, *PI* 241–42)

> How could human behavior be described? Surely only by showing the actions of a variety of humans as they are all mixed up together. Not what *one* man is doing *now*, but the whole hurly-burly, is the background against which we see an action. (Wittgenstein, *RPP* II §624: 629)

Our ethical lives cannot be captured with a half a dozen words like 'ought', 'right', 'duty', 'responsibility', 'fairness', 'justice', and the like: our ordinary language, as Austin has shown in his "A Plea for Excuses", is much more refined and "sharp-eyed", better at drawing differences. What matters is not so much moral judgment or understanding as perception, synoptic vision: an *ordinary* perception. Wittgenstein suggests a *Gestalt* approach in ethics, by bringing out the necessity of recourse to a narrative *background* and to define our vision: our particular moral views emerge from a background. Here is how Diamond defines this background:

> Our particular moral views emerge from a more general background of thought and response. We differ in how we let (or do not let) moral concepts order our life and our relations to others, in how our concepts structure the stories we tell of what we have done or gone through [Diamond, "Moral Differences and Distances" 1997, p. 220]

3 Ethics and Aesthetics of Attention

Wittgenstein pointed this out in his 1933 course about our uses of the words game, beautiful, good. The elements of the moral vocabulary have no sense except in the context of our customs and of a form of life. Better, they come to life against the background (the *praxis*) that "gives our words their sense". A moral sense that is never fixed and is always particular. "Only in the practice of a language can a word have meaning". Sense is determined not only by use, or "context" (as many analyses of language have recognized, whatever you might call it), but it is embedded and perceptible only against the background of the practice of language, which changes through what we do in it.

One might thus be tempted to take ethics in the direction of a particularist ontology—one that puts abstract particulars (derived, e.g., from perception) at the center of a theory of values or a realism of particulars. But that would be again to miss the import of the idea of family resemblance, which is precisely the negation of all ontology. Wittgenstein criticizes the craving for generality. Iris Murdoch, in "Vision and Choice in Morality", evokes in this connection the importance of attention in ethics (care: to pay attention, to be attentive. "Attention" thus would be a possible translation into French of "care" or "*Sorge*".)

Murdoch describes differences in ethics as differences of *Gestalt*:

> Here moral differences look less like differences of choice, given the same facts, and more like differences of vision. In other words, a moral concept seems less like a movable and extensible ring laid down to cover a certain area of fact, and more like a total difference of *Gestalt*. ("Vision and choice in morality", p. 82)

There are no univocal moral concepts that can simply be applied to reality to pick out a set of objects; rather, our concepts depend, for their very application, on the *vision* of the "area", on the narration or description we give of it, on our personal interest and our desire to explore: on what is important for us. Here, in the idea of importance, we have another formulation of care: what is important (what matters) to us, what counts.

Now activities of this kind certainly constitute an important part of what, in the ordinary life, a person "is like". When we apprehend and assess other people we do not consider only their solutions to specifiable practical problems, we consider something more elusive which may be called their total vision of life, as shown in their mode of speech or silence, their assessments of others, their conception of their own lives, what they think attractive or praiseworthy, what they think funny: in short the configurations of their thought which show continually in their reactions and conversation. These things, which may be overtly and comprehensibly displayed or inwardly elaborated and guessed at, constitute what, making different points in the two metaphors, one may call the texture of man's being or the nature of his personal vision (Id.).

Cavell pursues this line exactly, about film and the movies that matter to us:

> The moral I draw is this: the question what becomes of objects when they are filmed and screened—like the question what becomes of particular people, and specific locales and subjects and motifs when they are filmed by individual makers of film—has only one source of data for its answer, namely the appearance and significance of just these objects and people that are in fact to be found in the succession of films, or passage s of films, that matter to us. To express their appearances, and define those significances, and articulate the nature of this mattering, are acts that help to constitute what we might call film criticism [Cavell, "What Becomes of Things on Film", *Themes Out of School*, p. 183]

The importance of film lies in its power to make what is important, what matters, emerge: "to magnify the sensation and meaning of a moment" (Cavell). Attention to particulars is this specific attention to the invisible importance of things and moments, the covering over of importance in our ordinary life. To redefine ethics by starting from what is important, and its connection with the vulnerability of our experience, might be the starting point for an ethics of the *particular*. We can look to a whole cluster of terms, a language-game of the particular: attention, care, importance, what matters. Our capacity for attention is the result of the development of a perceptive capacity: to be able to see a detached detail, or gesture, against its background. Here the importance is in details.

> We do continually have to make choices—but why should we blot out as irrelevant the different backgrounds of these choices, whether they are made confidently on the basis of a clear specification of the situation, or tentatively, with no confidence of having sufficiently explored the details? Why should attention to detail, or belief in its inexhaustibility, necessarily bring paralysis, rather than, say, inducing humility and being an expression of love? (Murdoch, "Vision and Choice in Morality", p. 88)

Moral philosophy must change its field of study, from the examination of general concepts to the examination of particular visions, of individuals' "configurations" of thought: attention to detail of forms of life.

The task of ethical and of aesthetic understanding is inseparably to perceive "the texture of a human's being or the nature of his/her personal vision". It is in the use of language ("choice" of expressions, style of conversation) that a person's moral vision shows overtly or develops intimately. For Murdoch this vision is not a theory but a texture of being (the texture might be visual, aural, or tactile). This texture is not a matter of moral choices, but of "what matters", of what makes and expresses the differences between individuals. See again Diamond:

> But we cannot see the moral interest of literature unless we recognize gestures, manners, habits, turns of speech, turns of thought, styles of face as morally expressive—of an individual, l or of a people. The intelligent description of such things is part of the intelligent, the sharp-eyed, description of life, of what matters, makes differences, in human lives. (Diamond, *RS* 375)

What matters is what makes a difference. These are the differences that must be the object of a "sharpened, intelligent description of life". This notion of *human life* is connected to Wittgenstein's idea of a form of life, which also defines a texture. We might also think of the "open texture" that Waismann spoke of in verifiability referring to the dependence of our words and our claims on their uses. "Texture" thus refers to an unstable reality that cannot be fixed by concepts, or by determinate particular objects, but only by the recognition of gestures, manners, and styles. A form of life, from the point of view of ethics, can be grasped only in a perception—attention to textures or moral patterns. These patterns are perceived as "morally expressive". What is perceived is not, therefore, objects or a moral reality but moral expression, which is not possible or recognizable in the absence of the background provided by a form of life.

In "Moral Differences and Distances", Diamond finds an example of this in the life of Hobart Wilson as told in an article in *The Washington Post*. Or again, in characters as Henry James describes them, in teaching us to see them correctly. In his preface to *What Maisie Knew*, James explains how he wants to actually describe and depict, to really *see* (Wittgenstein: "don't think, look!"). The whole novel is a critique of perception, through which the description of perception of life is connected to the ability to really see, judge, appreciate what Maisie is. But film is the best approach to what it is to *get* to *see* something properly.

The background of a form of life is neither causal nor stuck like a décor, but living and mobile. One can speak here of forms of *life* (*life forms*, as Cavell says, instead of *forms of life*): the forms that our life takes under an attentive gaze, the "whirl" of life in language, and not, for example, a body of meanings or of social rules. Here two representations of ethics and two approaches to moral perception are opposed: that of the background (cf. Searle, for whom institutions constitute the fixed background that allows us to interpret language, to perceive, and to follow social rules), and that of the perceptual texture of life. The term "background" (*Hintergrund*) appears in Wittgenstein in order to designate a background of description that makes the nature of actions appear, and not, as Searle suggests, in order to *explain* anything. The background cannot have a causal role, for it is language itself in all its instability and its dependence on practice:

> Our particular moral views emerge from a more general background of thought and response. (Diamond, "Moral differences and distances", p. 220)

We perceive action, but taken in the midst of a bustle, the whirl of the form of life in which it emerges and which gives it its meaning and importance. It is not the same thing to say that the application of a rule is causally determined by a background and to say that it is describable against a background of human actions and connections. This is the heart of the difference traced by Cavell in *Conditions Handsome and Unhandsome* between a descriptive conception of ethics and a "conformist" conception that aims to justify our actions in terms of previously agreed-upon rule. The background does not determine ethical meaning (for there is no such thing). Rather it allows us to perceive what is important and meaningful for us (the important moment). The meaning of an action is given by the way it is perceived against the background of a form of life. The "accepted", given background does not determine our actions (no causality) but it allows us to *see* them clearly.

Here the conceptual adventure intervenes as part of moral perception. There is adventure in every situation that mixes uncertainty, instability, and "the sharpened sense of life". Diamond shows how Henry James articulates this adventurousness that belongs to the *form* of moral thought:

> A human, a personal 'adventure' is no a priori, no positive and absolute and inelastic thing, but just a matter of relation and appreciation—a name we

conveniently give, after the fact, to any passage, to any situation, that has added the sharp taste of uncertainty to a quickened sense of life. Therefore the thing is, all beautifully, a matter of interpretation and of the particular conditions; without a view of which latter some of the most prodigious adventures, as one has often had occasion to say, may vulgarly show for nothing. [James 1934, 286]

This taste of adventure is what Cavell is referring to in *Pursuits of Happiness* constantly about the "green world" and the adventurousness of the couples in the films, and especially about *The Philadelphia Story* and its sense of society being embarked in an adventure. Perception, defined as care, is activity, mobility, and improvisation. It is a mobility as much of the senses as of the intellect. Wittgenstein speaks similarly of a "spiritual mobility".

What is important is to *have* an experience (not to derive something *from* experience). Dewey and Emerson both make the point. To have an experience means to perceive what is important, what *matters*. What interests Cavell, in film, is the way his experience there makes (visually) emerge, makes visible what is important, what matters. It is the development of a capacity *to see what is important* that allows us to redefine experience—experience is the appearance and meaning of things (places, persons, patterns).

> It is part of the grain of film to magnify the feeling and meaning of a moment, it is equally part of it to counter this tendency, and instead to acknowledge the fateful fact of a human life that the significance of its moments is ordinarily not given with the moments as they are lived so that to determine the significant crossroads of a life may be the work of a lifetime. (Cavell, "The Thought of Movies", *Themes Out of School*, p. 11)

Experience itself, if one trusts it, becomes an adventure itself. Failure of attention to experience, failure to perceive what is important, makes one miss the adventure. Thus one can see experience as an adventure at once of intellect and of sensibility (one opens oneself to experience). Put another way, it is at the same time passive (one lets oneself be transformed, touched) and active. There can be no separation, in experience, of thought (spontaneity) from receptivity (vulnerability to reality). This is what, according to James, *constitutes experience*.

4   LIFE FORMS AND DIFFERENCES

This approach to expression, which makes it possible to respond, is a product of attention and of care. It is the result of an education of sensibility. Here we recall the Cavellian theme of "an education for grownups": in recognizing that education does not end with childhood, and that we still need, once grownup, an appropriate education, we see that education is not just a matter of knowledge. This is precisely the point of Wittgenstein's insistence on the idea of learning a language. Learning a language consists in learning, not meanings, but an ensemble of practices that could not be "founded" in a language or causally determined by a social and natural basis, but are learned at the same time as language itself, and that are the changing texture of our life.[1] The question of education, on Cavell's reading of Wittgenstein (by contrast with Lovibond's or McDowell's), is infused by skepticism: learning does not offer me a guarantee for the validity of what I do, only the approval of my elders or of the community can do that, and that approval is not something merely given or obvious. Nothing, in sum, founds our practice of language, except this practice itself—"this whirl of organism that Wittgenstein calls forms of life".

Here we can return to the way Austin defines the method of ordinary language philosophy, and the critique mounted by Wittgenstein against the "craving for generality" characteristic of philosophy. The attention to the ordinary that Wittgenstein advocates goes against our tendency, in science as in philosophy, to theorize the world, and our tendency to look for general meanings in our words independently from the context of expression and from the agreement on/in use.

> If we reach this agreement, we shall have some data ('experimental' data, in fact) which we can then go on to explain. Here, the explanation will be an account of the meanings of these expressions, which we shall hope to reach by using such methods as those of 'Agreement' and 'Difference'.) (Austin, *PP* 274).

Attention to our ordinary uses of language is then the way to know reality. As Austin says, "we are using a sharpened awareness of words to sharpen our perception of the phenomena".

---

[1] Cf. Wittgenstein on learning the word "pain": "Pain occupies *this* place in our life, it has *these* connections." Wittgenstein 1967, §§ 532–33.

> When we examine what we should say when, what words we should use in what situations, we are looking again not *merely* at words but also at the realities we use the words to talk about: we are using a sharpened awareness of words to sharpen our perception of, though not as the final arbiter of, the phenomena. For this reason I think it might be better to use, for this way of doing philosophy, some less misleading name than those given above—for instance, 'linguistic phenomenology', only that is rather a mouthful. (Austin, "A Plea for Excuses", *PP* 182)

To pay attention to language is to care for/about what others say and what we say, and mean, is a basic ethical principle but also a cognitive one. And this takes us back to the *ethics and aesthetics* of attention.

Perception, or more precisely misperception, misappreciation, is what can lead us to "miss the adventure": what Austin called, articulating moral and truth, "thoughtlessness, inconsiderateness". Here he mentions the importance of importance.

> What, finally, is the importance of all this about pretending? I will answer this shortly, although I am not sure importance is important: truth is. (Austin, "Pretending", *PP* 271)

Knowledge is not enough. Here the idea is that to get importance, we need to properly *appreciate* situations. Truth AND importance are important, as Austin very well explains:

> It happens to us, in military life, to be in receipt of excellent intelligence, to be also in self-conscious possession of excellent principles (the five golden rules for winning victories), and yet to hit upon a plan of action which leads to disaster. One way in which this can happen is through *failure at the stage of appreciation of the situation,* that is at the stage where we are required to cast our excellent intelligence into such a form, under such heads and with such weights attached, that our equally excellent principles can be brought to bear on it properly, in a way to yield the right answer. So too in real, or rather civilian, life, in moral or practical affairs, we can know the facts and yet look at them mistakenly or perversely, or not fully realize or appreciate something, or even be under a total misconception. (Austin, "A Plea for Excuses", *PP* 194)

Following the sociologist Erving Goffman, himself an admirer of Austin, we understand how misperception and misframing can involve us in "systematically sustained, generative error": a language that is entirely misguided, misleading in our lives.

> The issue is that an individual may not merely be in error, but that certain of these errors prove to be a matter of « misframing », and consequently involve him in systematically sustained, generative error, the breeding of wrongly oriented behavior. For if we can perceive a fact by virtue of a framework within which it is formulated [...] then the misperception of a fact can involve the importation of a perspective that is itself radically inapplicable, which will itself establish a set, a whole grammar of expectations, that will not work. The actor will then find himself using not the wrong word but the wrong language. If, as Wittgenstein suggested, « to understand a sentence means to understand a language », then it would seem that speaking a sentence presupposes a whole language and tacitly seeks to import its use. (E. Goffman, *Frame Analysis*, p. 309)

Ethics, then, has to take into account this vulnerability in our very use of language and ordinary lives: to become, as Austin suggests, a matter of *appreciation*—involving both accurateness and attention.

5 Realism

> Even thoughtlessness, inconsiderateness, lack of imagination, are perhaps less matters of failure in intelligence or planning than might be supposed, and more matters of failure to appreciate the situation. A course of E. M. Forster and we see things differently: yet perhaps we know no more and are no cleverer. (Austin, *PP* 194)

This is Cavell's main point about film. Knowing what is important to you is knowing yourself, and it is to trust your experience, which simply means being able to *have an experience*.

> To subject these enterprises and their conjunction to our experiences of them is a conceptual as much as an experiential undertaking; it is our commitment to being guided by our experience but not dictated by it. I think of this as checking one's experience (*PH* 10).

The interest, and also the specific difficulty of the definition and practice of philosophy of language, is that the speaking of language is speaking about what one is speaking about (and how, and where). Austin said it very clearly in "A Plea for Excuses", in his trademark mock superficial manner:

> When we examine what we should say when, we are looking again not merely at words (or 'meanings' whatever they may be) but also at the realities we use the words to talk about: we are using a sharpened awareness of words to sharpen our perception of, though not as the final arbiter of, the phenomena. (« A Plea for Excuses », Austin, *Philosophical Papers*, p. 182)

It is the notion of difference that will define the connection between a conscience sharpened for the use of words and our perception of the world. Cavell was actually the first to make this point:

> Too obviously, Austin *is* continuously concerned to draw distinctions, and the finer the merrier, just as he often explains and justifies what he is doing by praising the virtues of natural distinctions over homemade ones. [...] Part of the effort of any philosopher will consist in showing up differences, and one of Austin's must furious perceptions is of the slovenliness, the grotesque crudity and fatuousness, of the usual distinctions philosophers have traditionally thrown up. Consequently, one form his investigations take is that of repudiating the distinctions lying around philosophy—dispossessing them, as it were, by showing better ones. And better not merely because finer, but because more solid, having, so to speak, a greater natural weight; appearing normal, even inevitable when the others are luridly arbitrary; useful when the other seem twisted; real where the others are academic. [...] One sometimes has the feeling that Austin's differences penetrate the phenomena they record—a feeling from within which the traditional philosopher will be the one who seems to be talking about mere words. (Cavell, *Must We Mean What We Say?*, pp. 102–3)

The naturalness (or the necessity) of distinctions drawn in language makes them superior to distinctions drawn by philosophers, and in particular to distinctions established by an "analysis" of words. They are, says Cavell, more REAL.

The kind of realism involved here (a realism that cannot be claimed as a theory or a thesis) appears in a very illuminating way in this passage of Austin's "Truth":

To ask 'Is the fact that S the true statement that S or that which it is true of?' may beget absurd answers. To take an analogy: although we may sensibly ask 'do we *ride* the word « elephant » or the animal?' and equally sensibly 'Do we *write* the word and the animal?' it is nonsense to ask 'Do we *define* the word or the animal?' For defining an elephant (supposing we ever do this) is a compendious description of an operation involving both word and animal (do we focus the image or the battleship?) and so speaking about 'the fact that' is a compendious way of speaking about a situation involving both words and world. (Austin, *PP* 124)

Note again that the only place where Cavell comments, or at least uses, this Austinian point is (parenthetically) in *Pursuits of Happiness*:

(J.L. Austin was thinking about the internality of words and world to one another when he asked, parenthetically in his essay "Truth", "do we focus the image or the battleship?") (*PH* 204)

The matter of this internality, or of what Wittgenstein calls *Harmony* (between thought and language), is the matter of importance. This is a definition of *self-reliance*: getting to know what interests me, *what I care about*:

What I take Socrates to have seen is that, about the questions which were causing him wonder and hope and confusion and pain, he knew that he did not know what no man can know, and that any man could learn what he wanted to learn. No man is in any better position for knowing it than any other man—unless *wanting* to know is a special position. And this discovery about himself is the same as the discovery of philosophy, when it is the effort to find answers, and to permit questions, which nobody knows the way to nor the answer to any better than yourself. (Cavell *MWM*, xxviii)

So the task of philosophy is to discover importance not only through accurate perception but through our pain in being unable to see, our failure to perceive, our missing the subject. This is what Cavell calls skepticism and what Goffman calls vulnerability (vulnerability *of reality itself* to the failures of our perceptions).

This relocation of importance and interest is what in *CR*, following my reading of Wittgenstein's *Investigations* I call the recounting of importance, and assign as a guiding task of philosophy. (*CW* 262)

Again we find this preoccupation in Goffman:

> The issue is that an individual may not merely be in error—as when he adds a column of figures wrong—but that certain of these errors prove to be a matter of « misframing », and consequently involve him in systematically sustained, generative error, the breeding of wrongly oriented behavior. For if we can perceive a fact by virtue of a framework within which it is formulated [...] then the misperception of a fact can involve the importation of a perspective that is itself radically inapplicable, which will itself establish a set, a whole grammar of expectations, that will not work. The actor will then find himself using not the wrong word but the wrong language. If, as Wittgenstein suggested, « to understand a sentence means to understand a language », then it would seem that speaking a sentence presupposes a whole language and tacitly seeks to import its use. (Goffman, *Frame Analysis*, pp. 308-09)

My aim is to try to isolate some of the basic frameworks of understanding available in our society for making sense out of events and to analyze the special vulnerabilities to which these frames of reference are subject. I start with the fact that from an individual's points of view, while one thing may momentarily appear to be what is really going on, in fact what is really happening is a joke, or a dream, or an accident, or a mistake, or a misunderstanding, or a deception, and so on. And attention will be directed to what it is about our sense of what is going on that makes it so vulnerable to the need for these various rereadings (*id.* 10).

Vulnerability is another name for skepticism. This vulnerability is what constitutes experience and also constitutes a task for philosophy: "to discover the reality in one's experience"—a task common to philosophy and film—to overcome skepticism, defined as our inability to see what matters.

> Any of the arts will be drawn to this knowledge, this perception of the poetry of the ordinary, but film democratizes the knowledge, hence at once blesses and curses us with it. It says that the perception of poetry is open to all, regardless as it were of birth or talent, as the ability is to hold a camera on a subject, so that a failure so to perceive, to persist in missing the subject, which may amount to missing the evanescence of the subject, is ascribable only to ourselves, to failures of our character; as if to fail to guess the unseen from the seen, to fail to trace the implications of things—that is to fail the

perception that that there *is* something to be guessed and traced, right or wrong—requires that we persistently coarsen and stupefy ourselves. (*Themes Out of School*, p. 14)

This revelation of one's own pertinence, of the possibility and above all the necessity of making use of who one is, is something that all Cavell's readers and students owe him. This redefinition of the task of philosophy, and of the pursuit of happiness, through the search of importance (what is important to me, what is important to us) and the recognition of our failures to acknowledge importance, to "guess the unseen from the seen", may be his main teaching and could define the way Cavell matters in our ordinary and intellectual lives.

6 Missing the Subject

Here the conceptual adventure intervenes as part of moral perception and care. There is adventure in every situation that mixes uncertainty, instability, and "the sharpened sense of life". Henry James articulates this adventurousness that belongs to the *form* of moral thought.

This taste of adventure is what Cavell is referring to in *Pursuits of Happiness* in speaking of the adventurousness of the couples in the films, especially *The Philadelphia Story* and its sense of society being embarked in an adventure. In limiting oneself to a narrow conception (based on choice, action, etc.) of ethics, one risks moralism and *missing the adventure*—missing a dimension of moral life through lack of attention. More precisely, what one misses is the *face* of moral thought and what matters to us. Here the conceptual adventure intervenes as part of moral perception. There is adventure in every situation that mixes uncertainty, instability, and "the sharpened sense of life".

It is by thinking about lack of attention that we can best understand this sense of ethics. Absence of attention and of care, failure to perceive what is important, makes one "miss the adventure". Thus one can see moral life as an adventure at once of intellect and of sensibility.

> What happens to her becomes adventure, becomes interesting, exciting, through the quality of her attention to it, the intensity of her awareness, her imaginative response. What happens, though, if we are bad readers? Two things joined together. We do not see what that is exciting happens to her.

That passes for nothing with us; and we also do not see what is exciting, what is fine, what is secret and hidden in the book. A novel or poem, James says, does not give out its finest and most numerous secrets, except under the closest pressure, except when most is demanded from it, looked for in it; in other words, when what is in the book, through the quality of the reader's attention, becomes his own very adventure. The inattentive reader then misses out doubly: he misses the adventures of the characters (to him they 'show for nothing'), and he misses his own possible adventure in reading. (*RS* 314–15)

This is what makes perception itself an adventure. As Henry James writes, experience—our capacity to feel life in general and in detail—is constituted by our attention. He follows Emerson in his idea that the most difficult is not (as the European epistemology taught us) to learn (or derive knowledge) from experience, but in Dewey's words, to HAVE an experience.

The power to guess the unseen from the seen, to trace the implication of things, to judge the whole piece by the pattern, the condition of feeling life, in general, so completely that you are well on your way to knowing any particular corner of it—this cluster of gifts may almost be said to constitute experience. "Try to be one of the people on whom nothing is lost!" I am far from intending by this to minimise the importance of exactness—of truth of detail. (James, *The Art of Fiction*, pp. 10–11)

A use of literature consists in "taking the moral life as a site of adventure" and in making reading itself our adventure. But the flip side of this subject, as Diamond notes, is moral *in*attention, the narrowing of the spirit, and the refusal of adventure. Here one can bring in the topic of skepticism. Cavell takes more interest in the emergence of radical disagreements in ethics than in agreement. Ethics is defined by this possibility of radical incomprehension. The moral question depends on our agreements in language but also on a radical kind of disagreement, incomprehension, distance, a feeling of nonsense, or indignation. Diamond, in "Moral Differences and Distances", takes an interest in our capacity to recognize when someone's words seem to go beyond our shared conceptual world. This capacity is linked to our capacity to lose, and by the same token to extend, our (moral) concepts by using them in new contexts. Such an extension, like the measuring of its limits, is the work of the moral imagination, of our capacity or incapacity to put ourselves in a situation and to make sense of the words of another. This capacity and its limits appear when we measure our distance from another's moral vision. We can get an idea of this from reading the testimony that Diamond cites, in "Moral Differences and Distances", from readers of *The Washington Post* after the publication of the Chip Brown article.

All this connects again this approach to ethics to the idea of mattering, counting, and importance—it does not initiate so much a new approach in ethics as a transformation in the status of ethics itself. Redefining ethics by starting from the concept of importance. Again, to *have* an experience means (for Cavell, Dewey, and Emerson) to perceive what is important, what *matters*. What interests Cavell, again, in film, is the way experience there makes (visually) emerge, makes visible what is important. It is the development of our capacity *to see what is important* that allows us to redefine experience—experience is the appearance and meaning of things (places, persons, patterns).

> The question what becomes of objects when they are filmed and screened… has only one source of data for its answer, namely the appearance and significance of just these objects and people that are in fact to be found in the succession of films, or passages of films, that matter to us. (Cavell, "What Becomes of Things on Film", *TOS* 183)

This requires a particular attention to the meaning of this or that moment. Last question: how can we perceive what is important in our lives? Experience reveals itself as defined by our capacity for attention, a capacity to see the detail, the expressive gesture—an attention to what matters in the expressions and styles of another—what makes and expresses the differences between persons, which must therefore be *described*. Film is the privileged site of this perception, through the creation of a background that allows important differences among experiences and expressions to appear. Film then makes it possible to have confidence in experience, to learn to be attentive. Experience itself, if one trusts it, becomes an adventure itself. To refuse this trust is to miss the adventure—that of the characters as well as one's own. So failure of attention to experience, failure to perceive what is important, makes one miss the adventure. Mistrust of language—what Diamond calls "reluctance to see all that is involved in using it well, responding well to it, meeting it well"—is then a way to misperception and practical error. As Austin says, "we are using a sharpened awareness of words to sharpen our perception of the phenomena". Wittgenstein also has a say in formulating what has been Cavell's obsession throughout his work: the search for the right, fitting tone—at once conceptually, morally, perceptually, musically—which Cavell mentions in his first autobiographical essay with regard to his mother's musical talent and his father's jokes.

Knowing and meaning what we say:

> I mean, of course, the ordinary world. That may not be all there is, but it is important enough: morality is that world, and so are force and love; so is art and a part of knowledge (the part which is about the world); and so is religion (wherever God is). (Cavell, *MWM* 40)

And this takes us back to the ethics of importance, which is an ethics of attention to oneself, to our own experience, which means giving importance to your experience, coming to your own attention—as Cavell says in *Little Did I Know*: "taking yourself seriously".

Failure of perception, or more precisely misperception, misappreciation, is what can lead us to miss our own adventure: what Austin called "thoughtlessness, inconsiderateness". In order to understand importance, we need to *appreciate* situations. Appreciation is at the core of this aesthetic understanding. Austin explains.

Understanding has to become a task of appreciation, both conceptual and experiential, and goes back to the concepts of pawnbroking—involving both accurateness and attention, truth and importance.

Importance, or what we care about, defines my task and the task of philosophy: to discover importance not only through accurate perception but also through our inabilities and misperceptions and failures, our being unable to see, our failure to perceive, our *missing the subject*. This is "the relocation of interest and importance, the recounting of importance" that Cavell assigned as a guiding task of philosophy (*CW* 262): but now a further relocation is needed, because importance is also to be defined through our essential failure to see the importance of things.

> It is as if an inherent concealment of significance, as much as its revelation, were part of the governing force of what we mean by film acting and film directing and film viewing. (*TOS* 11)

"Missing the adventure" and "missing the importance" are then constitutive of our ordinary lives—we are permanently not only missing the adventure but also "missing the evanescence of the subject".

The search for importance requires the recognition and acceptance of our failures to acknowledge importance, to "guess the unseen from the seen". This can be seen in two different ways. Importance may be concealed *as* it is revealed to us as something more essentially hidden. This is something Diamond tells us about "missing the adventure" by studying a different kind of blindness: blindness to what is actually going on in a novel, because we are precisely caught in moral issues and, for example, care so much for a character that we are blind to what is happening to her. In *The Portrait of a Lady*, we like Isabel so much that we are blind to other readings and understandings of the situation.

> We readers of *The Portrait of a Lady* may find ourselves reading the novel with the question: Should Isabel or should she not go back to Osmond? … The moral issue *what she should do* so interests us, we like her so much, we hate so much her having to go back or thinking she must go back to this horrible man, that we do not actually see *her* fully; do not see her as the great maker of something out of what happens to her, we do not see the relevance of her genius for appreciation. We may miss the sense of what she does, miss her adventure, impoverish our own, through our very concern (care) for her. (*RS* 316)

What remains, then, to be explored, is the mode of appearance of this *hidden importance* of things, the way we are essentially blind to it, that is, *meant* to be blind to it, in order to share the adventures of the characters we like or hate or are interested in. Could importance *of some kind* be essentially dissimulated from us? To overcome skepticism and this vulnerability is to overcome our inability, our refusal, to *see what matters*: "to fail to guess the unseen from the seen, to fail to trace the implications of things—that is to fail the perception that that there *is* something to be guessed and traced, right or wrong". This is at the core of the redefinition of ethics, and of the pursuit of happiness, through the search of importance and the recognition of our failures to acknowledge importance.

Hence for Cavell the importance of film in understanding *what matters*:

> We involve the movies in us. They become further fragments of what happens to me, further cards in the shuffle of my memory, with no telling what place in the future. Like childhood memories whose treasure no one else appreciates, whose content is nothing compared to their unspeakable importance for me. (Cavell, *The World Viewed*, p. 154)

REFERENCES

Austin, J.L. 1994. *Philosophical Papers*. Oxford and New York: Oxford University Press and Clarendon Press, 1962 (PP).

Cavell, S. 1969. *Must We Mean What We Say?* Cambridge: Cambridge University Press (MWM).

———. 1971. *The World Viewed*. Cambridge, MA: Harvard University Press.

———. 1979. *The Claim of Reason*. Cambridge University Press (CR).

———. 1981. *Pursuits of Happiness*. Cambridge, MA: Harvard University Press (PH).

———. 1984. *Themes Out of School*. San Francisco: North Point Press (TOS).

———. 2005. *Cities of Words*. Cambridge, MA: Harvard University Press (CW).

———. 2010. *Little Did I Know*. Stanford University Press (LDIK).

Das, V. 2007. *Life and Words, Violence and the Descent in the Ordinary*. University of California Press.

Diamond., C. 1991. *The Realistic Spirit, Wittgenstein, Philosophy, and the Mind*. Cambridge, MA: MIT Press (RS).

———. 1997. Moral Differences and Distances. In *Commonality and Particularity in Ethics*, ed. L. Alanen, S. Heinamaa, and T. Wallgren, 197–234. London: Macmillan.

———. 2000. Ethics, Imagination, and the Method of Wittgenstein's *Tractatus*. In *The New Wittgenstein*, ed. A. Crary and R. Read. Routledge.

Laugier, S., ed. 2006. *Ethique, litterature, vie humaine*. Paris: PUF.

———. 2013. *Why We Need OLP*. Chicago: University of Chicago Press.

———. 2015a. *Recommencer la philosophie*. S. Cavell et la philosophie en Amérique, nouvelle ed. Paris: Vrin.

———. 2015b. The Ethics of Care as a Politics of the Ordinary. *New Literary History* 46 (2015): 217–240.

———. 2015c. Voice as Form of Life and Life Form. *Nordic Wittgenstein Review* 4 (2015): 63–81.

Laugier S. 2016a. Care, the Ordinary, Forms of Life. *Iride. Filosofia e discussione pubblica*, n° 1/2016: 109–121.

———. 2016b. Politics of Vulnerability and Responsibility for Ordinary Others, *Critical* Horizons. *A Journal of Philosophy and Social Theory* 17 (2). https://www.tandfonline.com/doi/abs/10.1080/14409917.2016.1153891.

Murdoch, I. 1997. Vision and Choice in Morality. In *Existentialists and Mystics: Writings on Philosophy and Literature*, ed. Iris Murdoch and Peter J. Conradi. London: Chatto and Windus.

Putnam H. 1994. *Words and Life*. Edited by J. Conant. Cambridge, MA: Harvard University Press.

———. 2000. Entretien avec J. Bouveresse (unpublished).

Wittgenstein L. 1953. *Philosophische Untersuchungen*. Edited by G. E. M. Anscombe, G. H. von Wright & R. Rhees. Oxford: Blackwell, second edition 1958 (PI).

CHAPTER 8

Achilles' Tears: Cavell, the *Iliad*, and Possibilities for the Human

David LaRocca

He who is unable to live in society, or who has no need because he is sufficient for himself, must be either a beast or a god: he is no part of a state.
—Aristotle[1]

Awesome—as when the grip of madness seizes one who murders a man in his own fatherland and flees abroad to foreign shores, to a wealthy, noble host, and a sense of marvel runs through all who see him—
—Homer[2]

---

[1] Aristotle, *Politics* in *The Basic Works of Aristotle*, trans. Richard McKeon (New York: Random House, 1941), Book I.2. It is my pleasure to have an occasion to thank those who have aided my research on this chapter, and for their generous insights, improved and enriched the present essay: Stanley Cavell, Kimberley C. Patton, the late Helmut Koester, the late Gordon D. Kaufman, Despina Kakoudaki, the late Newton Garver, J. M. Bernstein, Lawrence Rhu, William Rothman, Michael Shaw, David Glidden, and especially Garry L. Hagberg.

[2] Homer, *the Iliad*, trans., Robert Fagles (New York: Viking, 1990), Book 24, lines 563–66. Note, all quotations from the *Iliad* come from this edition and translation (unless

---

D. LaRocca (✉)
Ithaca, NY, USA
e-mail: davidlarocca@post.harvard.edu

© The Author(s) 2018
G. L. Hagberg (ed.), *Stanley Cavell on Aesthetic Understanding*, Philosophers in Depth,
https://doi.org/10.1007/978-3-319-97466-8_8

> Gone is the armor of power that formerly protected their naked souls; nothing, no shield, stands between them and tears.
> —Simone Weil[3]

As Stanley Cavell has articulated on many occasions over the years, "[n]othing could be more human" than "the power of the motive to reject the human."[4] Moreover, he observes that there is "inherent in philosophy a certain drive to the inhuman," and that we find in this drive "the most inescapably human of motivations."[5] To be human, on this register, means to wish or will the end or erasure of one's humanity—yet to become what instead? A beast or a god, in Aristotle's parlance? Or is the "motive to reject the human," paradoxically, part of an effort to understand the human—in effect to humanize oneself by means of an agonistic, self-imposed contestation? In Cavell's depiction of the human predicament, we are somehow endlessly caught up in questions about (human) knowing and (human) being, and therefore inclined to struggle with questions of solipsism and skepticism (or the world beyond our minds and bodies that we desire to address and comprehend); this network of concerns may be described with admiration as Cavell's attunement to the history of humanism, and also marking out his contribution to it.[6] We seem mired in

---

otherwise noted) and will be henceforth cited by book and line number, except when quoting from Bernard Knox's introduction, in which case the page(s) will be given.

[3] Simone Weil, *The Iliad; or, The Poem of Force* (Wallingford, PA: Pendle Hill Publications, 1993; originally published 1940), p. 15. See also Simone Weil, *The Iliad; or, The Poem of Force—A Critical Edition*, trans. James P. Holoka (New York: Peter Lang, 2003).

[4] Stanley Cavell, *The Claim of Reason: Wittgenstein, Skepticism, Morality, Tragedy* (Oxford: Oxford University Press, 1979/1999), p. 207.

[5] Stanley Cavell, "An Interview with Stanley Cavell," James Conant, in *The Senses of Stanley Cavell*, ed. Richard Fleming and Michael Payne, *Bucknell Review* 32, no. 1 (1989) and (Cranbury, NJ: Associated University Presses, 1989), p. 50. See also Richard Eldridge, "Between Acknowledgment and Avoidance," in *Stanley Cavell* (Cambridge: Cambridge University Press, 2003), p. 4; and David LaRocca, "The Education of Grown-ups: An Aesthetics of Reading Cavell," *The Journal of Aesthetic Education*, 47, no. 2 (Summer 2013): 109–31 and "Defying Definition: Opening Remarks on the Transcendental" in *The Bloomsbury Anthology of Transcendental Thought: From Antiquity to the Anthropocene*, ed. David LaRocca (New York: Bloomsbury, 2017).

[6] See *Stanley Cavell and Literary Studies: Consequences of Skepticism*, ed. Richard Eldridge and Bernard Rhie (New York: Continuum, 2011), pp. 4–5, and LaRocca (2013), p. 112.

our plea to resolve whether "I am inside my body or I am my body."[7] Something of this mystical befuddlement remains inexorable and vexing, a hallmark trait of a mind that must think of *and* for itself. In these self-reflexive trials befitting the *ouroboros*, our own metaphysical condition—what and who were are—is in danger of never reaching beyond the boundaries of our individual being. We become irrevocably, tragically, existential narcissists. To mediate our distress, Cavell turns us, with interpretations of characteristic candor and illumination, to the figure of the human in a multitude of fictitious forms—from Othello to Mélisande; C. K. Dexter Haven to Stella Dallas; Henry James' Morris Gedge to Ibsen's Nora—and how we might, I don't know, learn from their struggles for *our* struggles.[8] These figurations—as artfully realized in fiction as they are read with now-iconic transformation by Cavell himself (sometimes making them *more* pertinent to our human quandaries—in a word, more philosophical—than even their authors might have achieved or imagined). In these fictions, Cavell founds elemental qualities of our humanity so that we might, as individuals, find our own.

Yet if the foregoing is a Cavellian prelude to an essay that takes up most centrally a core scene in the *Iliad*, and in particular, a moment in which grown men weep together (over other grown men who have died, or who might), our question becomes: what does Cavell help us see about Homer's epic, especially as that indelible work relates to the ongoing, millennia-old conversation about the human that we, despite all, continue to have and contest within? Though Achilles shares fictional status with Othello and the rest, he is, unlike them, shall we say, not quite human, or rather *more* than human. He is a demi-god. And yet, as a half-god, we are forced to ask anew if that status makes him (also) *less* than human? Achilles' existential position, therefore, is a puzzle worth mulling over, if not just to illuminate the meaning of demi-gods in pagan antiquity, but also—especially for this occasion—to make an exhibition of our contemporary meaning(s) of the human, that is, what we think we are. Of course, such a statement about "the human" is too broad and (justifiably) stirs the ire of

---

[7] Cavell, *The Claim of Reason*, p. 397.
[8] See also David LaRocca, "'Eternal Allusions': Maeterlinck's Readings of Emerson's Somatic Semiotics," in *A Power to Translate the World: New Essays on Emerson and International Culture*, ed. David LaRocca and Ricardo Miguel-Alfonso (Re-mapping the Transnational, Donald Pease, Series Editor; Dartmouth College Press, 2015), pp. 113–35.

anti-essentialists and anti-foundationalists, but I am asking both more and less than that question: the purpose of drawing Cavell's remarks on the human toward Achilles' and the *Iliad* is to explore how they may give shape to our sense of what we can know (about ourselves and others) through an attunement to the manner in which people express their emotions before us—especially if the audience for these human emotions is, well, not (fully?) human, if he is, let us call him, Achilles. And conversely, what can we make when a demi-god performs his or her emotions before an audience of humans (in the principle scene of our action here, Achilles before Priam)? Where we imagined a human-to-human encounter, of men weeping together, we instead discover an ontological asymmetry. The one who "break[s] through men,"[9] and the king of Troy may share a tent, but what can we say they *share* in terms of their emotional expressivity, and thus mutual intelligibility—since, in our day, in *our* human-to-human encounters we often remain frightfully, painfully inaccessible to one another? If we can source the hurt of Priam's tears, what can we make of Achilles' tears—their affective significance, their symbolic evocation (to Priam, to us, even to Achilles himself), their production of sensibility; their plea for acknowledgment by another even as they may be said to authentically confess (*express*) this soldier's deepest grief?

With these questions at hand, Cavell's committed, inventive readings of fictional characters may have found a new (yet ancient) figure worthy of our reflection—namely, the man who appears to exhibit the most human of traits—*lacrimosus, dolorosus*—and yet, is not human himself; again, we need to decide whether it is fairer to say Achilles is "not fully human," or is "partially human"—and what then of the divine? How precisely, does the portion of humanity mix, if at all, with the portion of divinity? (These questions may need to remain at the level of conjecture, since they seem as metaphysical as they are metaphorical.) In an uncanny way, of course, in our turn back to Homer—to the indelible character of Achilles that haunts the literature of Western civilization—we are also, concomitantly, hurried to the present and future to ask similar, if not the same, questions about animals and artificial intelligence and so on, in effect, the broad sweep of the expanding landscape of the post-human and the trans-human.[10] Is the

---

[9] Among epithets for Achilles, we find him "breaking through men" (ῥηξ-ήνωρ).

[10] See Cary Wolfe, *What is Posthumanism?* (Minneapolis: University of Minnesota Press, 2010); Stephen Mulhall, *The Dying Animal: J. M. Coetzee and the Difficulty of Reality in*

demi-god Achilles, we are tempted to say, "human enough" to fathom Priam's pain as well as his own mortal losses (actual and imagined)? Can Achilles *feel* for his fellow man in a way that we, humans, know as our own? And more particularly, what does this half-god's behavior—the way he is moved to tears by the plea of another man—tell us about the nature of human empathy more generally, our knowledge of how *others* feel, and the possibility of the human as such? Sometimes it is those who are not fully human—gods, demi-gods, animals, the animated that may no longer be animate (and here we must call on the whole history of cinematic projections, as Cavell does: "It is an incontestable fact that in a motion picture no live human being is up there. But a human *something* is, and something unlike anything else we know.")[11]—who demonstrate, reinforce, or call out for questioning and denial of (our presumed) human traits.

Though we humans live among many thousands of distinct non-human species, we are prone to say, at least until recent history, that man is the only thinking animal, indeed a *homo sapiens*. Yet, if we are so confident of ourselves as the (only) kind of being that thinks, we remain vexed by the fact that we do not have a reliable way of reading the minds of others, nor of feeling precisely what others feel. We do not possess telepathic powers or extra-sensory perception; we are not mind readers. So though we may *want* to know what another feels (or thinks), we do not have access to such inner states; our "access," if any, can be said to operate (only) at the level of "reading" the performances of others—their embodied actions or their actions of speech.[12] We become "friends of interpretable objects," whether they be somatic movements or linguistic inventions.[13]

Literature and Philosophy (Princeton: Princeton University Press, 2010); David LaRocca and Ricardo Miguel-Alfonso, "Thinking Through International Influence," in *A Power to Translate the World* (2015), pp. 1–28; and David LaRocca, "'Profoundly Unreconciled to Nature': Ecstatic Truth and the Humanistic Sublime in Werner Herzog's War Films" in *The Philosophy of War Films*, ed. David LaRocca (Lexington: University Press of Kentucky, 2014), pp. 437–82.

[11] Stanley Cavell, *The World Viewed: Reflections on the Ontology of Film*, Enlarged ed. (Cambridge: Harvard University Press, 1979), p. 26.

[12] See David LaRocca, "Performative Inferentialism: A Semiotic Ethics," *Liminalities: A Journal of Performance Studies*, 9, no. 1 (February 2013), and "The False Pretender: Deleuze, Sherman, and the Status of Simulacra," *The Journal of Aesthetics and Art Criticism*, no. 3 (Summer 2011).

[13] See Miguel Tamen, *Friends of Interpretable Objects* (Cambridge: Harvard University Press, 2004).

Our sense of empathy pushes beyond sympathy (a feeling with) to become something like a presumption of feeling *within*; our narratives and definitions of empathy reinforce the impression that vicarious experience is somehow a form of bona fide knowledge.[14] Despite our skills for reading and interpreting, it remains a beguiling fantasy of knowledge, does it not?, to consider that by some sort of clarity about *our own* feelings (and minds) we can claim knowledge of the feelings (and thoughts) of others—as if, as an individual, a person were sufficiently representative of others to make reliable inferences about their interior realms that otherwise would appear to lie behind or beyond an impassable divide (though it be only the thickness of the human skull). Cavell has participated in the long history of this debate about other minds, and his work on the interaction between self-knowledge and knowledge of others—especially as it informs our emotional and affective capacities—becomes a guiding force in what follows. One of the "possibilities for the human," as alluded to in the subtitle, is that we can say something meaningful about our knowledge of others *because of* certain achievements of self-knowledge. Another is that knowledge is not the sort of thing we can (ever) claim about our relationship to the inner lives of others; on this second take, humans—regardless of the intimacy and intensity of communication (e.g., their successes as readers and interpreters of others' bodies, behaviors, and speech)—remain, as it were, strangers, and thus perpetually, permanently estranged. If this latter, bleak view holds, we will stand in need of some compensatory theory for thinking about the ways in which we *believe* we have (and do *achieve*) meaningful "knowledge" of others (e.g., their inner lives, their feelings, etc.); the quotation marks have been added to admit that it may be the wrong word, that, in fact, we should not use it in such contexts and that we are in need of some other way of describing what it is we wish to say

---

[14] Here as elsewhere, it may be useful to distinguish between empathy and sympathy. Adam Smith, for example, in *The Theory of Moral Sentiments* (1759), describes sympathy as "fellow-feeling for the misery of others." Other figures to consult for variations on these two terms include Rousseau (*pitié*), Hume, Herder, Dilthey, Schelling, Schleiermacher, the Schlegels, and Novalis. Indeed, as Robert Sinnerbrink writes: "Herder […] applied the notion of *Einfühlung* [empathy] to the interpretation of texts, arguing that one could experience the ideas of an artist or author through an 'empathic' projection that opens up a text's inner symbolic meaning." See *Cinematic Ethics: Exploring Ethical Experience through Film* (London: Routledge, 2016), pp. 89–90. For Herder, empathic projection not only applies to humans, as in our case, but to inanimate things as well.

we have accomplished. Still, what seems quintessentially human—our sociality, our desire of human congress, for example—may be founded on false premises and made from false promises. Evaluating these "possibilities for the human" is the critical project that underwrites the task of undertaking a close reading of the *Iliad* in league with an applied Cavellian sensibility for what he calls "the stake of the other."[15] Because human desire (erotic and intellectual) is often thwarted, the thing we think we have wanted may not be possible, and so we have to invent a story to slake our frustration. With Cavell's prodigious remarks on these varied and contested stories ready to hand, what can the *Iliad* tell us about the story we tell ourselves about human emotion—not just our own, and not just that of others, but what we can say about our *knowledge* of what others feel?

While we are discussing the meaning (practice? ability?) of self-knowledge, Cavell's work in company with the *Iliad* may lead us to ask if we are also in need of a notion of "self-acknowledgment"—for example, as a way to gloss the problem of narcissistic grieving, that is, when it seems our emotions for others are motivated by our feelings about ourselves. Can this notion—fledgling though it may be—possibly scan with Cavell's notion of acknowledgement (with its inherent sense of other-directedness)? Or does self-acknowledgement, in this nascent state of postulation, present something of a challenge to it, for example, troubling what we may think of as the *authenticity* of Cavellian acknowledgment (in the sense that it is even possible for us to *achieve* acknowledgment without the phenomenon being re-described or reassessed as a variant of self-acknowledgment)? In the light of such concepts and questions, Achilles becomes the troubling emblem of a provocation to think and re-think acknowledgment as a genuine possibility for human emotive expression, even as it bypasses its will to knowledge.

A reader should not take the sustained attention to the *Iliad* in what follows as a sign of neglecting Cavell's work, but rather regard the full sweep of the inquiry as informed by presiding, abiding Cavellian concerns, ones I have made explicit here, at the outset, and return to later, but also those that may remain (for lack of space) implicit, or related by indirect—but salient—connection to works by philosophers to which Cavell himself

---

[15] Stanley Cavell, "Othello and the Stake of the Other," in *Disowning Knowledge in Seven Plays of Shakespeare* (Cambridge: Cambridge University Press, 1987, updated edition, 2003).

has directly addressed his attention (e.g., Norman Malcolm).[16] Cavell's remarks on human emotion, the status of the human, his reading of empathic projection (especially from *The Claim of Reason*),[17] constitute the intellectual atmosphere of these proceedings.

Still more, the syntagma "aesthetic understanding" that presides over the contributions to the present volume may be invoked, at least in this more local precinct, to conjure our remembrance that Cavell's professional title glosses his work as falling under the banner of "aesthetics and the general theory of value." We are reminded, that is, how ethics and aesthetics are conceived under the shared category of "value theory." Yet, in what sense is (the) *aesthetic* related to understanding; in what way(s) is "aesthetic" modifying "understanding"—such that we say, for example: we do not merely *have* understanding, but something more, or less, or altogether different? Aesthetic understanding would therefore be a *kind* of understanding, and, as I am treating it, *akin* to ethical understanding. Value theory, as a category of philosophical description, or accountability for ideas, makes the case for me, since the lingua franca of ethics and aesthetics is *judgment*: of the good, true, and right (in the former case) and of the beautiful (in the latter). A theory of value—and thus of judgment—will, mutatis mutandis, draw us back to fundamental questions of humanistic inquiry, among them: how do I know my judgments to be sound, valid, and we might even add, my own?

The chapters in this book, and I hope my own, go some way to making more evident, explicit, and efficacious the ways in which aesthetic understanding is a significant part of our daily experience of what it means to be human (to achieve it, to know it), indeed, what we would *want* it to mean to be human. Though aesthetic understanding would seem a familiar presence—part of the everyday and ordinary experience we take for granted—my reading of Cavell, by way of the *Iliad*, suggests, on the contrary, that it is more *aspirational* than (already) factual and immanent. We are, thus,

---

[16] For example, Norman Malcolm's work becomes a point of shared interest between the present essay and Cavell's "Knowing and Acknowledging," though I draw from Malcolm's "Knowledge of Other Minds" (1964), while Cavell uses Malcolm's "The Privacy of Experience," in *Epistemology: New Essays in the Theory of Knowledge*, ed. Avrum Stroll (New York: Harper and Row, 1967), pp. 129–58; for the latter, see Cavell, "Knowing and Acknowledging," *Must We Mean What We Say?: A Book of Essays* (Cambridge, UK: Cambridge University Press, 1976), pp. 238–66, esp. 242n1.

[17] Cavell, *The Claim of Reason*, see esp. Part IV, pp. 420–55.

as likely to find ourselves failing at our expression or achievement of aesthetic understanding (e.g., under the term that Cavell names acknowledgment) as often as we fail at discerning what it means to do the right thing, or to have satisfied justice.

Cavell's definitive, nuanced conjuring of (Emersonian) moral perfectionism depends on our remembrance of its characteristics "onwardness," its steadily invoked "new, yet unattainable" status.[18] Aesthetic understanding, like, or in company with, moral perfectionism exists, for the most part, in a state of deferment. Reading the *Iliad* in Cavell's company illuminates the intimacies among, and overlaps between, aesthetic understanding and moral perfectionism; they are tandem enterprises, and both announce anew, with each new encounter, the human questions that vex our judgment, and thus our capacity to assess, define, and defend the pronouncements of value we hold so dear, or wish so desperately to defeat.

1 A Human Encounter?

In the final book of the *Iliad*, Priam travels to Achilles' tent to offer "priceless ransom" for the body of his slain son, Hector.[19] By this point, we know that Achilles killed Hector as a legitimate combatant enemy of the Achaeans, but also, more personally and pointedly, in revenge for Hector's slaying (albeit in a moment of misrecognition) of Patroclus, Achilles' mentor and dearest friend—Hector taking the son of Menoetius to be the "swift footed" son of Peleus. Indulging his enraged grief (he "kept on grieving for his friend, the memory burning on [...] the memories flooded over him, live tears flowing"),[20] Achilles has made sport of dragging Hector's corpse around Patroclus' tomb. Earlier, when Achilles heard of Patroclus' death a "black cloud of grief came shrouding over" him: "Antilochus kneeling near, weeping uncontrollably, clutched Achilles' hands as he wept his proud heart out—for fear he would slash his throat with an iron blade."[21] This gut-wrenching torment is a signature pretext of Achilles' emotional state when he is approached by Priam, and the men

---

[18] Stanley Cavell, *Emerson's Transcendental Etudes*, ed. David Justin Hodge (Stanford: Stanford University Press, 2003), p. 19.
[19] *The Iliad*, 24.587.
[20] *The Iliad*, 24.4–12.
[21] *The Iliad*, 18.25; 18.36–38.

weep together. In this revelatory encounter, we find men—who are sworn enemies, with long, complex histories of antagonism, and a recent killing that inextricably binds them—share a moment of weeping, and then, perhaps surprisingly, a sense of awe at each other's beauty. In this scene, these enemies make themselves vulnerable to each other, and in that exposure, confirm the commonality of their humanity and suffering. Discovering King Priam suppliant to Achilles' mercy, a father begging another man's son for leniency with the body of his own son (now dead), complicates their relationship of power, their status as enemies, and their positions as men—especially as they figure themselves in varying modes of surrogacy: one the imagined son (Achilles for Hector), the other the imagined father (Priam for Peleus).

We may observe, then, a way to approach male emotive weeping as it relates to Achilles' recognition of something in another human being that is not inert, that is not dehumanizing—not a (material) thing but an entity capable and worthy of emotional relationality. In a word, a human being. It would seem that tears humanize and interfere with the stolid economy of exchanging a (material) ransom for a (material) corpse. Do tears, on this occasion, transform the human being (even if a corpse) into something more than, as Simone Weil puts it, a thing?[22] Priam's plea, coextensive with his weeping, appears to activate Achilles' change of heart—"melt[s] his rage"—and this turn of affection, or shift in perception, "stir" Achilles' empathic projection.[23] (For those familiar with Cavell's discussion of the "active skeptical recital" in *The Claim of Reason*, we can gloss the parallels between our opposition—or coupling—of "a human" and "a thing," by way of Weil, and Cavell's concern "that skepticism with respect to others is, or can be, produced along the lines that produced skepticism with respect to the external world," that is, physical objects beyond the mind.)[24]

---

[22] See Section 3 below.

[23] *The Iliad*, 24.592–93; 24.146. The idea of empathic projection will be discussed further below, but I wish to note here a concern about the use of this modern theory for an analysis of an ancient Greek text and culture, principally, that there is arguably no concept in the Greek language that fully parallels our idea of empathy. For the Greeks, empathy was something more akin to "emotion in general" (Michael Shaw, Department of Classics, University of Kansas; private correspondence). Given this proviso, though, it should become clear in the course of the present argument that the ideas proposed by John Stuart Mill, Norman Malcolm, A. J. Ayer, Stanley Cavell, and others, regarding empathic projection bear a strong conceptual relationship to the experiences of characters in the *Iliad*, despite the lack of an isomorphic term or concept in the Greek language.

[24] Cavell, *The Claim of Reason*, pp. 420–21.

To summon a picture of the possibility that empathic projection is, for Achilles, a means or mode of relationality—both to his own internal states and those he encounters in others (or presumes to)—we can dwell on text that tells us how Priam's "words stirred within Achilles a deep desire to grieve for his own father."[25] In this moment of inwardness ("overpowered by memory"),[26] Achilles yet is *also* able to see his father when he looks at Priam, and so he *feels* toward Priam as he would toward his father: natively, intuitively recognizing that his father is more than a thing (and by association or overlap, so must be this father, Priam). Though tears proliferate in the *Iliad*, the tears shed and shared between Achilles and Priam—based on this special surrogacy of father for father, of son for son—elucidate something that has gone unacknowledged throughout the story: that men are, at last, capable of being more than corpses in the making. Achilles' status as a demi-god, doubtless, troubles our sense both of the theurgic power of his tears (what might they summon?), and by extension, what we can expect (of ourselves and others) as those who weep, shall we say, *merely* as humans. When Achilles spares Priam, and then heals him with food and rest, along with time to mourn and bury his son, he, nevertheless, exhibits this very human possibility.[27]

2 Weeping with the Enemy

The *Iliad* is comprised of myriad scenes of physical violence meted out from one man to another; almost every page of the epic registers the awful brutality of war—ever amidst the gritty proximity of armed men, fighting beard to beard—and the costs it demands in body and heart. To the enemy, the corpse of the offending party is a sign of victory, a purely material emblem of dominant power confirmed. The same corpse, however, held-in-arms by a comrade, is a dearly lost and irreplaceable friend; that body, bleeding over his hands, becomes an invitation to revenge—and, doubtless,

---

[25] *The Iliad*, 24.592–93.

[26] *The Iliad*, 24.594.

[27] Crying is a strictly human possibility according to some scholars—see, for example, Tom Lutz, *Crying: The Natural and Cultural History of Tears* (New York: W.W. Norton & Company, 1999)—but it is important to note (and reflect on) the striking fact that, in the *Iliad*, there are non-human criers, among them Zeus, who weeps when his son, Sarpedon, is killed (and then, not shedding watery tears but tears of blood); and Achilles' horses, who weep after the deaths of Patroclus and Achilles.

its moral justification. The cycle proceeds, as it does so tragically in our own time, line after glorious and gruesome line. Yet toward the end of the *Iliad* this familiar, seemingly intractable and commonplace economy of trade, either as a body for ransom (with Chryseis), or as a corpse understood as an incitement to avenge losses, is temporarily suspended. We enter a kind of asylum from the normal system of motivations and advantages, rationalizations and rage-induced retributions. We enter, it seems, a space in which tears have a genuinely transformative effect on the men who shed them. The result of this conversion, however provisional it may be, is nothing less than an occasion on which a man (or the human part of this demi-god) is humbly reminded of his humanity, and his connectedness with the world and to other men—which is to leave open, whether this connection can count as understanding or knowledge of them. Still, in this space, Achilles would seem to see his enemy as a man, not just as a commodity to be traded, or an object to be destroyed.[28] Concomitantly, Achilles sees himself as a man (or recognizes that part of him that is human) and thus capable of human emotion.

Priam arrives at Achilles' tent, having been escorted and protected along the way by Hermes (a god who assures safe passage through an otherwise impassable gauntlet of the Achaean fleet), and then Priam makes his first move of supplication to the imposing warrior:

> The majestic king of Troy slipped past the rest
> and kneeling down beside Achilles, clasped his knees
> and kissed his hands, those terrible, man killing hands
> that had slaughtered Priam's many sons in battle.[29]

Achilles has killed many of Priam's fifty sons, and yet, the king's approach to him is at once stealthy and unthreatening. Achilles is shocked to believe that any man—much less the king of the opposing army—would dare to enter his compound, or succeed in doing so; later he will realize that Priam was aided through the gates by the divine messenger. What is more, the man does not enter with spear in hand, poised to pierce the

---

[28] This assessment is complemented by Rachel Bespaloff, who writes: "The two adversaries can exchange looks without seeing each other as targets, as objects which there is merit in destroying" in "Priam and Achilles Break Bread," *Modern Critical Views: Homer*, ed. Harold Bloom (New York: Chelsea House Publishers, 1986), p. 35.

[29] *The Iliad*, 24.559–62.

heart of this despised murderer, but rather to engage his heart with a plea. Priam's direct contact with Achilles is not with the cold, sharp edge of a mottled sword, but with the softness of his warm lips pressed against the very hands that took so many precious lives, including his beloved Hector. "So Achilles marveled, beholding Priam."[30]

Achilles does not reach for a weapon himself nor commandeer his soldiers to apprehend the trespasser; still stunned by the king's divinely authorized entry, and by the extreme display of physical supplication (kneeling) and affection (kissing) as well as narrative bids for mercy, Achilles listens to Priam as he draws an analogical portrait of emotional pain:

> Remember your own father, great godlike Achilles—
> as old as *I* am, past the threshold of deadly old age!
> No doubt the countrymen round about him plague him now,
> with no one there to defend him, beat away disaster.
> No one—but at last he hears you're still alive
> and his old heart rejoices, hopes rising, day by day,
> to see his beloved son come sailing home from Troy.[31]

Priam's first effort is *not* to make himself known as the king of Troy, one who, according to the decorum of war, has a legitimate claim to his son's corpse, but rather to be seen by Achilles as if in the position of Achilles' own father, Peleus. Where Priam's kneeling and kissing were physical signs of his mendicancy (and to be sure, his genuine suffering), now we discover his efforts at a cognitive transformation in his charge that yet conveys the emotional reality that underwrites the purpose of his visit. In his cunning, however sincere, Priam appears to instigate a kind of affective legerdemain. It were as if Peleus, not Priam, had come to the tent to beg Hector to hand over Achilles' dead body. Invoking the memory of Peleus first makes Achilles vulnerable (or simply available, that is, able to hear, to feel in response) to Priam's attempted exchange of fathers. If this trade is convincing, then Achilles might release Hector to Priam from a successful appeal to fairness, again returning us to the moral economy of war—since he would want Hector to release his own body to Peleus, were

---

[30] *The Iliad*, 24.568.
[31] *The Iliad*, 24.570–76.

such an outcome conceivable. Priam takes a surprising, seemingly counterintuitive tack, however, since he doesn't stoke similarities between the fathers but rather *contrasts* Peleus' fortune with his own life, "so cursed by fate":

> I fathered hero sons in the wide realm of Troy
> and now not a single one is left, I tell you.
> ...   Many,
> most of them violent Ares cut the knees from under.
> But one, one was left me, to guard my walls, my people—
> the one you killed the other day, defending his fatherland,
> my Hector! It's all for him I've come to the ships now,
> to win him back from you—I bring a priceless ransom.
> Revere the gods, Achilles! Pity me in my own right,
> Remember your own father! I deserve more pity…
> I have endured what no one on earth has even done before—
> I put to my lips the hands of the man who killed my son.[32]

Even the god Ares, sworn protector of the Trojans, allowed Priam's many sons to perish. Indeed, as this translation handles it: the sons were brought to their knees. Now their father comes to Achilles on his knees, not because he was cut down to this level, but because he willed himself into this supplicatory position as a last attempt to honor (and recover what remained of) his most beloved son, "my best son!," Hector, through funerary rites.[33] First Priam has likened himself to Peleus, a father, and now to his fallen sons. In this way, he is both a father suffering for his son's death, as Peleus will someday be, and he is, like his sons, on his knees before a dominating force that has the power to spear him or spare him.

The trades of identity in Priam's brief soliloquy are manifold and complex, and they establish the context in which Achilles will weep. Priam's order of presentation, first as anonymous father to be taken as a surrogate for Peleus, and then as Hector's father to be regarded as deserving of Achilles' pity, forces Achilles to imagine Peleus weeping, and thereby to contend with the kind of pain a father suffers when losing a beloved son. In presuming his father's pain (that is, *imagining* it), as he bears witness

---

[32] *The Iliad*, 24.578–91.
[33] *The Iliad*, 24.288.

to Priam's pain, Achilles empathically projects an emotion (onto Priam), and by making this transference, he is stirred to tears.

As a moment of pause or digression—but with import—consider how such descriptions suggest a potentially useful linkage to Gilles Deleuze's work on Herman Melville's *Bartleby, the Scrivener*, especially when Deleuze describes the "relation of identification" between one character and another.[34] Of course Deleuze is speaking of Bartleby and his boss, the attorney, but we can hear the same point at issue between Achilles and Priam, namely, that this "relation of identification" is "a complex operation that passes through all of the adventures of resemblance, and that always risks falling into neurosis or turning into narcissism. A 'mimetic rivalry' as it is sometimes called. It mobilizes a paternal function in general: an image of the father par excellence, and the subject is a son, even if the determinations are interchangeable."[35] What catches my attention is the way "resemblance" allows for slippage in identities, and that—returning to Achilles and Priam—how robustly they court just this kind of re-identification (of father^1-for-father^2, or son-for-father^1, or son-for-father^2, and many other such permutations) in order to achieve a new perspective (in this ancient text, a view from the position of the other). Yet notice how even though Deleuze is, admittedly, millennia removed from the *Iliad*, he recognizes a pattern or structure that is uncannily relevant to our reading here, namely, in which these trades of identification—often made possible by the stirring or stoking of feelings, often disturbing passions and desperate emotions—may result not just in neurosis, but in narcissism; this is a matrix and an outcome we should be prepared to find in the "relation of identification" and the "paternal function" already in evidence, and at work, in Ilium, and very far from Bartleby's New York. By projecting oneself outward (e.g., as a son seeks a view from the position of the father), one seems to hazard returning to one's own position with an even more violently committed self-reflexivity.[36] Empathy would seem to stoke narcissism. Not for nothing, then, when Deleuze asks "[w]hat then is the

---

[34] Gilles Deleuze, "Bartleby; Or, The Formula," in *Essays Critical and Clinical*, trans. Daniel W. Smith and Michael A. Greco (Minneapolis: University of Minnesota Press, 1997), p. 76.

[35] Deleuze, "Bartleby; Or, The Formula," p. 76.

[36] Surprisingly, though very much focused on Melville's work, Deleuze does make reference to Achilles in the context of Kleist's *Penthesilea*—"an Ahab-woman who, like her indiscernible double Achilles, had chosen her enemy, in defiance of the law of the Amazons

biggest problem haunting Melville's oeuvre?" Deleuze's reply befits our thinking about the *Iliad*: "reconciling ... the inhuman with the human."[37]

With these notes in hand, we return to the private tent the two men share, where Priam makes four demands of Achilles: revere the gods; pity me, Priam, in my own right; remember your own father, Peleus; and I, Priam, deserve more pity. This concatenation of demands, albeit petitions made from a supplicant's position, activate the sequence of translations Achilles will have to make in order to see the situation from Priam's point of view—that is, for Achilles to feel (to "feel"?) Priam's pain, we are tempted to say, within himself, and to recognize the correspondence of emotion that would prompt him, Achilles, to return Hector's body; somewhat suddenly, the very notion of feeling what another feels seems hopelessly confined to a gesture, that is, to a metaphor. (Emerson has been slandered by some latter-day literary critics for callousness when he expresses his experience of this unanticipated perception in himself, as he grieves the loss of his own boy: "In the death of my son, now more than two years ago, I seem to have lost a beautiful estate,—no more. I cannot get it nearer to me. [...] it does not touch me: some thing which I fancied was a part of me, which could not be torn away without tearing me, nor enlarged without enriching me, falls off from me, and leaves no scar. It was caducous."[38] Yet Emerson is not in congress and conversation with another; his experience is private, part of a conversation with himself, as he essays his grief—and then makes that report public, for us to read and reflect upon. Priam's meditations on his dead son are spoken to the person who caused the death; he doesn't address fate, which would *eo ipso* be fruitless, but instead makes a poem of his pain for the one who might modestly mitigate it. After Priam makes his thoughts known—are these lucid demands or febrile solicitations?—Achilles' response shows that he has been touched by more than gentle hands and soft lips:

---

forbidding the preference of one enemy over another." Deleuze, "Bartleby; Or, The Formula," p. 79.

[37] Deleuze, "Bartleby; Or, The Formula," p. 84. See also, David LaRocca, "The European Authorization of American Literature and Philosophy: After Cavell, Reading 'Bartleby' with Deleuze, then Rancière" in *Melville Among the Philosophers*, ed. Corey McCall and Tom Nurmi (Durham: Lexington Books, 2017), pp. 189–212.

[38] Ralph Waldo Emerson, "Experience," *Essays and Lectures* (New York: The Library of America, 1983), p. 473.

> Those words stirred within Achilles a deep desire
> to grieve for his own father. Taking the old man's hand
> he gently moved him back. And overpowered by memory
> both men gave way to grief. Priam wept freely
> for man-killing Hector, throbbing, crouching
> before Achilles' feet as Achilles wept himself,
> now for his father, now for Patroclus once again,
> and their sobbing rose and fell through the house.[39]

This moment is unlike any other in the *Iliad* in its depiction of men weeping together, specifically in terms of grieving shared between a father and a son, each a surrogate for the other: Priam as Peleus (for Achilles), and Achilles as Hector (for Priam). The tent is evidently crowded anew with these doubles and doppelgängers, real and imagined.

Yet, even with identities fabricated, duplicated, and traded, there is some question about the motivation for these tears, especially Achilles' tears. We may feel sure why Priam weeps: he grieves over his lost, dearest, last son. But why is Achilles weeping? And for whom does he weep? The text says he "grieves for his own father," and also for his fallen comrade, Patroclus. Achilles has wept for Patroclus before,[40] but why should he weep for his own father, since, after all, Peleus is still alive? The emotional logic on offer suggests that Achilles weeps when he remembers his father, and his father's grief—or is it better to say, thinks about some *future event* in his father's life, that is, this moment of Achilles' prospective death? Priam's pleas are aimed at mapping one identity (the generic father grieving over the generic dead son) onto another (the specific father weeping—in the future—over the specific dead son). According to this schema of substitution, we reach a startling conclusion: Achilles' tears are in fact *Priam's* tears. Achilles has projected Peleus onto Priam, and himself onto Hector. And since Achilles weeps Priam's tears (that is, a father's tears over his son), the conceptual rearrangement of these identities means that Achilles sheds tears *over himself*. He is weeping over his own death, a death he is sure will come (since his mother, Thetis, told him so; as she "mourned her brave son's fate, doomed to die, she knew, on the fertile soil of Troy"),[41] and *therefore* a death that will certainly cause surviving Peleus to

---

[39] *The Iliad*, 24.592–99.
[40] See *The Iliad*, 18.24.
[41] *The Iliad*, 24.104–05.

mourn over his lost son. Peleus, we are then forced to consider, will likely live to see his only son, Achilles, die. Because Achilles sustains Priam's demand for pity, and this demand engenders such comprehensive empathy, Achilles goes beyond merely feeling for the other: he feels for himself (that is to say, as if the phrase were a double entendre—that his intense emotions are not only his own but also are [only?] about *him*). In this way, it would seem he recovers that half of him that is human—and by a sort of bracketing of the divine—somehow makes it the whole of him. Aligning himself with men, and not the gods (such as his own mother), Achilles tells Priam: "What good's to be won from tears that chill the spirit? So the immortals spun our lives that we, we wretched men live on to bear such torments—the gods live free of sorrows."[42]

While I am here emphasizing a scene of male weeping, the foregoing logic—viz., that tears shed for another are in fact tears spilled for oneself—appears also in a scene of *female* weeping, for example, when Briseis mourns the death of Patroclus. There her grief channels the despair felt by many of the women who stood by her: "Her voice rang out in tears and the women wailed in answer, grief for Patroclus, calling forth each woman's private sorrows."[43] Mourning Patroclus *also* becomes a way of weeping for themselves—for their injury, hurts, and losses.

---

[42] *The Iliad*, 24.612–14. Given the significance and prevalence of film in Cavell's work, and indeed of the cultural uses that film is put in philosophy and elsewhere—often, we must admit, *in the place* of reading the literature on which it is based—we might benefit from a query into the adaptation of the *Iliad* as found in Wolfgang Petersen's *Troy* (2004). In the film, Achilles (played with sullen intensity by Brad Pitt) says that "we men are wretched things," just as we find it in Book 24. Yet what he goes on to tell Briseis, as in confidence, should surprise readers of Homer's epic: "I'll tell you a secret. Something they don't teach you in your temple. The gods envy us. They envy us because we're mortal, because any moment might be our last. Everything is more beautiful because we're doomed. You will never be lovelier than you are now. We will never be here again." Of course, these are not Homer's words but those of David Benioff, now perhaps more famous for being the creator and show-runner of *Game of Thrones*. As Charles C. Chiasson reminds us in "Redefining Homeric Heroism in Wolfgang Petersen's *Troy*," sentiments among the gods are "precisely the opposite" in the ancient text, for example where Apollo rebuffs Poseidon's challenge to a fight (drawing now directly from the translation in Chiasson): "Earthshaker, you would say that I am out of my mind / If I were to join battle with you for the sake of mortals, / Wretches, who like leaves at one moment enjoy / The prime of their lives, eating the fruit of the earth, / But the next moment dwindle and die. No, let us cease fighting / Immediately, and let the mortals themselves fight to the end" (21.462–67; in Chiasson, 200–01).

[43] *The Iliad*, 19.357.

Given this parallel scene with Briseis' tearful despair, we may be pushed to ask how important it is that these tears shed by Achilles and Priam are *male* tears? Can we make any kind of justifiable claims about the meaning of these tears as they depart from the human, that is, away from their gendered hosts? Perhaps, if we remain within the precincts of the *Iliad*, and venture out only to the question of male emotive weeping as it involves, say, the deaths of other men (even in our own time, e.g., in a time of war, such as we live in),[44] we may find ourselves on terra firma. To our contemporary ears, does the notion of "male tears" sound like a kind of emotional oxymoron—a syntagma of troubling force, and also striking incomprehension? Is it too general a remark, indeed, perhaps at once sexist and incorrect, to say that male tears often seem to arise at the *end* of a male emotional crisis: for example, as part of an admission of not being able to go on in a certain sense, or a sane sense, where, by contrast, literature and film seems replete with female tears that mark the *beginning* of a conversation aiming for (self and mutual) comprehension? Another way of sorting this apparent bifurcation may be to say that for women tears appear as an *invitation* to comprehension, whereas for men they are signs of the *culmination* of comprehension. In our scene in the tent, it is only after Priam speaks—sounds his lament, draws out the analogy of fathers and sons—that the men cry ("their sobbing rose and fell throughout the house").[45]

Such reflections, speculative though they may be (and therefore vulnerable to counter-instance), can find some measure of reason in our address to the text itself. Consequently, we ask: if we know Achilles is mortal (despite Thetis, his immortal mother), does that lack of a full-fledged "godly" quality (viz., immortality) reinforce our willingness to regard him as one of us? And moreover, are we to assume that his mortality aids his emotional range because (this time, like us) he knows he can die, knows he *will* die (in fact, with even more assurance and specificity than is common to man, owing to his mother's prophetic confession)? And, in a last question that we may not yet know what to do with, does his self-knowledge (as mortal) make him *more* of a narcissist—and thus, in that capacity, does his predicament (by association, resemblance, or identification) cast light on our own weeping and its implied meaning? Though the

---

[44] For more on contemporary warfare, including the depiction of male emotional expression, see *The Philosophy of War Films*, ed. David LaRocca (Lexington: The University Press of Kentucky, 2014).
[45] *The Iliad*, 24.599.

gods repeatedly exhibit formidable self-regard, we may wonder whether human mortality—the fact of death to come, what Heidegger calls our "ownmost possibility" (or "potentiality-of-being")—does not, in fact, make humans *more* self-regarding than the gods.[46] Narcissism on this reading would be a symptom of fearing death. Thinking of one's end—one's eventual nonexistence—may also stoke a re-evaluation of one's individual identity (what one is and is not); and here we find in Homer's ancient text a through line to Virgil's *Aeneid* centuries later, where Aeneas—second cousin to Priam's children, and another demi-god[47]—reveals, according to Garry L. Hagberg, a remarkably nuanced moral psychology and moral phenomenology, both of which draw us anew to thinking out the terms and conditions of the human, especially in terms of self-constitution.[48] Here is Aeneas in action:

> And from your criminal blood exacts his due.
> He sank his blade in fury in Turnus' chest.
> Then all the body slackened in death's chill.
> And with a groan for that indignity
> His spirit fled into the gloom below.[49]

Consider Hagberg's questions in the wake of this culminating scene, and how they bear relation to Achilles' "blade in fury" in Hector's chest, or, in contrast, to Achilles' tears in reaction to Priam's request to reclaim Hector's body: "Does this exemplify reflection-borne compassion? Is it to assess and respond to Turnus' vanquished appeal and to respond to the flash of humanity we see shining through the brutal exterior?"[50] If we moderns are confounded by the logic of the human in these scenes, it may prove elucidating to recall Alasdair MacIntyre's conviction that Homeric

---

[46] See Martin Heidegger, "Existential Project of an Authentic Being-toward-Death" (§53) in *Being and Time*, trans. Joan Stambaugh (Albany: State University of New York, 2010).

[47] Aeneas is the son of prince Anchises and the goddess Venus.

[48] Garry L. Hagberg, "Self-Defining Reading: Literature and the Constitution of Personhood," in *A Companion to the Philosophy of Literature*, ed. Garry L. Hagberg and Walter Jost (Oxford: Blackwell, 2010), p. 144. See also Garry L. Hagberg, *Describing Ourselves: Wittgenstein and Autobiographical Consciousness* (Oxford: Oxford University Press, 2008).

[49] Virgil, *The Aeneid*, trans. Robert Fitzgerald (New York: Random House, 1983), 12.938–52.

[50] Hagberg, "Self-Defining Reading," p. 144.

virtues are distinctive—and perhaps distinctively at odds with many contemporary virtues (as well those of Christ and St. Paul).[51] With narrative and emotional parallels running steadily through and between the *Iliad* and the *Aeneid*, we are given a chance to assess how demi-gods force us to come to terms with our identities and our emotions and thus with our humanity as readers and as agents.

The idea that tears humanize Achilles—or that his tears activate a certain heightened register of his humanity—is not merely a trope for an enhanced sense of compassion, or willingness to feel empathically. Achilles is, after all, the only man in the *Iliad* who is the child of a mortal (Peleus) and a goddess (Thetis).[52] We know that Achilles is mortal, but while he is alive—before the prophecy of his death is realized—there is some question, some doubt about what sort of being he is. Men on both sides of the battle marvel at his specialness—figured among many contending and complementary traits, this rare hybrid man seems capable of extra-human strength, speed, and punishing force. If he is not immortal, he fights well enough to give the impression that he is.

As Aristotle's line from the *Politics*, placed here as an epigraph, illustrates: one may conclude either that Achilles' power renders him more god-like or more animalistic—even monstrous. In either case, he is always more or less than human, but never quite human. Charles Segal has understood this alternation as posing two grave options that stand before the uncommon being who knows himself as part man and part god: "Achilles reaches out toward comprehending the mystery of his own spirit's terrible suspension between violence and ruth."[53] If Achilles behaved as if he were more than human (god-like) or reacted as if he were less than human (beast-like), then Priam might not have won his affection. Somehow Achilles finds the seam in between these options. Achilles' emotive response to Priam's plea accentuates the profound impression that he has experienced an unprecedented intimacy with his own humanity and by

---

[51] Alasdair MacIntyre, "The Nature of the Virtues," in *After Virtue: A Study in Moral Theory* (Notre Dame, University of Notre Dame Press, 1981), pp. 171–72. See also David LaRocca, "The Last Great Representative of the Virtues: MacIntyre After Austen," in *Jane Austen and Philosophy*, ed. Mimi Marinucci (Lanham: Rowman & Littlefield, 2016).

[52] Helen is the only female half-god in the *Iliad*—in her case, the child of a mortal, Tyndareus, and the god, Zeus.

[53] Charles Segal, *The Theme of the Mutilation of the Corpse in the Iliad* (Leiden, Netherlands: E.J. Brill, 1971), p. 67.

extension the fate that befalls all humans, namely, death.[54] This is why, more than *mere* empathy for Priam or Peleus, or paralleled identification with Hector, Achilles weeps for his own mortality—that it will come, and that others will suffer for it (including, most acutely, his father); returning again, briefly, to the notion of gendered tears, we may wonder what to make of Thetis' tears (presuming she will shed them for a son whose death she foretells), but then her pain is not invoked in the tent where men cry over themselves; still, it may be fittingly *inhuman* of the goddess Thetis to withhold her grief, that is, to avert showing it the way men—that is, mortals—do. "Achilles," says Bernard Knox, "has broken out of the self-imposed prison of godlike unrelenting fury, reintegrated himself in society, returned to something like human feeling; he is part of the community again."[55] Part of the *human* community, and perhaps not again but for the first time.

3   The Force of Generosity

Simone Weil concluded her legendary essay, "*The Iliad*; or, The Poem of Force," written in 1939 (and published the following year, just two years before her tragic death at thirty-four) by saying: "[…] nothing the peoples of Europe have produced is worth the first known poem that appeared among them."[56] Such a hyperbolic assessment, made at a time of unparalleled destruction on the continent, Weil's exaggerated esteem issued a scathing indictment by way of praise, though it may also read concomitantly as a prescient reminder of human failures—of the failure of human civilization(s)—in the last minutes of the final hour. Total annihilation deferred, we live, nevertheless, in the long wake of a war she did not see end, and so her remark becomes a sort of provocation for thinking

---

[54] Harold Bloom has noted that Achilles may be considered the only tragic hero in the *Iliad* precisely because he is the only half-god: "The epic is the tragedy of Achilles, ironically enough, because he retains the foremost place, yet cannot overcome the bitterness of his sense of his own mortality. To be half a god appears to be Homer's implicit definition of what makes a hero tragic.... Achilles can neither act as if he were everything in himself, nor can he believe that, compared even to Zeus, he is nothing in himself." *Homer's The Iliad* (New York: Chelsea House Publishers, 1987), p. 4. It is unclear, however, why Bloom claims that Achilles is the only half-god in the *Iliad*, since there are others, among them Helen, Sarpedon, Aeneas, and one of Achilles' Myrmidon commanders.
[55] Bernard Knox, *The Iliad*, p. 58.
[56] Weil, *The Iliad; or, The Poem of Force*, p. 37.

about the *Iliad* (and perhaps still coupled with a potent sense of impending doom). She is convinced that this poem, the *Iliad*, gives us the clearest portrait (yet) of what it means to be human and, perhaps more importantly, how we *fail* in being human, especially in so far as we fail to recognize others *as* human. For her, the pivotal concept—indeed, the transformative idea of the entire *Iliad*—is *force*. Invoking the place-holding signification of an algebraic equation, she says force is "that x that turns anybody who is subjected to it into a *thing*."[57] This unknown, this x as she calls it, has "the ability to turn a human being into a thing while he is still alive."[58] We are not, then, debating only whether corpses are things—no longer deserving, for example, of our respect, or standing in need of coins for the boatman. Since force can turn a person into a corpse "before anybody or anything touches him," it is not surprising that the topic of force should occupy such a central place in this founding poetic narrative.[11] Weil will later claim, more broadly, that the "main subject of Greek thought" was a "geometrical rigor" deployed to "penalize the abuse of force."[59] In her estimation, this endeavor of pre-Hellenic ethical perspicacity and conviction is "the soul of the epic." Weil's reading of the *Iliad* suggests the degree to which she struggled, in her own time (some twenty-seven centuries later), with the role of pacifism in the face of societal and martial evil.

Weil labored to create translations from the Greek that would honor the "human tenderness and pity that pervades the *Iliad*."[60] Consider this passage depicting Hector's end at the edge of Achilles' sword, a description that also serves to illustrate her claim about the transformative power of force:

> Thus spoke the brilliant son of Priam
> In begging words. But he heard a harsh reply:
> He spoke. And the other's knees and heart failed him.
> Dropping his spear, he knelt down, holding out his arms.
> Achilles, drawing his sharp sword, struck
> Through the neck and breastbone. The two-edged sword
> Sunk home its full length. The other, face down,
> Lay still, and the black blood ran out, wetting the ground.[61]

---

[57] Weil, *The Iliad; or, The Poem of Force*, p. 3.
[58] Weil, *The Iliad; or, The Poem of Force*, p. 4.
[59] Weil, *The Iliad; or, The Poem of Force*, p. 15.
[60] Simone Pétrement, *Simone Weil: A Life* (New York: Pantheon Books, 1976), p. 362.
[61] Weil, *The Iliad; or, The Poem of Force*, p. 5.

Again, a depiction of a man dropping to his knees, this time to plead that his own life be spared (or perhaps honorably run through)—with arms outstretched, and neck and chest made vulnerable to a looming piece of man-killing metal wielded by a man-killing man. Weil's translation is sparse, but heavy, rhythmically graceful without distracting from the grisly reality of the scene. Here we witness an occasion when brute force has rendered a living man a corpse *before* the cold tip of the sword has even broken the flesh of the man's taut, warm skin. What we see is how "a moment of impatience on the warrior's part will suffice to relieve" an enemy of his life.[62]

The scene invoked earlier, that I have highlighted most prominently, with Achilles stirred by Priam's plea for his son's corpse, leaves us wondering if the king conjured sufficient emotional regard from the warrior, Achilles, to assuage his impatience—and beyond that, what failure might betoken for we, humans, and what success, likewise, might indicate for human relationality (including mutual discernment and interpersonal comprehension). As temper vies with memory, as temperament contends with vanity, Achilles loses his patience, if momentarily, when Priam repeats his demand for Hector's body: "No more, old man, don't tempt my wrath, not now! ... Don't anger me now. Don't stir my raging heart still more. Or under my own roof I may not spare your life, old man—suppliant that you are—may break the laws of Zeus!"[63] Patience has its limit. And if that limit should be transgressed, Priam will become—perhaps even before the sword strikes him—no more than a thing to Achilles, another son of Troy felled by Achilles' rage-filled hands.[64] No wonder, then, that Weil signals generosity as the countervailing concept to force.[65] "To

---

[62] Weil, *The Iliad; or, The Poem of Force*, p. 6.

[63] *The Iliad*, 24.656; 24.667–69.

[64] If patience is lost, Achilles will become, as Katherine Callen King understands it, an animal: "Achilles attempts to comfort Priam with this exposition of generic human woe, but when Priam refuses comfort and asks only for the immediate return of the body, Achilles slips momentarily back into the anger that before had led to the merging of his human nature with that of god and beast. Human sympathy recedes. His mind reverts to the gods.... His mood, on the other hand, is bestial: he threatens Priam that, if provoked, he might kill him, suppliant though he is, and transgress the commands of Zeus; then he leaps to the door 'like a lion'" (*Homer's The Iliad*, 1987, pp. 42–43).

[65] Graham Zanker also writes of generosity, though without reference to Simone Weil's work: "Achilles' unique experience and knowledge of death enable him, alone among warriors before Troy, to attain to the companionship in suffering that he shares with Priam and the sublime generosity that he shows toward him, a generosity that ... outstrips even that of

respect life in somebody else," she says, "when you have had to castrate[66] yourself of all yearning for it demands a truly heartbreaking exertion of the powers of generosity. [...] Lacking this generosity, the conquering soldier is like a scourge of nature," and at the "touch of force" such men "become deaf and dumb."[67]

Weil again and again links her understanding of generosity to the figuration of tears, especially as generosity is understood as the inversion of force (the power that, we are meant to think, does not succumb to weeping—at least not when it is meted out). She notes that the battles waged in the *Iliad* are "in reality mere sources of blood and tears"; that slaves, being constrained, will always "keep tears on tap" for the death of a master since that is the only permissible occasion for such expression of grief; that women weep for lost sons, fathers, brothers, and husbands; that warriors weep over each other[68]; and, lastly, that the tears that fall between mortal enemies (who in this rare intimacy, if for an instant, have recognized that they share a human connection) obviate the ruling passions of force that would render them both mere carrion.[69] This last occasion for tears forms Weil's own comment on the foregoing, as it were ongoing, scene between Priam and Achilles, with her claiming that in the self-effacing father (Priam), and the tolerant, or least temporarily patient son (Achilles), we encounter the very definition of generosity. Weil identifies this scene as the most convincing expression in the *Iliad*—and given her esteem for the poem, perhaps anywhere in the literature of the Western world—of her notion of generosity:

---

the gods themselves, whose immortality debars them from the totality of Achilles' vision." *The Heart of Achilles: Characterization and Personal Ethics in the Iliad* (Ann Arbor: The University of Michigan Press, 1994), p. 125.

[66] The word "castrate" is a translation of Weil's French, and may strike the ear as being out of place, awkward, or simply the wrong word. In context, the word is used to characterize *constraint* such as soldiers are trained to endure. Weil writes: "For other men death appears as a limit set in advance on the future; for the soldier death *is* the future, the future his profession assigns him.... On each one of these days [that the soldier realizes his fate] the soul suffers violence. Regularly, every morning, the soul castrates itself of aspiration, for thought cannot journey through time without meeting death on the way." Weil, *The Iliad; or, The Poem of Force*, p. 22.

[67] Weil, *The Iliad; or, The Poem of Force*, p. 25.

[68] "The most beautiful friendship of all, the friendship between comrades-at-arms, is the final theme of The Epic." Weil, *The Iliad; or, The Poem of Force*, p. 29.

[69] Weil, *The Iliad; or, The Poem of Force*, pp. 9–10, 23, 28–29.

> The purest triumph of love, the crowning grace of war, is the friendship that floods the hearts of mortal enemies. Before it a murdered son [Hector] or a murdered friend [Patroclus] no longer cries out for vengeance. Before it—even more miraculous—the distance between benefactor [Achilles] and suppliant [Priam], between victor and vanquished, shrinks to nothing. [...] These moments of grace are rare in the *Iliad*, but they are enough to make us feel with sharp regret what it is that violence has killed and will kill again.[70]

Weil's deft—though hardly a conventional or intuitive—reading of the *Iliad* leaves us with the imposing suggestion that violence is, in final account, a form of impatience and a cessation of generosity. In other words, violence is impetuous and selfish, and makes the other a stranger—a bit of inert matter, a thing, even when the other is still alive (and regardless of social status: powerless slave and powerful warrior are equalized, entering a shared economy of value somewhere beyond or below the level of the human).

Coupling my account of the weeping that occurs between Achilles and Priam with Weil's idea of generosity, we might recognize how the portrayal of male emotive weeping in the *Iliad* suggests an emergent capacity for distinguishing between human beings and things (and also, though somewhat further afield, between our regulation of the power gods are said to possess and, on another tack, our sense of kindredness with or alienation from the animals we do not call human). Drawing Cavell back into the conversation more conspicuously, at this juncture, let us venture to ask if Weil's account of generosity (and its attention to the distinction between human and thing) leads us to a fund of knowledge or acknowledgment—that is, to a new (or renewed) reflection on justified true belief, or as Cavell re-writes the matter, a scenario of regard. Patience and generosity, as we find them expressed (literalized? literaturified? letteralized?) in the form of tears—in the "unthinging" of others—may be said to function as signs of human perception and judgment; this twin capacity would seem to gloss glancingly, if not define outright, what empathic projection is or alludes to, namely, a *choice* about how to take the existence of others in the world; a decision whether (or not) to treat others *as* human. The definition of the human, at last, may not be a matter definition or categorical traits but *an effect of ascriptional practice*. The "human" is not an

---

[70] I have added the brackets to name Weil's referents, and to emphasize how closely her account supplements the analysis offered in Part I; italics added. Weil, *The Iliad; or, The Poem of Force*, p. 29.

essence, neither an inherent nor a latent quality, but a choice that is always predicated on an assessment of knowledge, or more carefully put: on the *limits* of that knowledge—on the extent to which I can know about (or remain ignorant of) the pain another human being experiences and is said to express (often by way of tears shed, and, no doubt, words said).

4   Knowing Pain, Knowing Others

Achilles weeping with Priam may be the first instance in Western literature in which, as Stanley Cavell would understand it, acknowledgement has overcome knowledge. If Achilles were truly a skeptic with regard to the quality of Priam's sorrow, he would be unable to verify the father's pain on the terms and conditions available to him; the very notion of "verify" in relation to our knowledge of what others feel comes in for a reassessment, since what can we mean when we use such a term? One simply cannot, in a direct, self-identical sense, *know* the other's pain; the best one can hope for is a capacity to appreciate the way another's emotional life is *like* our own. This analogical trade is the hallmark of empathy, the belief that we understand how another feels because we have, in some sense, known that feeling in or for ourselves; not incidentally, this picture forms the basis upon which modern philosophy has come to understand what it calls "the problem of other minds." The *problem*, to be sure, admits that, like the emotions of others, other minds cannot be known in the way one knows one's own mind. Knowledge of others always arrives, if it does at all, as a derivation of or an extrapolation upon self-knowledge. This is why we continue to brace for the suggestion that when Achilles weeps he weeps (merely?) over himself. Like all of us, all Achilles knows (of pain) derives from himself, and therefore, to have an authentic or true emotional response to Priam's pain, Achilles must (first) feel *his own* pain. Despite Weil's high regard for the *Iliad* as an epic—not least for its rare glimpse of generosity—we may be left, at this point, wondering whether a demi-god is a decent, or even reliable, representative for the feeling, expression, and knowledge of *human* suffering. Perhaps we would be served by integrating remarks from another, complementary source.

An associated account of the inner lives of others arises in Aristotle's *Rhetoric*, in his account of pity (*eleos*), which he defines as "a feeling of pain caused by the sight of some evil, destructive or painful, which befalls one who does not deserve it, and which we might expect to befall ourselves or some friend of ours, and moreover to befall us soon."[71] Pity involves an understanding of how something happening *outside* ourselves, in the minds of others, yet is, nevertheless, related to our own well-being, and perhaps immanently. In this way, the outside feels connected to—even coextensive with—the inside. To feel pity, then, requires that we can sufficiently imagine how it feels to be, for example, the victim of undeserved suffering; the more one can relate the presumed pain of another to one's own pain, and subsequently genuinely feeling "it" (in that mode of relation or projection), so the theory goes, the greater the degree of one's pity. However, according to Aristotle, being "panic-stricken" with fear disables a person's capacity for feeling pity because the person is solely "taken up with what is happening" to himself.[72] In order to feel pity, genuine pity, then, we have to be aware of what we *believe* others feel.

Weil claims that characters in the *Iliad* rarely display patience and generosity, the very attributes that would allow a man (a demi-god) such as Achilles—in the central scene of male interaction before us—to empathetically project his inner, private emotional state "onto" another person (whether that person be his own [imagined] father, Peleus, or in his [imagined] position *as* a father, such as we find with Priam). Achilles weeping *with* Priam may be taken as the principal and rare instance of this translation occurring in the *Iliad*, and for its apparent singularity the scene is left to bear the weight of illustrating how it is that, in Weil's understanding, one can perceive and judge the difference between a human being and a thing—and, perhaps, more often than not, one can choose to forgo just such a perception and a judgment. Attempting a translation of our own, Weil's notion that perceiving the other as myself (assuring that I will judge him *as* human) would seem to underwrite the Cavellian shift from knowledge to acknowledgment—as noted above, a shift from identity to ascription, from the denotation of "is" to the connotation of "as," from the logic of the copula to the art of the analogy. On this braided or overlapping account, the vectors may also reverse so that denying the other's humanity (by refusing acknowledgment) entails denying one's own humanity. For Weil, the only way to affirm a common humanity is through

---

[71] Aristotle, *Rhetoric* in *The Basic Works of Aristotle*, trans. Richard McKeon (New York: Random House, 1941), II.8.15.

[72] Aristotle, *Rhetoric*, II.8.15.

patience and generosity—both taken in moods or modes that befit (and thus benefit from) acknowledgment. At the end of the *Iliad*, this commonality is achieved through Achilles' recognition of Priam's tears, and the pain that causes his tears to flow. We know that Achilles had mourned Patroclus with acute intensity, that Thetis "found him groaning hard, choked with sobs," and that Priam's wife, Hecuba, declared her rage over Hector's slaughter by saying of Achilles "Oh would to god that I could sink my teeth in his liver, eat him raw! *That* would avenge what he has done to Hector—."[73] But Priam does not indulge these modes of self-righteous grieving—however justified they may be—but instead trusts the god Iris, whom Zeus sent to say: "Achilles is no madman, no reckless fool [...]. Whoever begs his mercy he will spare with all the kindness in his heart."[74] And it is on these terms that Priam meets Achilles, can *appeal* to him, in a space of shared grieving over real and imagined losses, acknowledging the pain of another because it is predicated on the knowledge of one's own pain. As Weil comments on this rare, unprecedented intimacy: when "the distance between benefactor and suppliant … shrinks to nothing … ," there is no difference between one and the other. With some clarity about his own human emotions (however much we can say the human [in him?] stirred feelings of rage and revenge as it also, by turns, enabled him to suppress or expiate those feelings), Achilles, in this moment of Priam's conciliatory approach, would seem to feel beyond the limits of his own mind and body. Priam's pain is first Achilles' pain, and only Priam's second, since to know it as the other's pain, Achilles must first know it as his own.

5   The Known Unknown

Even as the Pyrrhonists initiated an account of the problem of other minds in antiquity, it was given one of its first, clear modern definitions by John Stuart Mill in *An Examination of Sir William Hamilton's Philosophy* (1865), where he declares soberly: "I bring other human beings, as phenomena, under the same generalizations which I know by experience to be the true theory of my own existence."[75] Mill's position is one that Norman

---

[73] *The Iliad*, 592.150; 595.252–54.
[74] *The Iliad*, 593.189–91.
[75] *The Oxford Companion to Philosophy*, ed., Ted Honderich (Oxford: Oxford University Press, 1995), p. 567 and 637.

Malcolm calls "representative" of what, in the discourse surrounding other minds, is commonly referred to as "the argument from analogy"—the central claim of the analogy being that I can base my knowledge of the existence of other minds on the existence of my own mind (and by extension, my knowledge of it).[76] A. J. Ayer lent his support to this argument in the following way:

> [… T]he only ground that I can have for believing that other people have experiences, and that some at least of their experiences are of the same character as my own, is that their overt behavior is similar to mine. I know that certain features of my own behavior are associated with certain experiences, and when I observe other people behaving in similar ways I am entitled to infer, by analogy, that they are having similar experiences.[77]

Ayer defends his interpretation of the argument from analogy by insisting that the "behavior" of others is "the only ground" on which he can base his knowledge of other minds. Away from Achilles' tent, and his tears, we can take up a more familiar scene of (shared) pain: When I see the behavior you exhibit after having stubbed your toe (bending over, clutching your foot, wincing, maybe weeping), I am summoned to draw upon my own experience of stubbing my own toe (e.g., drawing from personal memory, I feel sure that I know what I felt, and how I behaved because of the painful stimulus).[78] Remembering this, I can, so Mill and Ayer claim, know that you are having a "similar" pain. Ayer admits that I cannot know the way the other feels in the *same* way that I know the way I feel (or remember feeling), but I can "attain to states of highly probable opinion"

---

[76] Norman Malcolm, *Essays in Philosophical Psychology*, ed. Donald Gustafson (Garden City: Doubleday, 1964), pp. 365–76; see esp. Malcolm, 365.
[77] A. J. Ayer, "One's Knowledge of Other Minds," Gustafson (1964), pp. 346–64.
[78] The example of the stubbed toe is meant to isolate the nature of stimulus response, that is, something that generates both feeling and behavior. Yet, the example might at first blush be taken as a different sort of response than an *emotional* response, such as weeping. But this precisely illustrates the reason the analogical approach is problematic: it extrapolates from something that we might agree on, for example, that stubbing one's toe causes pain, or is painful, to something that seems impossible to agree on, namely, how that pain feels. Hence, the complexity of moving from a simple stimulus response initiated by a stubbed toe to the immensely more complex emotional response to experiences such as the death of one's father or son.

about such matters.[79] Ayer's commitment to such inductive reasoning is confidently revealed when he writes: "[…] certain properties have been found to be conjoined in various contexts to the conclusion that in a further context the conjunction will still hold."[80] If I know how I feel, the argument goes, I can infer how you feel. But does this (supposed) self-knowledge—which may, in fact, be closer in form to a memory, and thus liable to error—projected upon others qualify as knowledge of their minds? Should we want it to?

For those feeling dubious about the credentials of Mill and Ayer's approach, Norman Malcolm reports that the argument from analogy "enjoys more credit than it deserves."[81] He contends that Mill's is a good example of "*weak* inductive reasoning," and the same could be applied to the everyday example of stubbed toes.[82] The reasoning is weak because it seeks to draw a (general or generalizable) conclusion from the experience of a single event (say, one's private experience, which is then logged as a memory of an experience). The problem with the argument from analogy is that it begins with the assumption that there is *no criterion* for determining the existence of other minds; this lack of a criterion alone prevents a genuine attempt to analogize one's experience with the experience of others; as such, this particular argument from analogy collapses. Malcolm puts it this way: "If I do not know how to establish that someone has a pain then I do not know how to establish that he has the *same* as I have when I have a pain." Malcolm's criticism would apply more directly to Mill than to Ayer, since Ayer conceded that we could only have knowledge of the experience of others "similar" to our own. In any case, Malcolm objects to the positions Mill and Ayer maintain because those claims lead to "tenuous analogical reasoning that yields at best a probability"—as opposed to generating what we presume to want: certainty (about the content of the feeling). Ayer also admitted the point about our (mere) probabilistic knowledge, but that admission does not dilute Malcolm's pointed postulate that the absence of a criterion renders the argument from analogy an inescapable dilemma. On the issue of our

---

[79] Ayer, "One's Knowledge of Other Minds," p. 353.
[80] Ayer, "One's Knowledge of Other Minds," p. 364.
[81] Ayer, "One's Knowledge of Other Minds," p. 365.
[82] Malcolm, "Knowledge of Other Minds," p. 366; italics in original.

lack of an evidential criterion, and the errors that follow from taking "behavior" as the point of departure for the argument, Malcolm has this to say:

> Perhaps he makes a mistake *every* time! Perhaps all of us do! We ought to see now that we are talking nonsense. We do not know what a mistake would be. We have no standard, no examples, no customary practice, with which to compare our inner recognitions. The inward identification cannot hit the bull's-eye, or miss it either, because there is no bull's-eye.[83]

Drawing this deliberation back to the *Iliad* for a moment, we could point out that for all of the (potentially distracting) drama of Priam's arrival in Achilles' tent, Achilles himself may be making a mistake! What if Priam is the first Trojan horse of the epic, arriving under the guise of a bereft father in search of his son's corpse, pantomiming his way to proximity by the trick of prostration and kissing … only in that moment of tenderness to swipe a sharp blade across Achilles' throat? Vengeance satisfied, and the fulfillment of a now-familiar narrative arc and economy of hatred.

In his essay, "Knowing and Acknowledging," Cavell sustains an interest in varied, often conflicting or contradictory, meanings of knowing.[84] In particular, he is concerned that the fixation upon certainty regarding knowledge of other minds has given credence to the challenges levied by the skeptic. In showing how the skeptic's position is revelatory of the predicament in which the anti-skeptic is often caught, Cavell introduces another way of thinking about other minds, namely, a way to "go beyond knowledge," to what he calls acknowledgment.[85] Knowledge is, as it were, and as it is literally (one wants to say, again, letterally), *contained* within the concept of acknowledgment: "from my acknowledging that I am late it follows that I know I'm late [...] but from my knowing I am late, it does not follow that I acknowledge I'm late."[86] The importance of this difference suggests, for Cavell, that acknowledgment "goes beyond" knowledge in so far as it requires "that I *do* something or reveal something on the basis of that knowledge." Thus when you stub your toe and I see your

---

[83] Malcolm, "Knowledge of Other Minds," p. 373.
[84] Stanley Cavell, "Knowing and Acknowledging," *Must We Mean What We Say?: A Book of Essays* (Cambridge, UK: Cambridge University Press, 1976), pp. 238–66.
[85] Cavell, "Knowing and Acknowledging," p. 257.
[86] Cavell, "Knowing and Acknowledging," pp. 256–57.

behavior, and hear you say "I stubbed my toe and it really hurts," your pain, or better your expression of pain (both physically *and* verbally), "makes a claim upon me."[87] In order to express my knowledge of your pain I must acknowledge it. This means that I am doing or revealing something on the basis of my experience of you, and your expression of pain. Your claim has the character of trying to elicit sympathy from me, but this does not mean that I have it: as Cavell ruefully reports, "the claim of suffering may go unanswered."[88] Thus, my acknowledgment of another's pain may fail or succeed, and so with it may my knowledge of another's pain. Failure to acknowledge is not the absence of something, but the presence of it, for example, indifference or meanness.[89] Therefore, knowledge of another's pain is not reducible to an awareness of criteria; rather, it requires that I respond *to* those criteria, to what those criteria are *for*.[90]

When Priam exhibits pain behavior, such as he does when he kneels at Achilles' feet, kisses his hands, weeps, and states his plea, a claim is made upon Achilles—one that Achilles takes to be authentic. Will Achilles recognize this supplication, this tenderness, these tears? And if so, how does that recognition register itself (first) within Achilles and (secondly) by means of his response or responsiveness to Priam (because of that internal awareness)? As discussed earlier, Achilles responds to Priam's behavior by, among other actions, weeping; Achilles is not skeptical of the genuineness of Priam's behavior, and so allows Priam's appeal to make claims upon him. The question before us now is whether Achilles' response qualifies as a version of Mill and Ayer's view of *knowing* how others feel by means of analogy, or as an illustration of Cavell's view where knowing is no longer a matter of certainty (or the establishment of criteria for knowing), but instead of acknowledgment.

If we place in parallel our opening remarks on Achilles' existential status (as a half-god, and thus as a half-man—and as such potentially illuminating about our own condition) with these later notes on human knowledge (as it is impacted by the "threat of skepticism"),[91] we may be in a position

---

[87] Stephen Mulhall, *The Cavell Reader* (Cambridge, UK: Blackwell, 1996), p. 48.
[88] Cavell, "Knowing and Acknowledging," p. 263.
[89] Cavell, "Knowing and Acknowledging," p. 264.
[90] Stephen Mulhall, *Stanley Cavell: Philosophy's Recounting of the Ordinary* (Oxford: Clarendon Press, 1994), p. 111.
[91] Cavell, "Emerson, Coleridge, Kant (Terms as Conditions)," in *Emerson's Transcendental Etudes*, p. 63.

to recognize how Cavell's account of acknowledgment provides us with a novel way of thinking about the human itself. As I wish to present it here, consider, for instance, how giving up on knowledge (of others, of other minds, of inner states, of criteria, and the like)—and admitting the efficacy of acknowledgment—may encourage us to give up (also) on the repression (or denial or overcoming) of the human that seems, according to Cavell, to have become a hallmark trait of the species (as *homo sapiens*— "the wise ones," which may more often than not slip into "the knowing ones").

Human frustration with knowledge has seemed to inspire a sort of insidious self-hatred—a self-denial that comes in the form of rebellion against the human. Is it too much to say that Achilles—"swift footed" demi-god—helps us make what I am suggesting is a new, Cavellian concatenation? Namely, that the embrace of acknowledgment becomes an embrace of the human (in our limitedness, in our ignorance, in our mortality). If we remain in a state of mutual ignorance, at an impasse of comprehension, unknown to one another, it is a symptom of our insistence on knowledge as the only, the best, perhaps the truest form of comprehension—and, by extension, as the incorruptible but yet lamentable figure for the divisions that set men at arms against one another, perpetually deferring the patience and generosity that would take the place of violence and force; yet, if we accede to Cavell's counter-proposal, we may find that acknowledgment is not just a worthy variant of epistemic achievement but also a condition for the possibility of defensible humanism—and thus of a particular kind of peace. Here understanding and nonviolence seem a reasonable by-product of acknowledgment. In what remains in the lines to follow, I wish to explore some further valences of the *Iliad*—and Achilles' emotional experience within it—that may provide credence for recognizing the warrior's heuristic value to these perennial philosophical conundrums.

The environment of the *Iliad* is replete with the suggestion that contested economies of trade form the foundation of cultural, civic, political, martial, and personal value—for things human or otherwise; the poem is saturated with stories involving bargaining, ransom, surrogacy, exchange, substitution, transference, compensation, and various notions of accounting. All this is a way of saying that the kind of value being sought, or defended, is one of justice (at least, in the context of a pre-Socratic Greek culture). Though our attention has been trained on the trade with which the poem culminates, the first lines of the poem find Chryses (a priest of

Apollo in Troy) and Agamemnon (king of Mycenae, "lord of men")[92] deliberating over the value of an exchange: a woman for a ransom. But not just any woman: Chryses' daughter, Chryseis. "Just set my daughter free, my dear one ... here, accept these gifts, this ransom," pleads Chryses to Agamemnon (and his brother, Menelaus).[93] Yet while all Achaeans "cried out their assent: 'Respect the priest, accept the shining ransom!' [...] it brought no joy to the heart of Agamemnon."[94] The king was unmoved: "The girl—I won't give up the girl."[95] When Chryses' plea—and offer of ransom—is refused, the priest instigates a different sort of appeal, and a new kind of trade: "[Y]our arrows for my tears!" exclaims Chryses to "the distant deadly Archer," Apollo, asking for him to destroy the Achaean army because its commander has refused to release his daughter.[96]

Though Agamemnon initially refuses the offer, protesting that he ranks Chryseis "higher than Clytemnestra, my wedded wife," he eventually relents for reasons of political utility: "I'm willing to give her back, even so, if that is best for all."[97] Though the *Iliad* begins—as it ends—with scenes of desperate deals and compelling compensations made by fathers hoping to honor the lives of their children (perhaps itself a bit of narcissism—to celebrate the greatness of one's own progeny), the negotiation between the Apollonian priest and the king of the Argives does not illustrate Agamemnon's subtle talents for empathy, but instead his brute military calculus. Even still, male tears are shed, yet in this case they do not move men; rather, Chryses' tears are theurgic: they summon Apollo and spur him to unleash his silver bow.[98] By the end of the *Iliad*, tears come to different effect: they soothe a raging warrior, and force him to cope with the commiserative emotions of a father who also bears a ransom for his child.

Once Achilles and Priam are in the throes of their emotional paroxysm, we are meant to wonder "Who is feeling what for whom?" The permutations of reply are indeed dazzling, yet we note just the relevant examples: Priam weeping for his son (Hector), for his other lost sons, and maybe,

[92] *The Iliad*, 1.8.
[93] *The Iliad*, 1.22–23.
[94] *The Iliad*, 1.25–27.
[95] *The Iliad*, 1.33.
[96] *The Iliad*, 1.49; 1.16.
[97] *The Iliad*, 1.132–33; 1.135–36.
[98] *The Iliad*, 1.56.

because of losing his sons, for himself (his legacy, his patrimony, etc.); Achilles weeping for Priam, for Peleus, for Patroclus, for Hector, and for himself. Because these men weep beyond themselves, moved by the sight, thought, or memory of others (other men, living and dead), they reveal the degree to which their weeping depends on them believing in the legitimacy and efficacy of their tears for others; these are not crocodile tears—performative, ersatz, affectations. The images of surrogacy, allowing the trade of identities (father for father, son for son), and compensation, which underwrites the exchange of different goods with (purportedly) the same value (a life for a ransom, or a corpse for a ransom) support the practice, if not the truth, of empathic projection.

And yet the exercise of such empathic projection—perhaps more in the mode of Agamemnon's political calculus than the emotional nuance of grieving fathers and sons—leads to the further question: "Can one truly weep for another?" In the present context, the practice of weeping "for another" has a double sense: first, to weep because the other is weeping (even if based on one's speculation that another *would* weep, as with Achilles' fantasy of his father's tears for him) and, secondly, to weep in place of the other (either, again, for example, as Achilles may be understood to take Peleus' place as mourning for Achilles' death before it has transpired, or, perhaps—in another variation on the idea of exchange—to altogether take the place of another mourner, to claim another's grief as one's own). The first description is a function of projection, the second description concerns surrogacy—yet both are enactments of empathy. If Achilles weeps for Priam by means of projection, that means he presumes to feel what Priam *does* feel, or what Peleus *will* feel—in short, to know, or to know with, after Ayer, "highly probable opinion."[99] (Yet Malcolm raises his hand to remind us "Perhaps he makes a mistake *every* time! Perhaps all of us do!")[100] If Achilles weeps for Priam by the exchange made possible by surrogacy, that means he presumes to know what Priam feels (because Achilles is, so to speak, putting himself "in" Priam's position—another kind of empathic move). Yet, as noted, these two options come to the same thing: one cannot weep for the other (in both senses) without also weeping for oneself. Let us call this the unfortunate reversal of empathetic projection, and the point on which I shall conclude.

---

[99] Ayer, "One's Knowledge of Other Minds," p. 353.
[100] Malcolm, "Knowledge of Other Minds," p. 373.

6   Tears and Narcissism

It seems perverse to suggest that one understand the emotional lives of every other person as being like his or her own—here the terrors of solipsism take the form of a hideous narcissism. To live in such a world would entail believing that if one wants to know how others feel, one merely has to feel "it"—whatever the object of the queried emotion is—for oneself. This is the world that empathic projection renders for us, and the world that frames the experience of mutuality between enemies at the conclusion of the *Iliad*. With empathic projection as a model for understanding other people, however, we discover that we do not genuinely or assuredly know anyone, or any of their experiences, at all, after all. Such ignorance seems especially poignant and difficult to admit when dealing with the remarkable, some say definitively human, expression of weeping.[101] If weeping is, as some cultural historians have argued, what makes us human, there is a lot at stake in determining what we know when we weep, and what we know of others when they weep. And yet, if the world is not comprised merely of other men, of other minds, and empathic projection falters as an explanatory mechanism for accounting for human suffering, what can we claim about our tears—yours and mine? At minimum, it seems we can say: when we weep, we only weep over ourselves, since that is all that can be known. If this is unsatisfying (but why unsatisfying? because it seems unintuitive, or perhaps self-defeating?; or because the scope of such knowledge seems insufficiently capacious?), perhaps we ought to ask whether we are willing to endure the implications of living with the argument from analogy, among them that the other is but a version of me. Knowledge of others would be suddenly (and necessarily, in the logical sense) reduced to self-knowledge—a pitiable suggestion, if only because it reinvigorates a potentially debilitating and depressing subjectivism, solipsism, and skepticism. We have not advanced very far from the Pyrrhonists after all.

Part of the wonder of being human, we would rather hope, is caught up with the diversity of experiences (individual and otherwise), including the presumption that one does not, cannot be sufficiently self-regarding to believe that one is the condition for what all others feel; and likewise, to

---

[101] Lutz begins his book by claiming "weeping is a human universal" and "weeping is exclusively human" (*Crying: The Natural and Cultural History of Tears*, 1999, p. 17). In Homer, weeping is not an exclusively human experience: Zeus weeps, Thetis weeps, even Achilles' horses weep. See note 27 above.

our relief, others are similarly denied such totalizing knowledge of us. The postulation, or better *fact*, of emotional remainders—namely, that there are emotional experiences that exceed (one's) comprehension—would confirm, in effect, the need for human community; others do not quite know what it is like to be me, and I do not quite know what it is like to be them. Our limitedness—our constraints, the obstructions that divide us one from the other, and encode our differences, then—delivers the better motivation to suppress vanity and cultivate genuine interest in one another. Ignorance of others, how much of ourselves, would be constitutional—a function of how we build ourselves, how we forge bonds with others, including how we seek mutual comprehension.

If Achilles was moved by Priam's tears, by the sentiment embodied in their intimate encounter, and able, in some measure, to imagine how this specific person was feeling at this specific moment—do we wish to make the further claim that such an emotional evolution would be an attractive, effective way to be or become *humanized* (if because one is already god-like, or, as the case may be, beast-like)?; could it be the only way? How humanizing is empathic projection after all, if at all? Is it possible that empathic projection is a form of delusion, and in its most developed forms, a kind of madness (a derangement born of skepticism—a familiar trope of a mind ill-at-ease); a theory made by solipsists for narcissists? Consider that "feeling for the other" (having empathy, being compassionate, or insisting on some mode of exchange or surrogacy) is predicated on a dubious premise, namely, that one can appreciate another's pain as that other feels it; and yet, of what kind, to what degree? Is this a partial feeling, or a total one? Recall that Ayer said we can only hope to "attain to states of highly probable opinion" about what others feel, even if it is not the same feeling.[102] Even with its strongest advocates making the case, the emotional analogy is a less than full option.

A hazard arises, does it not, when one believes that one's compassion for another reaches beyond a mere inference, or superficial analogical connection? The danger becomes even more pronounced when one is tempted to call that belief a form of knowledge, since such knowledge can be used to devastating effect. The presumption of such justified true belief itself seems to invite a kind of hubris—shown variously in contempt and wrath—something sure to quell the diversity of human expressions and interac-

---

[102] Ayer, "One's Knowledge of Other Minds," p. 353.

tions, and the richness of its communications. Thus, when one believes that one *knows* how another feels, the social—*humanizing*—benefits of empathic projection may begin to unravel and reverse. With a faith in the reality of empathic projection, one ceases, in some sense to be (or behave as a) human, and so may (returning again to Aristotle's hierarchy) descend to carnal, beast-like qualities or aspire to ascend to god-like ones—and both lurches would summon crises in our mental states. Likewise, in both appeals the space of the human is evacuated.

I conclude, then, by wondering over the character of Achilles' empathic projection. Does Achilles have what we might call a sane presumption of empathy for Priam (one that must be coupled with his capacity to judge that Priam's pleas are authentic and not, instead, a savvy set-up for attempted assassination)? Or, does Achilles' display of emotive weeping confirm something like a comprehensive scope for narcissism, encompassing the breadth of his self-concern and his self-pity? Since the scene between Achilles and Priam occurs at the end of the *Iliad*, and it is in an undeniable sense the emotional denouement of all the preceding carnage, it is perhaps understandable that Achilles is often read as being softened, touched, or moved by Priam's weeping.[103] An alternative to these views, however, may lie in seeing how Achilles is stirred—by Priam's plea, his physical contact (the laying on of hands, of lips applied in a kiss), and his tears—to an extreme form of self-concern or self-regard. In this way, bearing witness to Priam's outward behavior (kneeling, pleading, touching, kissing, weeping) only stimulates Achilles' own inward sensibilities, how valuable he is and how sad it will be when he dies, a realization that, in turn, brings him to tears. What happens to the conclusion of the *Iliad* if we read Achilles' weeping as an exaggerated, distorted form of empathic projection, which in its distension, even derangement, confirms that

---

[103] On the subject of what Priam provokes in Achilles, Katherine Callen King writes: "The generic grief that mingles his tears with Priam's issues in a new personal response, pity. This pity leads into an assertion of their common humanity in sorrow as distinguished from the carefree existence of the gods" (*Homer's The Iliad*, 1987, p. 42). James M. Redfield links Achilles' revitalized perception of humanity with Priam's presence: "Achilles' rending sense of his own mortality … becomes a bond with others, even with his enemy. At the moment Achilles feels himself most a mortal man, he stands away from his men, as the gods do, and sees himself one with other mortals…. In their common mourning, Achilles and Priam together experience the limiting finitude of the heroic consciousness" (*Homer's The Iliad*, 1987, pp. 84–85).

Achilles weeps only for himself? If this is a compelling and plausible way to read Achilles' emotional status, then we may have come across, in this work of pagan antiquity, a way to think ourselves past empathic projection, beyond knowledge as a basis for human contact and comprehension—that is, toward Cavell's bid for the humanizing merits of acknowledgment.

Along similar lines, it may be preferable to keep Weil's paired notions of patience and generosity separate from empathic projection since, from her view, one need not presume knowledge of another mind—for instance, its pain—in order to act humanely. Weil proposes that we merely (in the good sense of constraining our ambitions) respect the humanity of the other, without pressing further to map one's own specific, private experience onto the experience of another—as if by analogy, as if by projection. We need then only train ourselves in patience with and for the other, thereby preparing ourselves for, while practicing, the best case for knowing the other's pain. Yet Weil asks remorsefully: "But then how many men do we know, in several thousand years of human history, who would have displayed such god-like generosity? Two or three?—even this is doubtful."[104] If humans are by nature narcissistic, it is no wonder that empathic projection—from the *Iliad* to *An Examination of Sir William Hamilton's Philosophy*—has made such an indelible impression on our thinking about human others, provided a picture of relationality that far from confirming our shared humanity has, in some sense, confirmed our skepticism about just such an attribute. The question before us, then, is whether, in not being demi-gods ourselves, we can yet achieve such god-like generosity in our capacities as human beings. We could, then, truly weep with another, for another, without also weeping for ourselves.

Stanley Cavell's ratification of acknowledgment may supply us with a generative model of aesthetic understanding—one that will take us beyond our claims to and hopes for knowledge, and orient us to the more fecund task of studying our habits of regarding others, in pain and otherwise. Even as we are said to inhabit the anthropocene, the post-human era is dawning—these seemingly antagonistic phenomena would appear to join forces in providing chilling new testimony and momentum to the sentiment that began these proceedings, namely that, in Cavell's words, "[n]othing could be more human" than "the power of the motive to reject the human."[105] It is high time—belated, in Cavell's lexicon—that

---

[104] Weil, *The Iliad; or, The Poem of Force*, p. 25.
[105] Stanley Cavell, *The Claim of Reason: Wittgenstein, Skepticism, Morality, Tragedy* (Oxford: Oxford University Press, 1979/1999), p. 207.

we come to terms with our humanity, our humanness, before it is eclipsed by some further evolution. While the days and nights remain for us to consider what poetry and literature and cinema can avail to our philosophy, reinvigorated postulation of our humanness—what we want of it, for it, and from it—may yet bear instruction on our claims to knowledge and our willingness to forego them. As *homo sapiens*, such reflection could become the impetus for re-evaluating our values, and oddly, giving up on certain presumptions and pretensions. The insights we have sought for our epistemology may, at last, be found and founded in acknowledgment, as Cavell has figured it for us. We find ourselves, then, with a performative innovation that yields a genuine advance in aesthetic understanding—and more desperately, more necessarily, an enactment worthy of our aspirations to the human at the very moment we are pressed to move beyond it.

CHAPTER 9

Wittgenstein "in the Midst of" Life, Death, Sanity, Madness—and Mathematics

Richard McDonough

If in the midst of life we are in death, so in sanity we are surrounded by madness.
Wittgenstein, *Remarks on the Foundations of Mathematics* (IV. 53)[1]

One of Cavell's most striking themes,[2] which he associates with Wittgenstein, is the intimate connection between philosophy and madness, particularly in connection with the threat posed by scepticism to the sanity of reason. This chapter develops this theme in connection with

---

[1] MDM is repeated with a slightly different translation by Winch in *Culture and Value* (44). See note 4 below for an explanation of all the acronyms in this chapter.

[2] Abbreviations of Cavell's works are as follows: *Must We Mean What We Say?* (*MMS*); *The Claim of Reason: Wittgenstein, Skepticism, Morality, and Tragedy* (*TCR*); *This New Yet Unapproachable America* (*NUA*); *Conditions Handsome and Unhandsome: The Constitution of Emersonian Perfectionism* (*ECH*); *Philosophy the Day after Tomorrow* (*PDAT*); and *In Quest of the Ordinary* (*IQO*). All references to Cavell's works are by page number.

R. McDonough (✉)
Arium School of Arts and Sciences, Singapore, Singapore

© The Author(s) 2018
G. L. Hagberg (ed.), *Stanley Cavell on Aesthetic Understanding*, Philosophers in Depth,
https://doi.org/10.1007/978-3-319-97466-8_9

Wittgenstein's remark in *RFM* (IV. 53) that "if in life we are in the midst of death so in sanity we are surrounded by madness".[3] Call this Wittgenstein's "Midst of Death and Madness" remark or MDM![4] It is useful to distinguish the antecedent and consequent in MDM. Call the antecedent the "Death in the Midst of Life" remark or DML, and the consequent, the "Sanity Surrounded by Madness" remark or SSM. One can imagine such remarks being made by theologians, certain psychologists, poets or artists, but such literary remarks are not usually accorded much philosophical significance in mainstream philosophy: What can life in the midst of death or sanity surrounded by madness *really* mean in the philosophy of mathematics? A clue is found in Wittgenstein's Remark to Drury that he cannot help seeing problems from a religious point of view (hereafter, WRD) (Malcolm 1997, 1). For, the Latin "*Media vita in morte sumus*" ("In the midst of life we are in death") has a long history in religious literature. This chapter argues that MDM illustrates how Wittgenstein employs religious points of view as literary devices to shed light on problems in the philosophy of mathematics.

Section 1 discusses the link between philosophy and madness envisaged by Wittgenstein and Cavell. Section 2 discusses the religious-literary history of DML, including the Bible, Augustine, Luther, the Episcopalian and Anglican Books of Prayer, Milton and Rilke (several of which were admired by Wittgenstein). Section 3 contrasts Wittgenstein's view on death in DML with his views on life and death in his "early" *Tractatus Logico-Philosophicus* (hereafter *TLP*).[5] Section 4 shows how MDM functions in *RFM* (IV. 53) as an application of WRD to the philosophy of mathematics. Section 5 shows how Wittgenstein employs MDM as a prin-

---

[3] Wittgenstein's works are abbreviated as follows: *Tractatus Logico-Philosophicus* (*TLP*); *Notebooks, 1914–16* (*NB*); *Philosophical Investigations* (*PI*); *The Blue and Brown Books* (*BB*); *Remarks on the Foundations of Mathematics* (*RFM*); *Lectures on the Foundations of Mathematics* (*LFM*); "Lectures and Conversations on Aesthetics" (*LA*); "Notes for the Philosophical Lecture" (*NPL*); *Culture and Value* (*CV*); *Zettel* (*Z*); and *On Certainty* (*OC*). References to *TLP* are to proposition number, to *NB* and *CV* by page number, to *PI*, *Z* and *OC*, unless indicated otherwise, by paragraph number, to *RFM* by section and paragraph number.

[4] The acronyms used in the paper are: MDM = "Midst of Death and Madness"; DML = "Death in the Midst of Life"; SSM = "Sanity Surrounded by Madness"; and WRD = "Wittgenstein's Remark to Drury".

[5] By Wittgenstein's early philosophy is here meant *TLP* and *NB*. By his later philosophy is here meant all the works referenced in the present paper except his *TLP* and *NB*. Although it is difficult to draw the distinction between Wittgenstein's "early" and "later" philosophies with any precision, Wittgenstein did distinguish between his early and later ways of looking at things (Kripke 1982, 78, 120, 123).

ciple for bringing the deceptive sublimity of mathematics "down to earth" (where the people—and the madness are). Section 6 argues that MDM suggests that one look at mathematics as akin, in certain respects, to literature—without destroying its unique dignity and utility. Section 7 argues that despite obvious differences between Wittgenstein's "grammatical" method and the methods of certain great literary figures, such as Shakespeare, there is, as Cavell holds, an analogy between the two.

1   Philosophy and Madness

> "The philosopher is the man who has to cure himself of many sickness of the human understanding before he arrives at the notions of the sound human understanding" (*Remarks on the Foundation of Mathematics*, p. 157)—as though there were no other path to sanity save through madness.
> Cavell, *Must We Mean What We Say?* (126–27)

Cavell observes that "Every profound philosophical vision can have the shape of madness" (*MMS*, 126; see also *NUA*, 37–38, 64–65, 69). Thus, Wittgenstein (*PI*, 255) remarks that the philosopher's treatment of philosophical problems must be like the treatment of an illness. The treatment is daunting. The path to sanity requires a journey through madness (see epigraph above). The philosopher is not just mistaken due to some logical error, but, rather, their mistake is comparable to an illness. However, *RFM* (IV, 53) also states that in order to achieve sanity, the philosopher must cure his/her self. "Working in philosophy—like work in architecture, in many respects—is really more a working on oneself" (*CV*, 16). Philosophy is, as Husserl (1970, 2) remarks, "the philosopher's quite personal affair". Further, *RFM* (IV. 53) concludes with the "Midst of Death and Madness" remark or MDM (see epigraph at the beginning of the chapter). What is added by MDM to the parts quoted by Cavell is *prima facia* that this madness is not limited to philosophers but is present in *all* human life. The philosopher may normally be the one who notices this madness, but it is present in human life: "Human speech and activity, sanity and community, rest upon nothing more, but nothing less than … the whirl of organism Wittgenstein calls 'forms of life'" (*MMS*, 52). Cavell's point is that "forms of life" do not provide the sort of rational foundation for our beliefs that philosophers tend to favour—hence his remark that Wittgenstein's vision is "terrifying" (*MMS*, 52). This dovetails with Cavell's suggestion that the madness explored by philosophers is also explored by many of the great literary figures, such as Shakespeare and Beckett (*MMS*, 155, 267–353; *PDAT*, 12–13). For the great literary figures do not produce their works for the benefit of the philosophy department but for all humanity. Both the philosopher and some great literary figures explore the "madness" that normally lies unseen just beneath the surface of ordinary human life.

Wittgenstein and Cavell acknowledge the negativity of madness. Madness is an illness. It needs treatment. This reveals a negative aspect of philosophy. Certain philosophical arguments might push one to madness (*MMS*, 126–27). However, Wittgenstein and Cavell both emphasize the positive dimension of madness. Madness may, alas, be a necessary stop on the way to sanity. Cavell (*MMS*, 305) refers to the creativity of that "world creating" madness. In this respect, the illness associated with philosophy is different from ordinary illnesses. One does not normally attempt to become sick in order to reap the rewards that attend the cure. In normal illnesses, one is healthy, one (unwillingly) becomes ill, one is treated and, sometimes, one recovers and reaps certain rewards as a result. However, *RFM* (IV. 53) suggests that the philosopher can *only* achieve sanity by taking a journey through madness. The philosopher as such *begins* in madness and only achieves health, if they do, after curing the disease of philosophy, paradoxically, by more philosophizing (*TCR*, 34).

Thus far, Wittgenstein's and Cavell's views are consistent with the ordinary view that madness is an evil—if a necessary one. That is why "genuine philosophy" may begin in wonder but "continues in reluctance" (*MMS*, 127). Perhaps more disturbing, however, is Cavell's view that madness may be inextricably linked with ordinary human life. Referring to the characters in Beckett's *Endgame*, who seem to embody the various psychopathologies of modern life, Cavell suggests that the real point of the play is not the fashionable view that Beckett is popularizing these psychopathologies but that the conversations of his characters "sound, at once, of madness and of plainness" (*MMS*, 117). Cavell explains it this way:

> What this requires, as I read Wittgenstein, is learning to bear up under, and to take back home, the inevitable cracks or leaps of madness that haunt the construction of the world—to take the madness back to our shared home of language, and to take it back once for all …. (*IQO*, 186)

Madness is not just an unpleasant way station on the way to sanity. Rather, there is no such thing as pure unadulterated sanity. For madness is always present, lurking just beneath the surface of everyday "sanity", threatening to erupt into ordinary life. Since madness "haunts" the construction of the world, one must learn to accept it "into our shared home of language and take it back once for all". This is not just the view that the path to sanity must go through madness (*TCR*, 400), but the more radical view that even at "home" in sanity one is "haunted" by madness. The philosopher and certain great literary figures explore the madness that lies just beneath the surface of ordinary life with a view to learning how to make a home in it. Cavell (*ECH*, 127–28) remarks, in a discussion of Emerson's essays, that "a condition of philosophy … is a willingness to host an ecstasy in the midst of madness". If MDM is correct, there is no place else where one might host this ecstasy.

2 The Literary History of Wittgenstein's "Death in the Midst of Life" Remark

In the midst of life we are in death …
The [Episcopal] Book of Common Prayer (297)

It is useful, in order to understand MDM, to survey the literary history of its antecedent, DML. Philosophers are familiar with something like DML in Plato's view that philosophy is "practicing death" (*Phaedo*, 80e–81a). Plato's philosopher does not merely think about death, but practises it. Death is a way (form?) of life. Plato's philosopher lives "in the midst of" death, a fact that is illustrated, all too concretely, by the case of Socrates. However, "practicing death" is not for everyone because philosophy is not for everyone (*Republic*, 493e). Plato's DML is only for the genuine philosophical elites.

The idea that one lives in the midst of death may be more familiar to non-philosophers in the remark in Psalm 23 of the Hebrew Bible that one "walks in the shadow of death".[6] This is not the claim that one merely thinks about death but that one experiences its "shadow" in life. Death is not something encountered only at the end of life but something that haunts one's everyday life in the world.

This theme is also found in Augustine, who Wittgenstein "revered" (Malcolm 2001, 51):

---

[6] Psalm 23 is usually attributed to King David, who lived between 1040 and 970 BCE (Carr and Conway 2010, 58), long before Plato. It is worth noting that in the present context religious works are cited as works of literature rather than as endorsements of religious doctrine.

What have I to say to God, save that I know not where I came from, when I came to this life-in-death, or should I call it death-in-life? (*Confessions*, I. 6)

This image of death-in-life (or life-in-death) is present into various Christian prayers and hymns. It is found in the Anglican and Episcopal Book of Common Prayer (see epigraph above) and in Luther's (1884, 39) Hymn "*Mitten wir im Leben sind*".[7] Further, Wittgenstein had great respect for Milton (*CV*, 48), and the idea that death pervades life is found in the first lines of *Paradise Lost*:

> Of Mans First Disobedience, and the Fruit
> Of that Forbidden Tree, whose mortal taste
> Brought Death into the World, and all our woe, …

Once again, it is not just that it is a consequence of human disobedience that people became *aware* of death, but that this disobedience brought death and woe "into the World".

The imagery in DML also appears in a poem titled "*Schlußstück*" ("Closing Piece") by the Austrian poet Rilke, who was much admired by Wittgenstein (Malcolm 2001, 8):[8]

> *Der Tod ist groß.*
> *Wir sind die Seinen*
> *lachenden Munds.*
> *Wenn wir uns mitten im Leben meinen,*
> *wagt er zu weinen*
> *mitten in uns.*
>
>> Death is great,
>> We belong to him,
>> laughing mouths.
>> If we intend to be in the midst of life,
>> he dares weep
>> into our midst.[9]

---

[7] Luther, Martin. 1524. "*Mitten wir im Leben sind*", Project Gutenberg. http://gutenberg.spiegel.de/buch/martin-luther-kirchenlieder-268/14.

[8] Wittgenstein picked Rilke as one of the main beneficiaries of his fortune (Monk 1996, 108, 110).

[9] The English title and text are this author's own translation. Snow (see Rilke 1994, 252–53) translates the title as "Closing Piece" and the text as "Death is great/We are his

The basic idea is that while we feel secure, laughing in the "midst" of life, death owns us, and, ever in our midst, "dares" to destroy our fleeting laughter with tears.

The claim is not that Wittgenstein is an Anglican or Lutheran. It is, first, that virtually the same words found in *RFM* (IV. 53) are found in various modern religious writings with which Wittgenstein was familiar. When Wittgenstein's close friend Drury announced that he wanted to be ordained an Anglican priest upon leaving Cambridge, Wittgenstein responded that he would not "ridicule this for a moment", but he talks Drury out of it on the grounds that "the collar would choke you" (Monk 1991, 264).[10] Wittgenstein does not ridicule Drury's commitment to Anglicanism, but holds that it is the wrong personal choice for him. Second, the imagery, if not the precise words of DML, is also present in Augustine, Milton and Rilke (all admired by Wittgenstein). The following section argues that DML marks a major departure from the view of death that Wittgenstein had held in his early *TLP*.

3 Wittgenstein's Early Views on Death

Death is not an event in life: we do not live to experience death.
Wittgenstein, *Tractatus Logico-Philosophicus* (6.4311)[11]

MDM, in the original German, begins with an "if" ["*Wenn*"],[12] but this is a rhetorical "if", comparable to the "ifs" in Nietzsche's "The Seven Seals" at the end of Book III of *Thus Spoke Zarathustra*: "If I am fond of the sea and of all that is of the sea's kind, …". There is actually no "if" about it. Just as Zarathustra is fond of the sea, Wittgenstein's DML, in context, implies that we are, in life, "in the midst of" death.

TLP (6.4311), by contrast, states that we are, in life, not in the midst of death: "Our life has no end just in the way that our visual field has no limits" (*TLP*, 6.4312). Employing a mathematical idiom, *TLP* sees death

---

completely with laughing eyes/When we feel ourselves immersed in life he dares weep immersed in us".

[10] For the record, Drury later became a medical doctor and psychiatrist (Malcolm 2001, 112).

[11] See also *NB* (75)!

[12] "*Wenn wir im Leben vom Tod umgeben sind so auch in der Gesundheit des Verstands vom Wahnsinn.*" Although Anscombe's translation is not wrong per se, recall that in English "sanity" is a legal, not a psychological term, thereby losing Wittgenstein's emphasis on the health [*Gesundheit*] of mind referenced in the original German.

as analogous to the endpoint of a mathematical line, where the endpoint is a limit of the line, not a part of the line. *TLP* banishes death from life: "If we take eternity to mean not infinite temporal duration but timelessness, then eternal life belongs to those who live in the present" (6.4311). In this respect *TLP* endorses Spinoza's (*Ethics*, Prop. LXVII) view: "A free man thinks of death least of all things; and his wisdom is a meditation not of death but of life". *TLP* (6.45) borrows Spinoza's (2015, Part V, Prop. XXIII, Scholium) view that one should look at the world "*sub specie aeterni*" (*TLP*, 6.45).[13] Indeed, Wittgenstein chose the Latin title *Tractatus Logico-Philosophicus* to suggest an analogy with Spinoza's *Tractatus Theologico-Politicus* (Monk 1990, 143, 206).

One might reply that *TLP* does not banish death from life, but only from the life of those who do not "live in the present". But DML makes no such exception. By the time he wrote *RFM*, Wittgenstein saw *TLP*'s view that one can escape death by "living in the present" as an illusion. For, even when, with "laughing mouth" one thinks one is secure in the midst of life,[14] death is present just beneath the surface—ready to kill one's laughter with tears.

One might object that it is too strong to say that DML contradicts *TLP* (6.4311) because DML only implies that in life one is "in the midst of" death and does not explicitly state that in life one can experience death. However, *CV* (50), dated 1946 (in Wittgenstein's "later" period), describes the hero as one who "looks death in the face, real death, not just the image of death". Further, in *NPL* (455–56), Wittgenstein provides criteria for distinguishing between a "pretend" death (as in a performance of a play) and someone's "dying in reality". Wittgenstein's realization in his "later" period that ordinary language contains criteria that distinguish experience of fake deaths (20 people quickly shot off horses in a "cowboy movie" like clay targets at a carnival) and experience of real death (looking into a loved one's face as they pass away) has reversed his *TLP*-view that one cannot experience death in life.[15]

---

[13] Spinoza's and *TLP*'s views of the world "under the aspect of the eternal" contrast with the more "existential" views of the world from "the midst of" life in Wittgenstein's "later philosophy", as reflected in *RFM* (IV. 53) and in Heidegger (1962, § 53).

[14] Compare the idea of being in the "midst" of life with the idea of the centre of life in McDonough (2015) and McDonough (2017)!

[15] This is not the causal claim that Wittgenstein's changing views about criteria for the use of words changed his views about the possibility of experiencing of death. It is difficult to

In *PI* (Preface) Wittgenstein remarks that he has become aware of grave mistakes in *TLP*. Since the ostensible subject matter of *PI* is the philosophy of language, it is natural to assume that he is referring to mistakes in his earlier *TLP*-views of negation, naming, logical form and so on. The present argument shows that he has also recognized grave mistakes in the more *mystical* or *spiritual* aspects of *TLP*. Whereas *TLP* (6.45) presented a sublime logical point of view on the world "*sub specie aeterni*", his *DML* remark in *RFM* presents a point of view on the world from *within the midst of* the temporal world (in which we are *owned* by death).

4   THE PHILOSOPHY OF MATHEMATICS "FROM A RELIGIOUS POINT OF VIEW"?

When Wittgenstein was working on the latter part of the *Philosophical Investigations*, he said to his ... close friend ... Drury: ... "I am not a religious man but I cannot help seeing every problem from a religious point of view."

Malcolm, *Wittgenstein: From a Religious Point of View?* (1)

Having clarified the antecedent DML in MDM, one can now turn to MDM as a whole. Since the antecedent, DML, employs an actual historical religious saying, and the consequent, SSM, employs a psychological idiom, MDM states that just as some religious people say that life is penetrated by death, one might also say that the seeming sanity of mathematics is pervaded by madness (SSM). That is, MDM is a principle for replacing the religious imagery of DML by the psychological imagery of SSM. The religious perspective in DML, having served in subordinate purpose of suggesting a fruitful religious analogy, drops out in favour of the psychological idiom in SSM. Indeed, MDM, on this view, illustrates what Wittgenstein means when he says in WRD that although he is "not a religious man", he looks at philosophical problems from a religious point of view. WRD does not state that Wittgenstein imports religious views into philosophy. The MDM remark only replaces the religious idiom by a psychological one. Wittgenstein's WRD and MDM can both be consistently stated by an atheist. MDM's role is to replace the death-in-life idiom with the new non-religious psychological idiom introduced in SSM (See *MMS*, 155).

know what caused what here, but it may be that his changing views about life and death changed his views about linguistic criteria.

5 Bringing Mathematics Down to Earth, Where the People, and the Madness, Are

> Mathematics, as a form of art, is the very quintessential type of the classical spirit, cold, inhuman, and sublime. But the reflection that such beauty is sublime is already romanticism—it gives a shiver of feeling in which the Self has its share. The true classical spirit loses itself in devotion to beauty, and loses its relation to man.
>
> Russell, quoted in Monk, *The Spirit of Solitude* (152)

Wittgenstein's implied view in MDM that mathematics is surrounded by madness seems most paradoxical. Although Russell's view (see epigraph) may be unnecessarily cold, it is closer to the common view, tracing to Plato (*Rep.* 526b-e; *Laws*, 818b-d), that if anything defines reason and sanity, it is mathematics. Individual mathematicians (e.g., John Nash) may sometimes be mad, but there is no madness in mathematics itself. The core view of the Enlightenment is that mathematics is "the pride of reason" (Cassirer 1969, 12, 15, 200, 243). Art, literature, music and philosophy may sometimes be invaded by madness, but surely not mathematics. Russell may have feared that he is himself mad (Monk 1996, xix, n1), but it was for that very reason that he fled to mathematics—conceived on Plato's model of timeless unchanging rational perfection—as an escape from the madness of human life (Monk 1991, 268). Thus, Wittgenstein's suggestion that mathematics is surrounded by madness is most paradoxical—and threatening. To find madness there is to find it inside the walls of the citadel of reason. However, Russell was soon to obtain a glimpse of the "madness" that lay just beneath the surface of this "enchanted region" when he recognized that his logical system in *Principia Mathematica* was beset by unsolvable contradictions (Monk 1996, 124–25, 142, 187). Wittgenstein was eventually to conclude that these contradictions were only the beginning. Whereas Russell states to Helen Thomas that mathematics "is a really beautiful world" because "it has nothing to do with life" (Monk 1991, 142), Wittgenstein insists on asking precisely about the use of mathematical propositions in life—and that, for Wittgenstein, is the source of the madness that "surrounds" mathematics.

Although *RFM* (IV) ends with MDM, it begins with what seems to be a mundane question whether the expression "770" occurs in the expansion of π (IV. 9):

> We only see how queer the question is whether the pattern ... '770' ... will occur in the infinite expansion of π when we try to formulate [it] in a common or garden way ...

For Plato or Russell, the question seems unproblematic. They will admit that it might be hard in *practice* to decide whether "770" occurs in the infinite expansion of π or not, but surely it either does or it doesn't.[16] The reason Russell thinks this is clear is because he has

> a vague imagination of having *discovered* something like a space (at which point he thinks of a room), of having opened up a kingdom, and when asked about it he would talk a great deal of nonsense. (*RFM*, IV. 5)

It is only when one examines the way such expressions are used in a "common or garden" way (from "in the midst of life"), that one concludes that "it looks as if a ground for the decision were already there; [but] it [actually] has yet to be invented" (*RFM*, IV. 9; *OC*, 199–200). Plato and Russell think that the "ground [*Entscheidungsgrund*]" for the answer is already present in the infinite series and see it as a minor detail, deriving from human frailty, that people cannot survey the entire series to verify its presence there. Wittgenstein replies that it is not a minor detail: "However queer it sounds, a further expansion of an irrational number is a further expansion of mathematics" (*RFM*, IV. 9). The mathematician "is an inventor, not a discoverer" (*RFM*, I, 167; *LFM*, 22, 82, 92). It is in the invention of these "grounds" that the "madness" comes in.

Wittgenstein makes a relevant remark in his Lectures and Conversations on Aesthetics (*LA*) where he describes Freud's "explanations" involving the unconscious:

> Many of these explanations are accepted because they have a certain kind of charm. The idea of an underworld, a secret cellar. Something hidden, uncanny. Cf. Keller's two children putting a live fly in the head of a doll,

---

[16] Since much of *RFM* (§ IV) concerns problems pertaining to the infinite, one might think that MDM does not find "madness" in all mathematics, but only in the mathematics of the infinite. However, although the madness" referenced in MDM is most evident in the mathematics of the infinite, there is reason to believe he holds similar views about virtually all mathematics. See the discussion of proofs in finite mathematics at *RFM* (I. 38–46): "A demon has cast a spell around this position and excluded it from our space" (*RFM*, I. 45). For this reason, this chapter refers to the madness in mathematics, although it is admitted that there are reasons why Wittgenstein asserts MDM at the close of a section that is primarily concerned with the mathematics of the infinite.

burying the doll, and then running away. This is the sort of thing we do. A lot of things one is ready to believe because they are uncanny. (*LA*, 25)

The sorts of bizarre activities described by Keller seem like madness, but this is the sort of thing we do. People sometimes prefer an explanation *because* it is uncanny (supernatural, mysterious, eerie): "Imagine calculating with $\sqrt{-1}$ invented by a madman, who, attracted by the paradox of the idea, does the calculation as a kind of service, or temple ritual, of the absurd" (*RFM*, IV. 6). Wittgenstein goes on in the passage to contrast such charming (mad) explanations with the sort of explanations required in physics or engineering. In physics an explanation "should enable us to predict something", and in engineering "the bridge must not fall down". Wittgenstein's point is that there is a sense in which explanations in mathematics look more like uncanny Freudian explanations than those in physics or engineering.

Consider the view that the rational numbers cannot be "enumerated" because they cannot be counted. Wittgenstein sees in such views "the whole system of pretense … that by using the new apparatus [of mathematical logic] we deal with infinite sets with the same certainty as hitherto we [dealt] with finite ones"—even comparing these procedures with "alchemy" (*RFM*, IV. 15–16). It is as if in these logical-mathematical techniques, one transforms the lead of ordinary finite series into the gold of infinite series. These sorts of mathematical views are, like Freudian views, accepted because of the charm of the uncanny:

> What is typical of the phenomena I am talking about is that a mysteriousness about some mathematical concepts is not straight away [seen] as an erroneous conception … but … as something … to be respected. (*RFM*, IV. 16)

Wittgenstein sees such mathematical views as less like those in physics and engineering and more like those in Freudian psychology except that the "uncanny … secret cellar" of the unconscious is replaced by the uncanny secret parts of the infinite series that is somehow, mysteriously, both "always beyond our ken" (*RFM*, IV. 14) and also something about which amazing (charming) mathematical theorems can be proved.

Wittgenstein traces much of this "madness" in common views about the foundations of mathematics to "[t]he disastrous invasion of mathematics by logic" (*RFM*, IV. 24; *LFM*, 227). It is by the application of the logical techniques pioneered by Russell, with help at the time from

Wittgenstein himself (Monk 1990, 72), that mathematical concepts are made to appear more solid, more sane, than they really are. There is, therefore, a sense in which mathematics has a "weak foundation" (*RFM*, IV. 5)—certainly a weaker foundation than he had earlier thought when he was rehearsing Russell's proofs in *Principia Mathematica*.

One would, however, be mistaken, in thinking that Wittgenstein simply rejects such mathematical explanations. Consider an analogy! A casual student of Feyerabend's philosophy of science might conclude that by pointing out the "anarchy" in the development of scientific theories, Feyerabend (1993, 13) seeks to undermine science. On the contrary, referring to Galileo's "trickery", Feyerabend (1993, 76 n 22) holds that science "needs such trickery" because he holds that science evolves out of human nature, warts and all. Feyerabend's aim is to show that science is erected on a more shaky kind of "foundation" than one had believed—and, rather than bemoaning this fact, he holds that it has to be this way. Similarly, Wittgenstein's aim in *RFM* is to show that mathematics is built on a weaker, a more human, a more insane kind of foundation than one had thought, and rather than bemoaning this fact, he holds that it has to be this way if mathematics is to be used by human beings (warts and all): "The form of expression we use seems to have been designed for a god … For us, of course, these forms of expression are like pontifical which me may put on, but cannot do much with …" (*PI*, 426). Wittgenstein's bottom line is that this weaker foundation suffices for human life. Wittgenstein would, it seems, agree with the chorus in Heidegger's (1961, 123) Antigone: "There is much that is strange but nothing that surpasses man in strangeness."[17] Wittgenstein's aim in *RFM* is not, so to speak, to bury mathematics, but to praise it as the "human-all-too-human"[18] art that it is: "The mathematician too can wonder at the miracles (the crystal) of nature … [but is] it really possible as long as the object he finds astonishing and gazes at with awe is shrouded in a philosophical fog?" (*CV*, 57) His point is not that the mathematician cannot continue to view the objects of mathematics with awe after that philosophical fog is lifted. Read carefully, the passage suggests that the mathematician can continue to admire the objects of mathematics, but he holds that "[the mathematician's] admiration will

---

[17] Storr (1912, lines 332–33), roughly, replaces Heidegger's "strange" with "wonder".

[18] The expression "human-all-too-human" is from Nietzsche (2000), who has his own quarrel with other-worldly sublime entities that he sees as falsifying the creativity and dignity of human life.

have suffered a rupture that will need healing".[19] The healing process begins by dispensing the philosophical fog: "All that I can do is to show an easy escape from this obscurity and these glistening concept-formations" (*RFM*, IV. 16). Wittgenstein's aim is to produce a human philosophy of mathematics, but that means disclosing its roots in that charming "human-all-too-human" "madness".

Wittgenstein's debt to Nietzsche (Monk 1991, 121–23) is evident here:

> How could anything originate out of its opposite? For example, truth out or error? Or the will to truth out of the will to deception? Or the pure and sun like gaze of the sage out of lust? Such origins are impossible; … The things of highest value cannot be derived from this transitory, seductive, deceptive, paltry world, this turmoil of delusion and lust. Rather from the lap of Being, the hidden god, the "thing-in-itself"—there must be their basis, and nowhere else. (Nietzsche 1966, para. 1)

Nietzsche's point is that the things of the highest value, art, science, philosophy and mathematics, do have precisely such lowly origins.[20] Nietzsche makes this point by mobilizing numerous historical, psychological, philological and literary resources. Wittgenstein's *RFM* makes a similar point, that mathematical truth arises out of human "madness", but does it by paying close attention to the way proof and explanation in mathematics is used to change the grammar of mathematical language (*RFM*, I, 108, 128: Appendix II. 9; II, 31, 38, 39; V. 6).

---

[19] Recall that Wittgenstein's philosopher treats a philosophical problem as one treats an illness. The comparison between Wittgenstein's later philosophy and psychoanalysis is relevant here (Heaton 2000). Like the psychoanalytic patient, the patient's pride may be ruptured in the healing process, but once the healing is completed the patient (mathematician) can achieve a new healthy view of mathematical truth.

[20] Origen suggests that Jesus was the bastard child of a Roman soldier (Casey 2010, 152–54). Nietzsche (1968, 240) alludes to this story when he states that all of our "gods" are "motley bastards" created by "poet's prevarications". Although most scholars reject Origen's story for a lack of evidence (Casey 2010, 154), the idea of "virgin birth" as a euphemism for a bastard-birth may be seen in two very different ways. The idea that Jesus is bastard may be seen as a criticism intended to undermine Jesus with the Jews (Casey 2010, 153–54). On the other hand, it can be seen as a celebration of the miraculous fact that that the most noble of beings can arise out the lowest—that "the pure and sun like gaze of the sage" can arise "out of lust".

Socrates is credited by Cicero with bringing philosophy "down from heavens to earth" (Taylor 1952, 138). Unfortunately, Plato immediately took it back up to the heavens again, and, even further than that, to an inaccessible transcendent beyond. It fell, therefore, to Wittgenstein to bring it down to earth again: "[We] in a sense bring the question, 'what is meaning?' down to earth" (*BB*, 1). By bringing such questions down to earth, Wittgenstein brings them to the place where the people (and their madness) are—and, for the same reason, to the place where the poetry, the literature, the music—and the life—is.

6   Mathematics as Literature, Well, Sort Of

Imagine set theory's having been invented by a satirist as a kind of parody on mathematics.—Later a reasonable meaning was seen in it and it was incorporated into mathematics.

Wittgenstein, *Remarks on the Foundations of Mathematics* (IV. 7)

When Plato (*Phaedrus*, 244a–c) claims that "the greatest blessings come by way of madness", a kind of "inspiration" that is "heaven sent" by "divine dispensation", he does not mean that these blessings accrue from schizophrenia, manic depression, multiple personality disorder and the like. Wittgenstein's MDM is not making a psychiatric comment about the *causes* of mathematics. MDM is a literary remark: "What I invent are new similes" (*CV*, 19). The "madness" mentioned in MDM denotes the inspiration or imagination that so far exceeds the abilities of ordinary human beings that one feels that it must come about by divine inspiration. Plato speaks of philosophy as the best sort of divine madness (*Phaedrus*, 249d-d). At *Symposium* (218b) the "philosophical frenzy" is described as a "sacred rage". At *Sophist* (216d) it is said that the philosopher is "thought" to be mad. Similarly, "singing as they do, under the divine afflatus" poets are said to be among the "inspired", who with the help of "their Graces and Muses, often ... hit upon" truth (*Laws*, 682a).

Wittgenstein's point in MDM is not that mathematics arises out literal clinical mental illnesses, but that it arises out of the same kind of mad inspiration that produces poetry and philosophy.[21] That is, Wittgenstein's

---

[21] Despite Plato's vehement criticism of poetry (*Republic*, Bk. 10), his poets bear a significant, although admittedly not perfect, resemblance to his philosophers: "If there is a quarrel between poetry and philosophy, it is a feud among kin" (Gonzalez 2011, 108ff).

RFM sees mathematics as akin to literature rather than, as Plato and Russell see it, as a description of some kind of "room".[22] In his *TLP*-period, when he was collaborating with Russell to reduce mathematics to logic, Wittgenstein conceived of mathematics akin to the description of logical space (*TLP*, 6.22, 6.234). In *RFM* (I. 8) Wittgenstein describes his old way of seeing things (which he now rejects):

> Here what is before our mind in a vague way is that logic is a kind of ultra-physics, the description of the 'logical structure' of the world, which we perceive through a kind of ultra-experience (with the understanding).

That is, on Wittgenstein's old *TLP*-view, mathematics and logic are descriptions of a sublime supra-human space that is already there. One's human-all-too-human imagination must, therefore, play no role in its description: "Logic is not a field in which we express what we wish with the help of signs but rather one in which the nature of the natural and inevitable signs speaks for itself" (*TLP*, 6.124). The self and its troublesome inspiration and imagination drop out and "the nature of the natural and inevitable signs speaks for itself". All traces of the self must drop out because these can only distort these sublime supra-human structures.

In opposition to his former *TLP*-view, Wittgenstein now holds that "however queer it sounds, the further expansion of an irrational number [like π] is a further expansion of mathematics" (*RFM*, IV. 9). Since the "ground" for the decision whether "770" occurs in the expansion of π has to be invented (see Section 4), Wittgenstein now compares mathematical questions to a poet's questions: "[T]he poet might reply when asked whether the hero of his poem has a sister or not" that "So far there is no such thing as an answer to this question" (*RFM*, IV. 9). Once the poet makes their decision, there is a ground for the answer that formerly was not there (e.g., "I suddenly realized that I needed a hero inspired by a related female character, otherwise the whole thing would not make sense"). Similarly, once the mathematician makes certain decisions, the question about the expansion of π might be answered. One is deciding

---

[22] Cantor is often said to have discovered a "paradise" of amazing objects (Tiles 1989). In fact, the word "paradise" is etymologically related to "enclosure" or "room". See *Online Etymological Dictionary*. http://www.etymonline.com/index.php?allowed_in_frame=0&search=paradise.

(creating), not describing something already there. Further, the grounds for such decisions are often aesthetic: "The queer resemblance between a philosophical investigation (perhaps especially in mathematics) and an aesthetic one" (*CV*, 25). Wittgenstein holds that mathematics, as a product of human inspiration that resembles Plato's "divine madness", is more like poetry or literature (aesthetic productions) than he could have imagined in his *TLP*-period. Wittgenstein is not merely attempting to achieve an aesthetic understanding of mathematics, which might be pursued by anybody and requires no specific philosophical orientation and has no specific philosophical consequences. He holds that in order to develop a correct philosophy of mathematics—that is, to understand mathematics as such—one must cultivate an appreciation of its aesthetic foundations. Since mathematics does not fall, ready-made from some sublime supra-human realm, but, rather, is constructed by human beings, "the trail of the human serpent", to borrow James' (1981, 13, 33) expression, including, therefore, the human aesthetic instinct, is all over it.

Wittgenstein does not, however, hold that mathematics is like poetry in every respect:

> Strangely, it can be said that there is, so to speak, a solid core to all these glistening concept formations. And ... that is what makes them into mathematical productions (*RFM*, IV. 16).

Recall that the explanations in physics and engineering, unlike Freud's explanations, must enable predictions: "The bridge must not fall down" (see Section 4). It would not, however, be wise to use the battle scenes in Homer's *Iliad* to plan a real battle. What distinguishes the products of the mathematical imagination from those of the poetic imagination (as ordinarily understood) is that "we should not call something 'calculating' if we could not make such a prophecy [prediction] with certainty. This really means: calculating is a technique. And what we have said pertains to the essence of a technique" (*RFM*, II. 67).[23] Wittgenstein's *RFM* holds that mathematics is like literature in that both are the product of similar kinds

---

[23] It may seem a bit puzzling that Wittgenstein uses the word "prophecy" in this context, but he moves freely to the word "prediction" in the same passage. His point is, presumably, to illustrate that that there is more similarity between the inspired (mad) prophet and the cold rational scientific predictor than one had expected.

of "divine madness", but they are not exactly the same. Despite their common origins in this "transitory, seductive, deceptive paltry world, this turmoil of delusion and lust", they do play very different kinds of roles in human life. This is why Wittgenstein (*RFM*, IV. 6) asks the reader to imagine how infinite numbers are used in a "fairy tale [*Märchen*]", where what occurs in this fairy tale "surely makes sense".[24] Since "fairy tales" portray what happens in the life of the characters in the tale, Wittgenstein's point is that what transpires in the life of these characters as they apply infinite numbers displays how much "sense" these characters can attach to the mathematical language in their lives.[25]

Many poets and mathematicians have agreed, at least, on one thing—that Plato, one of the greatest poets in world civilization (Randall 1970, 3, 102), was fundamentally correct when he stated, with a touch both of irony and divine madness, that poetry and mathematics represent two completely opposite, even contradictory, tendencies of mind.[26] Thus, Plato holds that poetry must be banished from the city of the sane in order to make room for the sublime rational truth of mathematics (*Rep*. 398a, 568b; *Laws*, 659c-660a). Wittgenstein's response in *RFM*, summed up in his own poetic statement, MDM, is that Plato's view that one must choose only one of the two as the conveyor of truth and consign the other to fable and illusion is a false choice. Wittgenstein does not hold that poetry and mathematics are the same, but that they are, so to speak, close siblings that, despite the usual family squabbles, are more alike than either wants to admit. For both poetry and mathematics trace their lineage, as disconcerting at this sometimes is to both of them, to the same sacred source of "divine madness" that is the source of all human greatness. One cannot banish the madness underlying poetry without destroying the madness underlying mathematics as well.

---

[24] "*Märchen*" is often translated as "fairy tale" but it can also have the connotation in German of a fable, myth or tall story.

[25] By using this terminology (see note 24 above), Wittgenstein surely intends to suggest that our prized mathematical creations bear a certain resemblance to "fairy tales" or fables—with the important proviso, not to be minimized, that these "glistening" mathematical creations do possess a "solid core" lacking in fairy tales proper.

[26] In the Introduction to their anthology on "mathematical poetry", Robson and Wimp (1979) agree with Plato that poetry and mathematics are inherently antithetical and that it may be more useful to consider the differences rather than emphasize the similarities.

7 Philosophy, Literature, Scepticism and Madness

> I am sitting with a philosopher in the garden; he says again and again "I know that that's a tree", pointing to a tree that is near us. Someone else arrives and hears this, and I tell him "This fellow isn't insane. We are only doing philosophy".
>
> Wittgenstein, *On Certainty* (467)

Since there is a distressing resemblance between the sceptical statements by esteemed philosophers and statements of the clinically insane, many of Cavell's formulations concern the analogies between scepticism and madness (*MMS*, 60). However, this makes Cavell's point appear unnecessarily negative since it is bound up with sceptical positions that many philosophers, including Wittgenstein, do not take particularly seriously: "If someone said to me he doubted whether he had a body I should take him to be a half-wit" (*OC*, 257). Wittgenstein also states that certain philosophical doubts are "hollow", that they make no actual difference in human life and that a doubt which goes on without end "is not even a doubt" (*OC*, 312, 338–39, 625). One is not driven to *real* madness by hollow doubts, the ravings of a half-wit, abstract claims that make no difference in real life or "doubts" that are not really doubts. Descartes never really doubted that he knew a great many things about the world (Hatfield 2014, § 3.1). He used doubt as a method, what Wilfrid Sellars used to call "a philosophical pressure device", to disclose the real structure of the edifice of knowledge which it was his ultimate aim to defend. Similarly, Hume (1967, 264, 269) admits that his philosophical doubts appear "cold" and "ridiculous" as soon as he leaves his study. This is why Wittgenstein does not see the philosopher's doubts and madness as real doubts and real madness. Similarly, when Wittgenstein suggests that mathematics is surrounded by madness, he is not stating a *theory* about the genesis of mathematics in genuine clinical madness, but is making a *comparison*, inventing a *simile*, that he finds illuminating (*PI*, 130–31; *CV*, 14, 20, 26). One might, therefore, wonder whether Cavell's suggestion that the great literary figures are responding to the issues posed by philosophical scepticism can survive (*PDAT*, 12–13). For if this philosophical madness is not genuine madness, then since the great literary figures explore genuine issues in human life (not doubts that are not doubts), there is no reason why they would be interested in the "hollow" doubts of philosophical scepticism. Thus, it may appear that Wittgenstein's notion of the madness that pervades human life disclosed by his philosophical investigations is not the kind of madness explored by Cavell in literature.

This argument is, however, hasty. This can be seen by examining another more positive formulation in Cavell—that scepticism reveals "the inevitable cracks or leaps of madness that haunt the construction of the world" (see Section 1). That is, the application of the sceptical method discloses the "abysses" that attend the construction of mathematics (and by analogy all language and thought). Wittgenstein (*RFM*, II. 78) refers to these abysses in mathematics: "We went sleepwalking on the road between abysses [*Abgründ*]. ... Can we be certain there are abysses ... we do not see?" Wittgenstein's point is that these abysses do *not constitute* a real threat to everyday sanity. Discussing his own fear of madness, Wittgenstein refers more generally (not just in mathematics) to his fear of taking something to be "an abyss right at my feet, when it is nothing of the sort" (*CV*, 53). His point, again, is that there is no real need to fear these "abysses". He makes an analogous remark about an "honest religious thinker":

> He almost looks as though he were walking on nothing but air. His support is the slenderest imaginable. And yet it is really possible to walk on it. (*CV*, 73)

Wittgenstein sees the honest religious thinkers as much like philosophers of mathematics (Recall *WRD*). His remark that one "sleepwalks" past the abysses in mathematics means that they are not a problem unless one sees them (and decides, like Russell, to *make* them into a problem): "What the eye doesn't see the heart doesn't grieve over" (*RFM*, II. 78). A misguided philosopher of mathematics may feel that one cannot walk through a region of mathematics lacking a rational foundation, but "it really is possible to walk" there.

Cavell's more positive formulation of the link between philosophical scepticism and madness is that scepticism reveals the madness underlying the "construction" of the various "worlds" we inhabit. Since the "foundations" of the "worlds" of the King (Lear),[27] the daughter (Kate), the sister (Antigone) and so on, is just as tenuous as those of mathematics, there is no reason why the great literary figures should not be interested in explor-

---

[27] See Cavell's discussion at *MMS* (155)!

ing the "mad" "foundations" of these more ordinary "worlds".[28] Further, it might seem that Wittgenstein's "grammatical" investigations are different in kind from the investigations of the great literary figures. However, Cavell compares the "facts of [modern] life" that "tell us what kind of object a modern work of art is" with Wittgenstein's "grammatical remarks" (*MMS*, 229). One might also view some of the scenes in literary works as grammatical remarks. As an example, Cavell (*MMS*, 288) gives an interpretation of Lear's madness that he admits may be hard to make convincing. Is Lear puerile or senile? No, for "the nature of his madness, his melancholy and antic disposition, its incessant invention, is the sign, in fact and in Renaissance thought, of genius; an option of escape [that is] open only to minds of the highest reach" (*MMS*, 288). In brief, Shakespeare is making something like a grammatical comment about the Renaissance notion of the connection between madness and genius.[29] Shakespeare makes an analogous point in *A Midsummer's Night's Dream* (V, I, 7): "The lunatic, the lover, and the poet are of imagination all compact".

Wittgenstein writes: "Theology as grammar" (*PI*, 373). Why should one not add: "Literature as grammar"—not always, but sometimes, when, for example, literature explores the concepts of love, betrayal, courage, wisdom, knowledge, rules and the like in the sensuous medium of literature rather than the more abstract language of philosophy proper (much as Plato, arguably, did in his magnificent literary works 2500 years ago). Indeed, literature would seem to be a natural medium for illustrating the philosophical view that meaning resides, not in private mental constructs or lifeless Fregean abstract entities, but in human activities, that is, in human "forms of life" (*PI*, p. 226). This is why Wittgenstein quotes, approvingly, Goethe's Faust's remark, "*Im Anfang war die tat*" ("In the beginning was the deed") (*CV*, 31)—itself Faust's modification of the Biblical sentence, "In the beginning was the Word" (John 1: 1). For much literature is a description and exegesis of the *meaning* of *deeds* (human or divine) in the various arenas of human life.

---

[28] In fact, Wittgenstein's idea that mathematics can, so to speak, arise out of madness, is just a variant on the imagery in *Z* (608), which suggests that language and thought may, so to speak, arise out of chaos. Compare Cavell's (*MMS*, 305) talk of the creation of a world out of madness with the cosmological language of the emergence of language and thought out of chaos in *Z*, 608 (McDonough 2015, 2017). See also McDonough (2016/2017b)!

[29] For a discussion of the concept of madness in the Italian Renaissance, see Brann (2002, 90, 247–48, 312, 329, 363)!

References

Augustine. 1993. *Confessions.* Translated by F.J. Sheed. Indianapolis: Hackett.
The Book of Common Prayer According to the Episcopal Church in the United States. 1853. New York: D. Appleton and Company.
Brann, Noel. 2002. *The Debate over the Origins of Genius in the Italian Renaissance.* Leiden: Brill.
Carr, David, and Colleen Conway. 2010. *An Introduction to the Bible: Sacred Texts and Imperial Contexts.* New York: John Wiley & Sons.
Casey, Maurice. 2010. *Jesus of Nazareth: An Independent Historian's Account of his Life and Teaching.* London: A&C Black.
Cassirer, Ernst. 1969. *The Philosophy of the Enlightenment.* Princeton, NJ: Princeton University Press.
Cavell, Stanley. 1976. *Must We Mean What We Say?* Cambridge: Cambridge University Press.
———. 1979. *The Claim of Reason: Wittgenstein, Skepticism, Morality, and Tragedy.* Oxford: Oxford University Press.
———. 1989. *This New Yet Unapproachable America: Lectures after Wittgenstein.* Albuquerque: Living Batch Press.
———. 1990. *Emerson: Conditions Handsome and Unhandsome: The Constitution of Emersonian Perfectionism.* La Salle: Open Court.
———. 2005. *Philosophy the Day after Tomorrow.* Cambridge, MA: Harvard University Press.
Feyerabend, Paul. 1993. *Against Method.* New York: Verso.
Gonzalez, Francisco. 2011. The Hermeneutics of Madness: Poet and Philosopher in Plato's Ion and Phaedrus. In *Plato and the Poets*, ed. Pierre Destrée and Fritz Gregor Herrmann. Leiden: Brill.
Hatfield, Gary. 2014. Rene Descartes. *Stanford Encyclopedia of Philosophy.* http://plato.stanford.edu/entries/descartes/
Heaton, John. 2000. *Wittgenstein and Psychoanalysis.* Totem Books.
Heidegger, Martin. 1961. *Introduction to Metaphysics.* Translated by Ralph Manheim. New York: Doubleday.
———. 1962. *Being and Time.* Translated by John Macquarrie and Edward Robinson. San Francisco: HarperSanFrancisco.
Hume, David. 1967. *A Treatise of Human Nature.* Oxford: Clarendon.
Husserl, Edmund. 1970. *Cartesian Meditations.* Translated by Dorian Cairns. The Hague: Martinus Nijhoff.
James, William. 1981. *Pragmatism.* Indianapolis: Hackett.
Kripke, Saul. 1982. *Wittgenstein on Rules and Private Language.* Cambridge, MA: Harvard University Press.
Luther, Martin. 1884. *Mitten Wir in Leben sind.* In *The Hymns of Martin Luther*, ed. Lord Woosley Bacon. London: Hodder and Stoughton.

Malcolm, Norman. 1977. *Memory and Mind*. Ithaca, NY: Cornell University Press.
———. 1997. *Wittgenstein: From a Religious Point of View?* New York: Routledge.
———. 2001. *Ludwig Wittgenstein: A Memoir*. Oxford: Oxford University Press.
McDonough, Richard. 2015. Wittgenstein's Augustinian Cosmology in *Zettel* 608. *Philosophy and Literature* 39 (1): 87–106.
———. 2017a. A *Gestalt* Model of *Zettel* 608. *Idealistic Studies* 68 (2): 163–182. Online First (Dec. 1). https://www.pdcnet.org/pdc/bvdb.nsf/purchase?openform&fp=idstudies&id=idstudies_2017_0999_11_28_63.
———. 2016/2017b. A Music Model of *Zettel* 608: Haydn and Beethoven. *The Journal of Music and Meaning* 17: 21–40.
Monk, Ray. 1990. *The Duty of Genius*. New York: Penguin.
———. 1996. *Bertrand Russell: The Spirit of Solitude (1972–1921)*. New York and London: The Free Press.
———. 2001. *Bertrand Russell: 1921–1970, The Ghost of Madness*. New York: The Free Press.
Nietzsche, Friedrich. 1966. *Beyond Good and Evil*. Translated by Walter Kaufmann. New York: Vintage Books.
———. 1968. *Thus Spoke Zarathustra* in *The Portable Nietzsche*. Edited and translated by Walter Kaufmann. New York: Viking, 112–439.
———. 2000. *Human, All Too Human I*. Translated by Gary Handwerk. Redwood City: Stanford University Press.
Plato. 1968. *Republic*. Translated by Alan Bloom. New York and London: Basic Books.
———. 1969a. *Phaedo*. Translated by Hugh Tredennick. *The Collected Dialogues of Plato*. Edited by Hamilton and Cairns. Princeton, NJ: Princeton University Press, 40–98.
———. 1969b. *Phaedrus*. Translated by R. Hackforth. *The Collected Dialogues of Plato*. Edited by Hamilton and Cairns. Princeton, NJ: Princeton University Press, 475–525.
———. 1969c. *Sophist*. Translated by F.M. Cornford. *The Collected Dialogues of Plato*. Edited by Hamilton and Cairns. Princeton, NJ: Princeton University Press, 845–919.
———. 1969d. *Laws*. Translated by A.E. Taylor. *The Collected Dialogues of Plato*. Edited by Hamilton and Cairns. Princeton, NJ: Princeton University Press, 1225–1516.
———. 1997. *Symposium*. Translated by Alexander Nehamas and Paul Woodruff. *Plato: Complete Works*. Edited by John Cooper. Indianapolis and Cambridge: Hackett, 457–505.
Randall, John Herman. 1970. *Plato: Dramatist of the Life of Reason*. New York: Columbia University Press.
Rilke, Rainer Maria. 1994. Closing Piece. *The Book of Images*. Translated by Edward Snow. North Point Press, 252–253.

Robson, Ernest, and Jet Wimp. 1979. *Against Infinity*. Parker Ford, PA: Primary Press.

Spinoza, Benedict. 1991. *Tractatus-Logico-Politicus*. Translated by Samuel Shirley. Leiden: Brill.

———. 2015. *Ethics*. Translated by R.H.M. Elwes. CreateSpace Independent Publishing.

Storr, F. 2014. *Antigone in The Three Theban Plays*. CreateSpace Independent Publishing.

Taylor, A.E. 1952. *Socrates*. New York: Doubleday and Company.

Tiles, Mary. 1989. *The Philosophy of Set Theory: An Historical Introduction to Cantor's Paradise*. Mineola, NY: Dover.

Wittgenstein, Ludwig. 1958. *Philosophical Investigations*. 2nd ed. Translated by G.E.M. Anscombe. Oxford: Blackwell.

———. 1961. *Tractatus-logico-philosophicus*. Translated by David Pears. London: Routledge and Kegan Paul

———. 1965. *The Blue and Brown Books*. New York: Harper.

———. 1966. *Notebooks, 1914–16*. G.E.M. Translated by Anscombe. New York: Harper and Row.

———. 1969. *On Certainty*. Translated by Denis Paul and G.E.M. Anscombe. Oxford: Blackwell.

———. 1970. *Zettel*. Translated by G.E.M. Anscombe. Berkeley and Los Angeles: University of California Press.

———. 1972. *Remarks on the Foundations of Mathematics*. Translated by G.E.M. Anscombe. Cambridge, MA: MIT Press.

———. 1980. *Culture and Value*. Translated by Peter Winch. Chicago: University of Chicago Press.

———. 1989. *Lectures on the Foundations of Mathematics*. Chicago: University of Chicago Press.

———. 1993. Notes for the Philosophical Lecture. In *Philosophical Occasions*. Indianapolis: Hackett.

———. 2007. *Lectures and Conversations on Aesthetics, Psychology, and Religious Belief*. Berkeley: University of California Press.

PART IV

Reading Fiction and Literary Understanding

CHAPTER 10

Fraudulence, Knowledge, and Post-Imperial Geographies in John Le Carré's Fiction: A Cavellian Postcolonial Reading

Alan Johnson

[T]he dangers of fraudulence, and of trust, are essential to the experience of art.... The world is to be accepted; as the presentness of other minds is not to be known, but to be acknowledged.—Stanley Cavell[1]

[Britons] came to define themselves as a single people not because of any political or cultural consensus at home, but rather in reaction to the Other beyond their shores.—Linda Colley[2]

---

[1] Stanley Cavell, "Music Discomposed," pp. 188–89, and "The Avoidance of Love," p. 322, both in *Must We Mean What We Say?: A Book of Essays* (New York: Cambridge University Press, 1969); hereafter abbreviated Cavell.

[2] Colley, *Britons: Forging the Nation, 1707–1837* (New Haven, CT: Yale University Press, 2005), p. 6; hereafter abbreviated Colley.

A. Johnson (✉)
Idaho State University, Pocatello, ID, USA
e-mail: johnala2@isu.edu

© The Author(s) 2018
G. L. Hagberg (ed.), *Stanley Cavell on Aesthetic Understanding*, Philosophers in Depth,
https://doi.org/10.1007/978-3-319-97466-8_10

1   Introduction: The Argument in Context

This essay argues that John le Carré's fiction, particularly his 1974 spy novel *Tinker Tailor Soldier Spy*,[3] succeeds as serious art because it unflinchingly casts the typical Cold War spy's post-imperial world not as knowable, because previously mapped and colonized, but instead as a truer reflection of what Stanley Cavell calls an inherently contingent, unknowable world. It is in acknowledging, rather than avoiding, this contingent world, as Cavell might put it, that le Carré's protagonist George Smiley achieves his stature as an ironic rather than tragic hero. The novel's post-imperial Cold War setting is therefore not mere backdrop, as in a James Bond film, but an integral part of its moral vision, which conditions any meaningful understanding of Smiley's motivations, actions, and realizations. If "texts have ways of existing that … are always enmeshed in circumstance, time, place, and society—in short, … worldly,"[4] then we must ponder the implications of this worldliness in le Carré's fiction. And nothing is more worldly, in this case, than the seemingly insignificant locales—a Delhi jail cell, unlit London alleyways—in which le Carré places his characters. His spy world is an uncanny and ironic reflection of British colonialism's dream of omniscient, panoramic vision.

"I have always wanted to set a novel in Cornwall," le Carré tells us in his introduction to the 1991 re-issue of *Tinker Tailor*. He failed in this endeavor, he says, because he "wanted the entire story to play in contemporary time and not in the flashbacks I later resorted to." He finds such a "linear path forward" unworkable, and burns the manuscript. What he does eventually produce is a novel that exposes, as he accurately puts it, "the inside-out logic of double-agent operation."[5] This begs some questions that I believe are crucial to address if we're to appreciate le Carré's accomplishments more deeply: Why did he initially aim for a "linear" storyline, and what accounts for the success of the novel in its current form? Why is his desired Cornwall, rather than the eventual global, setting so difficult? More broadly, what accounts for le Carré's role in having "made the spy story into one of the most important literary genres of the

---

[3] John le Carré, *Tinker Tailor Soldier Spy* (New York: Penguin, 2011); hereafter abbreviated *Tinker Tailor*.

[4] Edward Said, *The World, the Text, and the Critic* (Cambridge, MA: Harvard University Press, 1983), p. 35.

[5] Le Carré, Introduction, *Tinker Tailor* (2011), pp. xi–xii.

mid-twentieth century," as John Cawelti and Bruce Rosenberg have argued?[6] Part of the answers to these questions lies, as Cawelti and Rosenberg point out, in le Carré's ability to transform a conventional "story of heroic ... triumph into a much more complex and ambiguous narrative of ironic failure in which the protagonists succeed only at the cost of becoming as dehumanized, as distorted in their conception of ends and means, as their adversaries" (179). Le Carré perceived that espionage and the catastrophe it anxiously and obsessively strives to prevent are reflections of an increasingly regimented, militaristic world, whose signature is the normalization of terror. Joseph Conrad had perceived this long before, with his 1907 novel *The Secret Agent*; but Conrad turns to espionage as a backdrop for other themes that interest him (such as a terrorist's personal motivations), as does Graham Greene after him.[7] Le Carré's novels, by contrast, emphasize the increasing regimentation of a post-World War II world haunted by both colonialism and nuclear destruction. Cornwall alone will not do as a proper setting for such widespread effects. Instead, Cornwall, like the public schools and country cottages that populate le Carré's stories, must be seen in relation to the alleyways and histories of seemingly distant global capitals, from Washington to Moscow, and from London to Delhi.

But if le Carré's protagonist Smiley becomes as alienated by modern life as his Russian counterparts, how is the reader to gain any clue to what I've called le Carré's "meaningful" narrative? Is there no difference, after all, between sides? Although there are no definitive answers, we can glean insights from the ways in which le Carré's series of novels featuring Smiley probe the changes he undergoes, from initial qualms about his work's amorality ("I honestly do wonder," he thinks at one point in another novel, "how I reached this present pass")[8] to his corruptive obsession with his Russian alter ego Karla. Like Walter White's character in the television phenomenon *Breaking Bad*, Smiley's increasing willingness to justify his

---

[6] John G. Cawelti and Bruce A. Rosenberg, *The Spy Story* (Chicago: University of Chicago Press, 1987), p. 157; hereafter abbreviated Cawelti and Rosenberg.

[7] For insightful analysis and context, see Tom Reiss's review, on the fourth anniversary of the 2001 9/11 attack, of Joseph Conrad's novels *The Secret Agent* (1907) and *Under Western Skies* (1911), "The True Classic of Terrorism," *The New York Times* Sunday Book Review (September 11, 2005); accessed June 14, 2014 at: http://www.nytimes.com/2005/09/11/books/review/11reiss.html?pagewanted=all.

[8] John le Carré, *The Honourable Schoolboy* (New York: Knopf, 1977), p. 523.

(or his side's) cruel acts by harping on the end result highlights the novels' exposure of systemic rot and its crippling psychological effects. The flashback technique is unavoidable for le Carré because his novels document, in part, the disappearance of one version of systemic rot, the Empire that, as Connie Sachs sardonically says in *Tinker Tailor*, many of MI5's agents had been "trained" to uphold (117). The imperial backdrop conditions these agents' motivations, just as it conditions the historical context in which Smiley and Karla act out their desires. At the same time, each of these characters must make individual choices. Being the first of the "Karla trilogy," *Tinker Tailor*—which was followed by *The Honourable Schoolboy* and *Smiley's People*—captures the catalysts for Smiley's evolution from honor-bound agent to the mirror image of Karla's ruthlessness.

This evolution is also a societal one, for it reflects the relinquishing of imperial self-certainty and the acknowledgment of the fluid state of a Cold War world that can no longer be defined "in reaction to the Other beyond" British shores, as Linda Colley summarizes the national-imperial strategy that shaped Britain for centuries (see epigraph above). Rather than having British spies seek the kind of certainty enjoyed by their more popular fictional counterparts, le Carré's Cold War protagonists (notably George Smiley) come to accept, in the way Cavell says we must, that their inability to obtain such certainty—about the enemy, about the world—misses the point. Instead, le Carré's characters frequently acknowledge (again, in Cavell's sense) the inherent contingency and moral ambiguity of human existence. This does not mean, as I've noted, that le Carré's fiction is amoral, as is sometimes assumed given its damning portrait of the intelligence establishment,[9] quite the contrary. In seeing that fraud and trust rest not on exalted notions of patriotism but on the acceptance, rather than avoidance, of irony in everyday life, characters like George Smiley and Peter Guillam, especially in *Tinker Tailor*, achieve a moral vision of the world that exceeds the boundaries of its Manichean geopolitics. The postimperial world is an inescapable part of this geopolitics, a point the older Smiley, who as a young man witnessed (like le Carré) the break-up of

---

[9] Le Carré himself seems to anticipate this stock reaction when the narrator of his first novel, *Call for the Dead* (1961), in which he introduces Smiley, tells us: "It intrigued him to evaluate from a detached position what he had learnt to describe as 'the agent potential' of a human being; ... This part of him was bloodless and inhuman—Smiley in this role was the international mercenary of his trade, amoral and without motive beyond that of personal gratification" (4).

imperial Britain, gradually discerns. In thus interconnecting post-imperial geopolitics and a Cavellian embrace of irony, le Carré addresses his readers' anxieties with this murky world by creating not a conventional spy who heroically ties up loose ends, but one who earns our trust by living with those anxieties.

Smiley earns our trust precisely because he is in many ways an everyman, decidedly unheroic and, more importantly, isolated and alone. When we first see him, in *Tinker Tailor*, he is in lonely retirement, his wife is estranged, and he talks to himself. Ironically, it is his mostly silent counterpart, the Russian spymaster, in whom Smiley sees himself reflected—with the difference that Smiley, despite acting in every way like a consummate detective, nevertheless conveys to us something of the impossibility of ever knowing the truth. Karla, who remains mostly silent in the novel, is never shown to have relinquished this common wish to know—although he, too, finally crosses into an uncertain future when he defects. Such lines, or boundaries, in le Carré represent the thin membrane between a Cavellian "avoidance" of unknowing and a wish to know (or to believe that one knows)—a thin but consequential demarcation.

2 *Tinker Tailor* in Context: Uncanny Spies and Unraveling Empires

When we read or watch even the most clichéd of spy stories, we understand that a certain kind of fraudulence lies at the heart of espionage. The typical spy-hero pretends to be someone he or she is not, and the ever-present danger of being found out, of being exposed as a pretender, generates much of the pleasure in the plot. The hero's skill with impersonation, and our wish for him or her to succeed, depends on a clearly defined conflict between two opposing forces, one generally on the side (our hero's side) of good, the other bad. This kind of story calls for fairly clear-cut presumptions about values like honor, patriotism, friendship, and romance, and likens impersonation to a mask that can be removed instantly and effortlessly. We trust in our hero's immutable goodness of heart, and in the author's unquestioned confirmation of that trust. We expect our hero to restore order in a chaotic world, and to do so by relying on a combination of bravery and cunning. We take pleasure in our hero's intimacy with a shadow-world of criminal intrigue, all while maintaining his (usually male) elegant civility, a juxtaposition of values whose exemplar is, of course, James Bond. His traffic in both abjection and urbanity—and often both at the same time—is simultaneously unsettling and thrilling. The popular spy story rarely compels us to ponder the moral consequences of this traffic, of the "unrecognizable alien lodged within a recognizable body."[10] We lend our hero the "license" not just "to kill," but to thrill by resorting to the kind of duplicity and disguise normally associated with sociopaths. For in this game, ends justify means, and we trust him with this license. The story comes to a satisfying resolution, and all's right with the world. An added pleasure is the ways in which a spy tale riffs on spy conventions, so that repetition operates more like the scaffolding to which "new meanings" accrue, as Alan Hepburn observes in his analysis of spy narratives (22).

There is, as le Carré's novels attest, a more serious variety of spy fiction that, even as it plays upon many of these conventions, obliges us to contemplate the consequential ethical fallout of espionage. By the final pages of such serious spy narratives, therefore, we are often left with more, not fewer, questions—questions not about the well-crafted plot or the ingeniously conceived spy traps, but about the characters' afterlives. By "serious" I mean novels in which, unlike the spies in popular fiction, characters inhabit a shadowy world of intrigue that, while familiar to the likes of Bond, is a far more ambiguous realm. Writers like le Carré, Eric Ambler, and Charles Cumming exhibit a willingness to embrace an irresolute denouement rather than a trite resolution of conflict that "reaffirm[s] ... conventional beliefs or perspectives" (Cawelti and Rosenberg, 98). In serious Cold War espionage fiction, spies on either side of the proverbial Iron Curtain prove to be more alike than not, so that the pleasure of reading actually depends upon the uncomfortable possibility that the geopolitical world, whatever the media might say, cannot be neatly split in two. Spies in this context are internally conflicted, with each new circumstance leading to a renewed moral questioning of their actions, producing a constant tension that the final seasons of the acclaimed television series *The Americans*, for example, conveys so well. Although popular spy stories sometimes acknowledge moral and global complexity, their outcome is more predictable, depending as they do on an unchanging hero. Serious spy novelists are far more acutely aware of the haphazard history that gave rise to this world, especially, as mentioned, the break-up of Britain's empire, and of their characters' unpredictable changes. By "world" I mean both a physical and psychological space that, in the best novels, reminds us of the disconcertingly thin line between civility and savagery—and even, as le Carré's narratives suggest, the fact that

---

[10] Allan Hepburn, *Intrigue: Espionage and Culture* (New Haven, CT: Yale University Press, 2005), p. 13; hereafter abbreviated Hepburn.

such a distinction may be illusory. On a psychological level, then, it is broadly true that all spy fictions forcefully convey, perhaps more than any other genre, the special unease of modern uncanniness, in Freud's sense of perceiving something as being at once familiar and strange. The genre does so, moreover, because of its characteristic gusto for the aforementioned mix of civility and abjection that post-war realpolitik seems to have engendered. But in addition to these broad themes, serious spy fiction knowingly grapples, as we will see in more detail, with the particular historical and geographical legacies of a British imperial world whose existence hinged on the fantasy of loyalty and the perennial threat (and fear) of betrayal, legacies that intensify the already-intense climate of Cold War intrigue.

There are two other, more-specific reasons for the lasting artistic success of le Carré's work. First, he benefitted from publishing well into the spy genre's twentieth-century evolution, which has provided him with a familiar scaffolding on which to build. Second, and more significantly, is his aforementioned recognition of the consequences of colonialism. The first reason is perhaps more obvious. As early as 1960, when he began his writing career, le Carré could assume his average reader was familiar with the ingredients of standard spy craft, which had been set decades earlier in Erskine Childers's hugely popular 1903 novel *The Riddle of the Sands*. Michael Denning, echoing Cawelti and Rosenberg, says that spy stories "are no longer one part of popular culture; they are at its centre."[11] It's useful to recall that when Childers began the modern spy genre, this was not yet true, though within just a decade, by the start of World War I, the ordinary public in western countries could read about fictional spies alongside real-life ones and see them enacted on screen.[12] Quite quickly, especially in a more disillusioned Europe following World War I, the threat of invasion from without, such as Germany's covert naval build-up as described in Childers's novel, becomes the threat of invasion from within, at least in European spy fiction.[13] By the time of the Cold War, American writers like Robert Ludlum had joined this British shift. Indeed, the opening of the 2004 film adaptation of Ludlum's 1986 novel *The Bourne*

---

[11] Michael Denning, "Licensed to Look: James Bond and the Heroism of Consumption," in *The James Bond Phenomenon: A Critical Reader*, ed. Christoph Lindner (New York: Manchester University Press, 2003), pp. 56–75; p. 56; and see Cawelti and Rosenberg, *The Spy Story*, p. 2.

[12] See the "Spy Film" entry in *Historical Dictionary of British Cinema*, ed. Burton and Chibnall (Lanham, MD: Scarecrow Press, 2013), p. 394.

[13] For more on the invasion motif in Britain, see, for instance, Hepburn, *Intrigue*, pp. 11–12.

Supremacy has star Matt Damon jogging on an idyllic beach in Goa, on the western coast of India. Here, amid churches built centuries ago by Portuguese colonizers, Jason Bourne thinks he has found sanctuary far from the spying world of Europe and North America. The location in India is not incidental to the story, for Goa serves as a way station, a place at the edge of the known (spy) world that emblematizes Bourne's outsider status. In other words, Bourne's physical location on this "edge"—relative to the world that "matters"—symbolizes his existential condition.

The Goa setting illustrates the second, less-discussed reason for the success of le Carré's fiction: his appreciation of the Cold War world as largely constituted by Europe's colonizing past. The Bourne novels miss this entirely, although *The Bourne Supremacy* film version, as mentioned, hints at it. Whereas for Bourne, Goa's mix of touristy sands and Portuguese façades echo Hollywood's habit of recasting postcolonial locales as places whose exoticism—or, as the case may be, "poverty porn"[14]—serves to spotlight the white hero's dislocation, such settings in le Carré instead highlight Cold War Britain's haunted relations with its former colonial theater and, more significantly, the complex effect of this on men like Smiley. In the Bourne film, by contrast, the hero moves through a clandestine geopolitics that is incidental to his search for identity—essentially a robot-like search for identifiable, finite answers rather than an acknowledgment of ambiguity. For this reason, Goa is disconnected from its Indian location to become a virtual extension of the Europe that stages Bourne's cat-and-mouse game. Equally significant is the conventional depiction of these "edges of Empire" as poor copies of Europe. The Portuguese churches look familiar to a western viewer, but they are also, at the same time, estranged from their ostensible home culture.[15]

It should be said that in these scenes, the film-makers arguably convey to western viewers a sense of uncanny recognition that matches the hero's disorientation. Consider how Damon's Bourne tries to elude a hit-man on Goa's byways. The viewer's perspective is mostly that of Bourne, who is driving, so that the car chase, as an action film set-piece, acts as a comforting contextual anchor in an otherwise chaotic setting—a setting that Bourne has grown somewhat familiar with, unlike his newly arrived

---

[14] Emily Wax uses this term in her article "Protests & Praise: 'Slumdog's' Mumbai Realism Is Divisive," *Washington Post*, January 23, 2009.

[15] For more on the dynamics of the British colonial understanding of "home," see my *Out of Bounds*.

European assailant. One could thus argue that the Goa setting is a fitting metaphor for, and apt prologue to, a story about accessing one's true identity. But the former colony proves to be no more disorienting, either for the unchanging Bourne or the viewer, than Berlin or New York City; it may even feel more familiar. To the standard viewpoints in the stock chase scene, then—its "psychological, physiological, and political [positions]" (Hepburn, 42)—we must add the spatial. We watch with Bourne as the hit-man is ultimately undone by the baffling maze of this the new-old environment. But then the film forfeits this potentially meaningful narrative vein by abruptly returning Bourne, and the viewer, to the more-familiar European context. For Bourne, the imperial set-up for today's clandestine world is a plot device, no more. For Smiley, it's everything.

If the spy plot overtly depends upon the tension between national loyalty and betrayal, le Carré's protagonists internalize this opposition without resolving it. In expressing this tension, they become tragic figures in whom readers see the reflection of their own lives, ones shaped by often violent colonial undoing and Cold War cynicism, and by economic and informational globalization. Rather than render the postcolonial world as exotic backdrop or neocolonial playground, le Carré acknowledges the influence of imperial attitudes and its complex geopolitical consequences, refusing to divorce the world of espionage from its historical contexts. Smiley, as we will see, does not avoid the recognition of Britain's historic shift during this period, from an active Empire that once encompassed the Central Asian world of Rudyard Kipling's 1901 novel *Kim* to a much-reduced post-imperial state, one that Thatcherite Britain sought to relive nostalgically in the 1980s.[16] Smiley's recognition of the simultaneously

---

[16] For more on the "Raj Revival" of the 1980s, see Rushdie's essay "Outside the Whale," in his essay collection *Imaginary Homelands: Essays and Criticism, 1981–1991* (New York: Granta; Penguin, 1991), pp. 87–101. Aside from this interlude, however, the pleasure of postwar spy narratives has not been the same as the pleasure that Edward Said, for example, found in reading Rudyard Kipling's 1901 spy novel *Kim*. Set in British India, the book's all-encompassing imperial reach, according to Said, belies the otherwise pleasurable fecundity of Kipling's description of the bicultural protagonist's youthful adventures in the Great Game. See Said, *Culture and Imperialism* (New York: Knopf, 1993), pp. 132–62. Although this reading overestimates the reach of Empire, it's true that the novel does not explicitly question the motivations of British governance. Today, by contrast, we expect spy narratives to question the very oppositions—"true" and "false," for instance—on which such governance is grounded. If spy characters are "emblems of doubt," as Hepburn puts it (p. 20), Smiley in *Tinker Tailor* earns our trust exactly because he probes the implications of doubt and conviction, disloyalty and loyalty—implications that Kim ponders but does not finally ascribe to imperialism.

familiar and estranged reaches of this post-imperial landscape enables him to recognize not only the classic duplicity of spies, but the interconnection between this duplicity and that of the late Empire. If Smiley is in many ways a reflection of his KGB nemesis Karla, so is British-built Calcutta a counterpart to imperial London—despite mainstream British society's best efforts to present these counterparts as opposites, one fraudulent (Karla, Calcutta) and the other authentic. Le Carré was born (in 1931) into this socially rigid social world, with its seemingly solid boundaries and its "heroic stories of romantic gentlemen pursuing moral purposes into … redemptive clandestine operations" (Cawelti and Rosenberg, 28). Following the transformative experiences of World War II and break-up of imperial Britain, however, le Carré turns, with a furious sense of having been conned, upon his predecessors' romantic illusions—illusions that their novels show to be alive and well in the Cold War's fixed beliefs. His work compels us to confront a world that is impossible to split into Truth and Falsehood. These oppositions instead prove to be each other's alter ego, intermixtures that, as we will see, Smiley and his KGB counterpart themselves represent.

3 Colonial Aesthetics: Loyalty, Betrayal, and Cavellian Fraudulence

Tinker Tailor appears in 1974, a period that David Cannadine has described as "nostalgic and escapist, disenchanted with the contemporary scene" as a result of the economic depression and anti-immigrant sentiment of the kind Enoch Powell infamously stoked in 1968.[17] Powell treated England as an island entire unto itself, ignoring the reality that supposedly quintessential English spaces have always been hybrid in practice, such as the colonial bungalow or the cricket pitch.[18] By way of illustration, we can consider nineteenth-century Calcutta, which, with its broad boulevards and western-educated Indian bureaucrats, or *babus*, was viewed by Britishers as an

---

[17] David Cannadine, *The Pleasures of the Past* (New York: W. W. Norton & Co., 1989), p. 258.

[18] For more on English colonial spaces, see Ian Baucom, *Out of Place: Englishness, Empire, and the Locations of Identity* (Princeton: Princeton University Press, 1999), p. 39; hereafter abbreviated Baucom.

inferior copy of London and its culture, a caricature of civility. In short, a fraud. Nor was it coincidental that this weaker copy was in fact a British invention, for colonial Calcutta, the capital of the Raj, was in many ways a necessary foil for Britain's imperious self-regard. In other words, London created urban Calcutta as imperial spectacle, an ostensibly civilizing bulwark against the tropical region's ever-threatening wilds. Calcutta was also a spectacle worthy (but not quite worthy) of London, allowing British-Indian residents to cultivate a homeliness that was alternately praised and caricatured by their brethren "back home." As Swati Chattopadhyay puts it, the British "attempted to create a safe and familiar sphere in [an] alien land.... What irked the colonizers most," however, "was *not* the unfamiliarity, but the suggestion of certain familiar practices in unexpected places."[19] The uncanny doubling of these two colonial-era cities, London and Calcutta, mirrored a spatial doubling within Victorian London itself, as Judith Walkowitz has shown, with the poorer, more racially and culturally diverse East End becoming a foil for the upper-class, all-white West End.[20] The latter's "monuments and government offices" were crucial symbols of Imperial Britain that either ignored or pontificated on the scandalous presence of "plague spots" in its midst (Walkowitz, 26–27). Thus, the exceptionally English spaces described by Powell had always been purely notional. In practice, they had always been uncanny hybrids.

Literary values were similarly hybrid. Scholars like Gauri Viswanathan have demonstrated how, in British India, European enculturation was most effectively implemented through the teaching of English literature, which made its first formal appearance as part of the effort to create, in T. B. Macaulay's words of 1835, "a class of persons, Indian in blood and colour, but English in taste."[21] If the best means of governing a subject

---

[19] Swati Chattopadhyay, *Representing Calcutta: Modernity, Nationalism, and the Colonial Uncanny* (New York: Routledge, 2006), p. 23.

[20] Judith Walkowitz, *City of Dreadful Delight: Narratives of Sexual Danger in Late-Victorian London* (Chicago: University of Chicago Press, 1992); hereafter abbreviated Walkowitz.

[21] Gauri Viswanathan, *Masks of Conquest: Literary Study and British Rule in India* (New York: Columbia University Press, 1989); and Thomas Babington Macaulay, "Minute on Indian Education" (1835), in *The Norton Anthology of English Literature* (New York: W. W. Norton & Co., 2014), "Norton Topics Online: Victorian Imperialism—Texts and Contexts," accessed June 27, 2014 at: https://www.wwnorton.com/college/english/nael/victorian/topic_4/macaulay.htm.

people is, as Frantz Fanon puts it, to inculcate "aesthetic forms of respect for the status quo,"[22] then English literature was an eminently successful tool. But what happens to this value system when Empire unravels, as Britain's did following World War II, a question le Carré's work implicitly asks? One answer is that the geographical break-up of Europe at this time was also a cultural break-up, a crisis of national and individual self-identification. If colonial governance was ever-anxious about the possibility of local rebellion, of what rulers liked to call their subjects' inherent tendency to "betray" their masters' interests, many British writers confronted colonialism's demise with a tone of bitter betrayal, this time a betrayal of the people by the state. As the character Guillam realizes "with a shudder" by the end of *Tinker Tailor*, he and his fellow intelligence officers, including Smiley, are "inquisitors" very like their Soviet counterparts or their historical religious namesakes (362). In many post-imperial writers' hands, Cold War spy craft is represented as a betrayal of much that western liberalism had pledged to uphold. Fictional spy worlds dramatize this political-historical-cultural crisis by giving the lie to the myth of European cultural superiority, and by showing modern life, with its addiction to image-making, to be a ceaseless peeling away of pretense. In this sense, modern spies are less "agents of order"[23] than discoverers (and sometimes exemplars) of political and cultural entropy. Since a spy is both a "perpetrator" and "victim of corruption," his or her "body is … a site of contradictions" (Hepburn, 9, 167).

Cavell might have been describing such spies in the following statement: "Within the world of art, one makes one's own dangers, takes one's own chances—and one speaks of its objects at such moments in terms of tension, problem, imbalance, necessity, shock, surprise … And within this world one takes and exploits these chances, finding, through danger, an unsuspected security …" (199). Cavell, writing about music in 1967, makes the still-pertinent observation that our attitudes toward art entail the "possibility of fraudulence" (188). That is, we commonly bring our culturally conditioned assumptions about what art should and should not be to our reading and viewing of particular stories—in fact, to our world—and we consign them to various categories to try to adjudicate their inher-

---

[22] Frantz Fanon, *The Wretched of the Earth* (1961), trans. Richard Philcox (New York: Grove Press, 2004), p. 3; hereafter abbreviated Fanon.

[23] Yumna Siddiqi argues this in *Anxieties of Empire and the Fiction of Intrigue* (New York: Columbia University Press, 2006), p. 24.

ent worth, such as by using terms like "escapist" and "serious." We try to do this, but, because each of us bases our evaluations on a combination of personal, cultural, and other attitudes, we can never definitely proclaim an art work to be authentic or perfect. The possibility of fraudulence proves, then, to be critical to any worthwhile evaluation. Such evaluations are conditioned by what Herbert J. Gans, updating eighteenth-century philosopher David Hume, calls "taste cultures,"[24] a premise on which I implicitly stake my broader argument. By this, Gans means each cultural context's generally agreed-upon standards and values that inform aesthetic evaluation (91–95). Cavell's point is that aesthetic judgment derives from a moral outlook on life rather than a check-list of prescribed attributes used to appraise the object at hand. Aesthetic judgment is, in other words, transactional and historically contingent, but never (ideally, at least) amoral. Curiously, spy fiction dramatizes this very tension even as it tends to be treated as escapist. For instance, even Umberto Eco, usually known for his inclusive views, falls into the trap of universalizing culturally bound evaluation in his well-known 1966 essay on James Bond[25] when he complains that Bond's inventor Ian Fleming, whose narratives, including *Casino Royale*, Eco shows to be skillfully structured as a series of oppositions—Bond and M, Loyalty and Disloyalty—betrays a "cynical" strategy in order to make his narratives "effective." Although Eco is primarily interested in a semiotic analysis of Fleming's novels, he betrays an interest in preserving the high art/low art divide when he accuses the author of squandering an evident talent for "literary" style by resorting to mere "fireworks," as in Fleming's "baroque" descriptions of violence. Fleming, argues Eco, has produced a collage of otherwise literary prose sections and gratuitously added "crude chronicle[s]" to suit his modern fantasy (51–55)—a charge that unwittingly reveals how the apparently

---

[24] As Hume wrote in 1757, in his essay "Of the Standard of Taste": "We are apt to call barbarous whatever departs widely from our own taste and apprehension: But soon find the epithet of reproach retorted on us." See http://www.csulb.edu/~jvancamp/361r15.html. A key distinction between Gans and Hume is that the latter, contradicting his acknowledgement of aesthetic taste's culturally-tied bias, maintains his own cultural privileging of educated vs. "common" views. See Gans, *Popular Culture & High Culture: An Analysis and Evaluation of Taste*, Revised ed. (New York: Basic Books, 1999), p. vii; hereafter abbreviated Gans.

[25] Umberto Eco, "Narrative Structures in Fleming" (1966), in *The James Bond Phenomenon: A Critical Reader*, ed. Christoph Lindner (New York: Manchester University Press, 2003), pp. 34–55; hereafter abbreviated Eco.

disjointed structure of Fleming's narrative undercuts precisely this kind of evaluative hierarchy. My point is that Eco echoes the still-dominant tendency to lump espionage stories together according to fairly conservative standards of taste.

Despite their differences, Cavell and Eco, writing within a year of each other in the 1960s—which is notably the height of a Cold War period steeped in political unease—are both interested in the degree to which art either fulfills or betrays its inherited standards, whatever those may be. This shared interest may be because characters like Bond, who had "became the Cold War's favorite agent, the spy whom the public loved" (Cawelti and Rosenberg, 50), resonated in Cavell's and Eco's minds with Horkheimer and Adorno's influential theory, first articulated in 1944, that bemoaned the power of the modern "culture industry" (especially Hollywood) to condition mass taste.[26] That is, the problem of taste acquired a heightened sense of urgency during a post-war period that Cawelti and Rosenberg describe as a societal "transition from a committed clandestinity to the chaotic state of suspicion, distrust and a concern [on the part of the state] for pure survival" (28). (Later revelations that CIA money funded the visits of some American artists to communist countries only amplified this view.) Ideological pressures compel popular trust in the state's ability to establish security, but when the state itself proves to have betrayed society, as with McCarthyism, Watergate, and CIA excesses, paranoia creeps into all levels of society (Cawelti and Rosenberg, 28–30). In this climate, art, especially in the form of spy fiction and film, becomes more ideologically charged than usual, and Eco and Cavell understandably worry about the implications for writers and musicians in ostensibly open societies.

The failing trust of western citizens in their governments during the Cold War also aided the efforts of nationalists around the world who fought for their independence from European powers, including Britain. Although the United States in many ways stepped into the vacuum left by Europe's global retreat, the post-imperial world remained in thrall to European value systems for a long time, especially in the context of educational institutions. As one scholar puts it, in Africa, "dominant intellectual

---

[26] See Max Horkheimer and Theodor Adorno, "The Culture Industry: Enlightenment as Mass Deception, in their *Dialectic of Enlightenment: Philosophical Fragments* (1944), trans. Edmund Jephcott (Stanford, CA: Stanford University Press, 2007).

paradigms" continue to be "products not of Africa's own experience but of a particular Western experience."[27] These paradigms include aesthetic evaluation, a fact that Nigerian novelist Chinua Achebe has described in his autobiographical essay collections. First-generation postcolonial writers like him had to work hard to unlearn colonial categories they had inherited in order to "call into question … childhood assumption[s] of the innocence of stories."[28] In this case, fraudulence is tied to the recognition of having been conned, much in the way that Cavell describes his sense that the flashy façade of a new musical composition can, with suitable training, belie its hollowness. For Achebe, the sense of betrayal stems from a one-sided education; for Cavell, betrayal follows a lack of generic discipline and appreciation for music's history. Although the personal and political consequences for Achebe's experience with colonialism are vastly different from Cavell's with music evaluation, both writers emphasize the importance of an honest—that is, ethical—treatment of art. For postcolonial writers like Achebe, the paranoia of Cold War Europe is a direct outcome of colonial hypocrisy, which has come home to roost—a belief that, as I've said, le Carré shares.

But what is colonialism if not territorial, as well as ideological, possession (and dispossession), a fact that conditions its twisted logic? This territorial imperative explains why writers like Achebe and le Carré turn to spatial metaphors to express the con games of colonialism and Cold War politics: "the no-man's land of the mind," Achebe says of his experience in colonial Nigeria (Achebe, 32), echoing the zone, the "half-world of ruin," between East and West Germany that le Carré describes in *The Spy Who Came in from the Cold*.[29] These uncanny spatial resemblances are important leitmotifs in spy fiction, as I've argued, for in echoing a world of colonial boundaries (a resemblance Greene makes explicit in *The Human Factor*), these writers encapsulate the struggle to first perceive and then traverse the boundaries of the "compartmentalized world" that colonialism bequeathed to the rest of the globe (Fanon, 3). That is to say, colonialism's obsession with boundaries is very much like that of Cold War

---

[27] Mahmood Mamdani, "Comment: Africa's Postcolonial Scourge," *Mail & Guardian* Online (May 27, 2011), p. 1. Accessed 1 June 2014 at: http://mg.co.za/article/2011-05-27-africas-postcolonial-scourge.

[28] Chinua Achebe, *Home and Exile* (New York: Anchor Books, 2001), p. 33; hereafter abbreviated Achebe.

[29] Le Carré, *The Spy Who Came in from the Cold* (1963) (New York: Penguin, 2012), p. 6.

geopolitics, whether in the form of physical or ideological walls. The ironic result, as we know, was a less-secure world, which generated the paranoia that le Carré so effectively conveys; for his protagonists perceive, as did a young Achebe, the apparatus behind the illusion. Their vision exemplifies the ethical outlook that Cavell advocates.

4   From Jekyll/Hyde to Smiley/Karla: Le Carré's Cold War Double

The aforementioned spatial doubling so characteristic of colonialism not surprisingly finds its correlative in the literary double, most famously embodied by the protagonists of Robert Louis Stevenson's 1886 novella *Strange Case of Dr. Jekyll and Mr. Hyde*.[30] The novella dramatizes both a split personality and a split cityscape, and therefore provides an index for the sense of the colonial uncanny that, as I've been arguing, haunts British spy narratives. Although not a spy story, Stevenson's novel is an antecedent to the genre, presaging an obsession with modern deception, and a fascination with what it means to remain loyal—to friends, to society, to one's principles. The obverse is betrayal, which is an anxiety at the heart of Stevenson's novel, of imperialism, and of spy fiction. *Jekyll and Hyde* lays the groundwork for later spy fiction, allegorizing as it does the kind of clandestine world of individual self-division characteristic imperial and post-imperial societies, whose segregated spaces contextualize their inhabitants' inner conflicts. One way to deflect the anxiety of possible betrayal is to repress it, which in literature takes the form of the doppelgänger, or double. This ghostly counterpart of a protagonist, such as in Joseph Conrad's 1910 short story "The Secret Sharer," often represents a character's projection of an unconsciously desired self, one that is familiar in certain ways but entirely alien, even monstrous, in other respects. The projected double is, however, simultaneously a willed (therefore controllable) creation and one that, as in Mary Shelley's 1818 *Frankenstein*, threatens to destroy the creator.

In Stevenson's tale, the respected Henry Jekyll denies to his friends that he is addicted to the potion that transforms him into the criminally minded Mr. Hyde, and it is not until after his final transformation and death that

---

[30] Robert Louis Stevenson, *Strange Case of Dr. Jekyll and Mr. Hyde* (1885) (New York: W. W. Norton & Co., 2003); hereafter abbreviated *Jekyll and Hyde*.

his friend, the lawyer Utterson, learns of the awful reality of Jekyll's socially and morally treasonable acts when he reads the doctor's confessional will. At one point, the narrator contrasts Dr. Jekyll's upper-class area of the city with the seedy, "dismal" Soho area that Hyde frequents, "with its muddy ways" and "slatternly passengers," prompting Utterson to think he is in "a district of some city in a nightmare" (23). It is nightmarish because it should not exist, just as Hyde should not exist—they are abominations of civilized society. When Utterson visits Jekyll's home and is told by the butler that the doctor is out and that Hyde "has a key" to the door, Utterson says, "Your master seems to repose a great deal of *trust* in that young man" (18; emphasis added). The word "trust" comes up again and again to imply that Hyde, like the Soho area, has betrayed that trust. This is due not only to Jekyll's harboring of the decidedly vulgar Hyde, but also to Hyde's audacity to cross from the seedy side of London to this urbane area of the professional class. The novel's setting perfectly matches the doubling of the Jekyll/Hyde character, for Victorian London is also a kind of split persona, its segregated spaces based on the well-heeled class's denial of its dependence on the poor's subterranean world.

To return to Cavell's point, we could say that the trust we, along with Utterson, have for Jekyll depends for its meaning upon the "betrayal" of Hyde—his violence, his hunched appearance, his visits to Soho. The novel ends, notably, with Jekyll's words, not Utterson's: "Here, then, as I lay down the pen and proceed to seal up my confession, I bring the life of that unhappy Henry Jekyll to an end" (62). Whatever happens, Jekyll writes resignedly, will involve "another than myself," as if to say that his double is not so much Hyde—he has, after all, killed both the Jekyll and Hyde parts of himself by his suicide—as anyone who learns about his life, which in this case is Utterson, for whose eyes alone Jekyll composes his confession. Utterson, we could say, is the Other (and notably a reader) whom Jekyll/Hyde requires in order to make sense of his existence. As readers, of course, we are privy to this confession, a sub-genre that is interleaved with others. The novel is, in fact, a collage of genres: letters, oral tales, straightforward narrative, a will. There is, as it were, no core; it is only in Utterson's and the reader's piecing together of various narratives that some sense of imaginative coherence arises, although this does nothing to dispel the "nightmare" that will, it is implied, continue to haunt the city.

That is to say, London, the British Empire's geographical core, is itself shown to have been turned inside out. Stevenson shows that not only do "the two parts of London imaginatively double[…] for England and Empire," as

Walkowitz puts it (143), but they are in fact inextricably interwoven. Material objects of Empire, such as Indian cloth and spices, were common in British homes, and exhibits and museums displayed art and artifacts from the imperial colonies. These objects, ranging from intricately carved wooden screens to the shrunken heads and stuffed tigers, reflected Europe's characteristically ambivalent view of non-European peoples, who were alternately noble and savage. Jekyll/Hyde embodies this split, with the doctor's "alchemy releas[ing] the ape-like barbarian ... who lives beneath the civilized skin."[31] But the barbarian Hyde and his getaway in Soho, where the chiaroscuro effect of "a marvelous number of degrees and hues of twilight" catches Utterson's eye, and where Hyde's room in this "nightmar[ish]" quarter is luxuriously furnished, fascinate the lawyer (*Jekyll and Hyde*, 23). Like the city itself, Jekyll's "two natures," as he writes in his will, "had memory in common" (55).

The ambivalence Stevenson describes exactly characterizes Britain's regard for its colonies from the late 1800s to the mid-1900s, a period that conditions Smiley's outlook. In fact, as scholars have demonstrated, the very notion of British identity became inseparable from the colonial culture that developed during this period.[32] Depictions of geography were an essential feature of this cultural entanglement, with the result that the British could, for example, visit an imperial exhibition in London, or, in India, re-trace points along a route they had read about. These points marked the subcontinent's natural wonders and ancient ruins, as well as British battle victories. The so-called Mutiny pilgrimage became popular with English visitors who wanted to see where their forebears had, as a 1924 guidebook stated, either been "betrayed" and "murdered" during the 1857 rebellion or had responded with furious and bloody vengefulness that is celebrated as "heroic." Such pilgrimages were a ritualistic reminder of a war that the British viewed as an act of betrayed trust (since Indian soldiers had rebelled against their British East India Company masters). Visits to the war's battle ruins were thus part of the attempt to create a coherent narrative of colonial rule (Baucom, 109). The visits to these sites and memorials, and their recollection, could only maintain this coher-

---

[31] Patrick Brantlinger, *Rule of Darkness: British Literature and Imperialism, 1830–1914* (Ithaca: Cornell University Press, 1990), p. 233.

[32] See, for example, Simon Gikandi, *Maps of Englishness: Writing Identity in the Culture of Colonialism* (New York: Columbia University Press, 1996), and Baucom, *Out of Place*.

ence through acts of retelling and returning; that is, acts of perpetual mourning that helped sustained the imperium.

After the Second World War, when Britain lost its Empire, many Britons projected this sense of mourning onto former colonial spaces—plantations in Jamaica, cities in India—which had been what Mary Louise Pratt has called "contact zones," "social spaces where cultures meet, clash, and grapple with each other, often in contexts of highly asymmetrical relations of power."[33] In the postcolonial Cold War period, such spaces became, especially in English narratives, tropes for post-imperial mourning and touchstones for the negotiation of English identity in a changed landscape. Nostalgia was part of this mournful remembrance, of course, but not the only ingredient, for nostalgia was intermixed with the changed realities on the ground. In Bond narratives, for instance, the English-speaking Caribbean simultaneously chimes the notes of a familiar, lost Empire but also the unfamiliar notes of local anti-imperialism, as well as a variety of positions in between. The Caribbean islands in these narratives are cultural and historical contact zones, functioning as links to Europe's past colonial era as well as sites of Cold War murkiness. As sites of temporal and spatial mixing, the islands therefore become—and this is the point I wish to emphasize—settings for betrayal (if a scene shows bad guys shooting at Bond, for example), loyalty, and eroticism (such as Bond's love-play in colonial-era resorts, where the British spy is nothing so much as an imperial agent), or an ambivalent combination of these. The Caribbean example indicates that the Cold War's loyalty/betrayal obsession is both similar to and different from imperial Britain's obsession with the same. The difference, of course, is that Britain's painful post-war diminishment in world affairs meant that it could no longer depend on defining itself in relation to "the Other beyond its shores" (Colley, 6), or on landscapes it had appropriated, such as the Indian "Mutiny" ruins. Instead, loyalty and betrayal now rested on ever-shifting ground, so that former colonial hubs, now delinked from the imperial web, became truly uncanny in British eyes.

Despite these dramatic changes, however, old colonial networks continued to be entwined in the new, global interconnections of espionage. London still maintained its commonwealth lines of communication, which explains why Smiley originally interrogates his Soviet nemesis Karla in a

---

[33] Mary Louise Pratt, "Arts of the Contact Zone," *Profession* 91 (1991), 33–40; p. 34.

New Delhi jail cell in the 1950s. Although India officially maintains a "non-aligned" status with respect to US-Soviet interests, the authorities there detain Karla "at our request," as Smiley tells Guillam (*Tinker Tailor*, 209). The scene, showing an electric fan rotating slowly above and the two men perspiring freely inside a small, drab room, encapsulates an ambivalent tone: India, relatively unchanged since British times in this compartmentalized cameo (just a decade or so after its independence in 1947), contrasts with the acceleration of Cold War tensions that we associate with Bond's technological enhancements. Yet these oppositions, the narrative suggests, depend on one another in much the way Smiley and Karla do, and in the way colonial constructs of the Other do. In this case, it is not a colonial Other but Smiley's European doppelgänger who functions as the necessary constituent of the Englishman's world. "I exchanged my predicament for his," Smiley confesses, for Karla "*looked* too complete to be alone in all his life" (215).

But it is a notably "confused" and mysterious world that Smiley describes (217), not least because his Soviet double refuses to communicate. The Cold War double, unlike the ostensibly more stable colonial Other mentioned above, mystifies a relationship that for a colonialist would have been part of a familiar, though by no means less unsettling, psychological dynamic. Here, as my use of the word "ostensibly" indicates, I refer to the situation of colonial mimicry, whereby the colonial subject is encouraged to imitate the European colonialist, but is prevented because of racial and other ideologies from ever "becoming" European, as Homi Bhabha has shown.[34] The result of this "flawed colonial mimesis" is the unintended mockery by colonized subjects of the tenets of European liberalism (Bhabha, 128). Despite obvious differences between colonial mimicry and the act of spying, both performances, because shaped by especially anxious power structures, expose doubts about normative values by throwing into relief the very act of imitation and its obverse, fraudulence. This is especially evident in novels, in large part because narration itself, through the narrator's commentary and the characters' thoughts,

---

[34] Homi Bhabha, *The Location of Culture* (New York: Routledge, 2004); hereafter abbreviated Bhabha.

advertises its theatrical nature.[35] By staging the Smiley-Karla meeting in recognizably colonial-era trappings—the austere tropical jail cell in Britain's former possession, the tropics' proverbially "[appalling] heat"—le Carré also points to an ambivalent relationship between different versions of history, one Soviet, the other European. Karla's mute presence before his British counterpart's volubility—in contrast to other literary doubles, such as Joseph Conrad's Captain and his Secret Sharer, who converse freely—adds to the scene's uncanny feel. Karla's only sign of communication is to accept Smiley's offer of a cigarette lighter that Ann, Smiley's estranged wife, had gifted him, an object that Smiley sees as "expressive of the bond between us" (217). When Smiley at one point sees a haggard Karla in the jail seated amidst Indians "on other benches," he says that Karla "looked very white among them" (218), as if to further persuade himself of their shared (racial and European) sense of alienation. Smiley's British sensitivity to old colonial places, with the specter of the nineteenth century's Great Game haunting his cultural memory of South Asia, as it were, gives him a false sense of commonality with Karla: They share many attributes, to be sure, but not this particular spatial-historical connection.

The ironies run deeper still, as Cawelti and Rosenberg have observed. The Karla-Smiley contest defines le Carré's important "Karla trilogy," and their meeting in Delhi and exchange of the lighter lend nuance to this pivotal psychological doubling. In allowing Karla to keep this gift from Ann, Smiley had hoped to persuade his nemesis to defect by trying to anoint their meeting with a small kindness. He hopes to make Karla, who is in danger of returning to a Moscow firing squad, see an escape from his utter vulnerability. In recalling this years later to Guillam, Smiley confesses his naiveté: "I thought it thoroughly appropriate that he should take her lighter; I thought it—Lord help me—expressive of the bond between us" (217). The irony is that the lighter, as we learn, ties together several nested tales of betrayal. It symbolizes Ann's infidelity with the traitor Bill Haydon, who has himself acted on Karla's instructions to seduce her, despite his homosexuality, in order to draw Smiley's suspicion away from his role as a mole. In doing so, Haydon injures Smiley's pride, thereby confirming (as

---

[35] Dorrit Cohn, "From Transparent Minds: Narrative Modes for Presenting Consciousness in Fiction," in *Theory of the Novel: A Historical Approach*, ed. Michael McKeon (Baltimore: Johns Hopkins University Press, 2000), pp. 493–514; p. 505.

Smiley sees by the end of the novel) Smiley's own vulnerability, one that he desperately wants to see reflected in Karla. In the face of Karla's expressionless "stillness," Smiley feels "unease" and a growing sense of confusion "creep over [him]" (213, 217). Conflicted in his desire to simultaneously identify with and distinguish himself from Karla's cold Soviet ruthlessness, Smiley is unable to exult in Karla's final defection, described in *Smiley's People*. This is because as Karla strides up to the MI-5 team waiting on the other side of the checkpoint, he drops Ann's lighter, which "glint[s] like fool's gold on the cobble" (373). This is "Karla's contemptuous gesture indicating that Smiley has become another Karla since he has been willing to exploit" the mental plight of Karla's daughter to get to him, just as Karla had exploited Ann (Cawelti and Rosenberg, 179).

The final irony is that it is not Karla, but a fellow Briton, Haydon, who proves to be at once closer to and more alienated from Smiley. The effect of Haydon's betrayal on Smiley, as on the reader, is the same disquieting realization that W. H. Auden had articulated about the real-life Cambridge spies Philby, Burgess, Maclean, and Blunt (a feeling both le Carré and Graham Greene admitted to), namely, that it is hard to disentangle one's own disenchantment with the state from the action of a friend who decides to actually cross the line.[36] A common reaction of government critics toward their defecting friends is sympathy. One reason is that many of these like-minded peers—Auden, Greene, le Carré—felt themselves to be outsiders, and so roamed the globe (Greene), emigrated (Auden), or looked askance not only at their nation but also their literary vocation (le Carré). If a sense of Britishness had been forged for centuries in "reaction to the Other beyond [its] shores" (Colley, 6)—that is, in the context of global rather than local affiliations—many Britishers now, in a post-war world, felt even less territorially rooted. For them, the spy perfectly embodied the outsider perspective and is "a flexible symbol,"[37] a figure who can lurk in the shadows of the nation-state and whose loyalties are less important than his or her ability to inhabit multiple personae. In another sense, therefore, the spy symbolizes the ventriloquistic power of fictional creation. Smiley's inability to elicit a word from Karla in his Delhi

---

[36] See le Carré's "Introduction" to *Tinker Tailor* and Toibin, Colm's "Introduction" to Graham Greene, *The Human Factor* (1978) (New York: Penguin, 2008), pp. ix–xv.

[37] Erin G. Carlston, *Double Agents: Espionage, Literature, and Liminal Citizens* (New York: Columbia University Press, 2013), p. 154.

cell tests this power, suggesting that "no reply" may trump any turn of phrase, as Cavell argues about Beckett's plays, because silence makes sense in a world unsure of its certainties (Cavell, 127).

The implied question the novel compels us to ponder, then, is: What differentiates Smiley's words—including his confessional reminiscence to Guillam—from Karla's silence? If they prove to be doubles, does Karla's silence in some way match Smiley's interrogation? How can you tell? The narrative troublingly indicates that it will not provide ready answers, such as a generic spy plot might be expected to deliver, but only present the paradox that confronts le Carré himself: How does one narrate a story grounded in absence, silence, and shadow, and whose speaker (in this instance, Smiley) is himself unsure of what he thinks ("I no longer knew what I felt" [217])? It is only in terms of one another that Smiley, Karla, and Haydon make sense, much as Colley says of British identity, which was partly formed in terms of how India and Britain defined themselves in relation to one another. Le Carré shows that the countries' dialectical relationship since India's independence is, on one level, a reflection of international Cold War gamesmanship. On another level, however, the two countries are still freighted with the complex dynamics of an imperial worldview. As a result, the young Smiley sees Karla through the scrim of colonial encumbrance, particularly visible in his understanding of the term "West": In Cold War terms, the West opposes Eastern Europe, whereas in colonial terms it opposed the East more generally. The two concepts are entangled in Smiley's mind. "I didn't make speeches to [Karla] about freedom—whatever that means—or the essential goodwill of the West," Smiley recalls to Guillam. "[B]esides, … I was in no clear ideological state myself" (219). The spatial connotation of "state" suggestively combines Smiley's remembrance of the scene as he speaks to Guillam with a specific physical locale (the jail), which itself elicits for a young Smiley, even after India's independence, the imperial worldview he is slowly learning to relinquish. This enlarges our understanding of why Smiley, visiting a Delhi jail that just a few years earlier would have held Indians protesting British rule, grows increasingly tense and confused during his one-way conversation with Karla.

The radically changed sense of Britain's place in the world is another reason why Smiley does not gloat, as others expect him to, when he eventually lures Karla to the West (described in *Smiley's People*). By way of instruction, he summarizes for his protégé Guillam the troubled "mood of the period": "Moscow Centre was in pieces … As a result, there was a fresh crop of defections among Centre officers stationed overseas. All over the place—Singapore, Nairobi, Stockholm, Canberra, Washington, I don't know where ..." (*Tinker Tailor*, 208). Smiley's use of the phrase "all over the place" and listing of representative cities indicate the bewildering rate of global re-ordering. This Cold War and, for Britain, post-imperial "mood" plays havoc with spy networks, both actual and fictional. "Those who had harbored idealistic hopes for Russia grew disillusioned," notes Anthony Blunt's biographer Miranda Carter[38]; spies defected to both sides, and, among many, patriotism morphed into McCarthyism. When his nemesis defects, Smiley, with something like the "shudder" Guillam feels upon realizing that MI5 agents are, like their KGB counterparts, "inquisitors" (362), sees that his and Karla's governments mirror each other in many ways. But Smiley's shudder is also, in a sense that the younger Guillam can't understand, induced by the still-painful recognition of imperial Britain's morally hollow history. What most terrifies Smiley, perhaps, is that he will never be able to disentangle in his mind the East that Karla represents from the East that his imperial predecessors represented. It is an ethical dilemma that no amount of speaking will clear up to his satisfaction. But speak he must, playing penitent to Guillam's confessor (a role the reader vicariously inhabits as well).

The role of inquisitor, together with the aforementioned sense of theatricality, of playing roles, are vital motifs in this novel, as they are in all of le Carré's work, and once more point the reader to Cavell's two-sided coin of fraudulence and belief. In trying to make sense of the mole Haydon's motivations, Smiley recognizes that Haydon had enjoyed "standing at the middle of a secret stage, playing world against world, hero and playwright in one" (379). Not coincidentally, Haydon is, as Smiley observes just before this insight, a failed artist whose "half-finished canvases" likely aggravated his sense of cultural inadequacy and, by extension, anger toward a country he felt had conned him (378). Like the real-life Anthony Blunt, who remained a prominent art historian throughout his spying career, Haydon fears a "loss of control" (to use Carter's words for Blunt [88]). Like Blunt, he fiercely denies any subliminal motivations for his double-agency, believing himself to be wholly in possession of his fate, wholly rooted in reality, as opposed to his belief that Smiley, for all his

---

[38] Miranda Carter, *Anthony Blunt: His Lives* (New York: Farrar, Strauss, Giroux, 2002), p. 355.

perspicacity, clings to the "illusion" of love (375). Here again, Freud's concept of uncanniness helps us understand such motivations. Haydon's sense that one's country has become familiar yet strange, a "trivial" vestige of a once-worthy culture now beholden to America (367), generates in him an anxiety that threatens his ego. His choice to go with the Soviets, he tells Smiley, is "an aesthetic judgement as much as anything" (368). Such aestheticism is clearly a pose rather than the kind of moral worldview le Carré, like Cavell, espouses. It is a choice that Haydon had hoped would preserve his vision of a world that, rather than being muddled, provides clear-cut answers. Given the sympathy le Carré has generated for Smiley, we instinctively want to side with him—but not for political or ideological reasons. We side with Smiley despite (or perhaps because of) his self-doubt. Haydon has lied to himself and become morally fraudulent, whereas Smiley at least acknowledges that he is no more certain of truth than Haydon. How, then (to reprise Cavell's original question [203]), are we to know what truth is? "Of all men living," Smiley concludes, "only Karla had seen the last little [Russian] doll inside Bill Haydon" (379). But Karla himself is an enigma, just as Smiley is to himself (as we all are to some degree, the novel implies).

The line between Blunt's and Haydon's aesthetic of life and that of their counterparts proves, in this particular context, to be a thin one. Smiley, as we've seen, increasingly ponders the "illusion" of difference between Cold War polarities: the words "truth" and "dream" bookend the novel in order to draw our attention to this world of mirrors. The unanswered, often unspoken question is: Can one be a moral citizen in a system like that of the Soviet Union? Smiley believes the answer is "no"— but also recognizes that it may be almost as hard to be so in the Cold War West, especially one distorted by its racial and colonial past. The novel ends by suggesting that a Britain whose official history of global conquest formed a coherent—that is, purpose-driven and ideological—narrative must now, with the end of conquest and ideological coherence, confront its unacknowledged past and open-ended present. In one sense, the novel implies, Haydon is on to something, for his motivation to betray his country is, like several real-life British spies, less a commitment to a cause than avowed disgust with his nation's misdirection. But Haydon is ultimately concerned only with Haydon: a self-absorbed, effete man who would, one guesses, have fit well into the colonial world, with its sense of self-certainty and derring-do.

Neither Smiley nor the reader, however, can bask in a self-certain contrast to Haydon, for the rug has been pulled out from under us. Le Carré's characters, Smileys and Haydons alike, demonstrate that the affective affinities linked to political intrigue are as consequential as human calculation. His characters gives life to the fact that geopolitical events turn on startlingly basic emotional responses that are not easily disentangled: personal and national pride, old and new jealousies, seasoned bitterness. Haydon, unable to see his ideal post-imperial image in the mirror he holds up to his familiar world, turns to the other, less familiar world of eastern Europe—but without leaving the familiarity of London. He has turned his old familiars into frauds, but has no sense of what a corresponding authenticity, for which he yearns, might look like. This is why the "Suez adventure of '56," when Britain failed, as a result of US and Soviet pressure, to force Egypt (which just four years earlier had thrown off Britain's proxy rule) to give up control of the canal, is the last straw for Haydon, who is "finally persuaded" of Britain's humiliated subordination to the United Sates. "The sight of the Americans sabotaging the British action in Egypt" confirms his bitter belief that his country has merely "spike[d] the advance of history" without "being able to offer anything by way of contribution" (371).

Tinker Tailor, by showing the Cold War world to be a hall of mirrors—a world whose "horrible" reality, as Auden put it, is that "one cannot be certain" of whom to trust (qtd. in Carter, 354)—thereby necessarily questions the very possibility of accurately documenting the past, of producing history-as-such. But what does it mean to read a book that confirms one's fears about the world? One implication is that (unless we prefer silence) it is left to artists, including novelists, to make sense of this past's affective consequences. This partly explains the conclusion of the novel, which presents us with the former spy Jim Prideaux having to recuperate emotionally with the help of schoolboy Bill Roach: "With time, Jim seemed to respond to treatment" (380). Prideaux, as we have learned, is traumatized by his old lover Bill Haydon's betrayal of him by having nearly delivered Jim to his death at the hands of Czechoslovakian soldiers; Haydon's betrayal of country is less at issue. Roach and Jim provide for each other the trust that has vanished in their lives (characteristically represented in le Carré by parental absence, in this case Roach's "broken home" [4], and a substitute family structure, with Roach acting as a maternal surrogate for Jim). Importantly, the novel ends with the word "dream": "The gun, Bill Roach had finally convinced himself, was, after all, a dream" (381). This is the narrative's leitmotif, that empirical evidence—Bill seeing his new friend Jim with a gun—is of less weight, finally, than our emotional remembrance of it, and our rationalizations in order to fit this remembrance into a meaningful, and often therapeutic, framework. Like his namesake Bill Haydon (another possible, if ironic, doubling), Bill Roach safeguards his worldview. The irony, of course, as le Carré delights in making clear, is that his own narrative framework (the novel one is reading) throws into relief exactly the sorts of troubling sights the two Bills seek to deny. Like Prideaux and Haydon, the novel's reader, too, may find the world's blurred boundaries—blurred topographically and historically, psychologically and politically—to be terrifying, and to therefore require the palliative of art.

5 Conclusion

It is telling that Miranda Carter, in her biography of Cambridge spy Anthony Blunt, quotes from le Carré's *Tinker Tailor* to illustrate her subject's motivation. Whatever the "game" being played, the double agent often wants, like Blunt, "to feel that he [or she] was acting rationally, out of pure motives"—even if those motives lead to the betrayal of that agent's homeland (Carter, 269–70). Paradoxically, this kind of person feels that others—his government or society—have betrayed *him*, and that spying against his country is an act of loyalty. This allowed people like Blunt to rationalize their actions to themselves. We find these lives fascinating because we, too, rationalize our actions daily. In an increasingly complicated and uncontrollable world, the spy gives us a taste of individual control over apparently uncontrollable events. The spy is "the link between the actions of an individual—often an 'ordinary person'—and the world historical fate of nations and empires. History is displaced … from politics to ethics."[39]

Spy characters thus elaborate for us the difficulty of differentiating between the real and the fake, which Cavell ponders at length. Spy stories, in other words, emphasize this fault-line between "trust" and "betrayal" both in their characters and in their form, and this perception of sham and

---

[39] Michael Denning, *Cover Stories: Narrative and Ideology in the British Spy Thriller* (New York: Routledge & Kegan Paul, 1987), p. 14.

façade explains much of the genre's appeal. As readers or viewers, we are drawn into the spy's inner world, only to find that it is inherently fragmented, composed of many worlds. We are drawn in because we recognize that spies, like us, thrive on role-playing, sometimes to the extent that they forget who they are. As John Scaggs has observed about hardboiled detective fiction, the Hollywood setting emphasizes this theme, which calls attention to a reality whose very existence we begin to doubt.[40] This fraudulence we see in the world is much like the fraudulence that Cavell says is a necessary part of defining whatever we think is valuable. Cavell seem to have more faith in the real than does much serious spy fiction, in which the "valuable" proves to be composed of layer upon layer of fabrication. But this does not mean that spy novelists are hopelessly cynical, only that they shine a light onto an important feature of how we shape and perceive the modern world. Indeed, le Carré's novels indict the amorality at the heart of modern espionage, an indictment his readers share. Novels like *Tinker Tailor* are the artistic expression of Cavellian insight, and their success in doing so rests to a large degree, as I've argued, on their exposure of the continued consequences of imperialism. Like the latter's conflicted need to duplicate its home abroad and also scorn that new home as a false copy, spies must continually choose to act in the interest of official histories, which are themselves, in a sense, false copies. Our very reading of such characters dramatizes this predicament, for we, too, must adjudicate among a variety of truth-claims.

---

[40] John Scaggs, *Crime Fiction (The New Critical Idiom)* (New York: Routledge, 2005), p. 71.

CHAPTER 11

Must We Do What We Say? The Plight of Marriage and Conversation in George Meredith's *The Egoist*

Erin Greer

In his two books about mid-century Hollywood film, *Pursuits of Happiness* and *Contesting Tears*, Stanley Cavell revives John Milton's seventeenth-century assertion that "a meet and happy conversation is the chiefest and the noblest end of marriage."[1] Cavell focuses on conversations in the films that allow him to elucidate the ethical relationship he calls "acknowledgment," a mode of being with others that hinges on the recognition that interpersonal intimacy is necessarily limited, and people will never achieve full mutual understanding with others. Cavell finds marriage to be one of the primary sites through which our culture imaginatively negotiates this ineluctable metaphysical fact, a site in which demands for intimacy are

[1] John Milton, *The Doctrine and Discipline of Divorce and the Judgement of Martin Bucer; Tetrachordon; & An Abridgment of Colasterion* (London: Sherwood, Neely, and Jones, 1820), p. 27; Stanley Cavell, *Pursuits of Happiness: The Hollywood Comedy of Remarriage* (Cambridge, MA: Harvard University Press, 1981), p. 87. Hereafter abbreviated *Pursuits*.

E. Greer (✉)
University of Texas at Dallas, Richardson, TX, USA
e-mail: erin.greer@utdallas.edu

especially high, and interpersonal difference may be experienced as especially threatening. It is through "happy" conversation, he suggests, that we might discover difference to be "a reasonable condition for a ceremony of union," rather than an excuse for solipsism, or a fact to be denied in dreams of romantic merger.[2]

Although Cavell's primary points of reference for his philosophical conjunction of marriage and conversation are mid-twentieth-century Hollywood "comedies of remarriage" and "melodramas of the unknown woman," he equally might have used Romantic and Victorian novels in his inquiry into the "form of life" represented by the "articulate responsiveness, expressiveness," as well as "consent and reciprocity" of good conversation (*Pursuits*, 87, 182). Indeed, in work published after his study of the "struggles for acknowledgment" enacted in conversations between lovers in the films, Cavell finds a similar convergence of conversation, intellectual reciprocity, and romantic partnership in fiction by Jane Austen and George Eliot (*Contesting*, 30).[3]

The present chapter looks at a work of late Victorian fiction that complicates the convergence of romantic aspirations and conversation, George Meredith's 1879 *The Egoist*. The novel's plot reverses the traditional formula of courtship and marriage: Clara Middleton promises to marry Willoughby Patterne near the beginning of the novel, and she spends the rest of the novel striving to disengage herself. Willoughby, too, is bedeviled by the tendency of language to *act* rather than simply *report*, finding that language attains "illocutionary" force when observed by the "world." In other words, *The Egoist* anticipates both the formal philosophical theorization of speech performativity offered by J.L. Austin in the middle of the twentieth century, and later post-structural and queer turns applied to Austin's work that interrogate the mutual reinforcement of linguistic and social convention, as well as the concept of personal agency in the context of performative language.

The action of *The Egoist* occurs in the temporal gap between what Austin would call a commissive performative utterance, Clara's engagement to marry Willoughby, and the fulfillment or non-fulfillment of this

---

[2] Stanley Cavell, *Contesting Tears: The Hollywood Melodrama of the Unknown Woman* (Chicago, IL: University of Chicago Press, 1996), p. 22. Hereafter abbreviated *Contesting*.

[3] For Cavell's reading of Austen and Eliot, see Stanley Cavell, *Philosophy the Day After Tomorrow* (Cambridge, MA: Harvard University Press, 2006), pp. 119–31.

promise. It is confined to the estate of its titular egoist, Patterne Hall, and, even more claustrophobically, the plot unfolds primarily in the conversations the various actors have in this restricted setting. These conversations illuminate the ethical and philosophical stakes of marriage, indicating "infelicities" (to borrow one of Austin's terms) in the marriage convention that are intrinsically both linguistic and social, while also hinting that a "meet and happy conversation" might indeed be the "chiefest and the noblest end of marriage." Conversation is a primary index in *The Egoist* of the unsuitability of the betrothed pair and the superior suitability of Clara and Willoughby's cousin Vernon, whom she loves unwittingly until the end. Willoughby's frequent invocation of Romantic tropes in conversations with Clara are comical (and frustrating to Clara) precisely because they indicate his utter lack of interest in "acknowledging" her as an actual speech partner, and his preference for fantasizing that he is enacting the plot of a second-rate novel rather than sharing the reality Clara attempts to impress upon him with her lucid speech. In Cavell's words, Willoughby "convert[s]" Clara "into a character and make[s] the world a stage for [her]."[4] Vernon, by contrast, grows out of his view of Clara as a "Mountain Echo," subservient to the speech of her mate, and comes to see her as possessing "a character" making her "fit [...] for the best of comrades anywhere."[5]

But *The Egoist* is principally about performativity, and the possibility for free and affirmative communication between intimates, given speech's tendency to *act*. By situating its study of speech performativity in a plot that reverses the conjugal trajectory of so many nineteenth-century novels, while simultaneously retaining hopes for the romantic acknowledgment Cavell discovers in "happy conversation," *The Egoist* combines its precocious theory of speech performativity with an inquiry into the possibility of intimacy in a world largely produced and governed by speech. The novel suggests that any theory of intimacy or community as negotiated in language must encompass the source of conversation's power to constitute a "form of life." A set of conventions underwrites this power, complicating the notion of autonomous self-expression and therefore also the intimacy that forms between linguistically expressive "selves."

[4] Stanley Cavell, *Must We Mean What We Say?* (Cambridge: Cambridge University Press, 1976), p. 333. Hereafter abbreviated *MWM*.
[5] George Meredith, *The Egoist* (New York: Penguin Books, 1968), pp. 66, 159.

In the first part of the chapter that follows, I elucidate how the conversations of Meredith's characters manifest what Cavell calls "struggles for acknowledgment." Out of these struggles emerges my primary subject: the novel's philosophy of language, and of intimacy problematically negotiated through the linguistic medium, which develops through its two protagonists' struggles against the illocutionary force of their words. Meredith may be, as Jami Bartlett has summarized, "a canonical writer generally agreed to be bad at writing," but *The Egoist* is critically prescient, and reading it in dialogue with Cavell and Austin produces a new perspective upon the conjugal entanglement of language and intimacy.[6] As we will see, Meredith's linked critique of language and marriage is devastating, and the novel culminates in a gesture toward intimacy beyond its own linguistic power of representation.

1 Meeting, Happily

The conversations that Cavell affirms in *Pursuits of Happiness* are performative aesthetic works. As performances, they are fleeting, but leave lasting effects upon the sensibilities; as aesthetic works, they possess what Immanuel Kant calls "merely formal purposiveness, i.e., a purposiveness without end."[7] They are not undertaken to meet ends beyond the "form of life" they enact and sustain.

Most crucially for Cavell—and most pertinently for *The Egoist*—the conversations between lovers at times manifest "struggles for acknowledgment" (*Contesting*, 30). Acknowledgment is a theme throughout Cavell's writing. In *Must We Mean What We Say?*, Cavell posits "acknowledgment"

---

[6] Jamie Bartlett, "Meredith & Ends," *ELH* 76, no. 3 (2009): 547–76, p. 547. Bartlett offers a summary of the critical disdain for Meredith and an exemplary reading that takes Meredith more seriously. Like the present chapter, Bartlett's founds its reading on resonances between Meredith's work and "the philosophy of language," focusing specifically on the philosophy implicit in the "granular descriptions" that, as she finds, tend to take the place of plot development.

[7] Immanuel Kant, *The Critique of Judgment*, trans. JH Bernard (New York: Hafner Press, 1951), §15, p. 62. Kant includes conversation among the "pleasant arts," which "are directed merely to enjoyment" (§44, p. 148). For the present chapter, this conception of conversation as a quotidian "pleasant art" suffices, but for a fuller investigation of the relation between aesthetics and conversation, see my article "A Many-Sided Substance: the Philosophy of Conversation in Woolf, Russell, and Kant" in the *Journal of Modern Literature* (Spring 2017).

as the ethical answer to the "problem of the existence of other minds," linking this "problem" to the more worldly skepticism posed by Descartes, Hume, Kant, and so on: "What skepticism suggests is that since we cannot know the world exists, its presentness to us cannot be a function of knowing. The world is to be *accepted*; as the presentness of other minds is not to be known, but acknowledged."[8] We accept the world's presence on the basis of something like faith: faith in our senses and their fidelity to the world as it is, and faith in our minds for translating sense perception into coherent cognitive representations of reality that are likewise faithful to "reality," at least to an acceptable extent. The concept of acknowledgment suggests that we take the "presentness" of other persons on something like faith, too: faith in other minds being somewhat like ours, or at least somewhat like the stories we tell to account for them—at any rate, of their being here, in some capacity, which we can only accept.

Many of the conversations between Meredith's protagonists enact Cavellian "struggles for acknowledgment," as Willoughby indulges in histrionics that prefigure several of the primary means Cavell identifies by which individuals evade "acknowledging" others. One such way a person might resist acknowledging another is through attempting to bridge the gap between the two, to merge with the other in the style recommended, for instance, in strands of romantic ideology. A version of this ideology is behind many of Willoughby's most excessive demands for Clara to commit herself in speech acts. In their engagement conversation, he makes her swear that she is "wholly" his, his "utterly," and that their "engagement is written above" (*The Egoist*, 73). Shortly after their engagement, he demands that she promise to be faithful to him even after he dies:

> "Clara! to dedicate your life to our love! Never one touch; not one whisper! not a thought, not a dream! Could you—it agonizes me to imagine ... be inviolate? mine above?—mine before all men, though I am gone:—true to my dust? Tell me. Give me that assurance. [...] Clara! my Clara! as I live in yours, whether here or away; whether you are a wife or widow, there is no distinction for love—I am your husband—say it—eternally [...]."
>
> "Is it not possible that I may be the first to die?" said Miss Middleton.

---

[8] Stanley Cavell, *Must We Mean What We Say?* (Cambridge: Cambridge University Press, 1976), p. 324. Hereafter abbreviated *MWM*.

> "And lose you, with the thought that you, lovely as you are, and the dogs of the world barking round you, might … Is it any wonder that I have my feeling for the world? This hand!—the thought is horrible. You would be surrounded; men are brutes; the scent of unfaithfulness excites them, overjoys them. And I helpless! The thought is maddening. I see a ring of monkeys grinning. There is your beauty, and man's delight in desecrating. You would be worried night and day to quit my name, to … I feel the blow now. You would have no rest for them, nothing to cling to without your oath."
>
> "An oath!" said Miss Middleton.
>
> "It is no delusion, my love, when I tell you that with this thought upon me I see a ring of monkey faces grinning at me; they haunt me. But you do swear it! Once, and I will never trouble you on the subject again. My weakness! if you like. You will learn that it is love, a man's love, stronger than death."
>
> "An oath?" she said, and moved her lips to recall what she might have said and forgotten. "To what? what oath?"
>
> "That you will be true to me dead as well as living! Whisper it."
>
> "Willoughby, I shall be true to my vows at the altar."
>
> "To me! me!"
>
> "It will be to you."
>
> "To my soul. No heaven can be for me—I see none, only torture, unless I have your word, Clara. I trust it. I will trust it implicitly. My confidence in you is absolute."
>
> "Then you need not be troubled." (85–86)

I will return to the explicit issue of these characters' relationships to speech acts—such as the eternally binding "oath" Willoughby demands of Clara—later in the chapter; for now, it is enough to observe that Willoughby's private melodrama makes him insensible to the woman speaking before him. The two are completely out of tune with each other, aligned in neither tone nor sentiment, to borrow a musical metaphor that Meredith himself frequently invokes.

The disconnect between Willoughby's comically exaggerated tone and Clara's levelheaded responses makes it clear that the two are not in each other's presence. Not only does Willoughby repress the meaning of Clara's words: he represses the fact of her presence before him as an autonomous other. Here is a prime example of Willoughby's tendency to, in Cavell's words, "convert" Clara "into a character and make the world a stage for [her]" (*MWM*, 333). For Cavell, willful insensibility manifests a (bad) form of acknowledgment, providing "as conclusive an acknowledgment that [others] are present as murdering them would be" (*MWM*, 332). But Willoughby goes further, denying acknowledgment altogether, which, according to Cavell, "does violence to others, it separates their bodies from their souls, makes monsters of them" (*Pursuits*, 109). "Acknowledgment" is not necessarily morally laudable, but its refusal is intrinsically brutal.

Fully entering into the presence of the other—acknowledging the other—means not only accepting the other's presence, but "put[ting] ourselves in the other's presence, reveal[ing] ourselves to them" (*MWM*, 332–33). This self-disclosure entails revealing one's own limitations and separateness: "It is only in this perception of them as separate from me that I make them present. That I make them *other*, and face them" (338). Accepting the condition of unbridgeable difference is alarming; it reminds us of our own mortality and limits, and it makes intimacy itself contingent upon incomplete understanding. Together, these alarming perceptions form what Cavell calls the "reasonable condition for a ceremony of union":

> [W]hat is wanting—if marriage is to be reconceived, or let's say human attraction—is for the other to see our separate existence, to acknowledge its separateness, a reasonable condition for a ceremony of union. Then the opening knowledge of the human is conceived as the experience of being unknown. To reach that absence is not the work of a moment. (*Contesting*, 22)

The kind of knowledge entailed in the "union" of acknowledgment is always incomplete. According to Cavell, it requires "reaching" an "absence," which I take to mean a state of humility, in which we might even appreciate insoluble mystery as the basis for a "ceremony of union"—a marriage, perhaps, but also possibly a conversation, seriously undertaken.

Willoughby does not want to accept "being unknown." As though his words could achieve what they assert—as though they could be performative—he tells Clara, "We are one another's […] So entirely one, that there never can be question of external influences. […] You have me, you have me like an open book, you, and only you!" (98–99). Denying his own limits, as well as Clara's, Willoughby's theatrical assertions that their love draws them into "oneness" deny the chance of actual "union," in the sense possible under the conditions of acknowledgment.

On the other hand, Willoughby's insistence upon the performative power of language offers his own weak form of acknowledgment. His constant demands that Clara undertake additional oaths demonstrate that he at least dimly perceives his own limits. He appeals to language to forge the bond he cannot otherwise guarantee. But this implicit acknowledgment betrays a misperception of what conversation can actually do. In the sort of conversation that follows acknowledgment, we speak from within, and on the premise of, the "absence" described above. In *Contesting Tears*, the study of the Hollywood "melodramas," Cavell explicitly equates "the logic of human intimacy" with "separateness," and calls this logic "the field of serious and playful conversation or exchange" (221). Willoughby's demands for words to bind Clara demonstrate an urge to overcome this separateness through a particularly charged kind of conversation or exchange.

2 Ceremonies of Union: The Commissive Speech Act

It is surprising, given the averred importance of J.L. Austin's work in Cavell's intellectual development, that Cavell did not draw speech acts into his constellation of marriage, ethics, and conversation. Drawing performativity into the constellation not only illuminates ways that performativity can be invoked in an attempt to evade acknowledgment, as in the discussion above; it also suggests the limits of any theory of intimacy that depends upon free and "purposeless" self-expression in language. *The Egoist* helps to make clear that a conception of the illocutionary force of speech underwrites the significance of talk in intimate relationships, throwing into relief the performativity shadowing even the most playfully purposeless conversations. It is precisely because speech *acts*—with both illocutionary and perlocutionary force—that words exchanged have the power to constitute a "form of life," and a "ceremony of union."[9]

---

[9]Austin terms the more psychological effects of utterances their "perlocutionary" consequences, as opposed to the performative consequences achieved by linguistic convention; like all of Austin's categories, however, this distinction between perlocutionary and illocutionary is blurry. Austin, J.L. *How to Do Things with Words* (Oxford: Clarendon Press, 1962), p. 101.

The marriage vow is paradigmatic in speech act theory.[10] *The Egoist* structures its plot and nascent philosophy of performative utterances around promising, however, which is an example of what J.L. Austin terms a "commissive" utterance. A commissive is less immediately and absolutely active than performative utterances like the marriage vow. Language, but not yet law, has entangled Clara with a man whose refusal to "acknowledge" her is evident in nearly every scene of interaction, and *The Egoist* suggests an engagement is nearly as difficult for a woman to escape as a marriage. The device through which this predicament is established—the illocutionary force of Clara's promise to marry Willoughby—completes a theoretical constellation of marriage, ethics, and speech that is both intuitive and illuminating.

Austin's discussion of commissives appears halfway through the lectures collected into *How to Do Things with Words*, as he begins to dissolve "the dichotomy of performatives and constatives […] in favour of more general

---

[10] As Eve Kosofsky Sedgwick has pointed out with characteristic wit, "The marriage ceremony is, indeed, so central to the origins of 'performativity' (given the strange, disavowed but unattenuated persistence of *the exemplary* in this work) that a more accurate name for *How to Do Things with Words* might have been *How to say (or write) 'I do,' about twenty million times without winding up any more married than you started out.* (Short title: *I Do-Not!*)." See Eve Sedgwick, "Queer performativity: Henry James's The art of the novel," *GLQ: A Journal of Lesbian and Gay Studies* 1, no. 1 (1993): 1–16, p. 3. What Sedgwick is directing attention to is the (queer) way in which Austin's own work "performatively" voids performative utterances of their illocutionary force. Austin writes a great deal about the necessity of particular circumstances in order to grant performative utterances effective force, and the various ways in which such utterances can be "infelicitous." For instance, reciting the marriage vow to your partner outside of the presence of an official of the state or church will not effect your marriage; nor will reciting "I do" accomplish a union if, like Rochester in *Jane Eyre*, one happens to have a wife already, locked in his attic; nor will it accomplish a marriage if the words are exchanged between two men, or two women, in a dwindling number of US states. But performative utterances are also "infelicitous" when offered in philosophy, just as in literature: when "it is as examples they are offered in the first place—hence as, performatively, voided in advance" (p. 3). In consequence, Sedgwick proposes a view of *How to Do Things with Words* that attends to its queerness: "*How to Do Things with Words* thus performs at least a triple gesture with respect to marriage: installing monogamous heterosexual dyadic church- and state-sanctioned marriage at the definitional center of an entire philosophical edifice, it yet posits as the first heuristic device of that philosophy the *class of things* (for instance, personal characteristics or object choices) that can preclude or vitiate marriage; and it constructs the philosopher himself, the modern Socrates, as a man—presented as highly comic—whose relation to the marriage vow will be one of compulsive, apparently apotropaic repetition and yet of ultimate exemption" (p. 3).

families of related and overlapping speech acts" (149). As many readers have noted, Austin's lectures begin by announcing the existence of a class of utterance hitherto unstudied in philosophy, the performative, but by their end, Austin has demonstrated that all speech has a performative dimension; he has moved from identifying "the performative" as a class of utterance, to demonstrating that performativity is an aspect of speech.[11] Commissives have less performative force than "verdictives" (the utterances of a jury, for instance) and "exercitives" (utterances that do what they say because of the relevant power of the speaker, such as issuing a formal warning, appointing someone to a position, etc.). "Typified by promising or otherwise undertaking," Austin explains, commissives "commit you to doing something, but include also declarations or announcements of intention, which are not promises, and also rather vague things which we may call espousals, as for example, siding with" (150–51). A commissive performs something immediately—in saying "I promise," one is doing the act of promising—but its performativity also relates in a more ambiguous way to the future act it anticipates.

There is a lapse of time between the speech act of promising and the execution of the promised act, of course. Judith Butler has thus invoked the figure of chiasmus to represent the relation between a commissive (in her discussion, a threat) and its associated act:

> The act of threat and the threatened act are, of course, distinct, but they are related as a chiasmus. Although not identical, they are both bodily acts: the first act, the threat, only makes sense in terms of the act that it prefigures. The threat begins a temporal horizon within which the organizing aim is the act that is threatened; the threat begins the action by which the fulfillment of the threatened act might be achieved. And yet, a threat can be derailed, defused, can fail to furnish the act that it threatens. The threat states the impending certitude of another, forthcoming act, but the statement itself cannot produce that forthcoming act as one of its necessary effects. This failure to deliver on the threat does not call into question the status of the speech act as a threat—it merely questions its efficacy.[12]

---

[11] For a thoughtful synopsis of Austin's initial theorization of performativity and a thorough review of the ways that performativity has been picked up by theorists following Austin, see Jonathan Culler, "Philosophy and Literature: The Fortunes of the Performative," *Poetics Today* 21, no. 3 (2000): 503–19.

[12] Judith Butler, *Excitable Speech: A Politics of the Performative* (New York: Routledge, 1997), p. 11.

Both a commissive and the event it promises are acts, and each requires the other in order to make full sense. If Clara and Willoughby did not have faith in the power of her "word" to guarantee the future event of their wedding, her promise to marry Willoughby could not compel the plot as it does. This faith situates her utterance and the promised wedding in the interweaving loop of chiasmus. But as Butler says of the threat, a promise can be unfulfilled, and it is precisely this possibility of "derailment" that interests Meredith in *The Egoist*.

It is worth observing that the temporal extension of the traditional, pre-modernist novel makes it the literary form best suited to revealing the narrative drama at the heart of everyday speech acts. By unfolding its primary plot in the space between a promise and its fulfillment or non-fulfillment, *The Egoist* illuminates the narrative aspect of speech acts and blurs the distinction between the literary, sociological, and material elements of language when spoken. Speech acts like promises depend upon "plots" to realize their full meaning, their final status as what Austin will call "felicitous" or "infelicitous."

Clara's initial promise to marry Willoughby is not directly represented in the novel. The narrative perspective is entirely limited to Willoughby's estate and surrounding neighborhood, and readers first learn about her existence through gossip, allusions to "hints […] dropping about the neighborhood" of a woman and a courtship unfolding elsewhere (65). These hints are made explicit in Mrs. Mountstuart Jenkinson's gossipy mash of sentimental cliché and material concern:

> He met her at Cherriton. Both were struck at the same moment. Her father is, I hear, some sort of learned man; money; no land. No house either, I believe. People who spend half their time on the Continent. They are now for a year at Upton Park. The very girl to settle down and entertain when she does think of settling. Eighteen, perfect manners; you need not ask if a beauty. Sir Willoughby will have his dues. We must teach her to make amends to him. (65)

Mrs. Mountstuart's information is evidently second-hand, if not from a further remove: she "hears" details about Clara's father and their material situation, and weaves these reports into an empty and unsubstantiated assertion that "both were struck at the same moment," culminating with an indication of the community's assumed role in the romance of others. The neighborhood must teach Clara to "make amends" for Willoughby's previous bad experience of being "jilted" (by a woman ironically and iconically named Constantia).

The presiding county gossip's report is followed in the next chapter by a fuller narrative description of the couples' courtship. Presented at this retrospective remove, and in a hasty summary, this description also assumes the air of gossip. Readers do not directly witness "the great meeting" between Clara and Willoughby, nor their subsequent courtship and engagement, but rather follow the narrator's synopsis. Willoughby has successfully asserted himself over other suitors, "while yet he knew no more of her than that he was competing for a prize," and he consequently feels that he has proven to "the world" that he is "the best man" (71–72). In this summary, readers also learn that Clara commits herself verbally to Willoughby only after much hedging and delay:

> She begged for time; Willoughby could barely wait. She unhesitatingly owned that she liked no one better, and he consented. A calm examination of his position told him that it was unfair so long as he stood engaged, and she did not. She pleaded a desire to see a little of the world before she plighted herself. She alarmed him; he assumed the amazing god of love under the subtlest guise of the divinity. Willingly would he obey her behests, resignedly languish, were it not for his mother's desire to see the future lady of Patterne established there before she died. Love shone cunningly through the mask of filial duty, but the plea of urgency was reasonable. Dr. Middleton thought it reasonable, supposing his daughter to have an inclination. She had no disinclination, though she had a maidenly desire to see a little of the world—grace for one year, she said. Willoughby reduced the year to six months, and granted that term, for which, in gratitude, she submitted to stand engaged; and that was no light whispering of a word. She was implored to enter the state of captivity by the pronunciation of vows—a private but a binding ceremonial. She had health and beauty, and money to gild these gifts; not that he stipulated for money with his bride, but it adds a lustre to dazzle the world; and, moreover, the pack of rival pursuers hung close behind, yelping and raising their dolorous throats to the moon. Captive she must be. (72–73)

Hardly "struck at the same moment," Willoughby and Clara evidently become engaged as a consequence of his pressuring and confusing her into "submission." Readers moreover learn that even after becoming formally engaged, Clara "enter[s]" an even further "state of captivity" by pronouncing additional vows. Willoughby strives to make her "captive" with her words, a verbal "ceremony of union" each considers binding.

Most crucially for the novel's inquiry into speech performativity, this scene spotlights the centrality of speech to Willoughby's strategy of subjugation, his extraction of verbal promises that enchain their utterers. He turns such speech acts into exaggerated performances: "He made her engagement no light whispering matter. It was a solemn plighting of a troth. Why not?" (73). As the account of this solemn plighting continues, readers learn that Willoughby has extracted from Clara more than the average recitation:

> Having said, I am yours, she could say, I am wholly yours, I am yours forever, I swear it, I will never swerve from it, I am your wife in heart, yours utterly; our engagement is written above. To this she considerately appended, 'as far as I am concerned'; a piece of somewhat chilling generosity, and he forced her to pass him through love's catechism in turn, and came out with fervent answers that bound him to her too indissolubly to let her doubt of her being loved. (73)

Clara's addendum "as far as I am concerned" implies that an engagement does not necessarily index possession that is entire, unchanging, and "written above" (God is appropriately figured as a writer exercising ultimate illocutionary efficacy). In granting Willoughby license to preserve his own liberty, swerve from the engagement or see it as purely human and contractual, Clara makes plain that she does not believe an engagement to be divine, transcendental, and permanently and wholly binding. She seeks to loosen the grip of her words as soon as she utters them by suggesting they are binding according to convention and will. His "fervent answers," moreover, demonstrate a confused belief that love vows assure lovers because of their performative, rather than expressive, power: love is to be deduced from the bonds a person has willingly spoken himself into, not from the content of any expressions of love. The indissolubility of their bond comes not from love, nor from the words "above" in which God has "written" of their bond, but from *Willoughby's* words.

Not only does Willoughby emphatically insist upon the solidity of bonds established through language, but he also enlists language throughout the novel in his efforts to shape reality. Two noteworthy instances occur in conversations between Willoughby and Laetitia, a woman he has known since childhood, twice encouraged to believe he would marry, and who has been openly pining for him throughout her entire adult life. As Willoughby becomes increasingly nervous that Clara will cut the bonds of her words and "jilt" him, he constructs a scheme in which he would preemptively jilt Clara, pair her with the cousin he thinks is undesirable, and marry Laetitia as though he has secretly loved the childhood friend all along. He tries to guarantee Laetitia's consent before releasing Clara to his cousin Vernon by attempting to make speech performative according to his own will, disregarding the circumstances typically necessary to make performative speech felicitous: "I am free," he tells Laetitia; "Thank heaven! I am free to choose my mate—the woman I have always loved! Freely and unreservedly, as I ask you to give your hand, I offer mine. You are the mistress of Patterne Hall; my wife" (474). His declaration "I am free" not only disingenuously implies that he has already broken his engagement with Clara, but it indicates and performs the actual freedom that he indeed has, unmatched by Clara. Moreover, it leads to the assertion that Laetitia is, or will become, his wife, which appears to be an effort at using what Austin calls an "exercitive" utterance (the class of utterance that names, appoints, and proclaims). Laetitia does not accept the nomination. Later, Willoughby attempts to secure her linguistically from the reverse direction, insisting that *her* words have performatively achieved something beyond her intention. Laetitia responds to a knock on the door, thinking it is Clara's knock, with, "Come in, dear." Willoughby enters and "seize[s] her hands," exclaiming, "Dear! [...] You cannot withdraw that. You call me dear. I am, I must be dear to you. The word is out, by accident or not, but, by heaven, I have it and I give it up to no one" (593).

As these last two instances with Laetitia show, Willoughby occasionally treats casual and conversational speech as equally performative as the more appropriately "binding" speech acts of promising and taking oaths. In all of the situations described above, he insists upon the effective value of spoken language, in contradiction of the purposeless play of conversation central to Cavellian descriptions of acknowledgment. This seeking of illocutionary force in ordinary conversation makes the same point that Austin eventually reaches in his lectures: lurking in all oral speech, all conversation, is potential illocutionary force. "What we need," Austin observes late in the lectures, is not "a list of 'explicit performative verbs,'" but rather, "a list of *illocutionary forces* of an utterance" (148–49, his emphasis). Certain utterances may have different illocutionary forces depending upon the circumstances in which they are said, their speaker's social position, their subjective context, and so on. In the instances described above, Willoughby wagers that illocutionary force might be managed by his intentions alone, irrespective of the intentions of his interlocutors. Willoughby's wager in fact points to a quandary raised by the relation between private intentions and public illocutionary utterances.

3   Doubtless Wrong, but No Misstatement

The performative force of language, *The Egoist* suggests, is problematic in a stratified world, in which speakers occupy such different positions within society that they relate to language differently. In Clara's case, it is her social position as a woman that makes it impossible for her to fully mean what she says, due to her historically guaranteed inexperience and restricted agency. Early in the novel, Willoughby's cousin Vernon reminds her that she is "in a position of [her] own choosing," referring of course to her acceptance of Willoughby's proposal. Clara recoils from this notion and makes an interesting qualification:

> "Not my choosing; do not say choosing, Mr. Whitford. I did not choose. I was incapable of really choosing. I consented."
> "It's the same in fact. But be sure of what you wish."
> "Yes," she assented, taking it for her just punishment that she should be supposed not quite to know her wishes. (196)

Consenting is, along with promising, among Austin's list of commissive verbs. In distinguishing between a commissive and the decision it supposedly indexes, Clara indicates not only that she succumbed after badgering, but that her succumbing was a matter of language, not a matter of inner decision. Insisting that she *consented*, but did not *decide*, Clara shifts emphasis to the speech act she committed rather than the intentionality behind it, signaling that she was "incapable" of having what Austin would call the "appropriate" intention when she performatively committed herself to marrying Willoughby.

Austin himself struggles with the issue of speaker intentionality, as though he anticipates the implications post-structuralists would later draw from his philosophy. He acknowledges, for instance, that a person can make a promise with no intention to carry out the promised action, in which case the promise "is not even *void*, though it is given in *bad faith*… doubtless wrong, … it is not a lie or a misstatement" (11). The person who says "I promise" is indeed, in that utterance, performing the act of promising, even if she or he has no corresponding intention to prove this utterance "felicitous" in subsequent action. As Jonathan Culler has observed, "the performative breaks the link between meaning and the intention of the speaker, for what act I perform with my words is not determined by my intention but by social and linguistic conventions" (507). Austin does not go as far as Jacques Derrida, for instance, in voiding utterances of intentionality, but his work nonetheless signals that speech operates somewhat independently of the intention of its speakers. There is no guarantee that "appropriate" intention underwrites the performative force of utterances. And as Clara finds, linguistic convention can hijack a person, enlisting her in a future she could not have intended.

The plot of *The Egoist* dramatizes the problems of citationality that Derrida, and later Judith Butler, make central to their retheorizations of performativity. An utterance achieves its institutional, performative effect only because it is recognizable as the appropriate utterance in a prescripted social formula. The utterance is a citation of other utterances, and the entire social history of speech underwrites its current meaning and efficacy. This citational element of speech constitutes what Derrida calls a "dehiscence" between the speaker's utterance and intentionality: "The intention animating the utterance will never be through and through present to itself and to its content. The iteration structuring it a priori introduces into it a dehiscence and a cleft [brisure] which are essential."[13] The iteration pre-exists the speaker, whose speech invokes this prehistory and takes its life from a system separate from the speaker's intention.

The prehistory, as Clara's situation exemplifies, makes it too easy for a woman to act, in speaking, beyond her full intentions. One could imagine that in Meredith's world, it would be possible to reform society in order to allow certain subjects to mean what they say: women could be more fully educated, given greater freedom and wider experience, and thus be ushered into the community of those who speak and act through language with full agency.[14] Along this vein, Clara asks Laetitia if it has ever struck

---

[13] Jacques Derrida, *Limited Inc.*, trans. Samuel Weber and Jeffrey Mehlman (Evanston, IL: Northwestern University Press, 1988), p. 18.

[14] Derrida, and those following in his legacy, would insist that the "brisure" hinted at by citationality does not disappear simply with the sociological empowerment of speakers to mean what they say. Language only means because its meanings have been sketched in advance of our use of it. This advance sketching of language, the very foundation by which anything has meaning, indicates that the agency and intentionality of any speaker of language is restricted. It is not, in other words, a problem unique to the "subaltern" of a society. *The*

her "that very few women are able to be straightforwardly sincere in their speech, however much they may desire to be?" (205). Laetitia implicitly affirms this attitude of skepticism regarding female sincerity, observing, "they are differently educated. Great misfortune brings it to them." Strangely exempting herself from this "they" who are differently educated, Laetitia alludes to the education that urges women to prevaricate rather than cause offense or discomfort. One consequence of this different education is evident in Clara's father's classically offensive and dangerous opinion that "Not to believe in a lady's No is the approved method of carrying that fortress built to yield" (527). But Clara's formulation suggests that the obstacle to female sincerity might lurk in speech itself, as well as desire.

Women are nonetheless bound by the words they utter. As Clara puts it, they "have their honour to swear by equally with men" (173). Society must logically affirm as much, she continues, even of "girls," when it makes them "swear an oath at the altar." The societal foreclosing of women's capacity to mean what they say, while yet holding them by their words, represents a provocative intertwining of linguistic and patriarchal convention. Willoughby, indeed, appears to intuit that linguistic and social convention are both on his side, as a male of the ruling class:

> I abhor a breach of faith. A broken pledge is hateful to me. I should regard it myself as a form of suicide. There are principles which civilized men must contend for. Our social fabric is based on them. As my word stands for me, I hold others to theirs. If that is not done, the world is more or less a carnival of counterfeits. (489)

This neo-Kantian case for behaving so as to make one's promise "felicitous"—a shifting of the categorical imperative from the realm of constative utterances into the realm of the performative—is, significantly, offered by a self-proclaimed "civilized man" with serious interest in maintaining the present "social fabric." Throughout the novel, Willoughby's

---

Egoist does not insist upon the same absolutist approach to language, and the novel's attitude seems much closer to that of "ordinary language philosophy" and specifically of Ludwig Wittgenstein, whose decoupling of language from the "metaphysical" realm returns agency to human speakers. For Wittgenstein, it is language *use* which determines language *meaning*, a view that corresponds to *The Egoist's* portrayal of Willoughby's insistence upon the "binding" *uses* of language.

behavior demonstrates what we already know: a "civilized" man's word is less binding when offered to a woman (or, presumably, to a servant, a colonized subject, etc.). But Willoughby's metaphor of the "social fabric" woven of pledges, in which to break one's pledge is to invite one's own social death, reveals truth in its hyperbole. Through performative force, words do in fact institute, and hold together, the social fabric.

Meredith's critique of the way that language serves the interests of patriarchy and aristocracy is firmly historical and materialist, illuminating the historical conditions of language use rather than implying an underlying correspondence between the formal structure of language and essential qualities of sex or gender. Language and patriarchy are mutually reinforcing, not due to something like the "phallogocentrism" that poststructuralists ranging from Derrida to Lacan, Irigaray, and Cixous would perceive a century after Meredith, but due to another chiasmatic loop, in this case between social inequality and language. Social inequality mediates a person's use of language, conditioning her ability to mean what she says, and certain linguistic conventions commit her to what she says even if she cannot "mean" it. That society holds subjects accountable for the performative conventions of language they cannot "mean" is a historical injustice, and the consequences that play out in language bear further historical and material consequences through the performative dimension of language. This method of critiquing patriarchy insists upon recognizing the profound significance of language in constructing reality, suggesting that a critique of any sort of social inequality must encompass an understanding of how certain historically imbedded uses of language magnify the inequality, increasing the vulnerability of those whose social position renders them less fluent in the languages of convention.

4 Performative Suspension

The Egoist's philosophy of linguistic efficacy unfolds a final crucial aspect in a climactic scene in which Willoughby attempts to drain language of all illocutionary force. The scene approaches questions about personal agency and the efficacy of language from the inverse direction of the performative utterance, a direction premised upon a view that speech "makes nothing happen" (to cite Auden on poetry) not only because it is *merely* talk, but because of the particularly vague character of the talk employed, which effectively forestalls definitive action. Willoughby, in this scene and for reasons I'll explain in a moment, undertakes a virtuoso conversation in which his talk becomes pure form: a structure of well-timed interruptions and ellipses, indeterminate demonstratives, and ambiguous gestures into which listeners invest meaning according to their preconceptions. It is an understatement to observe that the scene contains no performative utterances; it depicts a conversation deliberately drained of illocutionary (and "perlocutionary") efficacy.

As we will see, Willoughby makes indeterminacy an instrumental value, perverting the interminable "playful conversation" admired by Cavell and Milton (*Contesting*, 221). Indeterminacy, one might say, is essential to conversation in its pure form, distinguishing it from "discussion" and "debate." Willoughby's performance in the following scene shows that indeterminacy may also be instrumentally employed as a particular mode of denying acknowledgment. This clear instrumentalization of one of the central aspects of conversation produces a surrogate speech performance, which offers insight not only into Willoughby's pathological denial of acknowledgment to others, but also into the sociable aesthetic play of conversation in its "good" sense. As mentioned earlier, "happy" conversations may be seen as performative aesthetic works, exhibiting "purposiveness without purpose"; but the free play of language loses its ethical value when it becomes a game played alone, in the company of others reduced to bewildered spectators.[15]

The scene occurs near the end of the novel, when Willoughby has grown increasingly panicked about the apparent likelihood of Clara "jilting" him. As I have mentioned above, he proposes to Laetitia—the night before the scene at hand—without having broken his engagement with Clara. Laetitia declines and leaves Willoughby's house for her father's cottage on the estate. Their exchange has been overheard by a boy living with Willoughby, Crossjay, who accidently hints its content to another of Clara's would-be suitors, Colonel de Craye. The circulation of this story registers one way in which language, and narrative, assume an active and agentic role, trundling the plot toward its conclusion. De Craye first shares the news of Willoughby's proposal to Laetitia with Clara, who is astounded

---

[15] Stanley Cavell elaborates upon the interrelation of theatricality and acknowledgment in his reading of *King Lear*, describing a tendency to deny acknowledgment by "convert[ing] the other into a character and mak[ing] the world a stage for him" (*MWM*, p. 333). In this scene, the situation is reversed, and Willoughby converts the others into an audience. As we will see, the consequence is that he feels himself morphing into a "juggler" and finally "a machine."

because Willoughby has that morning renewed his pressure upon her. She confronts Willoughby in the presence of her father, Dr. Middleton, working her way up to a direct question about his alleged proposal to Laetitia. He tells her he was speaking on Vernon's behalf, which satisfies Dr. Middleton and stirs doubts in Clara. Meanwhile, the gossip Mrs. Mountstuart arrives, and de Craye intercepts her with news that Willoughby and Laetitia are now engaged. Her whispered congratulations inform Willoughby that a story is definitely abroad, and definitely inaccurate in its indication that Laetitia assented. A tense lunch is served, after which Willoughby, Vernon, Mrs. Mountstuart, and Clara all depart the house, leaving Dr. Middleton alone with Willoughby's aunts. Another visitor arrives: Laetitia's father, Mr. Dale, who is distressed at what he has ascertained from his daughter's odd behavior and gathering gossip about her engagement with an already-engaged man. Confusion mounts as Dr. Middleton, believing that Mr. Dale has come after learning that his daughter declined *Vernon*, reassures Mr. Dale that Laetitia can yet be persuaded to marry "the gentleman" whom Dr. Middleton so highly esteems (539). He comically extends the confusion by cautioning that "the circumstances" should not yet be treated as "public," and therefore "it is incumbent on us [...] not to be nominally precise."

The "public" then arrives, in the form of the dull-witted county gossips Ladies Busshe and Culmer. They, too, have heard that Laetitia and Willoughby are engaged. The scene becomes increasingly convoluted, with bits of dialogue representing the gradual piecing together of strands of gossip, until Lady Busshe screeches, "What whirl are we in?" She enjoins the gathering to "proceed upon system," the first step of which is to state everything known with explicit precision (545). "The Middletons are here," she reviews, "and Dr. Middleton himself communicates to Mr. Dale that Laetitia Dale has refused the hand of Sir Willoughby, who is ostensibly engaged to his own daughter!" Dr. Middleton has momentarily departed and cannot revise her nominally precise interpretation, and no one listens to Willoughby's aunts, who attempt to insist upon the version of the story Willoughby has told Dr. Middleton, that Laetitia refused his plea on Vernon's behalf.

Mrs. Mountstuart now reenters the scene, and although she is aware of Willoughby's plan to marry Laetitia himself and couple Clara with Vernon (in order to disappoint de Craye, his imagined rival for the affection of both Clara and the county at large), she luxuriates in the suspension of clarity. The conversation continues, very slowly illuminating the Ladies representing "the world," and someone even suggests that their conversation is itself determining the state of affairs: whether or not Vernon has been rejected by Laetitia, the unnamed speaker says, "is in debate, and at this moment being decided" (549). When Lady Busshe finally articulates aloud Willoughby's plan, and observes that "Dr. Middleton is made to play blind man in the midst," she comments that the length of time and convolutions of plot, which have led toward this projected "amicable rupture, and […] smooth new arrangement," have "improve[d] the story," firmly locating the affair in the realm of discourse. She moreover appears to credit "the county" with producing the story: "I defy any other county in the kingdom to produce one fresh and living to equal it," and as we will see, this attribution of power to the "county" of gossips is partially appropriate.

At this moment, Willoughby and Dr. Middleton both enter, and the former immediately perceives danger. Not certain what each person present knows, he nonetheless recognizes that he is suspended in a web of contradictory gossip about his engagement status. The upshot of this is that, while he is not definitively engaged to either Clara or Laetitia, neither is he quite disengaged from either, at least in the view of "the world" whose perspective he confuses with reality. He launches a conversation involving everyone present that seeks to preserve this state of indeterminacy, evidently believing that both futures remain open to him as long as the uncertainty lasts, and the observing world is made to believe indistinctly in each. He feels like a "fearfully dexterous juggler," keeping the various versions of truth in motion (563). Willoughby survives this scene because of what the narrator calls his "proleptic mind," a characterization that suggests his mind itself functions like a rhetorical figure, representing events as accomplished when they are still unfolding (551).

Willoughby's prolepsis combines ambiguous language, significant glances, and interruptions. He reassures Mr. Dale that Patterne is "[his] home," for instance, which Mr. Dale presumably interprets in relation to his daughter's proposed marriage to Willoughby, while Dr. Middleton interprets the words as an allusion to Laetitia's marriage to Vernon, who also lives at Patterne. To the county Ladies, his vagueness is a mode of hedging that denies them confirmation of the story Mrs. Mountstuart has communicated. At one point, Willoughby glances significantly at Lady Busshe, but "Lady Busshe would not be satisfied with the compliment of the intimate looks and nods," and she asks directly, "Which is the father of the fortunate creature?" (556). Willoughby's reply that "the house will be empty to-morrow" blatantly evades her question. He then bounces away to interrupt a threatening conversation between Dr. Middleton and Mr. Dale, intervening with gestures and words about Mr. Dale's health just when Dr. Middleton is about to specify by name the man whose "passionate advocate [he] proclaimed [himself]" (558). Willoughby's behavior throughout this scene provides an exaggerated substantiation of Cavell's observation that "We are [...] exactly as responsible for the specific implications of our utterances as we are for their explicit factual claims [...] Misnaming and misdescribing are not the only mistakes we can make in talking. Nor is lying its only immorality" (*MWM*, 11–12).

While Willoughby's evasion of the commitment that would follow linguistic precision seems to be a straightforward and ordinary, albeit self-serving and unethical, use of vagueness, the scene suggests deeper philosophical implications of this use of language.[16] Indeed, Meredith was writing at a moment of renewed philosophical inquiry into vagueness, a line of inquiry traceable at least as far back historically as Aristotle, which had fallen out of favor in philosophy until a revival in the nineteenth century.[17] According to one strand of this tradition, the vagueness of certain linguistic terms is an epistemic matter, vague language indexing incomplete knowledge of the world. Other philosophers saw linguistic vagueness as a problem arising from the intrinsic vagueness of the thing being represented. This second view, called the "supervaluationist approach," means that "for some sentences there is no fact of the matter whether they are

---

[16] As numerous linguists, philosophers, and sociologists have noted, "conversational implicature" plays a significant role in verbal communication. See, for instance, Erving Goffman, *Forms of Talk* (Philadelphia, PA: University of Pennsylvania Press, 1981), especially "Replies and Responses"; Dan Sperber and Deirdre Wilson, *Relevance: Communication and Cognition* (Cambridge, MA: Harvard University Press, 1986); and H. P. Grice, *Studies in the Way of Words* (Cambridge, MA: Harvard University Press, 1989), especially "Logic and Conversation" and "Presupposition and conversational implicature."

[17] For recent work on the ways novels have taken up the philosophical problem of vagueness, see Megan Quigley, "Modern Novels and Vagueness," *Modernism/modernity* 15, no. 1 (2008): 101–29, and Daniel Wright, "George Eliot's Vagueness," *Victorian Studies* 56, no. 4 (2014): 625–48. Quigley generally associates literary inquiry into vagueness with the "linguistic turn" evident in Modernism, whereas Wright argues that nineteenth-century literary realism was not strictly "realist" when it came to linguistic philosophy, and that numerous Victorian novelists were engaging in similar inquiry as their contemporary philosophers. My argument about Meredith's own "linguistic turn" and its invocation of vagueness tends to support Wright's historical claims.

true," and these different interpretations of vagueness can lead to two further philosophical positions: "on one view, once the semantics have been properly formulated, there is nothing more to be said; on another view, the semantic indeterminacy reflects some real indeterminacy in the non-linguistic world itself."[18]

The most interesting feature of Willoughby's semantic indeterminacy is that his oral vagueness is performative: not merely *reflecting* indeterminacy in the world, or indeterminate knowledge of the world, his language *achieves* worldly indeterminacy. If he were to speak truthfully and definitively, there would once more be a "realist" correspondence between language and world, but since he holds out hope for a world more advantageous to him than the one that increasingly looks most likely, he delays. Borrowing an anachronistic analogy from quantum physics, we might say that Willoughby's prolepsis turns the drawing room into a sociological version of Erwin Schrödinger's box, giving his engagement status something like quantum superpositionality. In Schrödinger's hypothetical box, an unfortunate cat is, theoretically speaking, both alive and dead until an observer peaks inside and the quantum atoms that have been (again, according to theory) in multiple positions snap into the position observed, in which they will have triggered or failed to trigger the release of a fatal gas.[19] Similar to the superpositional cat, Willoughby is in some senses engaged to both Laetitia and Clara as long as both fathers think he is

---

[18] R. M. Sainsbury and Timothy Williamson, "Sorites," *A Companion to the Philosophy of Language* (Ed. Bob Hale and Crispin Wright, Oxford: Blackwell, 2001), p. 466.

[19] Erwin Schrödinger, "The Present Situation in Quantum Mechanics: A Translation of Schrödinger's 'Cat Paradox' Paper," trans. John D. Trimmer, *Proceedings of the American Philosophical Society* 124 (1980): 323–38. In a bit more detail, Schrödinger's story (which he put forward in 1935) describes a cat placed in a steel box along with a glass tube of acid that, if released, will kill the cat. A hammer rests against the tube. Whether or not the hammer shifts and cracks the tube depends upon the state of a radioactive substance in a Geiger counter. According to quantum theory, the state of that substance would be represented by a wave function: it is equally probable that an atom of the substance decays and sets off the hammer, as it is probable that no atoms decay and the cat survives, and in fact, according to an interpretation of data showing that unobserved particles distribute their positions as a kind of "smear" across possible states, the atoms both decay and retain their integrity. But as soon as we peak into the box in which a cat's life depends upon an atom that can be in two positions at once, the atom has a position, and the cat proves to be alive or dead. Before we peak into that box, at least hypothetically speaking, the cat must be both alive and dead. The atom must be both in the state that would crack the glass of acid, and in the state that would leave the hammer unmoved. Schrödinger offers this parable in order to show that a moder-

engaged to their daughters, the women themselves have no true independent agency, and the observing gossips remain bewildered by the incidents and talk unfolding before them. A word of precision could reveal his duplicity and effectively make him engaged to neither of the women, but until then, a marriage to either woman remains possible.

In other words, Meredith's novel depicts a world so thoroughly mediated by discourse that not only is social reality determined by certain performative utterances, but, conversely, the coordinates of social reality can be suspended by indeterminate discourse. The Schrödinger analogy clarifies the significance of the observing witnesses: it is the gossips who have the power to arrest discursive play and make one solid reality out of the manifold. As long as they are uncertain, Willoughby is untethered. Talk itself becomes the quantum box—the space in which simultaneous oppositional states are "true"—a use of language that prefigures twentieth-century philosophy's turn from positivist-rooted investigations of the correspondence between language and truth to explorations of the power language possesses to make its own truth conditions. To adapt the Schrödinger analogy, this drawing room scene suggests that observers achieve the life or death of the "cat" not in the moment of observation, but in the moment of performatively uttering the content of that observation to the wider world. The gossips do not, of course, have the biblical power to speak with complete creative force, but they do have the power to compel changes in the social world through their interpretation of the discursive world. The scene indicates that the ultimate source of language's performative power is the public, and specifically, a public bent on interpreting, and therefore fixing, language's relation to fact.

The indeterminacy of this scene may moreover be seen as an intensified demonstration of the temporal and narrative dynamics of performative utterances. Clara's repeated delays of the promised marriage, during which she attempts to talk her way out of her promise rather than breaking it, are mirrored in Willoughby's delay of communicative meaning. Like Clara, Willoughby stalls, attempting to delay the illocutionary force that Meredith suggests all conversation will eventually have. Willoughby's suspension of illocution creates space for additional plot. One of the two women might change her mind, in which case agreeable meanings will settle retroactively on the indeterminate words. If neither woman agrees to marry him, he will at least have delayed being shamed in the eyes of "the world."

---

ately acceptable hypothesis about the superpositionality of microparticles becomes absurd when extrapolated to the case of macroforms, like cats.

The Ladies of "the world" function as much as communicative readers as they do scientific observers in this scene. When they leave Patterne Hall believing Willoughby to be engaged to Laetitia, Lady Busshe thanks him for "a lovely romance," and is described to be "thoroughly imbued […] with his fiction, or with the belief that she had a good story to circulate" (564). While Willoughby credits himself as the author of the fiction that the Ladies, having parsed, will circulate, the power seems to reside much more in the community of gossiping "readers," who insist upon making social fact out of conversational play. Their interpretation moreover entails collating observed words and behaviors with the norms that convey them into meaning, making the gossips exert a pull not only toward facticity but also toward normativity. Relatedly, this scene indicates that the aesthetic qualities of conversation—its indeterminacy and purposeless play—are not, in themselves, "good." The ethical value of conversation depends upon the circumstances in which it unfolds, and Meredith seriously challenges the possibility that a man and a woman of his era could have the kind of "meet and happy conversation" that legitimizes marriage in a Miltonian or Cavellian sense, because of the multivalent connections between language, gender, and power.

By the end of the novel, Willoughby's fixation on the observing "world" leaves him without independent agency. He labors to align reality with the "story" Lady Busshe will begin to circulate and realizes that he has lost his sense of independent selfhood: "his partial capacity for reading persons had fled. The mysteries of his own bosom were bare to him; but he could comprehend them only in their immediate relation to the world outside" (566). So molded by concern for the world's perception, he attempts and fails to "read" himself in the same "partial" manner in which he was once able to read others, his inner qualities a "bare" text to parse through the prism of the world's vision. Moreover, he finds himself to be a bad reader of a self that functions like "a machine," calculating and performing whatever will salvage its image before the world. Recalling Cavell's warning that, in refusing to acknowledge others, we "make monsters of them," it appears here that the same refusal can make "monsters" of ourselves. Willoughby's attempt to control a situation dependent upon others begins as an evasion of their authentic otherness, but it ends in making him fully "other" to himself. This version of alienation is the consequence of an extreme will to control his image and others' perceptions. Denying the limits of his power, Willoughby has forfeited his self.

5 Noblest Ends

In the novel's denouement, Willoughby achieves his new goals of Laetitia's promise to marry him (in a "binding ceremonial" in which she explicitly states that her commitment is verbal, not sentimental), and Clara's evasive reassurance that she will "engage to marry no one else" other than Vernon (569). The novel's pairing of Clara and Vernon would seem to represent the best-possible authentication of marriage in the world depicted by *The Egoist*. Vernon finds Clara witty and charming as a conversational partner, and she finds him enlarging and erudite, as well as kind. But in the final sentences of the novel, which suggest a union of sorts between the two, the narrator conspicuously declines to make explicit claims: "Two lovers met between the Swiss and Tyrol Alps over the Lake of Constance. Sitting beside them the Comic Muse is grave and sisterly. But taking a glance at the others of her late company of actors, she compresses her lips" (602).

The scene through which Vernon and Clara affirm their mutual attraction is likewise full of ellipsis that, in this novel, represents a critical deferral of the performativity of intimate conversation. To a question about whether or not she will join Vernon and her father on their proposed expedition to the Alps, Clara responds, "Yes, then: many times: all that can be uttered" (586). Vernon, never having proposed, nonetheless suggests in his follow-up question—"Do you consider what you are saying?"—that she is affirming a much greater commitment than that of accompanying them in Switzerland. Her deeply ironic assertion of "all that can be uttered" reinforces a sense that, in this world in which speech has a power divorced from its speaker's intentionality, utterance is itself at odds with the expression of deep and free feeling. This "all" is precisely what cannot be uttered: "it" may be indicated, but not contained, in elliptical language. Laetitia enters the scene a few lines later and witnesses "their union of hands," an embodied expression of tenderness that suggests their carving of a space for intimacy surrounded by, but not enacted through, language. In this case, linguistic vagueness preserves intimacy precisely by refusing to perform, by shaping a space for indeterminate union.

The final page's image of the Comic Muse "compress[ing] her lips" represents the strength of Vernon and Clara's connection precisely by refusing to name it, to draw it into the conventions of marriage (whose characterization Clara has not amended from her earlier pronouncement that it is a "dungeon") or language. This silence of the two lovers' meeting is playfully allegorized—they meet in the setting they have earlier associated with "comradeship," above a lake named to reflect both the ironic name of Willoughby's first fiancée and the ideal commonly associated with such romantic closures. The "lovers" are thus stranded in between narrative allegory and intimate privacy, and this raucous novel ends with an ambivalent gesture that signals, among other things, the incompatibility of a "meet and cheerful conversation" and marriage, in its contemporary form.

As Cavell notes, "If marriage is the name of our only present alternative to the desert-sea of skepticism, then for this very reason this intimacy cannot be celebrated, or sanctified; there is no outside to it. You may describe it as lacking its poetry; as if intimacy itself, or the new pressure upon it, lacked expression."[20] For Cavell, marriage is a poor representative of the best intimacy achievable in the condition of human separation and the potentially disfiguring skepticism this condition might provoke. Intimacy modeled by default on one relationship "lack[s] its poetry," as though celebration of the instituted inevitable is intrinsically empty. We can easily enumerate further problems with a situation in which marriage is the only "name" or symbolic relation through which a culture can imagine intimacy; such a culture is necessarily insensible to, or repressive of, not only non-normative romantic relations, but also various other forms of social configurations outside, against, and beyond the conjugal pair. This is bad news, Cavell suggests, for anyone seeking rescue from skepticism through marriage, just as it is repressive or heedless of other rich possibilities for connection.

For Meredith, the intimacy of romantic love lacks its Muse. Just as marriage lacks poetry if it cannot be undertaken in full freedom, the novel suggests that love lacks its literary representative because language itself, in Meredith's England, cannot be undertaken in freedom. The historically embedded performativity of speech, and its derivation of power from flawed social as well as linguistic conventions, means that finding a language for intimacy that is authentic and non-coercive, a poetics of intimacy outside the epithalamion, remains ultimately beyond the scope of *The Egoist*. What the novel offers instead is a quantum box, an intimate meeting space sketched and prepared by language but with sensibility preserved for an indeterminate, unuttered "all." In a sense, the scene suggests

---

[20] Stanley Cavell, *In Quest of the Ordinary: Lines of Skepticism and Romanticism* (University of Chicago Press, 1994), pp. 64–65.

a more positive ethic derived from the lesson of Willoughby's anti-illocutionary antics in the drawing room. The vagueness of the conclusion is the greatest freedom that the novel and its readers, interpolated as gossipy observers, can afford the lovers. If Clara and Vernon are to undertake a conversation worthy of Cavell's and Milton's accolades, it will need to articulate its own conventions of meaning, new utterances appropriate to a partnership not yet legible in Meredith's England.

CHAPTER 12

Within the Words of Henry James: Cavell as Austinian Reader

Garry L. Hagberg

It is in, of all places, his essay "Fred Astaire Asserts the Right to Praise"[1] that Stanley Cavell captures in microcosm the philosophical imperative that has motivated so much of his work across decades. Having just mentioned a philosophical culture that is willing to unquestioningly accept Quine's suggestion that philosophy be conceived as "a chapter of science," Cavell says that he by contrast has "tried proposing … that art be taken, in Walter Benjamin's phrase, as part of the history (or progress) of philosophy."[2] The counterproposal is oblique rather than contrary: Cavell is not saying that philosophy might be conceived as a chapter of art. What he is saying is that the arts could be acknowledged as part of, or as one might say deeply contributory to, the progress of philosophical understanding. Or: the arts make a contribution to philosophical understanding

---

[1] Stanley Cavell, "Fred Astaire Asserts the Right to Praise," in his *Philosophy the Day After Tomorrow* (Cambridge, MA: Harvard University Press, 2005), pp. 61–82.
[2] Cavell, "Fred Astaire Asserts the Right to Praise," p. 61.

G. L. Hagberg (✉)
Bard College, Annandale-on-Hudson, NY, USA
e-mail: hagberg@bard.edu

© The Author(s) 2018
G. L. Hagberg (ed.), *Stanley Cavell on Aesthetic Understanding*, Philosophers in Depth,
https://doi.org/10.1007/978-3-319-97466-8_12

of a kind that is not available or accessible in any other way; to leave the arts out of consideration in conceptual matters is not merely to reduce the number of illustrations of some select philosophical ideas. It is, rather, to diminish the scope and depth of philosophy itself. This is what the scientific image of philosophy systematically misses, and it is what Cavell's project has been devoted to rectifying.[3]

It is important to see from the outset that this is significantly different than Arthur Danto's view of the relation between philosophy and art; for Danto, art followed its developmental trajectory until it converged with (in Warhol, in Duchamp, in others) philosophy, until it became philosophy. That is not what Cavell has in view. Rather—and central to what I want to explore here—Cavell sees an intricate connection between the forms of understanding we achieve in philosophy, the instructively parallel forms of understanding we find in aesthetic experience, and the role that language, and specifically a certain relation to our words (to use Wittgenstein's phrase), plays in both of these. That conception (not a unifying or reductive *theory*) of language is initiated, and its importance shown, in Wittgenstein's work; it is developed in an individual way in the work of J. L. Austin; and it is explored adventurously (and in its way fittingly to both Wittgenstein and Austin) in the writing of Henry James. Cavell works with, and from, all three.

In this essay Cavell writes:

> I treasure James's achievement (perhaps over-fervently, deploring its neglect) because of its commitment—something that for me goes beyond what I get out of the pages I cited from Barthes and Foucault—to find the implication, the sustaining, of world catastrophe in our daily manners, in the way, for example, so to speak, we capitalize persons, or, as Wittgenstein puts the matter, sublime, hence metaphysicalize, our concepts. In one among his series of characterizations of his work, Wittgenstein observes: "What we do is to lead words back from their metaphysical to their everyday use." His is the most original philosophical account I know of how it is that we drive words *away* from us, into an uncontrollable structure of transcendent service.[4]

---

[3] It is of interest to note that the scientific image of philosophical content has been preserved intact within recent inclusions of the arts within philosophy—where that inclusion is made acceptable by bringing the arts under science first, that is, where studies in cognitive science or experimental psychology concerning visual perception are brought in as empirical evidence for conceptual claims. Not surprisingly, what Cavell has in view here has remained remote from those developments.

[4] Stanley Cavell, "Fred Astaire Asserts the Right to Praise," p. 66.

Cavell sees Henry James as an author capable of catching the very large in the very small (exaggerated, but nevertheless articulated, in "world catastrophe in our daily manners"), the broadly significant in the telling interpersonal detail. And Cavell sees an author who can with microscopic linguistic precision capture the ways we bring ourselves together in language,[5] and the innumerable ways we can separate ourselves, alienate ourselves, from others with linguistic tools as well (we can "capitalize" persons by making them formal and distant). Wittgenstein's philosophy, in its way, does the same: he wrote of condensing a cloud of philosophy into a drop of grammar. Cavell sees this connection well. If we "metaphysicalize" our concepts, we remove them from the contexts of our usage in the interest of finding a truth that transcends those particular usages. But then we risk the unwitting elimination of the circumstances that make those usages intelligible, usages that capture inflected meaning by being in the web of relations that make them what they in fact are. Wittgenstein, in finding routes back for our words from metaphysical to ordinary usage, reminds us of how our words *work*; this is a central part of what James shows with countless meaning-inflecting subtleties, reminding us of what *persons*, and not in a dehumanized way words unto themselves, mean.[6] An alienated relation to our words recapitulates an alienated relation to each other. One could express in a preliminary way that what Cavell has in view by saying something like this: Trying to comprehensively grasp the meaning of a word by studying it in isolation from speakers who use it would be all too like attempting to comprehensively grasp the moral depths of a person by staring at a stranger for an hour with no further knowledge. But we need to assemble a good deal more to comprehensively grasp what Cavell pressed into his encapsulation of his fundamental philosophical imperative.

In his essay "Henry James Returns to America and to Shakespeare,"[7] Cavell writes:

---

[5] On the way that shared metaphor can cultivate intimacy between persons, see Ted Cohen, *Thinking of Others: On the Talent for Metaphor* (Princeton: Princeton University Press, 2008).

[6] I discuss this matter at greater length in "A Person's Words: Literary Characters and Autobiographical Understanding," *Philosophy and Autobiography*, ed. Christopher Cowley (Chicago: Univ. Chicago Press, 2015), pp. 39–71.

[7] Stanley Cavell, "Henry James Returns to America and to Shakespeare," in *Philosophy the Day After Tomorrow*, pp. 83–110.

I mentioned my wish to reinvest the ground of philosophy with a concern for the conditions of possibility of the aesthetic that has no obvious precedent among the ways philosophy is formed on its English-speaking path (this is one reason I crave the companionship of Emerson's thinking), and my inclusion, on an equal footing in this investment, of the newest of the great arts, I mean cinema, can seem a mere idiosyncrasy. That I at the same time bring essentially to this task the issue of the ordinary (an issue that from Plato's *Republic* onward, or outward, pictured in its Cave, has been portrayed as the natural antagonist of philosophy), the ordinary as reappraised in the methods of J. L. Austin and the later Wittgenstein, stands to put off both those for whom Austin and Wittgenstein have an expected part in the analytical philosophical curriculum, as well as those, on the contrary, for whom an essential inclusion of aesthetic concerns derives from a Hegelian or Nietzschean or Heideggerian reception of Kant.[8]

One plainly sees here: it is not only the aesthetic, nor only the possibility of the aesthetic, but the conditions of the possibility of the aesthetic for which Cavell wishes to re-enliven a concern. This is anti-reductive, and it is in its way Kantian. Taking the latter, the Kantian aspect, first: in the Transcendental Aesthetic, within the *Critique of Pure Reason*, Kant was concerned to articulate the preconditions of our experiencing the world as we do—to arrive rationally at the conditions of our empirical experience. That is to speak of our experience on the ground of perception and action, but it is also to speak of more than that—he is after all Kant and not Locke, and so the cognitive contribution to what we before Kant thought of as external sensation or experience of an independent world is inseparably included. Cavell speaks of the aesthetic, of aesthetic experience, but also of more than that—he inseparably includes the conditions of language, of interpersonal understanding, and of the parallel aesthetic understanding. And so moving to the former, we begin to see more clearly why one needs to grasp something of Cavell's conception of language as a way of grasping his conception of the aesthetic, where each is comprehensible only with the other, where each is in this sense irreducible. For Cavell, philosophy along its Anglophone path has not properly or genuinely incorporated a concern for the conditions that make the aesthetic possible. And we might see in his mention of his special inclusion of film something deeply fitting here—film is the art in which we see persons using language

---

[8] Cavell, "Henry James Returns to America and to Shakespeare," p. 83.

where that language positions them with endless particular variations in regard to each other. But more important for present considerations is Cavell's itemizing his concern for the ordinary as essential to his project, his stating that the ordinary since Plato's cave has been assumed, as a corollary of the scientific methodological presupposition, that it is antithetical to what philosophy should desire and what it should properly pursue, and that it was Wittgenstein and Austin who (in Wittgenstein's terms) changed our way of seeing it and (in Austin's terms) lifted it into immediate philosophical significance by showing its role in preserving linguistic intelligibility. Cavell sees that his agenda will also put off philosophers in both analytic and continental traditions—but that is not of fundamental importance here. Cavell's inclusion of Austin, however, most certainly is, and it is this element in his work that as we shall see explains the philosophically important reasons for his fervent treasuring of James's achievement.

1 Wittgenstein, Austin, and the Meaning of a Word

In his *Blue Book*,[9] one of the major transitional if not revolutionary moments in modern philosophy and a style or form of philosophical investigation from which Cavell's work unfolds, Wittgenstein began by asking what on first glance can seem a simple and neatly self-contained question: "What is the meaning of a word?"

As is widely known, Wittgenstein begins his investigation into what this question is asking by considering, and rapidly demolishing, the answer that a word means the thing or object to which it refers. Ostensive definition is conceptual pointing: the word, conceived as a name, is thought to point at its object. But taking the case of a pencil, Wittgenstein shows that "This is a pencil"; "This is round"; "This is wood"; "This is one"; and "This is hard" all equally work when one points to the referent. (He follows this list by "etc. etc."; the familiar formula coming out of this is "ostension does not individuate.") And he turns to the next notion that presents itself here: the idea that there is a determinate mental event that is the interpretation of the word and that gives it its correct or incorrect content. This too suffers a harsh and rapid fate; if we are instructed to pick a red flower and in doing so imagine a mental color sample of red, we

---

[9] Ludwig Wittgenstein, *The Blue and Brown Books* (Oxford: Basil Blackwell, 1958).

carry within a criterion for the color red, for the meaning of "red." But this yields an obvious infinite regress problem: for that mental sample to be verified as correct we would have to compare it to another sample separate from it. (And so again, "etc. etc.".) These pictures of word meaning do not survive even preliminary scrutiny. But what Wittgenstein is doing here, and this is perhaps less well known, is challenging not only these pictures or conceptual models as answers to the question of word meaning; rather, he is challenging the question of word meaning itself—that is, the *general* question of word meaning. We may well be able to ask and answer innumerable individual questions concerning word meaning in real-life contexts of usage; it does not follow from this that we are thus able to ask and answer a global or universal question of word meaning as the logical prerequisite of answering all those individual questions. "What is the meaning of "parsimonious"?" is not a miniscule sub-set of the question "What is the meaning of not any word in particular but of a word in general?," where the answer to the former is made possible by preknowledge of the answer to the latter. It is not only that actual language—our language, as Cavell has been so centrally concerned to bring back into philosophical reflection—does not work like that; rather, and more deeply, it is that our language may not have room, logico-linguistic room, for the latter question. The question may appear intelligible because of the easy familiarity of the words that make it up, but the question as formed may in truth be only something that, in Cavell's sense, drives our words away from us, something that leads us into disorientation.[10] It was Austin who recognized so acutely what Wittgenstein was undertaking here and why it mattered so deeply to philosophical understanding.[11]

Austin wrote:

Having asked in this way, and answered, 'What is the meaning of (the word) "rat"?', 'What is the meaning of (the word) "cat"?' 'What is the meaning of (the word) "mat"?', and so on, we then try, being philosophers, to ask the

---

[10] For a particularly insightful discussion of the question of style as it emerges in Cavell, and Cavell's conception of Wittgenstein's confessional style and its significance for him, see Timothy Gould, *Hearing Things: Voice and Method in the Writing of Stanley Cavell* (Chicago: University of Chicago Press, 1998); see especially "Wittgenstein's Voices of Confession and the Words of Philosophy," pp. 68–72.

[11] On this connection see W. Harris and Elmar Unnsteinsson, "Wittgenstein's Influence on Austin's Philosophy of Language," *British Journal for the History of Philosophy* 26, no. 2 (2017): 371–95.

further *general* question, 'What is the meaning of a word?' But there is something spurious about this question. We do not intend to mean by it a certain question which would be perfectly all right, namely 'What is the meaning of (the word) "word"?': *that* would be no more general than is asking the meaning of the word 'rat', and would be answered in a precisely similar way.[12]

The contrast here is signally instructive: "What is the meaning of the word 'word' is *very* unlike the similar-looking question "What is the meaning of a word?" (Wittgenstein said at one point that great difficulty can be generated in philosophy by the way in which superficial similarities in language can obscure deep differences.) But at the same time, we do recognize a difference, because as Austin says here "we do not intend to mean by it a certain question which would be perfectly alright." But the pernicious superficial similarity between the two questions misleads us into believing that because the particular is readily intelligible, the general—composed of similar words with a similar construction—must be intelligible as well. If we feel a puzzlement, we attribute that puzzlement to the fact that we do not have an answer at hand in the way we do with "rat," "mat," and "cat" questions. And we thus misguidedly feel—against what Wittgenstein, Austin, and following them Cavell see here—that this is a place for philosophical analysis and philosophical theory. We should, rather, be questioning the question. Austin writes:

> Supposing a plain man puzzled, were to ask me 'What is the meaning of (the word) "muggy"?', and I were to answer, 'The idea or concept of "mugginess"' or 'The class of sensa of which it is correct to say "This is muggy"': the man would stare at me as at an imbecile. And that is sufficiently unusual for me to conclude that that was not at all the sort of answer expected: nor, in plain English, *can* that question *ever* require that sort of answer.[13]

Cavell wrote above of reintegrating a concern for the ordinary as a component of his incorporating a concern for the conditions of the aesthetic; as we are beginning to see through Austin, Cavell's concern for the ordinary is not a predilection for the quaint or the quotidian. It is a concern

---

[12] J. L. Austin, "The Meaning of a Word," in his *Philosophical Papers*, ed. J. O. Urmson and G. J. Warnock, 3rd ed. (Oxford: Oxford University Press, 1979), pp. 55–75, this passage p. 57.

[13] Austin, "The Meaning of a Word," p. 59.

for the logic of our language. It is a concern for sense—and for the preconditions of the possibility of sense in our shared language. As we will see, this underwrites Cavell's entire approach to aesthetics.

One way to characterize the achievement of what was called, for better and worse, ordinary-language philosophy is a both heightened and deepened sensitivity to the front and the back of a philosophical problem. That is, a special sensitivity to the often inexplicit presuppositions carried in with the formulation of a question, and a corresponding special sensitivity to the implications carried by a given formulation of a problem that determine, here too often in an inexplicit way, how an answer to that problem will proceed and the expectations that are set up in terms of what form an answer to it will take. What Wittgenstein, and Austin, and Cavell all see (and that Henry James sees in literature—but we will come to that) is that questions do not house their sense internally within the bounds of a given few words punctuated by a question mark, where that sense is invariant across contexts of usage and where that sense is thus "dropped in" from above. These authors ask: Who is asking the question? In what circumstance? With what "backstory"? In what way are the words as used inflected by the context in which a call for them arises? What fine distinctions are in play where those distinctions tell us more precisely about the subject at hand? (Was it unintentional, inadvertent, accidental, mistaken, happenstance, unaware, unconscious, half-deliberate, or countless other things throughout a range of subtle variations that it takes literature to show?) The content of a question is not pre-packaged. Austin thus writes:

> The general questions which we want to ask about 'meaning' are best phrased as, 'What-is-the-meaning-of (the word) "x"?'?' The *sort* of answer we should get to these quite sensible questions is that with which I began this discussion: viz. that when I am asked 'What-is-the-meaning-of (the word) "x"?', I naturally reply by explaining its syntactics and demonstrating its semantics.
>
> All this must seem very obvious, but I wish to point out that it is fatally easy to forget it; no doubt I shall do so myself many times in the course of this paper. Even those who see pretty clearly that 'concepts', 'abstract ideas', and so on are fictitious entities, which we owe in part to asking questions about 'the meaning of a word', nevertheless themselves think that there is *something* which is 'the meaning of a word'.[14]

---

[14] Austin, "The Meaning of a Word," p. 60.

Something which is "the meaning of a word." Austin is pointing out the fact that it is interestingly easy to fall almost immediately back into the presumption on the front of the question that Wittgenstein unearthed—the presumption that for the word or phrase to have a meaning (and here we are calling it *a* meaning, which itself is motivated by the underlying philosophical or conceptual picture) it must whatever else we say at bottom refer to some kind of thing. If that thing is not a material object, not a pencil or a chair, then it must be a different kind of object, such as a mental one. So on the back end of the question, Wittgenstein warns us about filling in the structure, the verbal architecture, of the question-template with an answer that does not in truth fit the facts of the case but that does fit the place reserved for it by the implicit expectations of the question. And Austin does the same:

> But this is the point: *if* 'explaining the meaning of a word' is really the complicated sort of affair that we have seen it to be, and *if* there is really nothing to call 'the meaning of a word'—*then* phrases like 'part of the meaning of the word *x*' are completely undefined; it is left hanging in the air, we do not know what it means at all. *We are using a working model which fails to fit the facts that we really wish to talk about.*[15]

Explaining the meaning of a word is a complicated affair precisely because it is not a question that can be asked both intelligibly and generically (It is not "What is the meaning of the word 'word'?"), that is, because it is disguised linguistic incoherence generated by misleading analogies and masquerading as the important general questions we must have answered before we move down to any particular ones. And it is a complicated affair because without situating any real question into a setting of human life as lived and human language as spoken with that life, as the ordinary-language philosophers demonstrated, we do not, in a very literal sense, know what we are talking about. Any real question of meaning will be situated; any answer within that situation will be lengthier and more intricate and more enmeshed within a web of interrelations than anything the formulation of the question would lead us to expect. And if we try to clean up the complexity, reducing language-as-used to any variant of an ideal language, we end up removing from consideration the very content that makes any given phrase, any given verbal exchange, any given actual usage, what it is in the first place.

---

[15] Austin, "The Meaning of a Word," pp. 62–63.

And so, and as if proclaiming the need for literature and a literary sensibility in contexts of philosophical and conceptual inquiry (and as if paving the way for Cavell's work), Austin writes:

> The difficulty is just that: there is *no* short description which is not misleading: the only thing to do, and that can easily be done, is to set out the description of the facts at length. Ordinary language breaks down in extraordinary cases. (In such cases, the cause of the breakdown is semantical.) Now no doubt an *ideal* language would *not* break down, whatever happened. In doing physics, for example, where our language is tightened up in order precisely to describe complicated and unusual cases concisely, we prepare *linguistically for the worst*. In ordinary language we do not: *words fail us*. If we talk as though an ordinary must be like an ideal language, we shall misrepresent the facts.[16]

Austin thus does not believe that any kind of reduction or analysis-down of meaning will be possible without misrepresentation. Or one could say: without obscuring what one is trying to clarify. For this reason, what Cavell called philosophical criticism is never reductive, never the kind of project where few cursory examples are briefly mentioned as mere illustrations of, for example, the nature of artistic meaning generally understood. Instead, Cavell has provided intricate, nuanced, and fine-grained studies of particular works of film, literature, theater, and music. The scale and level of detail of these philosophico-critical undertakings are appropriate to Austin's and to Wittgenstein's vision of language. Cavell, following them both, does not "metaphysicalize" aesthetic concepts. Nor, owing to an unfailing awareness of the need to "set out the description of the facts at length," does Henry James.

2   Expanding Descriptions

In the course of his essay "Henry James Returns to America and to Shakespeare," Cavell writes:

> I note that I take a particular interest in the question of modern negativity in criticism, one which is fed by my concern with an inheritance from Wittgenstein and from J. L. Austin. I have over the years variously taken into account their sometimes insouciant acknowledgments of their philosophical

---

[16] Austin, "The Meaning of a Word," p. 68.

destructiveness, as in this third quotation, from Wittgenstein's *Investigations* (§118).

> Where does our investigation get its importance from, since it seems only to destroy everything interesting, that is, all that is great and important?... What we are destroying is nothing but houses of cards.[17]

That negativity requires fuller articulation in order to avoid misunderstanding. It is the negativity that we have seen above, that is, the acute awareness at both ends of a question—again, its embedded presuppositions and its implications concerning its answer—that resist the habit of taking on the question as given, as traditionally or historically stated. ("Do we have free will?," taken globally, trans-historically, and in isolation from any context within which any of countless distinct questions of freedom and free action might arise.) So in truth the term "negativity" would apply only for those still wedded to what Wittgenstein is here referring to as "everything interesting," the "great and important" issues. From this perspective, the actual house of cards that is the question "What is 'the meaning of a word'?" that is expecting the name of a single substantive as an answer would be the great and important question, taken to be far grander than the local questions. But to remove those questions is to remove a blockade to a clear vision of the particularities that are the substance of sense. One could say "falsely negative" and capture more of what Wittgenstein, Austin, and Cavell have in mind.

Cavell is interested in the way in which a theme, an idea, a phrase, a word can "fan out"; in his philosophical criticism, he often sees how the development of an idea—in Shakespeare, in American film, in music, and perhaps especially in Henry James—is a matter of capturing in explicit language what was intimated implicitly prior to that articulation. Thus one variety of aesthetic understanding takes form as our seeing that something in the work that came before carried within it seeds of further development, or perhaps lines of implication that were present but as yet unstated. (The theme and variations form in music is the paradigm case here.) The importance of this at present is that this notion of an implication-range is the direct analogue of how language actually, within the wondrously rich, layered, and complex interactions of our discourse, *works*. The Wittgensteinian-Austinian vision of language is the model, the predecessor, the prototype—in his words the inheritance, for the Cavellian vision of art. Cavell writes:

---

[17] Cavell, "Henry James Returns to America and to Shakespeare," pp. 94–95.

> In one of James's prefaces to his novels (*The Spoils of Poynton*) he speaks ... of the "germ" of his story, and here requires of this incitement that it have the "power to penetrate as finely as possible," explaining that "this fineness it is that communicates the virus of suggestion, anything more than the minimum of which spoils the operation."[18]

Incitement is to make something happen that is not contained within the inciting itself; the virus of suggestion is something that grows beyond what it unto itself is. Those lines are compatible and consonant with the conception of language as being more than a sequence of words with internally contained meaning that remains invariant across context. But James's last line is the most interesting in connection with Cavell's conception of philosophical criticism. James claims, against a reasonable initial intuition, that anything *more* than the minimum spoils the operation. One might initially think that the maximum suggestion, the most articulated, would prove the most helpful. But there is a kind of paradox here: The less one has in precisely James's sense, the more one has. The minimum but still powerful germ of the idea, the minimum explicit content, leaves maximum room for creative movement, creative development. The theme, as in theme and variations, is set in place, but with a theme rich in implication the freedom is then left to the composer, the author, the poet, the painter, the filmmaker, the scriptwriter, to explore and move in the space of that implication-range as desired. Words, of course, can and are "fine" in James's sense and they can incite in Cavell's sense, and they work in the world just as do materials of works of art (including of course where those materials are literary words.) The interpretation of a work of art or literature moves within its opened space in the same way, sensing and then following out, fanning out, the implication-range contained within it. To spoil the operation in literary creativity is to have too much so that one is left with too little; to spoil the operation of critical interpretation of the kind that Cavell has followed out throughout his work in aesthetics is to have too much given, too much that is exhaustively and plainly evident so that there is too little room to move, too little space in which to assess and, to adapt Austin's phrase, "set out the description of the artwork at length."

In the light of these considerations I want to review a passage in which Cavell inventories the descriptive phrases that James employs of himself in

---

[18] Cavell, "Henry James Returns to America and to Shakespeare," p. 96.

his book about his return to the United States after twenty-five years, *The American Scene*. Cavell has discussed the aesthetic approaches and priorities of Benjamin and Adorno, and this passage simultaneously tells us something about (a) the nature of self-description, about (b) literary invention and exploration, and about (c) the unobvious relations between these that turn out to comport well with the views both of language considered above and the conception of aesthetic engagement that we are considering presently. Cavell writes:

> I alluded to the variety of self-descriptions that the writer creates for himself in *The American Scene*. I might take a moment ... to give an idea of them. The most frequent such description of himself is as "the restless analyst," a frequency that could hardly go unremarked by any commentator on *The American Scene*. It is one that easily goes with the extended effort to align James's critical practices with those of Benjamin and Adorno; so does the modification James sometimes introduces as "the brooding analyst." But here are a dozen or so others that do not seem compatible with ways in which Benjamin and Adorno can, or would wish to, cast themselves: James calls himself "the shuddering pilgrim," "the intelligent pilgrim," "the indiscreet listener," "the hovering kindly critic," "the seeker of stories," "the mooning observer," "the musing visitor," "the strayed amateur," "the charmed beholder," "the visiting shade," "the repatriated absentee," "the reinstated absentee," "the restored absentee."
>
> I take these further descriptions not as negating James's self-understanding, or self-exploration, as an analyst of a culture, but as specifying what kind of analyst he is becoming, one might say what the conditions are or the consequences, of this adventure. I note for further reference the heavy accent James gives to the idea of returning (absentee, pilgrim), as a ghost (shade), a sojourner (visitor), and an artist (a seeker of stories), mysteriously moved, absorbed, in his encounters (shuddering, charmed, musing). Are these not essential characterizations of his enterprise?[19]

First, concerning what Cavell describes as the self-descriptions that the writer creates for himself: this is important in connection with all the foregoing because it captures the creative aspect of using words self-referentially in a way that initiates a line of implication for self-understanding. That is to say, a given self-description on the part of James awakens one set of connotations or associations as it closes off others, and so further

---

[19] Cavell, "Henry James Returns to America and to Shakespeare," pp. 100–01.

self-descriptions will unfold the "logic" of the earlier ones. There are closer, or tight, relations, and there are more extended ones; "the brooding analyst" is close, but still a significant and association-awakening variation on, the theme of "the restless analyst." (And as Cavell mentions, these are closer in descriptive spirit to the self-descriptions appropriate to Benjamin and to Adorno.) The two varieties of pilgrim, joined at the noun, are separated in adjective: "shuddering" sets off a set of associations and establishes expectations that "intelligent" never would. And of course the contrast itself establishes a line of implication concerning a kind of shuddering born of an especially acute discernment or sharply intelligent perspicuity. And we have the conceptual placement of this particular pilgrim into the class of earlier actual American pilgrims, opening yet another line of implication. An indiscreet listener listens across borders of privacy and so we are now asking an intimate ethically inflected question: does he tell what he should not?; a hovering kindly critic, elevated or floating above the scene, is viewing the scene (we now say "the scene below" within this spatial metaphor) while moving inside the distance that as we saw earlier is opened between interpretive critic and literary text, and of all possible descriptions of that scene, these will be kind; a seeker of stories organizes what he observes into a structured narrative, so we are now thinking about the imposition of a literary pattern onto messier or less intrinsically structured experience. A musing visitor is reflective perhaps to a degree of being lost in reflection as he witnesses what he sees, and this leads us into an avenue of our reflection on the saturation of sensation with cognitive or reflective content—so that we now wonder if there is such a thing as direct perception. That is, are we all in a way musing visitors? "Strayed," "charmed," and the three varieties of absentee do their work, awaken their context-dependent implications, while "the visiting shade" implies ghostliness, immateriality, disembodied selfhood, and a form of watching presence that is invisible or only dimly, perhaps eerily, sensed by those watched. It is a form of presence secretly in, but not of, the scene silently observed.

But second, what Cavell says about these self-descriptive variations is more important still: these varying descriptions do not negate any prior description that carries self-understanding within its words, but rather continue James's unfolding process of self-exploration as intertwined with his exploration of the America to which he has finally returned. These descriptive variations capture various aspects of himself as an analyst of culture, and they show us what he sees and, more self-revealing, how he sees them. But then comes the most important observation: these phrases specify *what kind of analyst he is becoming*. Language here is not mere, or flat, description of facts or features that exist prior to and separate from that language. Rather, there is an intricate negotiation underway here between language and the self, between what James says and what James is. The ostensive-definition model of meaning is wholly inadequate here. What we see in action, and what I believe Cavell here sees in action, are the conditions of the possibility of self-understanding, where this again stands parallel to, or as a model for, aesthetic understanding.

The conditions of that understanding are anything but this: the inert and fixed world external to us, and a directly corresponding language that describes it. Rather, in James's vision and in Cavell's conception as it follows Austin and Wittgenstein, the world is of such multitudinous complexity that selection, ordering, indeed composition, is required to bring coherence to it. It is not given. Thus James, in *The American Scene*, writes:

> The facts themselves loom, before the understanding, in too large a mass for a mere mouthful: it is as if the syllables were too numerous to make a legible word.[20]

It is not only that the image is perfect to the case at hand; it is also that the "facts"—the place and the culture within which it is situated and which it reflects—are too large for speech in unitary or encapsulated or reductive form. It is a *word* that they cannot form. There is no such thing as a single, non-relationally embedded perception, and there is no such thing as a single word that corresponds to it. In Austin's sense, we have to set out the whole complex situation to capture what we have in view. And so Cavell writes:

> This level of the difficulty of cultural engagement—a difficulty not of polemic but of producing order out of chaos—seems to me to match the complex range of James's self-descriptions I noted a moment ago, hence to suggest the need for a stricter understanding of James's sense of his task of cultural analysis as continuous with his task of literary criticism and with, indeed, his founding task as a writer, or painter, of narrative fictions.[21]

---

[20] Quoted in Cavell, "Henry James Returns to America and to Shakespeare," p. 102.
[21] Cavell, "Henry James Returns to America and to Shakespeare," p. 102.

The projects of self-understanding, of cultural understanding, and of aesthetic understanding go together. Or: they are themselves, in their way, intertextually interwoven. Complexity, of the kind Austin and Cavell are taking as necessary for genuine understanding, emerges in cultural engagement, in self-description, and in the interpretation of works of art. And the investigation and articulation of that complexity is James's "founding task."

3 "The Jolly Corner" and Who We Would Have Been

In Henry James's "The Jolly Corner," the protagonist, Spencer Brydon, returns to the United States, and specifically to New York City, after thirty-three years abroad. He inherited, and has lived in Europe for those decades on the proceeds from, two buildings on "the jolly corner" of his youth, the house in which he grew up and its larger neighbor, which is now being renovated as an apartment building. Brydon has lived as a gentleman of leisure for all these years, regarding the kind of work required to renovate and manage a building as vulgar and dismayingly materialistic, but he has in a slowly and steadily increasing way found that he is good at such work—indeed that he is so good at it that this previously undetected ability is spoken of as a gift. Brydon's gradual emergence into this role—a role he will come to see as a possible alternative identity—is represented by James through a series of growing, evolving, and implication-tracing descriptions and self-descriptions. (The parallel to his experience and to his progress of self-description in *The American Scene* is evident.) Brydon's old friend and perhaps more, Alice Staverton, a person who has been in New York all the while, often leads him as a Virgil to his Dante through the series of self-descriptions, where these are not merely descriptive in the way considered above. They *begin* as descriptions analogous to hypotheses, but many of them quickly solidify into character traits and then, as correct descriptions, as phrases of self-understanding.

The story, like a number of James's tales, is classified as one of his "ghost stories," but that is almost never accurate—indeed it is too brief, in Austin's sense, to be accurate. Rather, this story, as with a number of those so-classified stories, is a tale of intricate moral psychology; the "ghosts" are the real ones we have in life, that is, the ones—the memories and thoughts, the possible counterfactuals, the things which might have been—by which we are haunted intellectually and what one might call imaginatively-emotionally. Brydon, with his alternative identity slowly but inexorably emerging from within himself through a complex chemical-like interaction of words and deeds, begins to sense the presence of an entity within the house that is in varying ways of him, external to him, a threat to him, and something he thus has a growing need to confront. The result of this psychic externalization of something growing within himself is that he begins prowling the empty and dark house at night in search of the entity, half looking for it, half afraid to find it. Finally, he does have an encounter: what it is is left within the space of "Jamesian ambiguity," within a range of possible interpretations that are left inexplicit as a way of preserving imaginative space and preserving lines of implication to be articulated in the mind of the reader. In the interest of solidifying the close relation between James's experience as a person returning to America and James's fulfilling of his founding task as a writer of acute and telling Austinian detail, Cavell quotes a final passage, and it begins, fittingly, with the sound of James's language:

> We must have fresh before us the sound of late Jamesian conversation: I take you to some experts overheard from the concluding pages of "The Jolly Corner." As Spencer Brydon regains consciousness, after climatically encountering the special stranger he has been stalking through his vacant house in New York as "his other self," he finds himself as if brought to life being held by Alice Staverton, who will say:
> "I've known all along that you've been coming," [that is, coming back to his blank house]… "I knew you would."
>   "That you'd persist, you mean?"
>   "That you'd see him."
> "Ah but I didn't!" cried Brydon with his long wail. "There's somebody—an awful beast; whom I brought, too horribly, to bay. But it's not me."
>   At this she bent over him again, and her eyes were in his eyes.
> "No—it's not you."[22]

Here I want to interrupt Cavell's quotation and add some articulations of content of a broadly Wittgenstein-Austinian kind concerning meaning and its interpretation.

---

[22] Cavell, "Henry James Returns to America and to Shakespeare," p. 103.

Knowing him for years, Staverton saw something, or the seeds of something, within him that she knew he had to return to work through as an inner necessity. She sees who he is in an enlarged frame of understanding: the possibilities he carried within himself from earlier times, the actuality that he became during his decades in Europe living in a way that closed off the possibility of his "New York" self emerging there, and the need he would face later in life to look from actuality across an imaginative gulf into long-suppressed possibility. That is the meaning of the phrase "I knew you would." And so, in response to his uncomprehending question about what she meant, about whether she meant that she would persist in encouraging him to come back until he finally did, she redirects incomprehension toward comprehension with the powerful and implication-pointing words, "That you'd see him"—where this means he would come to see, to confront, his other non-actualized self. "Ah but I didn't!" is a wailing expression of psychic resistance, a repudiation of the growing need to gaze across that gulf, and the "awful beast" is described as "somebody" brought horribly to bay, but first and foremost: "not me." Her answer in turn is linguistically profound and humanely beautiful: with her eyes "in" his, itself not a small determinant of meaning, in gently saying "No—it's not you," she is saying: I understand your conception of yourself presently; I understand the descriptions of your selfhood that you regard as essential and those you regard as alien; I understand that through the experience you are presently having, the former is being threatened by the latter; I understand the delicacy of this self-reflective situation and the power that you fear of such internally constitutive descriptions (in Austinian terms, self-descriptive performatives); and I understand that your way of preserving what you presently regard as your internal integrity is to hermetically fence off the former while externalizing the latter, telling yourself that this is not the confrontation of now-past but still mentally present possible self but rather the meeting of a separate haunting entity who is as separate from you as is another person.

If words were simple, if meaning were reductive, if context did not inflect, if we generically omitted what Cavell called the difficulty of cultural engagement and of producing order out of chaos that in degree of difficulty matches the complex range of James's self-descriptions, we could say, "No, it's not you" means No, it's not you. That would be a language for robots, it would be an anemic conception of meaning that could not survive Wittgenstein's and Austin's reflections, and it would fail to incorporate the personal voice to which so much of Cavell's work has been devoted.

But given what Alice Staverton understands, leaving Brydon in this self-fenced state would not be consistent with the love and corresponding depth of imaginative understanding she has shown so far. Having redirected toward comprehension, she needs to move him closer to the necessary inner consolidation. (From a sign in her dream she knows that Brydon had fully encountered the entity).

Cavell continues the quotation:

"*He* didn't come to me."
"You came to yourself," she beautifully smiled.[23]

It is of particular interest that Cavell here inserts a comment on this exchange; he writes:

[That is, neither quite accepting nor denying Brydon's assertion.]

The linguistic move in this language-game is intricate, and it shows the psychologically exacting mimetic fidelity exemplified throughout James's literary language. What Cavell means by this remark, I think, is this: Staverton acknowledges, in Cavell's sense of the term,[24] both that (a) Brydon has a self-concept both made of and supported by networks of descriptions (like James's self-descriptions in *The American Scene*), and that (b) that self-understanding has been gradually but steadily rupturing as the "ghost" grows in content and sharpness of profile. But she sees as well that (c) this is the moment of inward recognition for him, particularly the recognition that he as a self is composed, to put it one pictorial way, of two Venn diagrams. The smaller one, contained wholly within the much larger one surrounding it, is his self-image and self-understanding as he has developed it over his decades in Europe. But that is surrounded by larger sets of possible selves[25] that are in the sense being developed here *realistically possible*; he might in fact have been those things, become those

---

[23] Cavell, "Henry James Returns to America and to Shakespeare," p. 103.

[24] The theme of acknowledgement is woven throughout Cavell's work; for an introduction one might consider his "Knowing and Acknowledging" in *Must We Mean What We Say?* (Cambridge: Cambridge University Press, 1979), pp. 238–66.

[25] I offer a discussion of this issue in "Self-Defining Reading: Literature and the Constitution of Personhood," in *The Blackwell Companion to the Philosophy of Literature*, ed. Garry L. Hagberg and Walter Jost (Oxford: Wiley-Blackwell, 2010), pp. 120–58.

selves. That is one thing she already knew about human selfhood, and one thing she already knew with specificity about him. And this is the content of what he is presently learning in his return to New York, both about himself and about the nature of human selfhood. But she knows (d) he is not prepared to be "slammed" with a blunt declarative proposition, and yet (e) he needs, beyond what he presently realizes, her gentle and sensitive assistance—humane, imaginative assistance, in becoming his larger self, the self that understands itself to have actualized the smaller Venn diagram but living inside the world of expanded possibility of the larger. It is a subtle language-game of self-knowledge, and she quietly manages it masterfully. (In this sense the story appears to be primarily about him—far more words are dedicated to him. But in truth—truth that rests beneath all the other language in the tale—she is the hero. As she leans down to kiss him with his head in her lap, she holds his head in her hands; this literalizes the metaphorical fact that his consciousness, his prospects for an integrated and fully self-aware life, rests in her hands.)

So neither quite accepting or denying? The sentence "You came to yourself" has two halves: the "you" in "You came" refers to and acknowledges the smaller self, the established self, the European man of leisure living on the profit from the houses. The "yourself" in "to yourself" refers to the enlarged self that is in the process of integrating where he came from, where he has been recently (in the house, with all that that means), and what he might have become. And "yourself," as the larger diagram, incorporates the "ghost," so that the "you" and the "yourself" are, under her gentle tutelage, merging. She is thus not accepting his repudiating assertion, nor is she denying it. Language is no simpler than Wittgenstein or Austin thought it to be, and it certainly does not reduce at some imagined bottom to true or false, or accepted or negated propositions.

James also finds in this—he sees the humane depth of his own character by seeing the significant lines of implication stemming from her own words as if they were separate from his imagination—a truth concerning the contingency of selfhood[26] and a correlative truth concerning the nature of our references to selfhood. Cavell's quotation continues:

---

[26] See on this matter Richard Rorty, "The Contingency of Selfhood," in his *Contingency, Irony, and Solidarity* (Cambridge: Cambridge University Press, 1989), pp. 23–43.

"But this brute... He's none of *me*, even as I *might* have been," Brydon sturdily declared.

But she kept the clearness that was like the breath of infallibility.

"Isn't the whole point that you'd have been different?"

Cavell adds another bracketed comment:

[That is, if you hadn't left, to return.][27]

Sturdy declarations can be as they appear—sturdy; or they can be what Aristotle warned about concerning a too-common misapprehension, that of taking obstinacy for moral strength. Alice Staverton, of course, is the truly sturdy one, and James shows this in the words "the clearness that was like the breath of infallibility." Brydon's words "none of *me*," and "even as I *might* have been" are conceptually confused: the presumption here is that he would be who and what he is regardless of external circumstance, regardless of the external relations or webs of circumstances into which he has entered, the relational circumstances he has missed, and the relational circumstances he has avoided. Or to put it linguistically, his unconsidered presumption is that the referent of the word "me" remains invariant across contexts, and that the meaning of that pronoun is fixed over and above circumstance. He is making the mistake concerning word meaning that Wittgenstein and Austin uncovered and that Cavell has been centrally concerned to correct. The phrase "Even as I might have been" repeats the mistake: the first-person pronoun is presumed to be invariant, so that whatever he might have been, the present self would still have been intact. This picture of selfhood, a conceptual picture of the fixed entity to which the first-person pronoun refers, and the very notion of ostensive meaning-determinants is powerfully challenged by her question: "Isn't the whole point that you'd have been different?"

There is thus a sense in which Brydon puts a generalized theory of human selfhood in place of human selfhood; this is analogous to Austin observing how we can ask the generalized pseudo-question concerning the meaning of a word in general as opposed to asking for the meaning of a word (including, as we saw above, the word "word"). Staverton sees more acutely and more clearly, and she sees individual persons, not

---

[27] Cavell, "Henry James Returns to America and to Shakespeare," p. 104.

invariant or fixed-entity referents of pronouns. In Cavell's sense, she acknowledges rather than theorizes.

Returning to the deep similarities between the making sense of or comprehending engagement with a place or culture, the understanding of words, and the understanding of works of art, Cavell writes of James's *The American Scene* that James encounters his ghosts in his finally-returned-to America, and that with phrases from that book in mind,

> It is sounding, with its spectral appeals and its quasi-hallucinations, quite like what James makes into a ghost story. His return in *The American Scene* turns out to be a matter of adapting words from "The Jolly Corner."[28]

It is, I want to suggest, the matter of adapting words that shows us the most here: The multiple descriptions of himself as returner in *The American Scene* and the ranges of implications opened by those descriptions, the ways in which descriptions of selfhood both trace and create the kind of observer he is becoming, and the negotiation of the world through the lens, or the terms of, literature already forming in James's mind as he travels, are all in interactive play here. This too is a complex Wittgensteinian language-game, and the theme of return itself here resonates within a larger Venn diagram than the one explicitly circumscribed. Cavell links the rediscovery of one's country to the rediscovery of human companionship (in the way that Spencer finds Alice and finds himself through his connection to Alice). And Cavell links both of these to philosophy's deliberate estrangement of itself from the human, from the ordinary in Wittgenstein's and in Austin's sense, in the name of the Quinean scientific model to which he proposed an oblique alternative. Here Cavell refers to "philosophy's task of showing the human as strange to itself." And he adds, making explicit his perceived relation between an approach to philosophy and the condition of Brydon, "and one could say, haunted by itself." That is to say, for Cavell philosophy can be haunted by what it has left behind in another "country," another methodology that banishes the ordinary and the voices of persons, just as it banishes the arts as irrelevant to its aims. So Cavell's suggestion is that philosophy's need to reunite and reintegrate can be satisfied by its reunification with and reappropriation of what he called at the outset of this paper the conditions of the possibility of the

---

[28] Cavell, "Henry James Returns to America and to Shakespeare," p. 106.

aesthetic. In Henry James, words are always already employed in situ, they show us what it is, where it is, to be back from their metaphysical use, and they show us our concepts in action and our minds in motion. Works of this kind provide a service that philosophy does not get elsewhere. Or perhaps better: they house philosophical significance that it is difficult to see from the scientific image of philosophy.

4   "The Beast in the Jungle" and the Range of Implication

James's tale, "The Beast in the Jungle," is thematically closely related to "The Jolly Corner": the protagonist, John Marcher, lives inside the feeling that a life-shaping event, either great or terrible or both, will leap from the "jungle" of the world and attack him as the defining moment of his life. As a result, Marcher lives in a special kind of retreat from life; because of his sense—foreboding, expectation, anticipation, and temporizing unreality all psychically woven together—he lives as a person sitting quietly whose number has not yet been called to come up to the counter for service. At the close of the story this sense transmutes into the polemically opposed sense that nothing will come, that the defining feature of his life is that he will be the person to whom nothing happens (about which, he will be in an unexpectedly recursive way, ruinously wrong). His original sense and its opposite both place him at a distance—as we will see a tragic distance—from the main person in his life-in-waiting, May Bartram. In light of the above themes in Wittgenstein, in Austin, and in "The Jolly Corner," Cavell sees a good deal here, and in this section I want to discuss a number of his passages about this story in some detail. Cavell writes:

> A late paragraph in James's story begins "He [Marcher] found himself wondering," which I read as suggesting that he came to know himself in the philosophical mood of wonder. And the cause of the wonder was a change he reports as absolute between his old sense and his new, namely between his old expectation of something revelatory to come and his new sense of nothing left to come. In the next paragraph he expresses this new vision as of "the lost stuff of consciousness," and identifies his quest of it—or his wager, either to "win it back or have done with consciousness for ever"—as becoming for him "as a strayed or stolen child to an unappeasable father." This to my mind takes him to Emerson's identification of himself in "Experience" as the father of a child lost, who finds that grief teaches only

that he cannot grieve, meaning perhaps that grief is not what he expected, it is not close enough to the fact, suggesting an insufficiency in human consciousness as such.[29]

A person of the mind, of reflection, Marcher senses a void within. That void is where the great inner sense lived or where he housed and cultivated it, and now, late in the story, with that gone, he finds his own consciousness aware of more absence than presence. "To have done with consciousness forever" would in this context be to rid himself of that sense by somehow dispensing that sense of vacancy by throwing himself into the world of action and outward engagement so that his reflective life would be wholly crowded out—one senses in the story that as he says this he knows he could not actually do it; the mind is not a private, hermetically sealed Cartesian theater over which one has immediate and transparent volitional control. And Cavell in his distinctive way sees this: the connection to Emerson, who, as father to his own lost child, finds that "grief" is not the name of an inner item of consciousness that one can turn on or off at will: grief as a concept and as an experience does not work like that, and he learns in a way parallel to what Marcher experiences within himself here that grief is not what he expected—where that expectation was established by a misled philosophical picture of consciousness.

Cavell continues with a densely thoughtful passage:

> The other context I take initially to measure the range in the concept of loss appears in the second paragraph of the story, where John Marcher is affected doubly by May Bartram's face, namely both "as the sequel of something of which he had lost the beginning," and as conveying "that the young woman herself hadn't lost the thread." So are we to take it that May Bartram presents herself to him as a descendant of Ariadne, who holds the thread for Theseus of his return from the maze; that accordingly the Beast in the Jungle is an interpretation of the Minotaur in the maze; that in the modern world, call it America, we know that obstacles to our desires are no longer at the center of a construction (say stories we tell ourselves), but that we are the Daedaluses of our own haunted, empty mazes, constructed in memory of, say in the loss of, romantic, monstrous quests; that we wander into the unsurveyable alleys of doubt and disorientation in order not to see what

---

[29] Stanley Cavell, *Cities of Words: Pedagogical Letters on a Register of the Moral Life* (Cambridge, MA: Harvard University Press, 2004), pp. 392–93.

stares us in the face; that the monster to find whom we are willing to risk losing ourselves in the maze is the one we flee, namely the young woman holding the thread?[30]

This passage is densely thoughtful precisely because it identifies and articulates much of the range of implication established by the words James sends to work together.

"The range in the concept of loss" itself speaks of a range of implication, but it is what Marcher sees, or senses, in May Bartram's face that itself tells a tale here. Her face for him, as the sequel of something of which he had lost the beginning, beautifully captures a moment of depth in the understanding of persons, and it functions here in a way that is interwoven with linguistic and aesthetic understanding. He sees in her expression that there is more—more of a backstory, more of a temporally reversed range of implication—than he can presently articulate. He senses it, but he cannot presently say it. What he sees before him stands in the middle of a story of which he not only does not recall the beginning, but also of which he is himself centrally involved. His self-disorientation is thus an inner call for the kind of understanding of the expanded sense-determining context that Wittgenstein called for, a call for a fuller grasp of the expression of the face as a parallel to the intelligible comprehension of a question and its answer that Austin demanded, and a deeper self-understanding that, again, is intertwined with aesthetic understanding. And in seeing that she has not lost the thread, he sees plainly that there is knowledge to be had and that he needs it; it is a moment of Socratic ignorance—he knows what he does not know.

But beyond these issues, Cavell sees Bartram as Ariadne. This places what we are reading into a pattern-life, into a narrative structure, that shapes both our understanding and our expectations of what will subsequently unfold. Marcher's beast thus is seen as Minotaur, and in mentioning the stories we tell ourselves Cavell is bringing to the surface the power of narrative self-descriptions that, as we saw in James's varying self-descriptions in *The American Scene*, establish lines of implication so strong as to not only describe but also to constitute, to solidify, the self-image and correlative self-understanding of the person. And here Cavell observes that the modern consciousness portrayed by James in the character of

---

[30] Cavell, *Cities of Words*, p. 393.

Marcher does not in a simple way confront and surmount external obstacles to the satisfaction of our desires; rather, we ourselves become Daedaluses of our own empty mazes, haunted as was Spencer Brydon. Those mazes are described by Cavell as having been created in memory or loss of romantic and monstrous quests—mazes that we cannot excise from consciousness by a simple act of inner volition, yet mazes that we have created as constructions of a literary self-narrative, our self-imposed pattern-life with which we then do Oedipal battle. But then consider also Cavell's next phrase: "that we wander into the unsurveyable alleys of doubt and disorientation in order not to see what stares us in the face." Those words as used here are a description of an inward traveler, an interpretation of a literary character and his psychic circumstance. It is in the realm of the aesthetic. And as a description of the mental circumstance of a character, it is also fairly evidently a description of one state of human consciousness. However, less evidently, it also describes with considerable precision the condition that both Wittgenstein and Austin labored to lift us out of in philosophy. How so?

After noting the close conceptual connections between this story and "The Jolly Corner," Cavell asks, "why does May Bartram not inform John Marcher of his mistake, since she seems always to have known the truth?"[31] That is, throughout the story Bartram is in the possession of the knowledge that Marcher senses—he feels this line of implication—but does not know. Why not just openly say to him that she herself is the great thing he has missed, she herself could have been the life-transforming event when they were younger, and now because time is lost the possibility that she represented in his life is the missing mental object, the thought now gone, that has opened the vacancy within his consciousness? Perhaps because their time was not truly lost until the moment of her death. Cavell writes:

> Is what she knows unsayable, let's say unnameable? (This is an important concept in Emerson's "Experience.") At the end (in the penultimate paragraph of the story) Marcher will evidently name the "it" that was to happen to him: "The name on the table [the gravestone] smote him ... and what it said to him, full in the face, was that *she* was what he had missed ... He had been the man of his time, *the* man, to whom nothing on earth was to have happened." So the stone says something to him, something that the woman

---

[31] Cavell, *Cities of Words*, p. 393.

could not say. But in what sense "could not"? For her to say "I am what you have missed" would not have been true, so long as she had the strength to say it. So did it become, as it were, true—only when she was dead? And then who was there to inform him of the truth? Who can inform you of what you either already know or can never really know?[32]

This is a presentation of a *person* speaking or not speaking over many years, a *person* using or not being able to use words. It is a presentation of the circumstances within which our words can play the roles that they do. It is a presentation of the circumstances within which a thing we say can be true, and the circumstances that can sometimes encircle a possible sentence and render it unsayable. And it is the gravestone that finally speaks to him, that finally delivers to him genuine and non-delayed understanding, at the dramatic close of this cautionary tale. The great event did finally happen, tragically too late, and it was constituted by the very stuff of consciousness that he carried for so long: the beast turned out to come from within, and it lunged in the form of his gravesite realization that his own lifelong expectation (and then toward the end, its negation replacing presence with its correlated absence) had itself been the thing that transformed, ruinously, his life, by placing him at the distance discussed above. What, then, of the philosophy in this? Cavell continues:

> Some of you will recognize this last formulation as a problem addressed in Wittgenstein's *Investigations*. I give it expression here because the disarmingly casual opening sentence of the James story flags an interest in the conditions of speech, of what can be said, of what is worth saying, by both declaring and denying the interest: "What determined the speech that startled him in the course of their encounter scarcely matters, being probably but some words spoken by himself quite without intention—spoken as they lingered and slowly moved together after their renewal of acquaintance." And everything that follows seems to turn on why something was said or on forgetting something that was said or on beseeching someone to say something or on characterizing the topic of speech.[33]

Knowledge is not a unitary kind of thing that can invariably be presented in declarative propositions so that anyone can be informed of any article of

---

[32] Cavell, *Cities of Words*, pp. 393–94.
[33] Cavell, *Cities of Words*, p. 394.

knowledge at any time or in any circumstance. As James is here showing, the concept of knowledge—the real concept of knowledge as used by speakers in an Austinian sense—does not work like that because it does not reduce to that. It makes sense that Cavell wants to defend, to fervently champion, Henry James.

As Austin showed above, cases in which we ask and answer questions of meaning will show us what meaning is; cases of linguistic usage will similarly show us what language is, the complex network of things it is. That something is said can be very different from why something is said; the significance of having forgotten something that was said may be a significance that we sense is there without knowing or being able to articulate, until we later remember or are told what was said, what that significance is; the meaning of beseeching someone to say something is very different from asking them to say it, or to repeat it, or to reformulate it. And characterizations of speech and, differently, the topic of speech will be as varied as are James's descriptions of himself as returner. James investigates all of these topics in this story (as he does in many other of his writings), and the benefits to an attentive and conceptually engaged reader can be as varied in form as language itself.

With his remarks on the maze in mind, Cavell writes:

> Now what am I doing in speculating about such possibilities? Am I suggesting that James's prose is a maze, that to follow its thread is an act of seduction designed to have us "watch" with its characters (as May Bartram contracts to do with John Marcher early in the story), in which case we are warned that our (reading) lives depend upon our not missing something, and in all fairness allowing ourselves to ask and to say what it is we get out of it, what compensates us for attending to this complex, famous, late, difficult, writing, a writing that divides audiences, who may find it inviting and opulent, or uninviting and evasive? To respond to the tale seems to require matching, or competing with, its prose. And I have barely begun.[34]

Just as "The Figure in the Carpet" can put the reader in the same position with regard to the story as the protagonist is with regard to his interpretive target,[35] this story can recapitulate the experience of the maze in its

---

[34] Cavell, *Cities of Words*, p. 394.

[35] I offer a discussion of this tale in connection with Wittgenstein's philosophy of language in *Meaning and Interpretation: Wittgenstein, Henry James, and Literary Knowledge* (Ithaca: Cornell University Press, 1994), pp. 139–48.

reader (and we are distant from or spectators of the world of the text just as Marcher is distant from or spectator to the life he does not live). That maze-experience itself can be a kind of exercise, an etude, in the process of achieving aesthetic understanding. But it is Cavell's last remark just above that I want to focus upon for the moment.

In saying that responding to the tale requires matching or competing with its prose, Cavell of course does not mean that we have to become Henry James in order to understand Henry James, that we have to rewrite James's story in order to fathom it. But he is saying that in seriously engaging with this work of fiction that we have to move, intelligently and perspicaciously, within the space opened up for its interpretation, and that this will be a matter of articulating implication-ranges that James's language works to create. We have seen Cavell momentarily do this in the densely thought passage above, and the process is strikingly similar to the perspicacious employment of conceptually instructive examples in the ordinary-language philosophical methodology that Cavell has been determined to keep alive. It is strikingly like, in Wittgenstein's sense, a philosophical investigation. Of such investigations, Wittgenstein asserted that we are never done (Cavell's "and I have barely begun"), precisely because false leads—what we might now call unsurveyable alleys of doubt and disorientation—call out to us and lead us along in ever-new ways. And haunted, empty mazes? "What is the meaning of a word?" is empty in this sense; "What is the meaning of the word 'word'?", or another particular word, is not. Cavell is not looking away from philosophy when he looks to literature. And so again: it is not a predilection for the quotidian that drives his interest. Nor does any such predilection have anything to do with the methodological imperative and underlying insight driving ordinary-language philosophy.

5 Words of Self-Description

May Bartram and John Marcher are not quite done with us. We see their words unfold within sense-determining circumscribed language-games, and we see James working within the range of implication opened by his characters' exchanges. Nothing in James is simple; portrayals of the mind in James are as complex as, well, the mind. Cavell writes:

> James's words depicting this moment of insight (or insight still missed) are more elaborated. I quoted earlier the sentence in which May Bartram's

tomb is described as saying something to John Marcher that May Bartram could not say, namely that she, or rather that missing her, was his beast. The conjunction of saying and missing is rubbed in in the preceding sentence: "He gazed, he drew breath, in pain; he turned in his dismay, and, turning, he had before him in sharper incision than ever the open page of his story." James is famous for his indirection. But he is, because of it, also violently direct. He had said a few paragraphs before this one: "The open page was the tomb of his friend."[36]

James is able to say what he does about Marcher suddenly recognizing his story (within the story) because of what he has said before; the possibility of the phrase is opened by the earlier remark. And James's word is not "vision," it is "incision": the word "incisive" is perhaps half way between the two words, but James goes to the extreme and awakens connotations of cutting, connotations of opening what will be a wound from which to recover (or not), and connotations of seeing something visually that in its way speaks something linguistically that, as we say, cuts him to the core. And with an "open page," Marcher is "reading" the world just as we are reading his story and reflecting on our endlessly varying roles we play as Marchers. Cavell captures this:

> The open page before us of James's story, which John Marcher recognizes as his story, declares itself to be a tomb, in which something which is the object of desire—our desire, if we read the story with desire—is buried, something we have missed. (This is I suppose the deepest connection of James's story and Emerson's "Experience.")
> This makes the story ours.[37]

Or perhaps: James makes it possible for us to make the story ours by making it possible to make the words in the story of self-description into our words of self-description. These are the conditions of possibility of the aesthetic. And these conditions bring meaningful language, aesthetic experience, and self-understanding together in the same place at the same time. How might we capture, in brief scope, what James is achieving here? Cavell follows his earlier passage:

---

[36] Cavell, *Cities of Words*, p. 404.
[37] Cavell, *Cities of Words*, pp. 404–05.

But is James counting merely on the idea that what makes it ours is some universalization of the experience of missing out on one's life, his text the tomb of our desires? (It is a characteristic enough American experience, from Jay Gatsby to Citizen Kane to Blanche DuBois to the James Stewart character in *It's A Wonderful Life*.) Or is James at the same time specifying something about the story before us, open as a tomb, namely that in however much time, in whatever interval of our life, we have spent with it, we have missed something? This seems to imply that James has undertaken to compose in a finite space a work of infinite implication. Something of the sort may be taken as defining the ambition of serious writing.[38]

To present in a finite space words of infinite implication is indeed one way of describing what great literature does, and it interweaves very well with the considerations concerning language that we saw in Wittgenstein and Austin above. It would be an odd claim to insist that because one could give the narrow or brief dictionary-entry meaning of every word in *The Golden Bowl* or *The Ambassadors* or *The Wings of the Dove* that one thereby and for that reason knows the meaning of these entire works. (Of course, following Austin, the very idea of *the* meaning of these entire works is very much in question.) The reason no one has ever made such as claim is that everyone recognizes in some way what Cavell here calls "infinite implication." What is true of words in literature has already been suggested of our words in life: they do not work like that. And further making the point, they do not in truth work like that in *The Oxford English Dictionary* either. Austin wrote:

> Anyone who wishes to see the complexity of the problem, has only got to look in a (good) dictionary under such a word as 'head': the different meanings of the word 'head' will be related to each other in all sorts of different ways at once.[39]

So all of the foregoing, integrating elements of language, self, and text, helps to articulate the opening of a range of implication as what Cavell called above the condition of the possibility of the aesthetic. Cavell, referring to "John Marcher's expedition—and his own sense of expectation—of redemption in one unnameable experience,"[40] draws attention to the

---

[38] Cavell, *Cities of Words*, p. 405.
[39] Austin, "The Meaning of a Word," p. 75.
[40] Cavell, *Cities of Words*, p. 407.

reverberations between the two stories under consideration here, and we are brought by his discussion to vividly see the connections between texts, the connections between art and life within the connections between James's self-understanding in *The American Scene* and the issues of self-understanding in his stories, the connections between characters (e.g. "But this was still one man conquering, that is, facing, the ghost of his missed life, with the help of a philosophical woman to teach him that what is missed is always the present"),[41] and the connections between varying forms of understanding persons as they are presented in James's writings. In all of this interpretive labor in philosophical criticism, Cavell says his intention is "to suggest routes of the dispersal of these texts of James ... into the endless complexity of the real," that is, to establish the conditions within which we can, in the above sense, make these stories our own. Or: to bring this literature to life, to see the world in it and to see the world through it.

6 "To Guess the Unseen from the Seen"

In writing on Cavell on film, Andrew Klevan[42] uncovers a deep and illuminating connection between James and Cavell in the special kind of sustained aspiration they share to be alive to the world, alive to art, and alive to the creative interactions between them. Klevan discusses the famous passage from James that Cavell regards as particularly methodologically important in his essay "The Thought of Movies."[43] James wrote:

> The power to guess the unseen from the seen, to trace the implication of things, to judge the whole piece by the pattern, the condition of feeling life in general so completely that you are well on the way to knowing any particular corner of it—this cluster of gifts may almost be said to constitute experience ...Therefore, if I should certainly say to a novice "Write from experience and experience only," I should feel that this was a rather tantalizing monition if I were not careful immediately to add, "Try to be one of the people on whom nothing is lost."

---

[41] Cavell, *Cities of Words*, p. 407.

[42] Andrew Klevan, "Guessing the Unseen from the Scene: Stanley Cavell and Film Interpretation," in *Contending with Stanley Cavell*, ed. Russell B. Goodman (Oxford: Oxford University Press, 2005), p. 118.

[43] Stanley Cavell, "The Thought of Movies," in his *Themes Out of School: Effects and Causes* (San Francisco: North Point Press, 1984), p. 6.

Klevan rightly discerns in this a kind of moral-aesthetic model or in Cavell's terms perhaps a perfectionist[44] ideal that is the target of an aesthetic aspiration. (Klevan notes the words "well on the way," "may almost," and "try"—all words intimating a process of reaching-for rather than of instantly or unproblematically grasping or achieving.) Klevan sees that "Cavell, like James, is tactfully alive" to this, and he observes that this "expresses more than an inclination." Rather, "it expresses a continuing aspiration."[45] There is a sustained, or indeed relentless, attentiveness very much like this in Wittgenstein's approach to language.

To (a) guess the unseen from the seen is to see within a larger frame, to expand one's vision to encompass more than a single item of inspection. To (b) trace implications is to fathom and (in tracing) to articulate lines of significance beyond what is materially given. To (c) judge the whole piece by the pattern is to see connections, to integrate elements, and to comprehend how meaning is inflected though the interaction of parts. To (d) see so acutely as to be able to see into the corners of life is to be aware of meaning-determining elements that may not initially be obvious. To (e) write from experience is to acknowledge that experience in a non-reductive way and to give it its due. To be a person on whom nothing is lost is to be all of this at once and, in Austin's sense, they "will be related to each other in all sorts of different ways at once." All of these Jamesian desiderata in the context of his essay are meant to describe the ideal conditions and characteristics of the writer. But in addition, they describe an interpreter's approach to the world of literature and the arts, and they describe with equal force and insight an approach to language and an approach to human selfhood, to the acknowledgement and understanding of persons, and to self-understanding. And so we see again, now from this vantage point, how these themes are intrinsically interwoven. Virtually all of Cavell's work explores these intersections. Of the philosophical significance of James's writing and his positioning of his characters in relation to each other, Cavell writes that this significance "awaits articulation." Precisely. And he adds that (at least of the stories considered here, but I think Cavell's point extends much further across James's literary world)

---

[44] This topic also weaves itself throughout much of Cavell's writing; one might begin with "Moral Perfectionism," in *The Cavell Reader*, ed. Stephen Mulhall (Oxford: Blackwell, 1996), pp. 353–68.

[45] Klevan, "Guessing the Unseen from the Scene," p. 118.

these stories "are involved in coming to terms with our relation to the work that art does, and hence, according to the way I read James, in our knowledge of the existence of others."[46] One wants to add: in all that that means.

At the outset of this discussion we saw Cavell offer a counterproposal to Quine's conception of philosophy as a chapter of science. To see philosophy as a humanistic discipline, as a form of humane investigation that is receptive to the contribution to philosophical understanding that the arts can provide, is to see philosophy in an expanded field. It is a view that does not methodologically emulate science—or imitate a falsely reductive image of science; by contrast it remains open to, it acknowledges, the deeper importance of aesthetic experience, and as Cavell develops it, it brings together in mutually illuminating and inseparable ways the relations, as we have variously seen them, between Wittgensteinian and Austinian inquiries into language and linguistic meaning, questions of self-understanding and the intricate relations between self-description and self-composition, and the writings of Henry James as they contribute to these themes with microscopic exactitude and painstaking fidelity to mental life, to moral psychology. And so one might ask if we can now encapsulate the ground covered into a summary statement or a formula, so that the view of the role of the arts and literature advanced and explored by Cavell can be expressed in brief scope. But here we might recall Austin, now in this context: "The difficulty is just that: there is *no* short description which is not misleading." Wittgenstein on word meaning, Austin on questioning the question, and Cavell on the philosophical significance of the arts are not reducible, because—and this is fundamental to understanding the points they make—they do not reduce to "isms" or to small sets of thesis-stating declarative propositions.

Speaking of his philosophical approach and the need for detail and length and patience and precision—exactly what Wittgenstein, Austin, and Cavell all in their distinctive ways defend—Austin said, "Otherwise we shall overlook things and go too fast."[47] Even with all the foregoing in mind, one could nevertheless say: Cavell is an Austinian reader. But to understand that—as is true, as his work has shown, of aesthetic under-

---

[46] Cavell, "Fred Astaire Asserts the Right to Praise," p. 64.

[47] Austin, *How to Do Things with Words*, ed. J. O. Urmson and Marina Sbisa (Cambridge, MA: Harvard University Press, 1962), p. 123.

standing—one would have to see that seemingly isolated sentence in the context and against the backdrop of all that has preceded it. And, activating networks of connotations, we would need to articulate much in the expansive range of implication that it opens.

INDEX[1]

A
Ace in the Hole, 5
Achilles, xvi, 197–237
Acknowledge/acknowledgment, xiii, xiv, xvii, 3–32, 39n5, 40–42, 44, 48–51, 53, 55, 67, 68, 82n12, 85, 99, 101, 106, 107, 110, 111, 113, 114, 121, 130, 133, 135, 145, 146, 149, 152–155, 158–162, 170, 182, 189, 193, 200, 203, 205, 222–225, 228–230, 236, 237, 242, 265, 266, 268, 270, 272, 273, 277n24, 289, 293, 295–301, 306, 307, 311, 311n15, 317, 321, 330, 339, 339n24, 340, 342, 353, 354
Aesthetic judgment, 204, 277
Aesthetic understanding, xii–xiv, xvii, xviii, 4, 22, 38, 106, 111, 167, 173, 180, 192, 204, 205, 236, 237, 255, 324, 331, 335, 336, 345, 349, 354
Alchemy, 250, 282
Aldrich, Robert, 8
Allegory, 87, 95–97, 97n39, 99, 100, 102, 103, 280, 318, 319
Ambivalence, 282–285, 319
America, xviii, 18n9, 289, 334, 337, 342, 344
The American Scene, xviii, 333, 335, 336, 339, 342, 345, 352
Anglican and Episcopal Book of Common Prayer, the, 244
Aristotle, 118, 197, 197n1, 198, 217, 223, 224, 235, 314, 341
Astaire, Fred, 321
Augustine, xvii, 58, 240, 243, 245
Austin, J.L., xi, xii, xviii, 10, 10n6, 61–63, 65, 67, 167–172, 177, 183–187, 192, 294–296, 300–303, 300n9, 301n10,

---

[1] Note: Page numbers followed by 'n' refer to notes.

© The Author(s) 2018
G. L. Hagberg (ed.), *Stanley Cavell on Aesthetic Understanding*, Philosophers in Depth,
https://doi.org/10.1007/978-3-319-97466-8

358 INDEX

302n11, 306–308, 322, 324–332, 335, 336, 338, 340–343, 345, 346, 348, 351, 353, 354
Ayer, A.J., 206n23, 226, 227, 229, 232, 234

B

Barthes, Roland, 322
Bartleby (Melville), 211
Bauer, Nancy, 53n25
"The Beast in the Jungle," xviii, 343–349
Beckett, Samuel, xii, 241, 242, 287
Benjamin, Walter, 321, 333, 334
Berlant, Lauren, 43n15
Betrayal, 19, 34, 48, 54, 60, 61, 259, 271, 273–283, 285, 286, 289–291
Bible/Biblical, 240, 243, 259, 316
The Big Sleep, 5
Biographical fallacy, 4n1
Blanchot, Maurice, 64, 66–70, 66–67n18
Blindness, 75, 77, 78n4, 81, 82n11, 193
Blue and Brown Books (Wittgenstein), 325n9
The Book of Common Prayer According to the Episcopal Church in the United States, 243
Brann, Noel, 259n29
Butler, Judith, 302, 303, 308

C

Cantor, P., 80, 88, 92
Carr, David, 243n6
Cartesian theater, 344
Casey, Maurice, 252n20
Cassirer, Ernst, 248

Cavell, Stanley, xi, 3, 37, 52–54, 57, 75–80, 109–131, 133, 167, 197–237, 239, 265, 293, 321–355
Character, xii–xiv, xviii–xix, 4n1, 5, 6, 9, 18, 18n9, 19, 21–23, 26n12, 49, 53, 54, 54n27, 54n28, 76, 77, 79n5, 81, 85, 88, 90–95, 97n39, 98–100, 99n45, 102, 104, 106, 107, 121, 121n26, 123–127, 130, 137, 138, 141, 142, 147, 153, 159–161, 180, 188, 190, 191, 193, 200, 206n23, 211, 224, 226, 229, 235, 242, 254, 256, 266–268, 270, 273n16, 276, 278, 280, 281, 284, 290, 291, 295, 296, 298, 311n15, 336, 340, 345, 346, 348, 349, 351–353
Chinatown, xiii, 3–32
Cicero, Marcus Tullius, 115n14, 116, 128, 128n40, 130n41, 253
The Claim of Reason, 10, 25, 62–65, 111n6, 112, 173, 204, 206
Cold War, xvii, 266, 268, 270–274, 276, 278–291
Coleridge, Samuel Taylor, xiv, 77, 86–90, 92, 94, 95, 108
Colonialism, 266, 267, 271, 276, 279, 280
Comedy, xiv, xv, 37, 38, 39n5, 41–46, 42n11, 42n12, 46n21, 53, 58–66, 71, 110, 110n1, 111, 121–131, 135, 144
Commissive utterance, 294, 301, 302
Connotations, 224, 256n24, 287, 333, 350, 355
Consciousness, xii, 162, 235n103, 337, 340, 343–347
Contesting Tears, xiv, 21n11, 38, 39, 41–44, 42n11, 43n15, 55, 58, 70n26, 71, 293, 294, 296, 299, 300, 311

Contingency, xvii, 268, 340
Conversation, xiii, xiv, xvii, xviii, 23, 25, 26, 39, 41, 42, 46n21, 49, 52, 59, 61–65, 71, 71n29, 175, 179, 180, 199, 212, 215, 222, 242, 287, 293–320, 337
Conway, Colleen, 243n6
Counterfactuals, 336
Cultural understanding, 336
Culture and Value (Wittgenstein), 239n1, 241, 244, 246, 251, 253, 255, 257–259

D

Danto, Arthur, 322
Death, xvii, 10, 11, 26, 28, 46, 60, 66, 95, 95n32, 96, 98, 107n55, 122, 205, 207n27, 210, 212–218, 220n65, 221, 221n66, 226n78, 232, 239–259, 280, 290, 298, 310, 316, 346
Dehumanized, 52, 206, 267, 323
De Lauretis, Teresa, 53n25
Deleuze, Gilles, 201n12, 211, 211n34, 211n36, 212, 212n37
Derrida, Jacques, 66, 67, 308, 308n14, 310
Descartes, Rene, 47, 48, 58, 110–112, 110n3, 118n23, 120n25, 128, 131, 139, 257, 297
Description, xvii, 13, 24, 47, 94, 117, 139, 143, 171, 178, 180, 181, 187, 204, 211, 219, 232, 254, 259, 273n16, 277, 304, 306, 330–336, 338, 339, 342, 346, 348, 354
Detective, 4, 5, 9, 11, 13, 14, 27, 46, 269, 292
  private, 9
Direct perception, 334

Drury, Maurice O'Connor, xvii, 240, 245, 247
Duchamp, Marcel, 322
Durgnat, Raymond, 6

E

Education, 41, 42n11, 42n12, 44, 45, 117n21, 183, 279, 309
The Egoist, xvii, xviii, 293–320
Eldridge, Richard T., 38n3, 53n25, 136n9, 198n5
Emerson, Ralph Waldo, xv, 60, 66–69, 71, 172, 182, 190, 191, 199n8, 212, 243, 324, 343, 344, 346, 350
Empire, 268–274, 276, 281–283, 291
Engagement/betrothal, xi, 58, 294, 297, 301, 304–306, 311–313, 315, 333, 335, 336, 338, 342, 344
Enlightenment, the, 95, 143, 149, 151, 161, 248
Erasmus, 116, 116n19
Ethics, 4n1, 118, 124, 149, 167–194, 204, 291, 300, 301, 320
Everyday, 13, 70, 204, 227, 242, 243, 258, 268, 303, 322
Explanations, 21, 47, 86n18, 89, 91, 98, 99, 101, 103, 104, 154, 183, 239n1, 249–252
  scientific, 250, 255

F

Faust (Goethe), 259
Feminism, xiv, 39, 42, 52–54, 55n29
Feyerabend, Paul, 251
"The Figure in the Carpet," 348
Film, xii, 4, 37, 57, 108, 111, 135, 170, 214n42, 266, 293, 324
Film noir, 4, 6, 7, 23
Forms of life, xi, xviii, 22, 41, 177, 178, 180, 181, 183, 241, 243, 259, 294–296, 300

Foucault, Michel, 66, 322
Foundations, philosophical, 241, 258
Fraudulence, 265–292
Frege, Gottlob, 176
Freud, Sigmund, 249, 255, 271, 289

G
Gailey, Samantha, 4n1
Galileo, 251
Gaslight, 37–55, 66
Genre
  comedy, 42, 63
  melodrama, 42n11, 42n12, 45, 58–60
Geography, 18, 265–292
Ghosts, 50, 333, 336, 339, 340, 342, 352
Goethe, Johann Wolfgang von, 259
Gonzalez, Francisco, 254n21
Gossip, 47, 303, 304, 312, 313, 316, 317, 320
Gould, Timothy, 38n3, 326n10
Grammar, philosophical, 323

H
Hammer, Espen, 38n3, 111n6
Haneke, Michael, 15n8
Hatfield, Gary, 257
Heaton, John, 252n19
Heidegger, Martin, xiii, 216, 246n13, 251, 251n17
Homer, 197, 197n2, 199, 200, 214n42, 216, 218n54, 233n101, 235n103, 255
Houses of cards, 331
How to Do Things with Words, 300n9, 301, 301n10
Hume, David, 111, 202n14, 257, 277, 277n24, 297
Husserl, Edmund, 241

I
Iliad (Homer), xvi, 122, 197–237, 255
Implication, xv, 5, 8, 46n21, 51, 87, 108n58, 110, 114, 119, 138, 142, 150, 188, 190, 193, 233, 266, 273n16, 278, 290, 307, 314, 322, 328, 331–334, 337, 340, 342–349, 351–353, 355
Incapacity, 17, 19, 85, 98, 99, 101–105, 191
  moral, xv, 75–108
Insight, xii, xvii, 19, 81, 160, 161, 197n1, 237, 267, 288, 292, 311, 326n10, 349, 353
Interpretation, xiv, 14, 18, 26n12, 29, 30, 53, 54, 58, 75, 77, 80, 86n18, 87, 88, 90, 91, 95, 96, 98, 99, 103, 107, 110n1, 113, 126, 127, 147, 181, 182, 199, 202, 202n14, 226, 259, 312, 313, 315–317, 315n19, 325, 332, 334, 336, 337, 344, 346, 348, 349, 352
Intimacy, xvii, 7, 17, 19, 20, 23, 26, 30, 38, 40, 141, 202, 205, 217, 221, 225, 269, 293, 295, 296, 299, 300, 318, 319, 323n5
Irony, 46, 48, 70, 72, 82n12, 122, 137, 152, 155, 156, 158, 171, 175, 218n54, 256, 266–269, 280, 285, 286, 291, 304, 318, 319
Isolation, xi, xii, 5, 5n2, 46n21, 59, 63–66, 79n5, 99, 105, 154, 161, 188, 226n78, 269, 323, 331, 355

J
James, Henry, xviii, 176, 180–182, 189, 190, 199, 301n10, 321–355
James, William, 255
Johnson, Samuel, 95–97
"The Jolly Corner," xviii, 336–343, 346

K

Kant, Immanuel, 53n26, 69, 70, 111, 296, 296n7, 324
Kaplan, E. Ann, 43n14, 43n15
King Lear (Shakespeare), xiv, 75–108, 110, 110n1, 121n26, 311n15
Kiss Me Deadly, 5
Klein, Melanie, 17
Klevan, Andrew, 352, 352n42, 353
Knowing and acknowledging, xiii, 3–32, 39, 111n6, 204n16, 228, 339n24
Knowledge, xi, xiii, 4n1, 38, 67, 110, 134, 167, 201, 257, 265–292, 299, 323
  of another person, xiii, 8, 13, 17, 40
Kripke, Saul, 240n5

L

L.A. Confidential, 5, 6
Language, xi–xiv, xviii, 10, 24, 26, 41, 44n20, 45, 46n21, 48, 68–70, 77, 82, 83n13, 123n35, 126, 135, 138–140, 161, 169, 174, 175, 177, 178, 180, 181, 183–188, 190, 191, 206n23, 242, 246, 247, 252, 256, 258, 259, 259n28, 294–296, 300, 301, 303, 305–308, 308–309n14, 310, 311, 313–319, 322–333, 335, 337–340, 348–351, 353, 354
  game, 179, 339, 340, 342, 349
Laugier, Sandra, xv, xvi, 53n25, 55n29
Laura, 5
Laws (Plato), 248, 253, 256
Le Carré, John, xvii, 265–292
Lectures and Conversations on Aesthetics (Wittgenstein), 249, 250
Lectures on the Foundations of Mathematics (Wittgenstein), 249, 250
Linguistic, 138, 139, 201, 247n15, 294–296, 300n9, 308–310, 314, 314n17, 318, 319, 323, 325, 329, 339, 345, 354
  usage, 348
Literature, xii, xiii, xvii, 58, 76, 86, 108n58, 125, 135, 141, 175, 180, 190, 200, 214n42, 215, 221, 223, 237, 240, 241, 243n6, 248, 253–256, 275, 276, 280, 301n10, 328, 330, 332, 342, 349, 351–354
Locke, John, 324
Logical space, 254
Love, 6, 33, 46, 48–50, 77–92, 78–79n5, 80n8, 83n13, 86n18, 93n27, 94, 95, 96n34, 97, 97n37, 98, 101, 103–107, 121, 126, 127, 130, 134, 149–152, 154, 162, 179, 192, 222, 246, 259, 278, 289, 295, 297–299, 304–306, 319, 339
  filial, 83, 85, 104, 105
Luther, Martin, xvii, 116n19, 240, 244

M

Madness, xvi, xvii, 48, 49, 54, 66, 79n5, 80, 81, 86, 89, 129, 197, 234, 239–259
Malcolm, Norman, 204, 204n16, 206n23, 225–228, 232, 240, 243, 244, 245n10, 247
The Maltese Falcon, 6
Marriage, xiii, xiv, xvii, xviii, 11, 12, 37–39, 39n5, 41–52, 42n11, 42n12, 43n16, 55, 59, 62–64, 89, 94, 95n33, 113, 143, 170, 293–320

Mathematical logic, 250, 254
Mathematics, xvii, 175, 239–259
McCarthy, Cormac, 18n9
  Blood Meridian, 18n9
McDonough, Richard, xvi, xvii, 246n14, 259n28
Meaning, xv, xvii, xviii, 6, 48, 69, 87, 88, 100, 123n35, 126, 126n39, 127, 133, 134, 134n5, 138, 140, 141, 168, 178, 179, 181–183, 186, 191, 192, 199, 202n14, 203, 215, 228, 253, 259, 281, 298, 303, 308, 308–309n14, 311, 316, 317, 320, 323, 325–330, 332, 335, 337, 338, 341, 344, 348, 349, 351, 353, 354
Melodrama, xiv, 21n11, 38, 38n3, 39, 39n5, 42–47, 42n11, 42n12, 43n15, 43n16, 44–45n20, 46n21, 51–55, 55n29, 57–72, 298, 300
Melville, Herman, 211, 211n36, 212
Meredith, George, xvii, 293–320
Metaphysical, 13, 17, 18n9, 40, 52, 70, 102, 113, 118, 123, 141, 176, 199, 200, 293, 309n14, 322, 323, 343
A Midsummer's Night's Dream (Shakespeare), 64, 110n1, 259
Mill, John Stuart, 84, 206n23, 225–227, 229
Milton, John, xiii, xvii, xviii, 240, 244, 245, 293, 311, 320
Misunderstanding, 23, 40, 72, 148, 175, 188, 331
Model, 14, 54, 101, 133, 154, 233, 236, 248, 319, 326, 329, 331, 335, 342, 353
Modernism, xiv, 15n7, 314n17
Modernity, 15, 15n7, 109, 133, 135, 146, 155, 161, 162

Modleski, Tania, 43n15
Moi, Toril, 53n25
Monk, Ray, 244n8, 245, 246, 248, 251, 252
Montaigne, Michel de, xv, 109–131
Moran, Richard, 22, 25
Mulholland Drive, 8
Mulvey, Laura, 43n15
Must We Mean What We Say?, 63, 111n6, 113, 168, 186, 204n16, 241, 265n1, 296, 339n24
Mystical, 199, 247

N
Nash, John, 248
Nietzsche, Friedrich, 70n26, 149, 245, 251n18, 252, 252n20
Notebooks, 1914–16 (Wittgenstein), 240n3, 240n5
"Notes for the Philosophical Lecture" (Wittgenstein), 246
Novels, xvii, 75, 137, 152, 180, 190, 193, 230, 266–274, 268n9, 273n16, 277, 280, 281, 284, 286–292, 294–296, 303, 305, 307, 309, 309n14, 314n17, 316–320, 332
Now, Voyager, 38, 43, 65, 66, 68, 71

O
On Certainty (Wittgenstein), 249, 257
Opera, 46, 139, 159
Ordinary language, xvi, 10, 177, 183, 246, 309n14, 328–330, 349
Organism, 183, 241
Origen, 252n20
Ostensive definition, 325, 335
Othello, 113, 114, 120, 121, 127, 139, 159, 199

INDEX   363

Other minds
  problem of, xiii, 3, 37–39, 45, 51, 52, 55, 134, 223, 225
  skepticism, xiii, 112
Others, knowledge of, 12, 13, 32, 134, 135, 140, 202, 223, 226, 228, 233
Out of the Past, 5

P
Paradox/paradoxical, 32, 65, 136, 198, 242, 248, 250, 287, 291, 332
Patriarchy, 146, 161, 310
Perfectionism, xii, xiv–xvi, 59–63, 71, 205
Perfectionist, xiv, 60, 61, 169, 170, 172, 353
Performative utterance, 67, 294, 301, 301n10, 310, 311, 316
Performativity, xvii, 294, 295, 300, 301n10, 302, 302n11, 305, 308, 318, 319
Persons, xi, xviii, 3, 8, 12, 13, 16, 17, 22, 24, 25, 26n12, 31, 33, 40, 71, 76, 79n5, 81, 85, 103, 104, 106, 114, 121, 124, 141, 143, 144, 160, 178, 180, 182, 191, 202, 212, 219, 224, 233, 234, 275, 291, 297, 305, 307, 308, 310, 317, 322–324, 336–338, 341–345, 347, 352, 353
Phaedo (Plato), 243
Phaedrus (Plato), 253
Philosophical Investigations (Wittgenstein), 140, 151, 169, 172, 175, 177, 241, 247, 251, 257, 259
Photography, 6, 11, 14, 21, 22
Pippin, Robert, 26n12
Plato, 115n15, 243, 243n6, 248, 249, 253–256, 253n21, 256n26, 259, 324, 325

Polanski, Roman, xiii, 4, 4n1, 8, 27, 33
Popular art, 52–55
Possibility, xiii, xv, xvi, 5, 5n2, 8, 14, 22, 29–32, 38, 40–42, 44–46, 49, 51, 52, 54, 55, 63–65, 75, 79n5, 80, 110–112, 118, 122, 130, 137, 139, 142, 146, 149, 150, 156, 159, 168, 189, 190, 197–237, 246n15, 270, 276, 277, 290, 295, 303, 317, 319, 324, 328, 335, 338, 340, 342, 346, 348, 350, 351
Postcolonial, 265–292
Post-imperial, xvii, 265–292
Principia Mathematica (Russell), 248, 251
Promising, 42n12, 58, 301, 302, 306, 307
Propositions, 176, 240n3, 248, 340, 347, 354
Psalm 23, 243, 243n6
Psychoanalysis, xii, 59, 65, 252n19
Puritan, 125, 125n38, 126
Pursuits of Happiness, xiii, 37, 38, 41, 42, 61, 64, 167, 168, 172, 182, 187, 189, 293, 296

Q
Quine, Willard Van Orman, 321, 354

R
Randall, John Herman, 62, 256
Rape, 27, 28, 30
Reason, 4n1, 10, 10n6, 14, 26, 29, 40, 78, 79, 80n8, 109, 117, 118, 126, 129, 133, 134, 151, 152, 158, 160, 184, 215, 226n78, 231, 239, 248, 249, 249n16, 253, 257, 258, 271, 272, 286, 287, 289, 324, 325, 330, 351
Relational circumstances, 341

364 INDEX

Relations, xii, xiii, xv, xviii, 9, 11, 12, 16, 18, 42n11, 42n12, 50, 52, 58, 59, 66, 68, 70, 77, 87, 100n49, 135, 141, 143, 154, 160, 175, 177, 181, 211, 216, 223, 224, 248, 267, 272, 283, 287, 296n7, 301n10, 302, 307, 313, 316, 317, 322, 323, 333, 334, 337, 341, 342, 353, 354
Remarks on the Foundations of Mathematics (Wittgenstein), xvi, 239–242, 245–256, 246n13, 249n16, 258
Renaissance, the, 109, 116n21, 259
Republic (Plato), 243, 253n21, 324
Responsibility, 7, 13, 15, 16, 20, 27, 31, 134, 135, 154, 177
Rilke, Rainer Maria, xvii, 240, 244, 244n8, 245
Robson, Ernest, 256n26
Romanticism, 248
Rorty, Richard, 340n26
Russell, Bertrand, 248

S

Sanity, xvii, 29, 30, 100, 239–259
Scepticism, 10, 11, 13, 14, 17, 24, 25, 30, 31, 75, 115n16, 116n19, 116n21, 117, 123, 133–135, 138, 140–142, 146, 154, 159, 161, 239, 257–259
Schlegel, Friedrich, 67, 70–72, 96, 107, 202n14
Schrader, Paul, 6, 7
Schrödinger's cat, 315, 315n19, 316
Scientific image, 322, 322n3, 343
Self-descriptions, 333–336, 338, 339, 345, 349–352, 354
Selfhood, 317, 334, 338, 340–342, 353

Self-understanding, xiv, xviii, 4, 333–336, 339, 345, 350, 352, 353
Sellars, Wilfrid, 257
Sensibility, 182, 183, 189, 200, 203, 235, 296, 319, 330
Separateness, 5, 16, 17, 26, 29, 40, 41, 299, 300
Sextus Empiricus, 115–117, 116n16, 128, 128n40
Shakespeare, William, xii, xiv, xv, 38n4, 76, 77, 82, 92, 94–97, 97n39, 99, 99n45, 100, 105, 107, 107n55, 109–131, 139, 158, 241, 259, 323, 330, 331
Sherlock Holmes, 5, 6n4
Sight/vision, xii, xvii, 30, 54, 75, 77, 78n4, 81, 82n11, 86–90, 92, 95–101, 106, 108, 151, 176–180, 191, 221n65, 223, 232, 241, 266, 268, 280, 289–291, 317, 330, 331, 335, 343, 350, 353
Skepticism
  comic, xv, 109–131
  Pyrrhonean, 115n14
  tragic, 114
Social inequality, 310
Socrates, 119, 168, 187, 243, 253, 301n10
  ignorance, 345
Sophist (Plato), 253
Spatial metaphor, 279, 334
Speaker intentionality, 307
Speech, xvii, xviii, 48, 79, 83, 84, 88, 97, 101, 135, 136, 139–141, 159–161, 168, 178, 180, 201, 202, 241, 287, 294, 295, 297, 298, 300–311, 318, 319, 335, 347, 348
  acts, 168, 297, 298, 300–307
Spinoza, Baruch, 246

Spy fiction, 270, 271, 277–280, 292
Storr, F., 251n17
Sub specie aeterni, 246, 247
Symposium (Plato), 253

T
Taylor, A. E., 253
Theology, 259
Tiles, Mary, 254n22
Touch of Evil, 5
Tractatus Logico-Philosophicus (Wittgenstein), xvii, 174, 240, 240n5, 245–247, 246n13, 254, 255
Transcendence, 59, 63, 64, 66–72
The Trial, 8
Twelfth Night, xv, 64, 123–125, 130

U
Uncanny, 18, 18n9, 200, 249, 250, 266, 269–275, 279, 280, 283, 285
Unsayable, 346, 347

V
Vagueness, 313–315, 314n17, 318, 320
Vertigo, 8
Vice, 87, 88, 90, 92, 95, 103, 104, 107, 125
Virtue, 54, 87, 95–99, 96n34, 101–103, 107, 108, 137, 185, 186, 188, 216, 217
Volitional necessity, 76

W
Warhol, Andy, 322
Warshow, Robert, 54n27
Weil, Simone, xvi, 91n26, 105n53, 107, 198, 206, 218–225, 220n65, 221n66, 222n70, 236
Welles, Orson, 8
Wimp, Jet, 256n26
Winch, Peter, 239n1
Wittgenstein, Ludwig, xi, xii, xvi, xvii, 22, 23, 27, 62, 65, 67–70, 134, 134n5, 136, 138, 139, 150, 169, 170, 172–174, 176–178, 180–183, 185, 187, 188, 192, 239–259, 309n14, 322–331, 335, 338, 340–343, 345–347, 348n35, 349, 351, 353, 354
Words, xii, xiv, xvi, xviii, 11, 21, 22, 27, 30, 48, 59, 67, 68, 70, 76, 80, 82–93, 83n13, 96, 97, 99, 101, 103, 105, 110, 119, 120, 122n30, 123, 124, 127, 137, 138, 140, 150, 152, 158, 159, 169–172, 175–178, 180, 183–188, 190, 192, 199, 202, 206, 207, 213, 214n42, 219, 221n66, 222, 223, 236, 245, 246n15, 254n22, 255n23, 272, 275, 277, 281, 284, 286, 288–291, 294–296, 298–300, 301n10, 303–306, 308–310, 308n14, 313, 314, 316, 321–355
  meaning, 48, 140, 183, 186, 298, 316, 317, 325–330
The World Viewed, xii, 14, 194

Z
Zettel (Wittgenstein), 259n28